P9-CKT-421

A Reader of Ancient Near Eastern Texts

A READER OF

ANCIENT NEAR EASTERN TEXTS

Sources for the Study of the Old Testament

MICHAEL D. COOGAN

New York   Oxford

OXFORD UNIVERSITY PRESS

Oxford University Press is a department of the University of Oxford.
It furthers the University's objective of excellence in research,
scholarship, and education by publishing worldwide.

Oxford   New York
Auckland   Cape Town   Dar es Salaam   Hong Kong   Karachi
Kuala Lumpur   Madrid   Melbourne   Mexico City   Nairobi
New Delhi   Shanghai   Taipei   Toronto

With offices in
Argentina   Austria   Brazil   Chile   Czech Republic   France   Greece
Guatemala   Hungary   Italy   Japan   Poland   Portugal   Singapore
South Korea   Switzerland   Thailand   Turkey   Ukraine   Vietnam

Copyright © 2013 by Oxford University Press

For titles covered by Section 112 of the US Higher Education Opportunity
Act, please visit www.oup.com/us/he for the latest information about
pricing and alternate formats.

Published by Oxford University Press
198 Madison Avenue, New York, NY 10016
www.oup.com

Oxford is a registered trademark of Oxford University Press.

All rights reserved. No part of this publication may be reproduced,
stored in a retrieval system, or transmitted, in any form or by any means,
electronic, mechanical, photocopying, recording, or otherwise,
without the prior permission of Oxford University Press.

Library of Congress Cataloging-in-Publication Data
Coogan, Michael David.
A reader of ancient Near Eastern texts : sources for the
study of the Old Testament / Michael D. Coogan.—1st ed.
    p. cm.
  Includes bibliographical references.
  ISBN 978-0-19-532492-1
  1. Middle Eastern literature—Relation to the Old Testament.   2. Bible.
O.T.—History of contemporary events—Sources.   3. Bible. O.T.—
Comparative studies.   4. Middle East—Religion—Sources.   5. Middle East—
Civilization—To 622—Sources.   I. Title.
  BS1184.C66 2012
  221.9'5—dc23   2012024144

Printing number: 9 8 7 6 5 4 3 2 1

Printed in the United States of America
on acid-free paper

FOR

FRANK MOORE CROSS
beloved teacher, mentor,
colleague, and friend

CONTENTS

1
MYTHS

2
EPICS

3
HISTORIOGRAPHIC TEXTS

PREFACE

THIS READER OFFERS to students a representative sample of ancient Near Eastern texts that will enhance their appreciation of the larger world in which the Old Testament came to be.

The reader is organized according to literary genres. Other ways of organizing the material are possible, but this most respects the integrity of the works themselves: understanding them on their own terms is necessary before comparing them to biblical texts. Within each genre, the sources are usually arranged geographically. This makes it possible for a student interested in, say, Egyptian texts, to access them easily. Some works are given in their entirety, but because of space limitations, others are excerpted. In general, the materials closest to the biblical sources both geographically and chronologically are more complete.

No individual scholar is capable of translating all of the more than a dozen languages of the texts given here. I have therefore selected what in my judgment are the best translations available, except when I am able to retranslate them myself. For consistency throughout the book, proper names are spelled the same, even when the original translations use different spellings. Standard English equivalents have been used, including those found in the Bible (e.g., "Jerusalem" for "Uru-salim," "Gilgamesh" for "Gilgamish"). All spelling and punctuation has been normalized to American usage and style.

I have also provided a brief introduction to ancient Near Eastern texts, their languages, and their writing systems and writing materials. Each text is preceded by essential information about it. Explanatory footnotes are of two types. Some provide identifications of the names of deities, rulers, places, and the like, as far as these are known. Others point to biblical parallels, using the chapter and verse numbering of the New Revised Standard Version; for the most part, these parallels indicate shared language and motifs rather than literary dependence.

Each chapter begins with an illustration. Taken together, these provide samples of the languages, scripts, and writing mediums used in the ancient Near East for the texts.

Several factors have influenced my choice of texts from the vast amount of material available. First is their relevance to the Bible, including not only nonbiblical sources that mention individuals or events also known from the Bible but also similar genres, diction, and the like. Second is their geographical and chronological proximity to the biblical writers. I include a greater proportion of texts from the first millennium BCE and in Hebrew, as well as in Phoenician, Aramaic, Moabite, and other closely related languages, than those in other languages and from other times. To be sure, these texts are also less numerous because of the vagaries of preservation and discovery. Although in recent years there has been a proliferation of texts, especially in Hebrew, the provenance of many of them is dubious, and many are demonstrable forgeries; I have not included such texts here.

Finally, personal favorites are also included: these are texts that over the years have spoken to me, not just because of their direct and indirect relevance for interpreting the Bible, but also because, in a broader humanistic way, they give insight into the men and women of the ancient Near East, who were as concerned as their Israelite neighbors with the human condition and humans' relationship with the divine, and as thinkers of all times and places have always been.

As always, I am grateful to my ever-patient and ever-supportive editor Robert Miller, and his talented assistants, especially Emily Krupin, Kristin Maffei, and Christina Mancuso.

TEXT CREDITS

Note: The number preceding the bold decimal refers to the chapter number; the number following the bold decimal refers to the reading number. **1.1:** Stephanie Dalley, *Oxford World's Classics: Myths from Mesopotamia, Creation, the Flood, Gilgamesh, and Others.* Copyright © 2000. Reprinted by permission of Oxford University Press. **1.2:** Reprinted by permission of Joseph Jensen, The Catholic Biblical Association of America, on behalf of Richard J. Clifford. **1.3:** Reprinted by permission of Mark E. Cohen, President, CDL Press. **1.4:** William Kelly Simpson, *The Literature of Ancient Egypt,* Yale University Press, © copyright 2003. **1.5:** Translation by Michael D. Coogan and Mark S. Smith, *Stories from Ancient Canaan* (Louisville, KY: Westminster John Knox Press, 2nd ed., 2012). Reprinted by permission of Michael D. Coogan and Mark S. Smith. **1.6:** *Hittite Myths,* by Harry A. Hoffner, Jr. © 1998. Reprinted by permission of the Society of Biblical Literature. **1.7:** *Hittite Myths,* by Harry A. Hoffner, Jr. © 1998. Reprinted by permission of the Society of Biblical Literature. **1.8:** *Hittite Myths,* by Harry A. Hoffner, Jr. © 1998. Reprinted by permission of the Society of Biblical Literature. **1.9:** *The Ancient Egyptian Pyramid Texts,* by James P. Allen © 2005. Reprinted by permission of the Society of Biblical Literature. **1.10:** *The Ancient Egyptian Pyramid Texts,* by James P. Allen © 2005. Reprinted by permission of the Society of Biblical Literature. **1.11:** *Ancient Egyptian Literature,* by Miriam Lichtheim © 1973 by the Regents of the University of California. Published by the University of California Press. **1.12:** *Ancient Egyptian Literature,* by Miriam Lichtheim © 1973 by the Regents of the University of California. Published by the University of California Press. **2.13:** Stephanie Dalley, *Oxford World's Classics: Myths from Mesopotamia, Creation, the Flood, Gilgamesh, and Others.* Copyright © 2000. Reprinted by permission of Oxford University Press. **2.14:** Stephanie Dalley, *Oxford World's Classics: Myths from Mesopotamia, Creation, the Flood, Gilgamesh, and Others.* Copyright © 2000. Reprinted by permission of Oxford University Press. **2.15:** Translation by Michael D. Coogan and Mark S. Smith, *Stories from Ancient Canaan* (Louisville, KY: Westminster John Knox Press, 2nd ed., 2012). Reprinted by permission of Michael D. Coogan and Mark S. Smith. **2.16:** Translation by Michael D. Coogan and Mark S. Smith, *Stories from Ancient Canaan* (Louisville, KY: Westminster John Knox Press, 2nd ed., 2012). Reprinted by permission of Michael D. Coogan and Mark S. Smith. **2.17:** *Hittite Myths,* by Harry A. Hoffner, Jr. © 1998. Reprinted by permission of the Society of Biblical Literature. **2.18:** *Hittite Myths,* by Harry A. Hoffner, Jr. © 1998. Reprinted by permission of the Society of Biblical Literature. **2.19:** *The Ancient Egyptian "Tale of Two Brothers,"* by Susan Tower Hollis (Bannerstone: 2008). Reprinted by permission of The David Brown Book Company. **3.20:** *Mesopotamian Chronicles,* by Jean-Jacques Glassner (2004). Permission granted by Societiy of Biblical Literature. **3.21:** Reprinted by permission of Mark E. Cohen, President, CDL Press. **3.22:** William Kelly Simpson, *The Literature of Ancient Egypt,* Yale University Press, © copyright 2003. **3.23:** Reprinted by permission of Linguistic Society of America. **3.24:** *Ancient Egyptian Literature,* by Miriam Lichtheim © 1973 by the Regents of the University of California. Published by the University of California Press. **3.25:** Excerpts from *The Raging Torrent: Historical Inscriptions from Assyria and Babylonia Relating to Ancient Israel* by Mordechai Cogan (2008). **3.29:** Excerpts from *The Raging Torrent: Historical Inscriptions from Assyria and Babylonia Relating to Ancient Israel* by Mordechai Cogan (2008). **3.30:** Excerpts from *The Raging Torrent: Historical Inscriptions from Assyria and Babylonia Relating to Ancient Israel* by Mordechai Cogan (2008). **3.31:** Excerpts from *The Raging Torrent: Historical Inscriptions from Assyria and Babylonia Relating to Ancient Israel* by Mordechai Cogan (2008). **3.32:** Excerpts from *The Raging Torrent: Historical Inscriptions from Assyria and Babylonia Relating to Ancient Israel* by Mordechai Cogan (2008). **3.33:** Excerpts from *The Raging Torrent: Historical Inscriptions from Assyria and Babylonia Relating to Ancient Israel* by Mordechai Cogan (2008). **3.34:** Excerpts from *The Raging Torrent: Historical Inscriptions from Assyria and Babylonia Relating to Ancient Israel* by Mordechai Cogan (2008). **3.36:** Excerpts from *The Raging Torrent: Historical Inscriptions from Assyria and Babylonia Relating to Ancient Israel* by Mordechai Cogan (2008). **3.37:**

Excerpts from *The Raging Torrent: Historical Inscriptions from Assyria and Babylonia Relating to Ancient Israel* by Mordechai Cogan (2008). **3.39:** Excerpts from *The Raging Torrent: Historical Inscriptions from Assyria and Babylonia Relating to Ancient Israel* by Mordechai Cogan (2008). **3.40:** Excerpts from *The Raging Torrent: Historical Inscriptions from Assyria and Babylonia Relating to Ancient Israel* by Mordechai Cogan (2008). **4.41:** Selections from *Law Collections from Mesopotamia and Asia Minor,* Second Edition, by Martha J. Roth used by permission of the Society of Biblical Literature. **4.42:** Selections from *Law Collections from Mesopotamia and Asia Minor,* Second Edition, by Martha J. Roth used by permission of the Society of Biblical Literature. **4.43:** Selections from *Hittite Diplomatic Texts* by Gary Beckman used by permission of the Society of Biblical Literature. **4.44:** Selections from *Hittite Diplomatic Texts* by Gary Beckman used by permission of the Society of Biblical Literature. **4.45:** Selections from *Hittite Diplomatic Texts* by Gary Beckman used by permission of the Society of Biblical Literature. **4.46:** Selections from *Hittite Diplomatic Texts* by Gary Beckman used by permission of the Society of Biblical Literature. **4.47:** *Ramesside Inscriptions,* by Kenneth A. Kitchen (John Wiley and Sons). Permission granted by Copyright Clearance Center. **4.49:** *Neo-Assyrian Treaties and Loyalty Oaths* (1988), edited by Simo Parpola and Kazuku Watanabe. Permission granted by Gaudeamus Helsinki University Press. **4.50:** *Neo-Assyrian Treaties and Loyalty Oaths* (1988), edited by Simo Parpola and Kazuku Watanabe. Permission granted by Gaudeamus Helsinki University Press. **4.51:** *Neo-Assyrian Treaties and Loyalty Oaths* (1988), edited by Simo Parpola and Kazuku Watanabe. Permission granted by Gaudeamus Helsinki University Press. **5.74:** Selections from *Hittite Diplomatic Texts* by Gary Beckman used by permission of the Society of Biblical Literature. **5.75:** Selections from *Hittite Diplomatic Texts* by Gary Beckman used by permission of the Society of Biblical Literature. **5.76:** Selections from *Hittite Diplomatic Texts* by Gary Beckman used by permission of the Society of Biblical Literature. **5.77:** Selections from *Hittite Diplomatic Texts* by Gary Beckman used by permission of the Society of Biblical Literature. **5.78:** William L. Moran, *The Amarna Letters* (Johns Hopkins University Press: 1992). **5.79:** William L. Moran, *The Amarna Letters* (Johns Hopkins University Press: 1992). **5.80:** William L. Moran, *The Amarna Letters* (Johns Hopkins University Press: 1992). **5.81:** Reprinted by permission of Mark E. Cohen, President, CDL Press. **5.89:** *Letters from Ancient Egypt,* by Edward Wente (1990). Permission granted by the Society of Biblical Literature. **6.94:** *Texts from the Amarna Period in Egypt,* by William J. Murnane (1995). Permission granted by

the Society of Biblical Literature. **6.95:** Reprinted by permission of Mark E. Cohen, President, CDL Press. **6.96:** Reprinted by permission of Mark E. Cohen, President, CDL Press. **6.97:** Reprinted by permission of Mark E. Cohen, President, CDL Press. **6.98:** Reprinted by permission of Mark E. Cohen, President, CDL Press. **6.99:** Reprinted by permission of Mark E. Cohen, President, CDL Press. **6.100:** Reprinted by permission of Mark E. Cohen, President, CDL Press. **6.101:** William Kelly Simpson, *The Literature of Ancient Egypt,* Yale University Press, © copyright 2003. **6.102:** Reprinted by permission of Mark E. Cohen, President, CDL Press. **6.103:** Reprinted by permission of Mark E. Cohen, President, CDL Press. **6.104:** Reprinted by permission of Mark E. Cohen, President, CDL Press. **6.105:** Reprinted by permission of the Semitic Museum, Harvard University. **6.106:** Reprinted by permission of Mark E. Cohen, President, CDL Press. **6.107:** *The Lamentation over the Destruction of Sumer and Ur,* reproduced courtesy of Eisenbrauns, Winona Lake, IN; © copyright 1989. **6.108:** William Kelly Simpson, *The Literature of Ancient Egypt,* Yale University Press, © copyright 2003. **6.109:** Reprinted by permission of Mark E. Cohen, President, CDL Press. **6.110:** Reprinted by permission of Mark E. Cohen, President, CDL Press. **6.111:** Reprinted by permission of Mark E. Cohen, President, CDL Press. **6.112:** Reprinted by permission of Mark E. Cohen, President, CDL Press. **6.113:** Reprinted by permission of Mark E. Cohen, President, CDL Press. **6.114:** Reprinted by permission of Mark E. Cohen, President, CDL Press. **6.115:** Reprinted by permission of Mark E. Cohen, President, CDL Press. **6.116:** Reprinted by permission of Linguistic Society of America. **7.119:** *Voices of Ancient Egypt,* R. B. Parkinson, University of Oklahoma Press, © copyright 1991. **7.120:** Raymond O. Faulkner, *The Egyptian Book of the Dead: The Book of Going Forth by Day* (San Francisco: Chronicle Books, 1994). **7.121:** Raymond O. Faulkner, *The Egyptian Book of the Dead: The Book of Going Forth by Day* (San Francisco: Chronicle Books, 1994). **7.122:** Raymond O. Faulkner, *The Egyptian Book of the Dead: The Book of Going Forth by Day* (San Francisco: Chronicle Books, 1994). **7.123:** *Ancient Egyptian Literature,* by Miriam Lichtheim © 1973 by the Regents of the University of California. Published by the University of California Press. **7.124:** Raymond O. Faulkner, *The Egyptian Book of the Dead: The Book of Going Forth by Day* (San Francisco: Chronicle Books, 1994). **7.125:** Raymond O. Faulkner, *The Egyptian Book of the Dead: The Book of Going Forth by Day* (San Francisco: Chronicle Books, 1994). **9.157–61:** William Kelly Simpson, *The Literature of Ancient Egypt,* Yale University Press, © copyright 2003. **9.162–68:** *Ancient Egyptian Literature,* by Miriam

Lichtheim © 1973 by the Regents of the University of California. Published by the University of California Press. **10.169:** Richard B. Parkinson, *Oxford World's Classics: The Tale of Sinuhe and Other Ancient Egyptian Poems 1940–1960 BC.* Copyright © 1998. Reprinted by permission of Oxford University Press. **10.170:** William Kelly Simpson, *The Literature of Ancient Egypt,* Yale University Press, © copyright 2003. **10.171:** *Prophets and Prophecy in the Ancient Near East,* by Martti Nissinen © 2003. Reprinted by permission of the Society of Biblical Literature. **10.172:** *Prophets and Prophecy in the Ancient Near East,* by Martti Nissinen © 2003. Reprinted by permission of the Society of Biblical Literature. **10.173:** *Prophets and Prophecy in the Ancient Near East,* by Martti Nissinen © 2003. Reprinted by permission of the Society of Biblical Literature. **10.174:** *Prophets and Prophecy in the Ancient Near East,* by Martti Nissinen © 2003. Reprinted by permission of the Society of Biblical Literature. **10.175:** *Prophets and Prophecy in the Ancient Near East,* by Martti Nissinen © 2003. Reprinted by permission of the Society of Biblical Literature. **10.176:** © with kind permission of Verlag Herder GmbH, Freiburg im Breisgau. **10.177–79:** *Prophets and Prophecy in the Ancient Near East,* by Martti Nissinen © 2003. Reprinted by permission of the Society of Biblical Literature. **10.180:** Reprinted by permission of the Semitic Museum, Harvard University. **11.181:** *Ancient Egyptian Literature,* by Miriam Lichtheim © 1973 by the Regents of the University of California. Published by the University of California Press. **11.182:** Richard B. Parkinson, *Oxford World's Classics: The Tale of Sinuhe and Other Ancient Egyptian Poems 1940–1960 BC.* Copyright © 1998. Reprinted by permission of Oxford University Press. **11.183:** William Kelly Simpson, *The Literature of Ancient Egypt,* Yale University Press, © copyright 2003. **11.184:** Richard B. Parkinson, *Oxford World's Classics: The Tale of Sinuhe and Other Ancient Egyptian Poems 1940–1960 BC.* Copyright © 1998. Reprinted by permission of Oxford University Press. **11.185:** William Kelly Simpson, *The Literature of Ancient Egypt,* Yale University Press, ©

copyright 2003. **11.186:** *Voices of Ancient Egypt,* R. B. Parkinson, University of Oklahoma Press, © copyright 1991. **11.187:** W. G. Lambert, *Babylonian Wisdom Literature* (Oxford: Clarendon Press, 1960). **11.188:** W. G. Lambert, *Babylonian Wisdom Literature* (Oxford: Clarendon Press, 1960). **11.189:** W. G. Lambert, *Babylonian Wisdom Literature* (Oxford: Clarendon Press, 1960). **11.190:** W. G. Lambert, *Babylonian Wisdom Literature* (Oxford: Clarendon Press, 1960). **11.191:** W. G. Lambert, *Babylonian Wisdom Literature* (Oxford: Clarendon Press, 1960). **11.192:** Reprinted by permission of Mark E. Cohen, President, CDL Press. **11.193:** Reprinted by permission of Mark E. Cohen, President, CDL Press. **11.194:** *Hittite Myths,* by Harry A. Hoffner, Jr. © 1998. Reprinted by permission of the Society of Biblical Literature. **11.195:** James M. Lindenberger, *The Aramaic Proverbs of Ahiqar* (Baltimore: The Johns Hopkins University Press: 1983).

CHAPTER OPENING IMAGE CREDITS

Page xvi: The Rosetta Stone, Alfredo Dagli Orti/The Art Archive at Art Resource, NY; **Page 8:** The Baal Myth, Réunion des Musées Nationaux/Art Resource, NY; **Page 38:** The Tale of Two Brothers, © Trustees of the British Museum; **Page 64:** Black Obelisk of Shalmaneser III, © Trustees of the British Museum; **Page 86:** Code of Hammurapi, Réunion des Musées Nationaux/Art Resource, NY; **Page 114:** Sealed Document, bpk, Berlin/Ägyptisches Museum, Staatliche Museen, Berlin/Art Resource, NY; **Page 124:** Akhenaten and His Family Praying to the Solar Disk, Gianni Dagli Orti/The Art Archive at Art Resource, NY; **Page 146:** Funerary Stela of Kuttamuwa; **Page 160:** Pyrgi Dedicatory Inscription, Universal Images Group/Art Resource, NY; **Page 166:** Wife of Nebamun, Werner Forman/Art Resource, NY; **Page 172:** Reconstructed Text from Deir Alla, André Lemaire, adapted from a drawing by G. Van Der Kooij; **Page 182:** The Gezer Calendar, Erich Lessing/Art Resource, NY.

A Reader of Ancient Near Eastern Texts

The Rosetta Stone
A fragment of a stela written during the reign of the Pharaoh Ptolemy V
in 196 BCE. Made of granodiorite, it is 45 inches (114 cm) high and 28.5
inches (72 cm) wide. The top panel is written in Egyptian hieroglyphics, the
middle in Egyptian demotic, and the bottom in Greek, which enabled the
modern decipherment of ancient Egyptian in the early nineteenth century. It
is named after the town of Rosette or Rosetta (Arabic Rashid).

INTRODUCTION

BY LATE ANTIQUITY, many of the languages of the ancient Near East had been forgotten. But in the early nineteenth century CE, scholars began to be able to read texts in those languages, starting with Egyptian. The mysterious writing on Egyptian monuments had been continuously visible, but what those hieroglyphs meant was no longer known until, in 1799, a soldier in Napoleon's army in Egypt discovered a large stela that came to be called the Rosetta Stone. It had three panels of writing, the top in hieroglyphics, the middle in demotic, and the bottom in Greek. Because Greek could be read, the top two panels were deciphered some twenty years later, and suddenly the literature of the ancient Egyptians became accessible. By the mid-nineteenth century, European explorers had discovered thousands of texts in other languages and writing systems, and these texts too were eventually deciphered. The flood of discoveries has continued to the present, so that we now have access to millions of texts from the ancient Near East. Although they are only a sample—one estimate is that 90 percent of ancient literature is still underground or lost—they have provided a window into the larger world to which the biblical writers belonged. Access to the writings of the Egyptians, the Sumerians, the Babylonians, the Assyrians, the Canaanites, the Hittites, the Phoenicians, the Israelites, and many other peoples has transformed the interpretation of the Bible.

WRITING SYSTEMS

Toward the end of the third millennium BCE, writing was invented in the two great riverine civilizations of the ancient Near East, in Mesopotamia and in Egypt, and people have been writing—and reading—ever since. For many centuries, however, literacy was restricted to a small fraction of populations because of the writing systems used. The Sumerians in Mesopotamia used a writing system that was pictographic: a drawing of an object, often stylized, represented the word for that object. Because there were so many objects—and concepts—there were also many signs to learn, and only a specially trained corps of scribes could master them. Eventually this pictographic system was adapted for other languages, most notably Akkadian, and many of the signs were given one or more syllabic values. Egyptian writing—called hieroglyphic—also used pictograms, as well as signs that represented sound clusters and grammatical elements; writing Egyptian, of necessity, also required extensive training. In the early second millennium BCE, a third type of writing was developed, in which a picture represented not an object, a concept, or a syllable, but simply a sound, usually the first sound or phoneme of the name of the picture. This system, called alphabetic, was extraordinarily adaptable and came to be used for a large number of languages, including, eventually, our own.

1

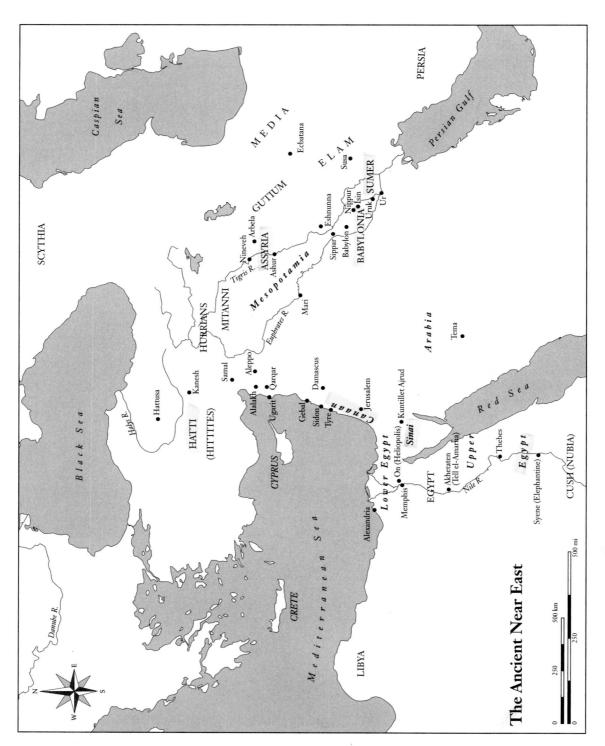

The Ancient Near East

Thanks to the invention and diffusion of writing, we are able to read the texts presented in this book, the literature and records of the distant past.

LANGUAGES

In the ancient Near East, several dozen languages and dialects were used, some of which are not yet fully understood or even deciphered. The principal languages of the texts translated in this book are as follows.

Egyptian. The Egyptian language, used principally only in Egypt, was written in several forms. In hieroglyphic texts, a picture represents a word or sound; hieroglyphic writing can be either vertical or horizontal, and either right to left or left to right or both. Hieratic is a simplified, cursive form of hieroglyphic, usually used on papyrus, generally written horizontally from right to left. In the mid-first millennium BCE an even more simplified script, known as demotic, was developed.

Sumerian. In Mesopotamia, the earliest known language is Sumerian, spoken by the residents of southern Mesopotamia during the third millennium BCE. Its writing is pictographic, and the principal system is known as cuneiform (literally, "wedge shaped"), in which the stylized pictures were impressed on damp clay with the tip of a cut reed, which gave them their distinctive shape. Although Sumerian stopped being spoken around 2000 BCE, it continued to be used for literary and religious purposes for another two thousand years, much as Latin continued to be a scholarly and liturgical language in the West long after it was no longer spoken by ordinary people. The Sumerian cuneiform writing system was used for other unrelated languages.

Akkadian. Akkadian is a scholarly term for the principal Semitic language of Mesopotamia from the third millennium BCE into the early Common Era. It eventually divided into Babylonian, in southern Mesopotamia, and Assyrian, in northern Mesopotamia; local dialects of Akkadian are also known. The first writers of Akkadian adopted the cuneiform writing system of their Sumerian neighbors but adapted it especially in the use of a syllabic system.

Hittite. Hittite is a general term for a language of ancient Asia Minor closely related to the Indo-European languages. It also used the originally Sumerian cuneiform system and flourished in the period of supremacy of the kingdom of Hatti (the Hittites) during much of the second millennium BCE.

Hurrian. Hurrian was originally the language of the Hurrian people, whose homeland was in southern Armenia. Hurrian texts, also written in cuneiform, have been found at sites throughout the Near East; one long text comes from Egypt. They date to the second millennium BCE.

Ugaritic. Belonging to the group of languages called Northwest Semitic, Ugaritic was the native language of the small kingdom of Ugarit on the northern Mediterranean coast of Syria during the latter part of the second millennium BCE. Although other languages and writing systems were used at Ugarit, its scribes also adapted cuneiform writing to an alphabetic system in which only thirty signs were used for the sounds of their language.

Closely related to Ugaritic and to each other are other Northwest Semitic languages, many of which emerged ca. 1000 BCE. All are written in similar-looking alphabets; they include:

Hebrew. The language of ancient Israel and its components, the northern kingdom of Israel and the southern kingdom of Judah and their political successors, especially Judea. It gradually stopped being used as a spoken language, being largely replaced by Aramaic (see below), but continued to be used by scholars and in worship. Revived as a spoken language in the late nineteenth century CE, it is now the principal language of the modern state of Israel.

Phoenician. The language of ancient Israel's northern neighbors, in modern Lebanon. Because of the Phoenicians' extensive trading and colonization, Phoenician inscriptions have been found at sites all over the Mediterranean, as well as in Asia Minor.

In the western Mediterranean, Phoenician developed into a dialect called Punic, especially in North Africa, where it continued to be spoken into the Common Era. The Phoenician version of the alphabet was borrowed by the Greeks and thus became the basis of all western alphabets in use today.

Moabite. The language of ancient Moab, located in Transjordan east of the Dead Sea. Only a few texts in Moabite have been found.

Ammonite. The language of ancient Ammon, located in Transjordan north of the Dead Sea. Only a few texts in Ammonite have been found.

Aramaic. Originally the language of the kingdoms of Aram in western Syria. By the mid-first millennium BCE, Aramaic had come to be used widely as a kind of lingua franca and eventually replaced languages such as Hebrew as the ordinary vernacular. For this reason, Aramaic texts are found throughout the Near East and Egypt and as far east as Pakistan and Afghanistan. In late antiquity and into the Middle Ages, Aramaic continued to be used by Jews and Christians (in the latter case in a dialect known as Syriac), and forms of Aramaic are still spoken in a few parts of the Near East.

WRITING MATERIALS

As in the present, many different surfaces were used in antiquity for writing texts. The most durable are on stone, whether still in its original setting or carved, and on clay, which was subsequently fired. Sometimes already fired pottery was used as a writing surface on which texts were either incised or written with ink; broken pieces of pottery with writing on them are generally called ostraca. Also fairly durable, although infrequently used, were ivory and metal. Least durable, and therefore in most climates often lost to natural processes of decomposition, are organic material, including leather, wood, and papyrus. Plaster was also used as a writing surface, although it too has rarely survived.

Because of their durability and widespread use, fired clay tablets are one of the two most frequently found mediums. The other is papyrus, which in the arid climate of Egypt and a few other places has survived in abundance.

GENRES

In this reader, the texts selected have been organized by genre or type, as follows:

Myths. Works in which deities are the principal characters.

Epics. Heroic tales in which humans are the principal protagonists, although deities are often also characters.

Historiographic Texts. Narratives or records of historical events or personalities.

Legal and Commercial Texts. Collections or codes of laws, various types of contracts, records of commercial transactions, and texts on jars and weights used in commerce.

Letters. Official and private correspondence.

Hymns, Prayers, Laments, and Rituals. Texts of praise and petition to the gods, along with medical texts that have a ritual component and other texts containing instructions for the offering of sacrifices and other ritual matters.

Burial Texts. Texts used in funerary rituals and texts written in tombs and on sarcophagi and tombstones.

Commemorative and Dedicatory Texts. Texts on monuments erected to commemorate an event or a person, to celebrate the completion or dedication of a building, and on votive offerings.

Love Poetry. Poems celebrating human love.

Prophetic Texts. Texts in which a divinely given message is relayed through a prophet to a king or other individual.

Wisdom Literature. Texts that deal with the human condition, in instructions, proverbs, dialogues, and other genres. Also included here are texts that deal with the scribal profession, because scribes were responsible for the creation and collection of wisdom literature, and texts that illustrate scribal education.

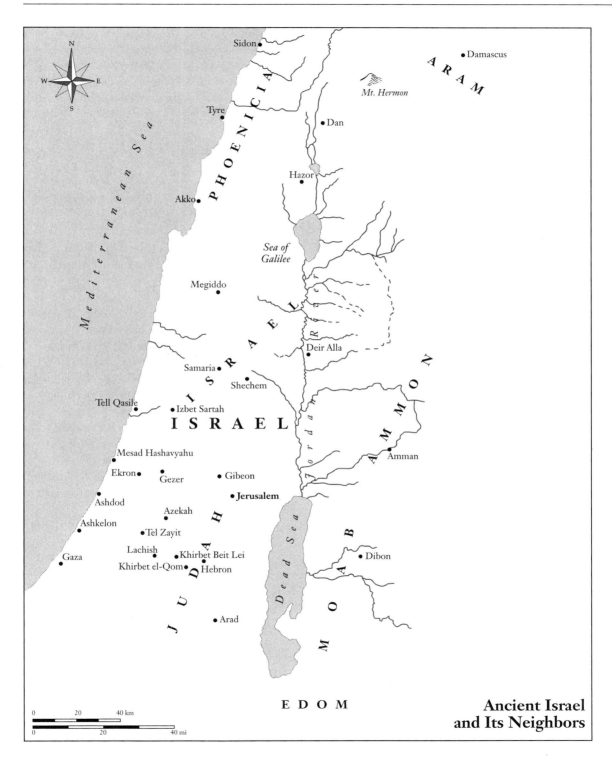

Ancient Israel and Its Neighbors

Within each of these divisions, the material is usually subdivided according to the culture from which it originated or the language in which it was written.

These categories are admittedly somewhat porous. Thus, mythical elements occur in many genres, treaties often contain extended historical sections, hymns were part of burial rituals, proverbs occur in prophetic and other texts, and so forth. But the organization adopted here illustrates how writers at different times and places shared both modes of expression and the ideas expressed.

Finally, not all of these texts are literature in any high sense, but even mundane texts contain valuable linguistic, historical, and religious information.

BIBLIOGRAPHY

For general introductions to ancient Near Eastern literature, see:

Ehrlich, Carl S., ed. *From an Antique Land: An Introduction to Ancient Near Eastern Literature.* Lanham, MD: Rowman and Littlefield, 2009.

Sparks, Kenton L. *Ancient Texts for the Study of the Hebrew Bible: A Guide to the Background Literature.* Peabody, MA; Hendrickson, 2005.

Series

These series consist of individual volumes focused on a particular language, genre, or period. Individual volumes from these series, of which there are many, are not listed in the following sections.

Writings from the Ancient World. A series published by the Society of Biblical Literature, with individual volumes focused on a particular genre or period. See further http://www.sbl-site.org/publications/Books_WAW.aspx.

Texte aus der Umwelt des Alten Testaments, published by Gütersloher Verlagshaus in a new edition since 2004.

Littératures anciennes du Proche-Orient, published by Les Éditions du Cerf, Paris.

Anthologies

There are several comprehensive collections of ancient Near Eastern texts:

Chavalas, M. W., ed. *The Ancient Near East: Historical Sources in Translation.* Malden, MA: Blackwell, 2006. Historical texts in cuneiform from the Sumerians to the early Persian period.

Hallo, W. W., and K. L. Younger, Jr., eds. *The Context of Scripture.* 3 vols. Leiden: Brill, 1997–2002. This has become the standard reference anthology.

McCarter, P. Kyle, Jr. *Ancient Inscriptions: Voices from the Biblical World.* Washington, DC: Biblical Archaeology Society, 1996. A detailed catalog to accompany a slide set.

Pritchard, J. B., ed. *Ancient Near Eastern Texts Relating to the Old Testament.* Princeton, NJ: Princeton University Press, 3d ed., 1969. Although dated, and now superseded by Hallo, this remains an important reference work.

Egyptian Literature

Lichtheim, Miriam. *Ancient Egyptian Literature.* 3 vols. Berkeley, CA: University of California Press, rev. ed., 2006 (original 1973–1980).

Simpson, W. K. *The Literature of Ancient Egypt.* New Haven, CT: Yale University Press, 3d ed., 2003.

Mesopotamian Literature

The Electronic Text Corpus of Sumerian Literature. Faculty of Oriental Studies, University of Oxford, 2003–2006. http://www-etcsl.orient.ox.ac.uk/. Translations of many important Sumerian texts.

Cogan, M. *The Raging Torrent: Historical Inscriptions from Assyria and Babylonia Relating to Ancient Israel.* Jerusalem: Carta, 2008.

Dalley, S. *Myths from Mesopotamia: Creation, the Flood, Gilgamesh, and Others.* Oxford: Oxford University Press, rev. ed., 2000.

Foster, B. R. *Before the Muses: An Anthology of Akkadian Literature.* Bethesda, MD: CDL, 3d ed., 2005.

Lambert, W. G. *Babylonian Wisdom Literature.* Oxford: Clarendon, 1960.

Persian Empire

Kuhrt, Amélie. *The Persian Empire: A Corpus of Sources from the Achaemenid Period.* London: Routledge, 2007.

Northwest Semitic

General

Aḥituv, Shmuel. *Echoes from the Past: Hebrew and Cognate Inscriptions from the Biblical Period.* Jerusalem: Carta, 2008.

Gibson, J. C. L. *Textbook of Syrian Semitic Inscriptions.* 3 vols. Oxford: Clarendon, 1971–1982.

Ugaritic

Coogan, M. D., and M. S. Smith. *Stories from Ancient Canaan.* Louisville, KY: Westminster John Knox, 2d ed., 2012.

Hebrew

Davies, G. I. *Ancient Hebrew Inscriptions: Corpus and Concordance.* 2 vols. Cambridge: Cambridge University Press, 1991; 2004.

Dobbs-Allsopp, F. W., et al. *Hebrew Inscriptions: Texts from the Biblical Period of the Monarchy with Concordance.* New Haven, CT: Yale University Press, 2005.

Aramaic

Porten, Bezalel. *The Elephantine Papyri in English: Three Millennia of Cross-cultural Continuity and Change.* Leiden: Brill, 2d ed., 2011.

Porten, Bezalel, and Ada Yardeni. *Textbook of Aramaic Documents from Ancient Egypt.* 4 vols. Jerusalem: The Hebrew University of Jerusalem; Winona Lake, IN: Eisenbrauns, 1986–1999.

The Baal Myth
A clay tablet containing part of the Ugaritic myth of Baal. Written in alphabetic cuneiform, it is 5.7 inches (14.5 cm) high and 6.1 inches (15.6 cm) wide. (See Text 5.)

MYTHS

MESOPOTAMIA

1. Enuma Elish

Enuma Elish takes its name from its opening words, which mean "when above." Sometimes called the *Babylonian Creation Epic,* it is a lengthy narrative hymn, written on seven tablets in over a thousand lines, describing how Marduk, the storm god and chief god of the city of Babylon, became king of the gods, just as Babylon became the dominant city of Mesopotamia.

The myth describes a conflict between two generations of gods. The older gods, headed by Tiamat, the goddess of salt water,[1] and Apsu, the god of fresh water, produced several generations of gods, and then tried to exterminate these younger gods. Tiamat was finally defeated by Marduk, who then established the cosmos and created humans.

When *Enuma Elish* was written is debated, although some time in the late second or early first millennium BCE seems likely. We know from other sources that it was recited in Babylon during the annual New Year festival. In a variant form it is told of Ashur, the chief god of Assyria.[2]

---

[1]Her name is related to the Hebrew word *tehom,* "deep."
[2]Translation by Stephanie Dalley, *Myths from Mesopotamia: Creation, the Flood, Gilgamesh, and Others* (Oxford: Oxford University Press, rev. ed., 2000), 233–274.

TABLET 1

When skies above were not yet named
nor earth below pronounced by name,
Apsu, the first one, their begetter
and maker Tiamat, who bore them all,
had mixed their waters together,
but had not formed pastures, nor discovered
    reed-beds;
when no gods were yet manifest,
nor names pronounced, nor destinies decreed,
then gods were born within them.

[*The birth of several generations of gods is recounted, including the birth of Anshar, the older sky god, and Kishar, the earth goddess, who in turn become parents of Anu, the sky god, who also had offspring.*]

The gods of that generation would meet
    together
and disturb Tiamat, and their clamor
    reverberated.
They stirred up Tiamat's belly,
they were annoying her by playing inside
    Anduruna.[3]
Apsu could not quell their noise
and Tiamat became mute before them;
however grievous their behavior to her,

---

[3]The home of the gods.

however bad their ways, she would indulge
    them.
Finally Apsu, begetter of the great gods,
called out and addressed his vizier Mummu,
"O Mummu, vizier who pleases me!
Come, let us go to Tiamat!"
They went and sat in front of Tiamat,
and discussed affairs concerning the gods
    their sons.
Apsu made his voice heard,
and spoke to Tiamat in a loud voice,
"Their ways have become grievous to me;
by day I cannot rest, by night I cannot sleep.
I shall abolish their ways and disperse them!
Let peace prevail, so that we can sleep."
When Tiamat heard this,
she was furious and shouted at her lover;
she shouted dreadfully and was beside herself
    with rage,
but then suppressed the evil in her belly:
"How could we allow what we ourselves have
    created to perish?
Even though their ways are so grievous, we
    should bear it patiently."

[*Despite Tiamat's opposition, Apsu decided to exterminate the younger gods who interfered with his sleep.
But they learned of the plot, and Ea, god of wisdom,
cast a spell on Apsu, putting him to sleep, and killed
him. Then he and Damkina, his consort, became the
parents of Marduk. Even as an infant, this storm god
caused trouble.*]

Anu created the four winds and gave them
    birth,
put them in Marduk's hand, "My son, let
    them play!"
He fashioned dust and made the whirlwind
    carry it;
he made the flood wave and stirred up
    Tiamat.
Tiamat was stirred up, and heaved restlessly
    day and night.
The gods, unable to rest, had to suffer....
They plotted evil in their hearts, and
they addressed Tiamat their mother, saying,
"Because they slew Apsu, your lover, and
you did not go to his side but sat mute,

he has created the four fearful winds
to stir up your belly on purpose, and we
    simply cannot sleep!
Was your lover Apsu not in your heart?
And vizier Mummu who was captured? No
    wonder you sit alone!
Are you not a mother? You heave restlessly
but what about us, who cannot rest? Don't
    you love us?
Our grip is slack, and our eyes are sunken.
Remove the yoke of us restless ones, and let
    us sleep!
Set up a battle cry and avenge them!
Conquer the enemy and reduce them to
    naught!"
Tiamat listened, and the speech pleased her.
"Let us act now, as you were advising!..."
They crowded round and rallied beside Tiamat.
They were fierce, scheming relentlessly night
    and day.
They were working up to war, growling and
    raging.
They convened a council and created conflict.

[*Encouraged by the older gods, Tiamat prepared for
battle, creating all sorts of monsters. She then appointed
Qingu, her lover, as leader of the gods.*]

Over the gods her offspring who had
    convened a council for her
she promoted Qingu and made him greatest
    among them,
conferred on him leadership of the army,
    command of the assembly,
raising the weapon to signal engagement,
    mustering combat troops,
overall command of the whole battle force.
And she set him upon a throne:
"I have cast the spell for you and made you
    greatest in the gods' assembly!
I have put into your power rule over all the
    gods!
You shall be the greatest, for you are my only
    lover!
Your commands shall always prevail over all
    the Anunnaki!"[1]

---

[1]The assembly of the gods.

She gave him the Tablet of Destinies and
    made him clasp it to his breast:
"Your utterance shall never be altered! Your
    word shall be law!"

TABLET 2

[*The plans of the older gods were reported to Ea, who
in turn reported them to Anshar. At his command,
first Ea and then Anu went to face Tiamat, but they
retreated in fear. The Igigi, the assembly of the gods,
was terrified. Finally, at his father's suggestion, Marduk, now grown, came forward and agreed to face
Tiamat, on one condition:*]

"If indeed I am to be your champion,
if I am to defeat Tiamat and save your lives,
convene the council, name a special fate,
sit joyfully together in Ubshu-ukkinakku:[1]
My own utterance shall fix fate instead of
    you!
Whatever I create shall never be altered!
The decree of my lips shall never be revoked,
    never changed!"

[*In Tablet 3, after repetition in epic style of much that
has preceded, the gods assembled.*]

TABLET 4

[*The gods formally gave Marduk supreme power,
which Marduk proceeded to demonstrate.*]

They founded a princely shrine for him,
and he took up residence as ruler before his
    fathers (who proclaimed),
"You are honored among the great gods.
Your destiny is unequalled; your word has the
    power of Anu.
From this day onward your command shall
    not be altered.
Yours is the power to exalt and abase.
May your utterance be law, your word never
    be falsified.
None of the gods shall transgress your
    limits.

May endowment, required for the gods'
    shrines
wherever they have temples, be established for
    your place.
O Marduk, you are our champion!
We hereby give you sovereignty over all of the
    whole universe.
Sit in the assembly, and your word shall be
    preeminent!
May your weapons never miss the mark, may
    they smash your enemies!
O Lord, spare the life of him who trusts in you,
but drain the life of the god who has espoused
    evil!"
They set up in their midst one constellation,
and then they addressed Marduk their son,
"May your decree, O Lord, impress the gods!
Command to destroy and to recreate, and let
    it be so!
Speak and let the constellation vanish!
Speak to it again and let the constellation
    reappear!"
He spoke, and at his word the constellation
    vanished.
He spoke to it again and the constellation was
    recreated.
When the gods his father saw how effective
    his utterance was,
they rejoiced, they proclaimed: "Marduk is
    King!"[2]
They invested him with scepter, throne, and
    staff of office.
They gave him an unfaceable weapon to
    crush the foe.
"Go, and cut off the life of Tiamat!
Let the winds bear her blood to us as good
    news!"
The gods his fathers thus decreed the destiny
    of the lord
and set him on the path of peace and
    obedience.
He fashioned a bow, designated it as his
    weapon,
feathered the arrow, set it in the string.
He lifted up a mace and carried it in his right
    hand,

---

[1]The hall in which the divine assembly met.

[2]Cf. Psalms 93:1; 95:3; 96:4, 10.

slung the bow and quiver at his side,
put lightning in front of him,
his body was filled with an ever-blazing flame.
He made a net to encircle Tiamat within it,
marshaled the four winds so that no part of
    her could escape:
South Wind, North Wind, East Wind, West
    Wind,
the gift of his father Anu, he kept them close
    to the net at his side.
He created the *imhullu*-wind,[1] the tempest,
    the whirlwind,
the Four Winds, the Seven Winds, the
    tornado, the unfaceable facing wind.
He released the winds which he had created,
    seven of them.
They advanced behind him to make turmoil
    inside Tiamat.
The Lord raised the flood-weapon, his great
    weapon,
and mounted the frightful, unfaceable
    storm-chariot.

[*Marduk then went to confront Tiamat and, although
initially frightened, engaged her in battle.*]

Face to face they came, Tiamat and Marduk,
    sage of the gods.
They engaged in combat, they closed for
    battle.
The Lord spread his net and made it encircle
    her,
to her face he dispatched the *imhullu*-wind,
    which had been behind:
Tiamat opened her mouth to swallow it,
and he forced in the *imhullu*-wind so that she
    could not close her lips.
Fierce winds distended her belly;
her insides were constipated and she stretched
    her mouth wide.
He shot an arrow which pieced her belly,
split her down the middle and slit her heart,
vanquished her and extinguished her life.
He threw down her corpse and stood on top
    of her....

[*Tiamat's allies fled in panic and were captured.*]

As for Qingu, who had once been the greatest
    among them,
he defeated him and counted him among the
    dead gods,
wrested from him the Tablet of Destinies,
    wrongfully his,
sealed it with his own seal and pressed it to
    his breast.
When he had defeated and killed his
    enemies,
and had proclaimed the submissive foe his
    slave,
and had set up the triumphal cry of Anshar
    over all the enemy,
and had achieved the desire of Nudimmud,[2]
    Marduk the warrior
strengthened his hold over the captive gods,
and to Tiamat, whom he had ensnared, he
    turned back.
The Lord trampled the lower part of Tiamat,
with his unsparing mace smashed her skull,
severed the arteries of her blood,
and made the North Wind carry it off as good
    news.
His fathers saw it and were jubilant: they
    rejoiced,
arranged to greet him with presents, greetings
    gifts.
The Lord rested and inspected her corpse.
He divided the monstrous shape and created
    marvels from it.
He sliced her in half like a fish for drying:
half of her he put up to roof the sky,
drew a bolt across and made a guard hold it.
Her waters he arranged so that they could not
    escape.[3]

[*Marduk then built temples for his divine allies.*]

TABLET 5

He fashioned stands for the great gods.
As for the stars, he set up constellations
    corresponding to them.
He designated the year and marked out its
    divisions,

---

[1] Evil wind.

[2] A name of Ea.
[3] Cf. Genesis 1:6–8; Job 38:8–11; Psalm 89:9–11.

apportioned three stars each to the twelve
    months.
When he had made plans of the days of the
    year,
he founded the stand of Neberu[1] to mark out
    their courses,
so that none of them could go wrong or stray

[*Marduk then established the moon to mark the
months. A lengthy break follows. Marduk then disposed of Tiamat's body.*]

Raising winds, making rain,
making fog billow, by collecting her poison,
he assigned for himself and let his own hand
    control it.
He placed her head, heaped up ...
opened up springs: water gushed out.
He opened the Euphrates and the Tigris from
    her eyes,
closed her nostrils....
He piled up clear-cut mountains from her
    udder,
bored waterholes to drain off the catchwater.
He laid her tail across, tied it fast as the
    cosmic bond,
and ... the Apsu beneath his feet.
He set her thigh to make fast the sky,
with half of her he made a roof; he fixed the
    earth.

[*Marduk completed the work of creation, establishing
the temple rituals and Babylon as the center of worship. The gods acclaimed his victory and acknowledged
his rule over them.*]

TABLET 6

When Marduk heard the speech of the gods,
he made up his mind to perform miracles.
He spoke his utterance to Ea,
and communicated to him the plan that he
    was considering.
"Let me put blood together, and make bones
    too.
Let me set up primeval man: Man shall be his
    name.

Let me create a primeval man.
The work of the gods shall be imposed on
    him, and so they shall be at leisure.
Let me change the ways of the gods
    miraculously,
so they are gathered as one yet divided in
    two."
Ea answered him and spoke a word to him,
told him his plan for the leisure of the gods.
"Let one who is hostile to them be
    surrendered up,
let him be destroyed, and let people be
    created from him.
Let the great gods assemble,
let the culprit be given up, and let them
    convict him."
Marduk assembled the great gods,
gave them instructions pleasantly, gave orders.
The gods paid attention to what he said.
The king addressed his words to the
    Anunnaki,
"Your election of me shall be firm and
    foremost.
I shall declare the laws, the edicts within my
    power.
Whosoever started the war,
and incited Tiamat, and gathered an army,
let the one who started the war be given up
    to me,
and he shall bear the penalty for his crime,
    that you may dwell in peace."
The Igigi, the great gods, answered him,
their lord Lugal-dimmer-ankia,[2] counselor of
    the gods,
"It was Qingu who started the war,
he who incited Tiamat and gathered an army!"
They bound him and held him in front of Ea,
imposed the penalty on him and cut off his
    blood.
He created mankind from his blood,
imposed the toil of the gods on man and
    released the gods from it....

[*Marduk finished assigning their roles to the gods,
and in return they constructed his temple Esagila in
Babylon.*]

---

[1]The planet Jupiter.

[2]A title of Marduk, meaning "king of the gods of heaven and
earth."

When they had done the work on Esagila,
and the Anunnaki, all of them, had fashioned
    their individual shrines,
the three hundred Igigi of heaven and the
    Anunnaki of the Apsu all assembled.
The Lord invited the gods his fathers to
    attend a banquet
in the great sanctuary which he had created
    as his dwelling.
"Indeed, Bab-ili[1] is your home too!
Sing for joy there, dwell in happiness!"
The great gods sat down there,
and set out the beer mugs; they attended the
    banquet.
When they had made merry within,
they themselves made a *taqribtu*-offering in
    splendid Esagila.
All the decrees and designs were fixed.
All the gods divided the stations of heaven
    and earth.
The fifty great gods were present, and
the gods fixed the seven destinies for the cult.
The Lord received the bow, and set his
    weapon down in front of them.
The gods his fathers looked at the net which
    he had made,
looked at the bow, how miraculous her
    construction,
and his fathers praised the deeds that he had
    done.
Anu raised the bow and spoke in the
    assembly of the gods;
he kissed the bow: "May she go far!"
He gave the bow her names, saying,
"May Long and Far be the first, and
    Victorious the second;
her third name shall be Bowstar, for she shall
    shine in the sky."
He fixed her position among the gods her
    companions.[2]
When Anu had decreed the destiny of the
    bow...
the great gods assembled
and made Marduk's destiny highest; they
    themselves did obeisance.
They swore an oath for themselves,

and swore on water and oil, touched their
    throats.
Thus they granted that he should exercise the
    kingship of the gods
and confirmed for him mastery of the gods of
    heaven and earth....

[*In the rest of Tablet 6 and most of Tablet 7, the gods
recite the fifty names of Marduk.*]

TABLET 7 *Conclusion*

NEBERU:[3] he does indeed hold the crossings of
    heaven and earth.
Neither up nor down shall they cross over;
    they must wait on him.
Neberu is his star which is bright in the sky.
He controls the crossroads; they must look to
    him,
saying: "He who kept crossing Tiamat without
    respite,
shall have Neberu as his name, grasping her
    middle.
May he establish the paths of the heavenly
    stars,
and may he shepherd all the gods like sheep.
Let him defeat Tiamat, constrict her breath
    and shorten her life,
so that for future people, till time grows old,
she shall be far removed, not kept here,
    distant forever."...
With fifty epithets the great gods
called his fifty names, making his way
    supreme.
May they always be cherished, and may the
    older explain to the younger.
Let the wise and learned consult together,
let the father repeat them and teach them to
    the son.
Let the ear of shepherd and herdsman be open,
let him not be negligent to Marduk, the Enlil[4]
    of the gods.
May his country be made fertile, and himself
    be safe and sound.
His word is firm, his command cannot alter;

---

[1]The Akkadian spelling of "Babylon," which means "gate of god."
[2]Cf. Genesis 9:13.

[3]"Crossing place," referring to the planet Jupiter.
[4]I.e., the leader of the gods. Enlil was an older storm god who had
control of human affairs.

no god can change his utterance.
When he is angry, he does not turn his neck
    aside;
in his rage and fury no god dare confront him.
His thoughts are deep, his emotions profound;
criminals and wrongdoers pass before him.
He[1] wrote down secret instruction which
    older men had recited in his presence,
and set it down for future men to read.
May the peoples of Marduk whom the Igigi[2]
    created
weave the tale and call upon his name
in remembrance of the song of Marduk
who defeated Tiamat and took the kingship.

2. A CREATION MYTH FROM SIPPAR

This incomplete myth features Marduk as the creator deity, as in *Enuma Elish* (Text 1). It is preserved in a bilingual Sumerian and Akkadian text from the sixth century BCE, but the original is significantly older.[3]

A holy house, a house of the gods, had not
    been built in its holy place;
a reed had not come forth, a tree had not
    been produced;
a brick had not been laid, a brick mold had
    not been built;
a house had not been made, a city had not
    been built;
a city had not been made, a living creature
    had not been placed in it;
Nippur had not been made; Ekur[4] had not
    been built;
Uruk had not been made; Eanna[5] had not
    been built;
the Apsu[6] had not been made, Eridu had not
    been built;
a holy house, a house of the gods and its
    foundations, had not been made.

All the lands were sea,
    the spring in the midst of the sea was only a
    channel.
Then Eridu was made, Esagila[7] was built,
Esagila that Lugaldukuga[8] erected in the heart
    of Apsu,
Babylon was made, Esagila was completed.
The gods, the Anunnaki, he divided into two
    equal parts,
they called it the preeminent city of the gods,
    the dwelling pleasing to them.
Marduk constructed a raft on the waters;
he created dirt and piled it on the raft.
In order to settle the gods in the dwelling
    pleasing to them,
he created humankind.
Aruru[9] created the seed of humankind with
    him.
He created the wild animals and all the
    animals of the steppe.
He created the Tigris and the Euphrates and
    set them in place,
giving them a favorable name.
He created the grass, the rush of the marsh,
    the reed, and the woods;
he created the green herb of the field,
the land, marshes, and canebrakes,
the cow and her young, the calf; the ewe and
    her lamb, the sheep of the fold;
the orchards and forests,
the wild sheep, the ibex....

[The rest of the text is broken and then missing.]

3. A CREATION MYTH FROM ASHUR

This bilingual text, written in Sumerian and Akkadian, comes from the library of the Assyrian king Tiglath-pileser I (ruled ca. 1114–1076 BCE), although the original may be older.[10]

When heaven had been separated from earth,
    in pair established,

---

[1]Perhaps the scribe.

[2]The assembly of the gods.

[3]Translation by Richard J. Clifford, *Creation Accounts in the Ancient Near East and in the Bible* (Washington, DC: Catholic Biblical Association of America, 1994), 62–63.

[4]The main temple of the city of Nippur.

[5]The main temple of the city of Uruk.

[6]The subterranean fresh waters, ruled by the god Enki, whose temple was in the city of Eridu.

[7]The temple of Marduk in Babylon.

[8]The father of the god Enlil.

[9]The mother goddess.

[10]Translation by Benjamin R. Foster, *Before the Muses: An Anthology of Akkadian Literature* (Bethesda, MD: CDL Press, 3d ed., 2005), 491–493.

when the mother goddess had appeared,
when the earth had been founded, the earth
    built up,
when they had established the plans for
    heaven and earth,
and, to regulate watercourses and irrigation
    canals,
had established the Tigris and Euphrates
    channels,
An, Enlil, Ninmah, and Ea, the great gods,
and the Anunnaki, the great gods,
took their places on their sublime daises;
they conferred among themselves.
Since they had established the plans for
    heaven and earth,
had laid out watercourses and irrigation
    canals,
and established the Tigris and Euphrates
    channels,
Enlil said to them:
"What should we do next?
What should we make now?
O Anunnaki, great gods,
what should we do next?
What should we make now?"
The great gods who were present,
and the Anunnaki, ordainers of destinies,
both replied to Enlil:
"In Uzumua,[1] the linking-place of heaven
    with earth,
let us slaughter Alla-gods,[2]
let us create humankind from their blood.
Their labor shall be labor for the gods:
to maintain the boundary ditch for all time,
to set pickaxe and workbasket in their hands,
to make the great dwelling of the gods,
worthy to be their sublime sanctuary,
to add field to field!
To maintain the boundary ditch for all time,
to regulate irrigation works for you,
to water the four abodes of the earth,
to make the plant life flourish,
. . . rainfall. . . ."
For maintaining the boundary ditch,
for heaping up piles of harvested grain . . .

for making the fields of the Anunnaki yield
    in plenty,
for making great the prosperity of the land,
for celebrating the gods' festivals as they
    should,
for libating cool water,
for making the great house of the gods worthy
    to be their sublime dwelling,
you shall call their names Ullegarra and
    Annagarra."[3]
To increase cattle, sheep, wild beasts, fish, and
    birds,
for prosperity in the land,
Enul and Ninul,[4] affirming, using their holy
    words,
and Aruru,[5] worthy to be mistress of them all,
laid down the master plans themselves:
skilled upon skilled, unskilled upon unskilled,
making many of them spring out of the earth,
    like grain,
a pattern as unalterable as the stars of heaven!
To celebrate the gods' festival, day and night,
    as they should,
Anu, Enlil, Enki, and Ninmah, the great
    gods,
laid down the master plans themselves!
Where humankind was created,
there also was Nisaba[6] cherished.[7]

4. DUMUZI AND INANNA

This cycle of Sumerian texts describes the relationship between the god Dumuzi (biblical Tammuz) and
Inanna (Akkadian Ishtar, the goddess of love and
war): their courtship and marriage, followed by his
death and seasonal revival. They originally date to
the late third millennium BCE.

  a. In this text, Inanna and her brother, the sun
god Utu, discuss her preparation for the marriage
with Dumuzi.[8]

---

[1]A district in the temple of Inanna in Nippur.
[2]Gods of an older generation; cf. the slaughter of Qingu on
page 13.

[3]Names having to do with abundance.
[4]The god and goddess of abundance.
[5]The mother goddess.
[6]Goddess of grain and writing.
[7]The text concludes with a note by the scribe suggesting that this is
esoteric doctrine suitable only for the truly wise.
[8]Translation by Thorkild Jacobsen, The Harps That Once. . . :
Sumerian Poetry in Translation (New Haven, CT: Yale University
Press, 1987), 16–18.

"My sister, what did you do in the house?
My little one, what did you do in the house?"
"I showered in water, rubbed myself with soap,
showered in the water of the bright copper
ewer,
rubbed myself with soap of the shiny stone jar,
anointed myself with the jar's sweet oil,
and dressed in the queenly robe, the robe of
the queenship of heaven.

"Thus freshened up, I roamed around in the
house.
I put kohl on my eyes,
the hair on the nape of my neck stood up—I
straightened it.
I tied on my hipflask, was filling it with water,
I designated a weapon that will make the
years of reign pleasant for him.
The hair of my head was tangled; I
straightened it.
The tresses of my crest had become loose; I
combed them,
and let them fall on the shoulders and nape of
the neck.
Rings of gold I put on my hands,
little stone-beads I hung around my neck,
straightened their counterbalance on the
nape of my neck."

"Sister, in seeking a husband for you I went
leading the way for your heart,
for your heart, the loving heart, I went.
Your tutelary goddess has given you bloom of
health.
Sister, you are radiant, the honey of the
mother who bore you!
My sister, worth any five to me,
my sister, worth any ten to me!
Since she[1] has perfected your shape for you
he will be wanting to come, O my most
pleasant and radiant sister!"

"Bring in my bridegroom from the palace!
May you send a man there about a wedding
wassail.
Let me, to start with, pour wine for him,
thus may his heart rejoice,

thus may his heart be pleased.
Let him come! Let him come!
By any means, yes, let him come!"

"My sister, let me escort you into the chamber,
may a lamb come, like unto the ewe,
O may it come!
May a kid come, like unto the goat,
O may it come!
May the lamb be as pleasing as the ewe,
may the kid be as pied as the goat!
My sister, let me escort you into the chamber!"

"Now our breasts stand up!
Now our parts have grown hair!
Going to the bridegroom's loins, Baba,[2]
let us be happy for them!
Dance! Dance! Baba, let us be happy for our
parts!
Dance! Dance! Afterward they will please
him, they will please him." [3]

**b. In this episode, Dumuzi has been killed, and his
wife, mother, and sister mourn for him.[4]**

A reed pipe of dirges—
my heart wants to play a reed pipe of dirges in
the desert!
I, mistress of Eanna, who lays waste
mountains
and I, Ninsana, the lord's mother,
and I, Geshtinanna, ward of the god of
Heaven!

My heart wants to play a reed pipe of dirges in
the desert,
play where the lad dwelt,
play where Dumuzi dwelt,
in Arali, on The Shepherd's Hill.

My heart wants to play a reed pipe of dirges in
the desert,
where the lad dwelt, he who is captive,

---

[1]The tutelary goddess mentioned above.

[2]A term of endearment for Inanna.
[3]These lines are spoken by Inanna's companions; compare the "daughters of Jerusalem" in the Song of Solomon.
[4]Translation by Thorkild Jacobsen, *The Harps That Once. . . : Sumerian Poetry in Translation* (New Haven, CT: Yale University Press, 1987), 50–51; cf. Ezekiel 8:14 and see page 16.

where Dumuzi dwelt, he who is bound,
where the ewe surrendered the lamb—
my heart wants to play a reed pipe of dirges in
    the desert—
where the goat surrendered the kid.

Treacherous are you, numen of that place—
where, though the lad said to me, "May my
    mother join me!"
My heart wants to play a reed pipe of dirges in
    the desert—
he may not move toward me his prostrate
    hands,
he may not move toward me his prostrate feet.

She neared the desert, neared the desert—
the mother who gave birth,
what crushing blow awaits her in the
    desert?

At the lad's territory, his desert, she arrived,
at the shepherd's territory, his desert, she
    arrived,
to Inanna's husband's territory,
—the mother who gave birth,
what crushing blow awaits her in the desert?

She will be able to see her slain wild bull,
will be able to see his face!
—The mother who gave birth,
what crushing blow awaits her in the
    desert?
What shudder befell her?"

• • •

The lady drew near for her to look closely.
Beside the son she stayed the foot.
—The mother who gave birth,
what crushing blow awaits her in the desert?

"It is you!" she says to him,
"You have changed!" she says to him.

What crushing blow is waiting for her,
in woe for her house,
in woe for being made to dwell away from her
    home!

UGARIT

5. BAAL

The body of this myth is preserved on six tablets, not all equally well preserved (see page 8), which recount three interrelated episodes concerning the storm god Baal: his defeat of Prince Sea and his assumption of power among the gods; his building a palace fitting his royal status; and his temporary defeat by the god of the underworld.[1] It dates to ca. 1350 BCE.

[The first tablet is poorly preserved. At the beginning of the second, Prince Sea/Judge River sends two messengers to the gods, assembled in council under the leadership of the high god El:]

    "Leave, lads, do not delay;
        now head to the Assembly in council,
        to the midst of Mount Lalu.
    Do not fall at El's feet,
        do not prostrate yourselves before the
            Assembly in council;
    still standing speak your speech,
        recite your message;
    and address the Bull, my father El,
        recite to the Assembly in council:
    'Message of Sea, your master,
        your lord, Judge River:
    Give up, gods, the one you obey,
        the one you obey, O multitude;
    give up Baal that I may humble him,
        the son of Dagan[2] that I may inherit
            his gold.'"
    The lads left; they did not delay;
        they headed to the midst of Mount Lalu,
        to the Assembly in council.
    There the gods had sat down to eat,
        the holy ones to a meal;
        Baal was standing by El.
    As soon as the gods saw them,
        saw the messengers of Sea,
        the legation of Judge River,
    the gods lowered their heads
        to the top of their knees,

[1]Translation by Michael D. Coogan and Mark S. Smith, *Stories from Ancient Canaan* (Louisville, KY: Westminster John Knox, 2d ed., 2012), 111–152.
[2]Cf. Judges 16:23; 1 Samuel 5:1–7.

and onto their princely seats.
Baal rebuked them:
"Gods, why have you lowered your heads
    to the top of your knees,
    and onto your princely seats?
Together will you gods answer
    the communication of the messengers
        of Sea,
    of the legation of Judge River?
Gods, raise your heads
    from the top of your knees,
    from your princely seats.[1]
For I myself will reply to the messengers of Sea,
    the legation of Judge River."
The gods raised their heads
    from the top of their knees,
    from their princely seats.
Then the messengers of Sea arrived,
    the legation of Judge River.
They did not fall at El's feet,
    they did not prostrate themselves before
        the Assembly in council;
still standing they spoke their speech,
    they recited their message.
They looked like a fire, or two;
    their tongues were like sharpened swords.
They addressed the Bull, his father El:
"Message of Sea, your master,
    your lord, Judge River:
Give up, gods, the one you obey,
    the one you obey, O multitude;
give up Baal so that I may humble him,
    the son of Dagan that I may inherit his
        gold."
And the Bull, his father El, replied:
"Sea, Baal is your servant;
    River, Baal is your servant,
    the son of Dagan your prisoner.
He will bring you tribute,
    like the gods, he will bring you payment,
    like the holy ones, gifts."

[*After a long break, the text resumes with the crafts-man of the gods, Kothar-wa-Hasis, promising Baal victory over Sea:*]

And Kothar-wa-Hasis spoke:
"Let me tell you, Prince Baal,
    let me repeat, Rider on the Clouds:[2]
Now, your enemy, Baal,
    now you will kill your enemy,
    now you will annihilate your foe.[3]
You will take your eternal kingship,
    your dominion forever and ever."[4]
Kothar fashioned two clubs,
    and he pronounced their names:
"As for you, your name is Driver:
Driver, drive Sea,
    drive Sea from his throne,
    River from the seat of his dominion.
Swoop from Baal's hands,
    like a vulture from his fingers.
Strike Prince Sea on the shoulder,
    Judge River between the arms."
The club swooped from Baal's hands,
    like a vulture from his fingers.
It struck Prince Sea on the shoulder,
    Judge River between the arms.
Sea was strong; he did not sink;
    his joints did not shake,
    his frame did not collapse.
Kothar fashioned two clubs,
    and he pronounced their names:
"As for you, your name is Chaser:
Chaser, chase Sea,
    chase Sea from his throne,
    River from the seat of his dominion.
Swoop from Baal's hands,
    like a vulture from his fingers.
Strike Prince Sea on the skull,
    Judge River between the eyes;
Sea will stumble,
    he will fall to the ground."
The club swooped from Baal's hands,
    like a vulture from his fingers.
It struck Prince Sea on the skull,
    Judge River between the eyes.
Sea stumbled;
    he fell to the ground;
    his joints shook,

---

[1] Cf. Psalm 24:7.

[2] Cf. Psalm 68:4, 33; Isaiah 19:1.
[3] Cf. Psalm 92:9.
[4] Cf. Psalm 145:13.

his frame collapsed.
Baal captured and pierced Sea;
   he finished off Judge River.
Astarte shouted to him by name:
"Hail, Baal the Conqueror!
   Hail, Rider on the Clouds!
Prince Sea is our captive,
   Judge River is our captive."

[*After his victory over Sea, Baal celebrates at a banquet. In the following excerpt, Baal is instructing messengers to go to his sister, Anat, the goddess of war,
who also has been victorious in battle.*]

"So then, lads, enter:
   at Anat's feet bow down and adore,
   prostrate yourselves, honor her,
and say to the Maiden Anat,
   recite to the Mistress of the Peoples:
'Message of Baal the Conqueror,
   word of the Conqueror of Warriors:
Remove war from the earth,
   set love in the ground,
pour peace into the heart of the earth,
   tranquility into the heart of the fields.
Hasten! hurry! rush!
Run to me with your feet,
   race to me with your legs.
For I have a word to tell you,
   a message to recount to you:
the word of the tree and the whisper of the
     stone,
   the murmur of the heavens to the earth,
   of the seas to the stars.
I understand the lightning that the heavens
     do not know,
   the word that people do not know,
   and earth's masses cannot understand.
Come, and I will reveal it:
in the midst of my mountain, divine Zaphon,[1]
   in the sanctuary, in the mountain of my
     inheritance,
   in the pleasant place, in the hill of my
     victory.'"

[*The text omits the journey of the messengers, whose
names are Gapn and Ugar.*]

As soon as Anat saw the gods,
   her feet shook,
   her back convulsed,
   her face broke out in sweat,
   her joints trembled,
   her vertebrae weakened.
She raised her voice and declared:
"Why have Gapn and Ugar come?
What enemy has risen against Baal,
   What foe against the Rider on the Clouds?
Didn't I demolish El's Darling, Sea?
   Didn't I finish off the divine River, the
     Mighty?
   Didn't I snare the Dragon and destroy him?
I demolished the Twisting Serpent,
   the seven-headed monster.[2]
I demolished El's Darling, Desire,
   I annihilated the divine calf, the Rebel;
I demolished El's bitch, Fire,
   I finished off El's daughter, Zebub.
I battled for the silver,
   I took possession of the gold.
Has Baal been driven from the peak of
     Zaphon,
   made to flee like a bird from his royal
     throne,
   from his resting place, from the seat of his
     dominion?
What enemy has risen against Baal,
   what foe against the Rider on the Clouds?"
Then the lads replied:
"No enemy has risen against Baal,
   no foe against the Rider on the Clouds.
'Message of Baal the Conqueror,
   word of the Conqueror of Warriors:
Remove war from the earth,
   set love in the ground,
pour peace into the heart of the earth,
   tranquility into the heart of the fields.
Hasten! hurry! rush!
   Run to me with your feet,
   race to me with your legs.
For I have a word to tell you,
   a message to recount to you:
the word of the tree and the whisper of the
     stone,

---

[1]See Isaiah 14:13; Psalm 48:2; Job 26:7.

[2]Cf. Job 7:12; Isaiah 27:1; 51:9–10; Psalm 74:13; Revelation 12:3; 13:1.

the word that people do not know,
and earth's masses cannot understand:
the murmur of the heavens to the earth,
of the seas to the stars;
I understand the lightning that the heavens
do not know.
Come, and I will reveal it:
in the midst of my mountain, divine
Zaphon,
in the sanctuary, in the mountain of my
inheritance.'"
Maiden Anat replied,
the Mistress of the Peoples answered:
"I will remove war from the earth,
I will set love in the ground,
I will pour peace into the heart of the earth,
tranquility into the heart of the fields.
Let Baal set his thunderbolts . . . .
And I have something else to tell you:
Go, go, divine powers;
you are slow, but I am swift.
Is not my mountain certainly far, O gods,
Inbubu far, divine ones?
Two fathoms under the earth's springs,
three lengths under the caves."
Then she headed to Baal on the peak of
Zaphon,
a thousand fields, ten thousand acres at
each step.
Baal saw his sister coming,
his father's daughter approaching;
he dismissed his wives from his presence.
He put an ox before her,
a fatling right in front of her.
She drew water and washed,
in the heavens' dew, the earth's oil,
dew that the heavens pour,
rain that the stars pour out.
She beautified herself with murex,
from a thousand fathoms in the vast
expanse of the sea.

[*Baal complains to Anat that he has no palace suitable to his status. Anat goes to El and threatens him with harm if he doesn't order a house built for Baal.*]

Maiden Anat spoke:
"Don't rejoice in your well-built house,
in your well-built house, El,

don't rejoice in the height of your palace.
Or else I will seize it . . . with my mighty arm.
I'll smash your head,
I'll make your gray hair run with blood,
your gray beard with gore."
El replied from the seven rooms,
from the eight enclosures:
"I know you, daughter, how furious you are,
that among goddesses there is no
restraining you;
what do you want, Maiden Anat?"
And Maiden Anat replied:
"Your decree is wise, El,
your wisdom is eternal,
a lucky life is your decree.
But our king is Baal the Conqueror,
our judge, higher than all:
all of us must bear his chalice,
all of us must bear his cup.
In lament he declares to the Bull El, his
father,
to El the King who brought him into being;
he declares to Asherah[1] and her sons,
to the goddess and her pride of lions:
'But Baal has no house like the
other gods,
no court like Asherah's sons:
El's home is his son's shelter,
Lady Asherah of the Sea's home,
the home of Pidray,[2] maid of light,
the shelter of Tallay,[3] maid of rain,
the home of Arsay,[4] maid of the wide world,
the home of the beautiful brides.'"

[*Apparently following El's advice, Baal seeks Asherah's support for his plan to build a palace. She agrees, and journeys to El.*]

Then she headed to El
at the source of the two rivers,
in the midst of the channels of the two
deeps.
She came to the encampment of El, and
entered

---

[1] El's wife, the mother goddess.
[2] A minor goddess, Baal's attendant, whose name means "misty."
[3] A minor goddess, Baal's attendant, whose name means "dewy."
[4] A minor goddess, Baal's attendant, whose name means "earthy."

the tent of the King, the Father of Time.
At El's feet she bowed and lowered herself;
    she prostrated herself and honored him.
As soon as El saw her,
    his brow relaxed and he laughed;
he put his feet on a stool,
    his fingers twirled with excitement.
He raised his voice and declared:
"Why has Lady Asherah of the Sea arrived?
    why has the Mother of the Gods come?
Are you hungry...
    or thirsty...?
Eat, please drink:
    eat some food from the table,
drink some wine from the goblet,
    blood of the vine from the golden cup.
Or does El the King's passion excite you?
    does the love of the Bull arouse you?"
But Lady Asherah of the Sea replied:
"Your decree is wise, El,
    your wisdom is eternal,
    a lucky life is your decree.
But Baal the Conqueror is our king,
    our judge, higher than all.
All of us must bear his chalice,
    all of us must bear his cup.
In lament he declares to the Bull El, his
        father,
    to El the King who brought him into
        being;
he declares to Asherah and her sons,
    to the goddess and her pride of lions:
'But Baal has no house like the other gods,
    no court like Asherah's sons:
El's home is his son's shelter,
    Lady Asherah of the Sea's home,
    the home of the beautiful brides,
    the home of Pidray, maid of light,
    the shelter of Tallay, maid of rain,
    the home of Arsay, maid of the wide
        world.'"
But El the Kind, the Compassionate, replied:
"So am I a servant, a slave of Asherah?
    So am I a servant who handles a tool,
    or a slave-girl of Asherah who molds bricks?
Let a house be built for Baal like the other
        gods,
    a court like Asherah's sons."
And Lady Asherah of the Sea replied:

"You are great, El, you are truly wise;
    your gray beard truly instructs you...
Now Baal will provide his enriching rain,
    provide a rich watering in a downpour;
and he will sound his voice in the clouds,
    flash his lightning to the earth.
Let him complete his house of cedar!
    let him construct his house of bricks!
Let it be announced to Baal the Conqueror:
'Call a caravan into your house,
    supplies into your palace;
the mountains will bring you much silver,
    the hills fine gold in abundance;
    the best ore will be brought to you:
and build a house of silver and gold,
    a house of purest lapis lazuli.'"
Maiden Anat was glad;
    she stamped her feet and left the earth;
Then she headed to Baal on the peak of
        Zaphon,
    a thousand fields, ten thousand acres at
        each step.
Maiden Anat laughed;
    she raised her voice and declared:
"Receive the good news, Baal;
    good news is brought to you:
A house will be built for you like your
        brothers,
    and a court like your kinsmen.
Call a caravan into your house,
    supplies into your palace;
the mountains will bring you much silver,
    the hills fine gold in abundance:
and build a house of silver and gold,
    a house of purest lapis lazuli."
Baal the Conqueror was glad;
    he called a caravan into his house,
    supplies into his palace;
the mountains brought him much silver,
    the hills fine gold in abundance;
    the best ore was brought to him.
He sent messengers to Kothar-wa-Hasis....
Baal the Conqueror spoke...
"Kothar, hurry a house;
    hurry, erect a palace;
hurry, you must build a house;
    hurry, you must raise a palace
    on the heights of Zaphon.
Let the house extend over a thousand fields,

the palace over ten thousand acres."
And Kothar-wa-Hasis replied:
"Listen, Baal the Conqueror,
    pay attention, Rider on the Clouds:
I should put an opening in the house,
    a window in the palace."[1]
But Baal the Conqueror replied:
"Don't put an opening in the house,
    a window in the palace."
But Kothar-wa-Hasis replied:
"You'll recall my words, Baal." . . .
They built his house,
    they erected his palace;
they went to the Lebanon for wood,
    to Sirion[2] for the finest cedar;
there — to the Lebanon for wood,
    to Sirion for the finest cedar!
Fire was set in the house,
    flames in the palace.
One day passed, then two:
    the fire burned in the house,
    the flames in the palace.
Three days passed, then four:
    the fire burned in the house,
    the flames in the palace.
Five days passed, then six:
    the fire burned in the house,
    the flames in the palace.
Then, on the seventh day,
    the fire went out in the house,
    the flames in the palace:
The silver had turned into blocks,
    the gold had become bricks.
Baal the Conqueror was glad:
"I have built my house of silver,
    my palace of gold."
Baal made preparations in his house,
    Haddu[3] made preparations in his palace:
he slaughtered oxen as well as sheep;
    he felled bulls, fatling rams,
    calves a year old, lambs of the flock, with
        kids.
He invited his brothers into his house,

his kinsmen in his palace;
    he invited Asherah's seventy sons.
He gave the gods lambs;
    he gave the goddesses ewes;
he gave the gods oxen;
    he gave the goddesses cows;
he gave the gods seats;
    he gave the goddesses thrones;
he gave the gods a vat of wine;
    he gave the goddesses a cask of wine.
Until the gods ate and drank their fill,
    he gave them sucklings to eat,
    with a sharp knife, a cut of a fatling.
They drank wine from goblets,
    blood of the vine from golden cups. . . .
He crossed from town to town,
    he toured from village to village.
Baal captured sixty-six cities,
    seventy-seven towns;
Baal sacked eighty,
    Baal sacked ninety;
Baal returned to his house.
And Baal the Conqueror said:
"I will put it in, Kothar, son of Sea,
    Kothar, son of the Confluence:
let a window be opened in the house,
    an opening in the palace;
so let a break be opened in the clouds,
    as Kothar-wa-Hasis said."
Kothar-wa-Hasis laughed;
    he raised his voice and declared:
"Baal the Conqueror, didn't I tell you:
    'You'll recall my words, Baal'?"
He opened a window in the house,
    an opening in the palace.
Then Baal opened a break in the clouds,
    Baal sounded his holy voice,
Baal thundered from his lips. . . .
    the earth's high places shook;
Baal's enemies fled to the woods,
    Haddu's haters took to the mountains.
And Baal the Conqueror said:
"Haddu's enemies, why are you quaking?
    why are you quaking, assailers of the
        Valiant One?"
Baal's eye guided his hand,
    as the cedar moved in his right hand.
So Baal was enthroned in his house:
"No other king or non-king

---

[1] The debate about whether the palace should have a window may be connected with a belief that death comes in through a window (see Jeremiah 9:21). In the next episode Baal becomes temporarily subject to the power of Death.

[2] Mount Hermon; see Deuteronomy 3:9, and cf. Psalm 29:6.

[3] One of Baal's titles; cf. biblical Hadad; Akkadian Adad.

shall set his power over the earth.
I will send a messenger to El's son Death,
    an envoy to El's Darling, the Hero,
that he may call to Death with his throat,
    instruct the Darling with his innards.
For I alone rule over the gods;
    I alone fatten gods and men;
    I alone satisfy earth's masses."
Baal declared to his lads:
"Listen, Gapn and Ugar...
Then head to Mount Targuziza,
    to Mount Tharummagi,
    to the mounds at the edge of the
        underworld.
Raise the mountain with your hands,
    the hill on top of your palms.
Then go down to the isolation ward of the
        underworld,
    you will be counted among those who go
        down into the earth.
Then head to the midst of his city, the
        Swamp,
    the Pit, his royal house,
    Filth, the land of his inheritance.
But, divine servants, be on your guard,
    don't approach El's son, Death,
lest he put you in his mouth like a lamb,
    crush you like a kid in his jaws,
Sun, the Gods' Torch, bums,
    the heavens shimmer.
    because of the power of Death, El's
        Darling.
A thousand fields, ten thousand acres at each
        step,
    at Death's feet bow down and fall,
    prostrate yourselves and honor him;
and speak to El's son, Death,
    recite to El's Darling, the Hero:
'Message of Baal the Conqueror,
    word of the Conqueror of Warriors:
I have built my house of silver,
    my palace of gold....'"

[In the broken text that follows, Baal's message is delivered and Death replies. When the text resumes, the
messengers are delivering Death's message to Baal:]

    "Message of El's son, Death,
        word of El's Darling, the Hero:

'So is my appetite like a lion's in the wild,
    or the desire of a dolphin in the sea?
Or is it like wild oxen that go to a pool,
    deer that go to a spring?
Or truly does my appetite consume a heap-full?
So do I eat with both my hands,
    or are my portions seven bowls' worth,
    or does my cup contain a whole river?
So invite me, Baal, with my brothers,
    summon me, Haddu, with my kinsmen,
to eat food with my brothers,
    and drink wine with my kinsmen.
Let us drink.... I will pierce you....
When you killed Litan,[1] the Fleeing Serpent,
    finished off the Twisting Serpent,
    the seven-headed monster,
the heavens withered and weakened,
    like the folds of your robe....
Now you must descend into the throat of El's
        son, Death,
    into the watery depths of El's Darling, the
        Hero.'"

[After a large gap, Baal's sentence is being announced
to him by messengers:]

    "One lip to the earth, one lip to the heavens;
        ...his tongue to the stars.
Baal must enter inside him;
    he must go down into his mouth,
like a dried olive,
    the earth's produce,
    the fruit of the trees."
Baal the Conqueror became afraid;
    the Rider on the Clouds was terrified:
"Go, speak to El's son Death,
    recite to El's Darling, the Hero:
'Message of Baal the Conqueror,
    word of the Conqueror of Warriors:
Hail, El's son Death!
    I am your servant, yours forever.'"
The gods left; they did not delay;
    then they headed to El's son Death,
to the midst of his city, the Swamp,
    the Pit, his royal house,
    Filth, the land of his inheritance.

---

[1]Biblical Leviathan; see Isaiah 27.1; Psalm 74:13; Job 3:8;
41:1–34.

They raised their voices and declared:
"Message of Baal the Conqueror,
    word of the Conqueror of Warriors:
Hail, El's son Death!
    I am your servant, yours forever."
El's son Death was glad. . . .

[*After a very large gap, Death concludes his instructions to Baal:*]

"As for you, take your clouds,
    your wind, your bolts, your rain;
take with you your seven lads,
    your eight noble attendants;
take with you Pidray, maid of light;
    take with you Tallay, maid of rain;
then head to Mount Kankaniya;
    raise the mountain with your hands,
    the hill on top of your palms;
then go down to the isolation ward of the
    underworld;
    you will be counted among those who go
        down into the earth;
    and the gods will know that you have
        died."
Baal the Conqueror obeyed;
    he loved a heifer in the pasture,
    a young cow in the fields on Death's shore:
He lay with her seventy-seven times,
    she made him erect eighty-eight times;
and she became pregnant,
    and she bore him a boy.

[*Here there is another large gap, which must have described Baal's descent into the underworld and his own death. When the text resumes, messengers are informing the gods of what has happened:*]

"We arrived at the lovely place, the desert
    pasture,
    at the beautiful fields on Death's shore.
We came upon Baal:
    he had fallen to the ground.
Baal the Conqueror has died,
    the Prince, the Lord of the Earth, has
        perished."
Then El the Kind, the Compassionate,
    came down from his throne, sat on his
        stool,

came down from his stool, sat on the
    ground.
He poured dirt on his head in mourning,
    dust on his skull in lamentation;
    he covered his loins with sackcloth.
He cut his skin with a stone,
    made incisions with a razor;
he cut his cheeks and chin,
    raked the length of his arms;
he plowed his chest like a garden,
    he raked his back like a valley.[1]
He raised his voice and declared:
"Baal is dead: what will happen to the
    peoples?
    Dagan's son: what will happen to the
        masses?
    I will go down into the earth after Baal."
Anat went about hunting
    on every mountain in the heart of the
        earth,
    on every hill in the heart of the fields.
She arrived at the lovely place, the desert
    pasture,
    at the beautiful fields on Death's shore.
    she came upon Baal, fallen to the earth.
She covered her loins with sackcloth.
She cut her skin with a stone,
    made incisions with a razor;
she cut her cheeks and chin,
    raked the length of her arms;
she plowed her chest like a garden,
    raked her back like a valley:
"Baal is dead: what will happen to the peoples?
    Dagan's son: what will happen to the masses?
    Let us go down into the earth after Baal."
Sun, the Gods' Torch, went down with her.
When she had finished weeping,
    had drunk her tears like wine,
she declared to Sun, the Gods' Torch:
    "Lift Baal the Conqueror onto me!"
Sun, the Gods' Torch, obeyed;
    she lifted up Baal the Conqueror;
    she put him on Anat's shoulders.
She brought him up to the heights of Zaphon;
    she wept for him and buried him;

---

[1] Traditional actions expressing grief; cf. Leviticus 19:28; Deuteronomy 14:1; Joshua 7:6; Job 1:20; 2:12–13; Jeremiah 16:6; Ezekiel 27:30; Lamentations 2:10; Ezra 9:3.

she put him into a great pit in the earth.
She slaughtered seventy wild oxen,
    as an oblation for Baal the Conqueror.
She slaughtered seventy plow oxen,
    as an oblation for Baal the Conqueror,
She slaughtered seventy sheep,
    as an oblation for Baal the Conqueror.
She slaughtered seventy deer,
    as an oblation for Baal the Conqueror.
She slaughtered seventy mountain goats,
    as an oblation for Baal the Conqueror.
She slaughtered seventy asses,
    as an oblation for Baal the Conqueror....
Then she headed to El at the source of the
    two rivers,
    in the midst of the channels of the two
    deeps.
She came to the encampment of El, and
    entered
    the tent of the King, the Father of Time.
At El's feet she bowed and lowered herself,
    she prostrated herself and honored him.
She raised her voice and declared:
"Now let Asherah and her sons rejoice,
    the goddess and her pride of lions:
For Baal the Conqueror has died,
    the Prince, the Lord of the Earth, has
    perished."
El called to Lady Asherah of the Sea:
"Listen, Lady Asherah of the Sea:
give me one of your sons,
    so I may make him king."
And Lady Asherah of the Sea replied:
"Why not make Yadi-Yalhan[1] king?"
But El the Kind, the Compassionate, replied:
"He's too weak to race,
    he can't compete in spear-throwing with
    Baal,
    compared with Dagan's son, he'd collapse."
And Lady Asherah of the Sea replied:
"Why not make Athtar the Awesome[2] king?
    Let Athtar the Awesome be king!"
Then Athtar the Awesome
    went up to the heights of Zaphon;
    he sat on Baal the Conqueror's throne.
His feet did not reach the footstool,

his head did not reach the headrest.
And Athtar the Awesome spoke:
"I can't be king on the heights of Zaphon."
Athtar the Awesome descended,
    descended from the throne of Baal the
    Conqueror,
    and he became king of the earth,[3] the god
    of it all....

[After a long gap, Anat takes revenge on Death:]

One day passed, then two;
    and Maiden Anat approached him.
Like the heart of a cow for her calf,
    like the heart of a ewe for her lamb,
    so was Anat's heart for Baal.
She seized Death by the edge of his clothes,
    she grabbed him by the hem of his
    garment;
she raised her voice and declared:
    "Come, Death, give me my brother!"
And El's son Death replied:
    "What do you want, Maiden Anat?
I was taking a walk and wandering
    on every mountain in the heart of the
    earth,
    on every hill in the heart of the fields.
My appetite longed for human beings,
    my appetite for earth's masses.
I arrived at my lovely place, the desert
    pasture,
    at the beautiful fields on Death's shore.
I approached Baal the Conqueror;
    I put him in my mouth like a lamb,
    he was crushed like a kid in my jaws."
Sun, the Gods' Torch, burned;
    the heavens shimmered
    because of the power of Death, El's son.
One day passed, then two;
    the days became months;
    Maiden Anat approached him.
Like the heart of a cow for her calf,
    like the heart of a ewe for her lamb,
    so was Anat's heart for Baal.
She seized El's son Death:
    with a sword she split him;
    with a sieve she winnowed him;

[1] One of Asherah and El's sons.
[2] Another of Asherah and El's sons.

[3] Probably the underworld.

with fire she burned him;
   with millstones she ground him;
   in the fields she sowed him.
Birds ate his flesh,
   fowl consumed his parts;
   flesh cried out to flesh!

[After another large gap, El has a dream indicating that Baal has been restored to life:]

In the dream of El the Kind, the
      Compassionate,
   in the vision of the Creator of Creatures,
the heavens rained down oil,
   the wadis ran with honey.
El the Kind, the Compassionate, was glad:
   he put his feet on a stool,
   his brow relaxed and he laughed.
He raised his voice and declared:
"Now I can sit back and relax;
   my heart inside me can relax;
for Baal the Conqueror lives,
   the Prince, the Lord of the Earth, is alive."
El called to Maiden Anat:
"Listen, Maiden Anat:
   speak to Sun, the Gods' Torch...
Maiden Anat left;
   she headed to Sun, the Gods' Torch;
   she raised her voice and declared:
"Message of the Bull, El your father,
word of the Kind One, your parent:
'Sun, the furrows in the fields have dried,
   the furrows in El's fields have dried;
   Baal has neglected the furrows of his
      plowland.
Where is Baal the Conqueror?
   where is the Prince, the Lord of the
      Earth?'"
And Sun, the Gods' Torch, replied:
"...I will look for Baal the Conqueror."
And Maiden Anat replied:
"Wherever you go, Sun,
   wherever you go, may El protect you,
   may you be protected, Sun...."

[Having been revived, Baal takes his revenge:]

Baal seized Asherah's sons;
   he struck Rabbim on the shoulder;

he struck Waves with his club;
   he trampled burning Death to the ground.
Baal returned to his royal throne,
   to his resting place, the seat of his dominion.
The days became months,
   the months became years.
Then, in the seventh year,
   El's son Death spoke to Baal the
      Conqueror;
   he raised his voice and declared:
"Baal, because of you I experienced shame:
   because of you I experienced splitting
      with a sword;
   because of you I experienced burning
      with fire;
   because of you I experienced grinding
      with millstones;
   because of you I experienced winnowing
      with a sieve;
   because of you I experienced scattering in
      the fields;
   because of you I experienced sowing in
      the sea.
Give me one of your brothers that I may eat,
   and my anger will turn away.
If you do not give up one of your brothers...,
   then I will consume humans,
I will consume the multitudes of the earth."

[After more damaged lines, Death speaks again:]

"See now, Baal gave my brothers for me
      to eat,
   my mother's sons for me to consume."
He turned to Baal on the heights of Zaphon;
   he raised his voice and declared:
"Baal, you gave me my brothers to eat,
   my mother's sons for me to consume."
They butted each other like champions;
   Death was strong, Baal was strong.
They gored each other like wild oxen;
   Death was strong, Baal was strong.
They bit each other like serpents;
   Death was strong, Baal was strong.
They trampled each other like running
      animals;
   Death fell, Baal fell.
Sun declared from above:
   "Listen, El's son Death:

How can you battle with Baal the Conqueror?
　　Will the Bull, El your father, continue to
　　　　listen to you?
Surely he will undermine the foundations of
　　　　your seat,
　　surely he will overturn your royal throne,
　　surely he will smash your scepter of
　　　　judgment."
El's son Death became fearful;
　　El's Darling, the Hero, was terrified;
　　Death was afraid of her voice.
He raised his voice and declared:
"Let Baal be enthroned on his royal throne,
　　on the resting place, the seat of his
　　　　dominion."

[*The remainder of the tablet is broken or obscure. The rest of the Baal cycle is known only in fragments.*]

HITTITE

6. EL-KUNIRSHA AND ASHERTU

This originally Canaanite myth survives only in Hittite translation, in several fragmentary tablets. It dates to ca. 1300 BCE.[1]

...Baal...went to the headwaters of the Euphrates River. He went to El-kunirsha,[2] the husband of Ashertu,[3] and entered the tent of El-kunirsha.

El-kunirsha looked at Baal and asked him: "Why have you come?" Baal said: "When I came to your house, Ashertu sent young women to me, saying: 'Come sleep with me.' I refused. Then she...spoke: 'Stay behind me, and I will stay behind you. Else I will press you with my word and stab you....' That is why I have come, my father. I did not come to you in the person of a messenger; I myself have come to you. Ashertu is rejecting you, her own husband. Although she is your wife, yet she keeps sending to me: 'Sleep with me.'" El-kunirsha replied to Baal: "Go threaten...my wife, and humble her."

Baal heard the words of El-kunirsha and went to Ashertu. Baal said to Ashertu: "I have killed your seventy-seven children. Your eighty-eight I have killed." When Ashertu heard the humiliating report, her mind within her became sad. She appointed mourning women. And she lamented seven years....

[*The text is broken here. When it resumes, Ashertu is speaking to El-kunirsha.*]

"...I will press Baal down with my word....I will stab him. And I will sleep with you." El-kunirsha heard and said to his wife: "Come take Baal as your prisoner, and do with him as you wish."

Anat-Astarte[4] heard those words. She became a cup[5] in El-kunirsha's hand. She became an owl and perched on his wall. Anat-Astarte heard the words which husband and wife spoke to one another. El-kunirsha and his wife went to bed and slept together. But Anat-Astarte flew off like a bird across the desert. In the desert she found Baal and said to him: "O Baal...Ashertu. Do not drink wine together...."

[*From what remains of the text, it seems that Baal is injured, perhaps even killed, and then brought back to life.*]

7. THE DISAPPEARANCE OF THE STORM GOD

Many Hittite myths feature the disappearance of a god. In this one, dating to the first half of the second millennium BCE, it is the Storm God himself. At his disappearance, fertility came to an end, as in the Ugaritic myth of Baal (see page 27).[6]

Mists seized the windows. Smoke seized the house. In the hearth the logs were stifled.

At the altars the gods were stifled. In the sheepfold the sheep were stifled. In the cattle barn the cattle were stifled. The ewe rejected her lamb. The cow rejected her calf.

---

[1]Translation by Harry A. Hoffner, Jr., *Hittite Myths* (Writings from the Ancient World 2; Atlanta, GA: Scholars Press, 2d ed., 1998), 90–91.
[2]I.e., El-qone-ars ("El the creator of the earth"), as in Genesis 14:19, 22; and Text 35.
[3]I.e., Asherah, the wife of El.

[4]If this is not a scribal error, then the two Canaanite goddesses have been combined.
[5]Perhaps an ancient mistranslation of a word for "owl."
[6]Translation by Harry A. Hoffner, Jr., *Hittite Myths* (Writings from the Ancient World 2; Atlanta, GA: Scholars Press, 2d ed., 1998), 21–22.

The Storm God of the Sky set out toward the steppe, the meadow, and the moor. He carried off plenty, prosperity, and abundance. The Storm God departed, and barley and wheat no longer ripened. Cattle, sheep, and humans did not become pregnant. And those who were pregnant did not give birth from that time.

The mountains dried up. The trees dried up. And the shoots did not come forth. The pastures dried up. The springs dried up.

The Sun God made a feast and invited the Thousand Gods. They ate, but couldn't get enough. They drank, but couldn't quench their thirst. The Storm God's father said: "My son is not there. He became angry and carried off everything good. He carried off grain, animal fecundity, plenty, and satiation."

All the gods began to search for the Storm God...sent the swift eagle: "Go search the high mountains. Search the deep valleys. Search the Blue Deep."

The eagle went, but did not find him. The swift eagle brought a report to the Sun God: "I searched the high mountains. I searched the deep valleys. I searched the Blue Deep, but I did not find him, the Storm God of the Sky."

The Storm God's father went to his (the Storm God's) grandfather and said to him: "Who sinned grievously, so that the seed perished and everything dried up?" The grandfather said: "No one sinned; you alone sinned grievously."

The Storm God's father said: "It wasn't I who sinned." The grandfather said: "I will trace this matter out, and I will kill you. So go search for the Storm God."

The Storm God's father went to Gulsa[1] and Hannahanna.[2] Thus said Gulsa and Hannahanna: "Why have you come, Storm God's father?" The Storm God's father replied: "The Storm God became angry, and everything dried up...and perished. My father says: 'It is your fault. So I will trace the matter out and kill you.' Now how shall I act? What has happened?"

Hannahanna said: "Don't be afraid. If it is your fault, I will make it right. And even if it is not your fault, I will still make it right. Go search for the Storm God before his grandfather hears."

The Storm God's father said: "Then where shall I go search?" Hannahanna replied: "I will give him to you. Go bring the bee here, and I myself will instruct it. It will search for the Storm God."

The Storm God's father said: "But if the great gods and the lesser gods searched for him and didn't find him, will this bee find him? Its wings are tiny, and it itself is tiny, and furthermore it is all by itself.

[*The text is broken here. The bee finds the Storm God and stings him to wake him up, and the Storm God returns home, bringing food and restoring fertility. The myth concludes with a description of a ritual to appease the Storm God's wrath in the future.*]

8. THE SONG OF KUMARBI

This Hittite version of an original Hurrian myth describes conflict for supremacy among the gods between Kumarbi, an underworld deity, and Teshub, the storm god; we find close parallels in Greek mythology. The text is not well preserved, even though it exists in several fragmentary copies, dating to the fifteenth century BCE.[3]

[*After a broken invitation to the gods to listen, the text begins:*]

Long ago, in primeval years Alalu was king in heaven. Alalu was sitting on the throne, and weighty Anu, the foremost of the gods, was standing before him. He was bowing down at his feet, and was placing in his hand the drinking cups.

For a mere nine years, Alalu was king in heaven. In the ninth year Anu gave battle against Alalu and he defeated Alalu. He fled before him and went down to the Dark Earth.[4] Down he went to the Dark Earth, and Anu took his seat on his throne. Anu was sitting on his throne, and weighty Kumarbi was giving him drink. Kumarbi was bowing down at his feet and placing in his hand the drinking cups.

For a mere nine years Anu remained king in heaven. In the ninth year Anu gave battle against Kumarbi. Kumarbi, Alalu's offspring, gave battle

---

[1] A goddess of fate.
[2] The mother goddess.
[3] Translation by Harry A. Hoffner, Jr., *Hittite Myths* (Writings from the Ancient World 2; Atlanta, GA: Scholars Press, 2d ed., 1998), 42–43.
[4] The underworld.

against Anu. Anu can no longer withstand Kumarbi's eyes. Anu wriggled loose from his hands and fled. He set out for the sky. But Kumarbi rushed after him, seized Anu by his feet, and dragged him down from the sky.

Kumarbi bit Anu's loins, and his manhood united with Kumarbi's insides as bronze (results from the union of copper and tin). When Kumarbi had swallowed the manhood of Anu, he rejoiced and laughed out loud. Anu turned around and spoke to Kumarbi: "Are you rejoicing because you have swallowed my manhood?

"Stop rejoicing within yourself! I have placed inside you a burden. First, I have impregnated you with the noble Storm God.[1] Second, I have impregnated you with the irresistible Aranzah River. Third, I have impregnated you with the noble Tasmisu.[2] And two additional terrible gods I have placed inside you as burdens. In the future you will end up striking the boulders of Mount Tassa with your head!"

When Anu had finished speaking, he went up to the sky and hid himself. Kumarbi, the wise king, spat from his mouth. He spat from his mouth spittle and semen mixed together.

[The remainder of the text is badly broken. Apparently Teshub emerges from Kumarbi and ousts him from the throne.]

EGYPT

Egyptian mythology is complex, in part because each major city had its own version. Moreover, unlike myths from elsewhere, much Egyptian mythic material is found not in fully developed works, but in funerary texts. Here is a sample, from the Pyramid Texts of the late third millennium BCE.

9. FROM THE PYRAMID OF PEPI I (CA. 2300 BCE)

A cosmogonic myth, which describes how the primordial god Atum created Shu, the god of air, and Tefnut, the goddess of moisture.[3]

Atum is the one who came into being as one who came with penis extended in Heliopolis. He put his penis in his fist so that he might make orgasm with it, and the two twins were born, Shu and Tefnut.

[Later Shu and Tefnut gave birth to Geb, the god of earth, and Nut, the goddess of sky.]

10. FROM THE PYRAMID OF PEPI II (CA. 2250 BCE)

An alternate version of Text 9.[4]

Atum Beetle! You became high, as the hill; you rose as the *benben*[5] in the Benben Enclosure in Heliopolis. You sneezed Shu and spat Tefnut. You put your arms around them as *ka*-arms so that your *ka*[6] might be in them.

11. THE MEMPHITE THEOLOGY

According to its introduction, this is an older work recopied in the reign of Pharaoh Shabaka (ruled 716–702 BCE); it may, however, be a late work deliberately written in an archaic style. Although the text seems to be a composite, much of it features Ptah, the chief god of the city of Memphis, whose Egyptian name means "house of Ptah." The text is broken, because the stone on which it was carved was subsequently used as a millstone. Its account of creation by divine speech has generic similarities to such passages as Genesis 1; Psalms 33:6, 9; 148:5; see also Text 1 (page 11).[7]

The living Horus: Who prospers the Two Lands; the Two Ladies: Who prospers the Two Lands; the Golden Horus: Who prospers the Two Lands; the King of Upper and Lower Egypt:[8]

---

[1]Teshub.
[2]Teshub's brother.
[3]Translation by James O. Allen, *The Ancient Egyptian Pyramid*

Texts (Atlanta, GA: Society of Biblical Literature, 2005), 164 (No. 475).
[4]Translation by James O. Allen, *The Ancient Egyptian Pyramid Texts* (Atlanta, GA: Society of Biblical Literature, 2005), 269 (No. 359).
[5]The primeval mound of earth that emerged from the waters at creation; the pyramid is a stylized representation of the *benben*.
[6]Life force.
[7]Translation by Miriam Lichtheim, *Ancient Egyptian Literature* (Berkeley, CA: University of California Press, 1976; 2006), 1.52–56.
[8]Upper Egypt is southern Egypt, and Lower Egypt is northern

Neferkare; the Son of Re: Shabaka, beloved of Ptah-South-of-his-Wall, who lives like Re forever.[1]

This writing was copied out anew by his majesty in the House of his father Ptah-South-of-his-Wall, for his majesty found it to be a work of the ancestors which was worm-eaten, so that it could not be understood from beginning to end. His majesty copied it anew so that it became better than it had been before, in order that his name might endure and his monument last in the House of his father Ptah-South-of-his-Wall throughout eternity, as a work done by the Son of Re Shabaka for his father Ptah-Ta-tenen, so that he might live forever....

Geb,[2] lord of the gods, commanded that the Nine Gods[3] gather to him. He judged between Horus and Seth; he ended their quarrel.[4] He made Seth king of Upper Egypt in the land of Upper Egypt, up to the place in which he was born, which is Su. And Geb made Horus king of Lower Egypt in the land of Lower Egypt, up to the place in which his father[5] was drowned, which is "Division-of-the-Two-Lands." Thus Horus stood over one region, and Seth stood over one region. They made peace over the two Lands at Ayan. That was the division of the Two Lands....

Then it seemed wrong to Geb that the portion of Horus was like the portion of Seth. So Geb gave to Horus his inheritance, for he is the son of his firstborn son.... Then Horus stood over the land. He is the uniter of this land, proclaimed in the great name: Ta-tenen, South-of-his-Wall, Lord of Eternity. Then sprouted the two Great Magicians upon his head.[6] He is Horus who arose as the king of Upper and Lower Egypt, who united the Two Lands in the Nome[7] of the Wall, the place in which the Two Lands were united.[8] Reed and papyrus were placed on the double door of the House of Ptah. That means Horus and Seth, pacified and united. They fraternized so as to cease quarreling in whatever place they might be, being united in the House of Ptah, the "Balance of the Two Lands" in which Upper and Lower Egypt had been weighed....

The gods came into being in Ptah....

There took shape in the heart, there took shape on the tongue the form of Atum. For the very great one is Ptah, who gave life to all the gods and their kas[9] through this heart and through this tongue, in which Horus had taken shape as Ptah, in which Thoth[10] had taken shape as Ptah.

Thus heart and tongue rule over all the limbs in accordance with the teaching that he is in every body and he is in every mouth of all gods, all men, all cattle, all creeping things, whatever lives, thinking whatever he wishes and commanding whatever he wishes. His Ennead[11] is before him as teeth and lips. They are the semen and the hands of Atum. For the Ennead of Atum came into being through his semen and his fingers.[12] But the Ennead is the teeth and the lips in this mouth which pronounced the name of every thing, from which Shu[13] and Tefnut[14] came forth, and which gave birth to the Ennead. Sight, hearing, breathing — they report to the heart, and it makes every understanding come forth. As to the tongue, it repeats what the heart has devised. Thus all the gods were born and his Ennead was completed. For every word of the god came about through what the heart devised and the tongue commanded....

Thus it is said of Ptah: "He who made and created the gods." And he is Ta-tenen,[15] who gave birth to the gods, and from whom every thing came forth, food, provisions, divine offerings, all good things, Thus it is recognized and understood that he is the mightiest of the gods. Thus Ptah was satisfied[16] after he had made all things and all divine words.

Egypt; according to Egyptian tradition, the country was unified under the first pharaoh of Dynasty 1 (ca. 3100 BCE).

[1]Pharaoh Shabaka is given his titles, which identify him with the god Horus, the son of Isis and Osiris, who is also identified with the sun god Re.

[2]The god of the earth.

[3]Also translated "the Ennead," the nine principal gods of ancient Egypt.

[4]A variant version of the myth found in Text 12.

[5]I.e., Osiris.

[6]The double crown, representing the union of Upper and Lower Egypt.

[7]An administrative subdivision of ancient Egypt.

[8]I.e., Memphis, whose Egyptian name means "House of Ptah." Horus and Ptah are equated.

[9]Life force.

[10]The scribe god.

[11]The nine principal gods of Egypt.

[12]See Text 9.

[13]The god of air.

[14]The goddess of moisture.

[15]The primeval mound from which life originated.

[16]Cf. Genesis 1:31. The word translated "satisfied" may mean "rested"; cf. Genesis 2:2.

He gave birth to the gods,
he made the towns,
he established the nomes.
he placed the gods in their shrines,
he made their bodies according to their
    wishes.
Thus the gods entered into their bodies,
of every wood, every stone, every clay,
every thing that grows upon him in which
    they came to be.
Thus were gathered to him the gods and all
    their *kas*,
content, united with the Lord of the Two
    Lands.

The Great Throne that gives joy to the heart
of the gods in the House of Ptah is the granary of
Ta-tenen, the mistress of all life, through which
the sustenance of the Two Lands is provided,
owing to the fact that Osiris was drowned in his
water. Isis and Nephthys looked out, beheld him,
and attended to him. Horus quickly commanded
Isis and Nephthys to grasp Osiris and prevent his
submerging. They heeded in time and brought
him to land. He entered the hidden portals in the
glory of the lords of eternity, in the steps of him
who rises in the horizon, on the ways of Re at the
Great Throne. He entered the palace and joined
the gods of Ta-tenen Ptah, lord of years.[1]

Thus Osiris came into the earth at the Royal
Fortress, to the north of the land to which he had
come. His son Horus arose as king of Upper Egypt,
arose as king of Lower Egypt, in the embrace of
his father Osiris and of the gods in front of him
and behind him.

12. THE CONTENDINGS OF HORUS AND SETH

The sky goddess Nut and the god of earth Geb had
given birth to two sets of twins, Seth and his sister
(and later, wife) Nephthys, and Osiris and his sister
(and later, wife) Isis. This is an exceptionally well-preserved account of how Horus, the son of Osiris and Isis,

avenged his father's murder by Seth and assumed his
kingship. Dating to the twelfth century BCE, its themes
of fraternal rivalry for succession also occur in "The
Tale of the Two Brothers" (Text 19) and other texts in
this book in the Bible, and in many other literatures.[2]

This is the judging of Horus and Seth, they
of mysterious forms, mightiest of existing princes
and lords. A divine youth was seated before the
All-Lord, claiming the office of his father Osiris,
he of beautiful appearances, the son of Ptah, who
brightens the netherworld with his luster, while
Thoth[3] presented the Eye to the great prince
of On.[4] Then spoke Shu,[5] the son of Re, before
Atum, the great prince of On: "Right rules might.
Do it by saying: 'Give the office to Horus.'" Then
Thoth said to the Ennead:[6] "That is right a million times!" Then Isis uttered a loud shout and
was overjoyed. She stood before the All-Lord
and said: "North wind, go west, give the news
to Wennefer!"[7] Then said Shu, the son of Re:
"Presenting the Eye to Horus seems right to the
Ennead." Said the All-Lord: "What is this, you
are making decisions on your own?" Then Onuris[8]
said: "Thoth shall take the royal name-ring to
Horus, and the White Crown[9] shall be placed on
his head!" Then the All-Lord was silent for a long
moment, for he was angry with the Ennead.

Then Seth, the son of Nut, spoke: "Let him
be sent outside with me, and I shall let you see
my hand prevailing over his hand in the presence
of the Ennead, since one knows no other means
of dispossessing him." Then Thoth said to him:
"Do we not know what is wrong? Shall one give
the office of Osiris to Seth while his son Horus is
there?" Then Re-Harakhti became exceedingly
angry, for it was Re's wish to give the office to Seth,
great of strength, the son of Nut. And Onuris

---

[1]This summarizes the myth of Osiris, according to which his
brother Seth killed him by drowning him in the Nile. His wife Isis
and Isis's sister (and Seth's wife) Nephthys rescued his body and
briefly restored him to life. Then he went to the underworld, where
he rules as king. See further page 60, n. 1 and page 150.

[2]Translation by Miriam Lichtheim, *Ancient Egyptian Literature*
(Berkeley, CA: University of California Press, 1976; 2006),
2.214–23.
[3]The scribe god, whose eye was the moon, here presented to the sun
god Re, who is generally called Re-Harakhti in this text.
[4]Heliopolis.
[5]The god of air.
[6]The nine principal gods of Egypt.
[7]A title of Osiris, to whom, in the underworld (the West), the news
is to be brought.
[8]The god of war.
[9]The crown of Upper (southern) Egypt.

uttered a loud cry before the Ennead, saying: "What shall we do?" Then said Atum, the great prince of On: "Summon Banebdjede, the great living god, that he may judge between the two youths."

They brought Banebdjede, the great god who dwells in Setit, before Atum, along with Ptah-Tatenen. He said to them: "Judge between the two youths, so that they will stop wrangling here every day!" Then Banebdjede, the great living god, replied to what he had said: "Let us not decide in ignorance. Have a letter sent to Neith the Great, the divine mother.[1] What she will say, we will do."

Then the Ennead said to Banebdjede, the great living god: "They have been judged once already in the hall 'Way-of-Truth.'" Then the Ennead said to Thoth in the presence of the All-Lord: "Write a letter to Neith the Great, the divine mother, in the name of the All-Lord, the Bull of On." And Thoth said: "I will, I will." He sat down to write the letter, which said: "The King of Upper and Lower Egypt: Re-Atum, beloved of Thoth; The Lord of the Two Lands, the Heliopolitan; the Aten[2] who illumines the Two Lands with his luster; the Hapi[3] mighty in his rising: Re-Harakhti; to Neith the Great, the divine mother, who shone on the first face, who is alive, hale, and young. The living ba[4] of the All-Lord, the Bull of On who is the good King of Egypt, says as follows: I your servant spend the night on behalf of Osiris taking counsel for the Two Lands every day, while Sobk[5] endures forever. What shall I do about these two people, who for eighty years now have been before the tribunal, and no one knows how to judge between the two? Write us what we should do!"

Then Neith the Great, the divine mother, sent a letter to the Ennead, saying: "Give the office of Osiris to his son Horus, and don't do those big misdeeds that are out of place. Or I shall get angry and the sky will crash to the ground! And let it be said to the All-Lord, the Bull of On: Double Seth's possessions. Give him Anat and Astarte, your two daughters.[6] And place Horus on the seat of his father!"

The letter of Neith the Great, the divine mother, reached the Ennead as they sat in the hall "Horned-Horus," and the letter was placed in the hand of Thoth. Then Thoth read it aloud before the All-Lord and the whole Ennead. And they said with one voice: "This goddess is right!" Thereupon the All-Lord became angry at Horus and said to him: "You are feeble in body, and this office is too big for you, you youngster whose breath smells bad." Then Onuris became angry a million times and so was the Ennead, the Council of Thirty.[7] The god Baba[8] got up and said to Re-Harakhti: "Your shrine is empty!"[9] Then Re-Harakhti felt offended by the answer given him, and he lay down on his back, shouting loudly at Baba and saying to him: "Go away; you have committed a very great crime!" And they went to their tents.

The great god spent a day lying on his back in his pavilion, his heart very sore, and he was alone. After a long while, Hathor, Lady of the southern sycamore,[10] came and stood before her father, the All-Lord. She uncovered her nakedness before him; thereupon the great god laughed at her. He got up and sat with the great Ennead; and he said to Horus and Seth: "Speak for yourselves!"

Then Seth, great of strength, the son of Nut, said: "I, I am Seth, the greatest of strength among the Ennead. For I slay the enemy of Re every day, standing in the prow of the Bark-of-Millions,[11] and no other god can do it. I should receive the office of Osiris!" Then they said: "Seth, the son of Nut, is right." Then Onuris and Thoth cried aloud, saying: "Shall one give the office to the uncle while the bodily son is there?" The Banebdjede, the great living god, said: "Shall one give the office to the youngster while Seth, his elder brother, is there?"[12]

Then the Ennead cried aloud to the All-Lord and said to him: "What are these words you spoke which are not worthy of being heard?" Then said Horus, the son of Isis: "It is not good to defraud

---

[1]The goddess of war and weaving, patron of the city of Sais.
[2]The sun disk; see Text 94.
[3]One of the sons of Horus, here identified with Re.
[4]The soul.
[5]The crocodile god.
[6]The Canaanite goddesses known from the Ugaritic texts, here identified as daughters of Re.

[7]The larger assembly of the gods.
[8]The baboon god, associated with Seth.
[9]Apparently meaning that he had lost his divine power.
[10]The cow goddess and a mother goddess.
[11]The boat that carried the sun god through the sky during the day and through the underworld during the night.
[12]In Egyptian mythology, Horus was sometimes Seth's nephew and sometimes his brother.

me before the Ennead and to take the office of my
father Osiris away from me!" And Isis was angry
with the Ennead, and she took an oath by the god
before the Ennead, saying: "As my mother lives,
the goddess Neith, and as Ptah-Tatenen lives, the
tall-plumed horn-curber of the gods, these matters
shall be laid before Atum, the great prince of On,
and also Khepri[1] in his bark!" Then the Ennead
said to her: "Don't be angry. Right will be given to
him who is right. All that you said shall be done."

Then Seth, the son of Nut, was angry with the
Ennead because of the words they had said to Isis
the Great, the divine mother. And Seth said to
them: "I shall take my scepter of 4,500 pounds and
kill one of you each day!" And Seth took an oath
by the All-Lord, saying: "I shall not contend in
court as long as Isis is in it!" Then Re-Harakhti said
to them: "Cross over to the Island-in-the-Midst and
judge them there. And tell Nemty, the ferryman:
'Do not ferry across any woman who looks like
Isis.'" So the Ennead crossed over to the Island-in-
the-Midst, and they sat down to eat bread.

Isis came and approached Nemty, the ferryman,
as he was sitting near his boat. She had changed
herself into an old woman who walked with a
stoop, and a small signet ring of gold was on her
hand. She said to him: "I have come to you in
order that you ferry me across to the Island-in-the-
Midst. For I have come with this bowl of flour for
the young boy who is tending some cattle on the
Island-in-the-Midst these five days, and he is hungry." He said to her: "I have been told: 'Don't ferry
any woman across.'" She said to him: "It was on
account of Isis that this was said to you." He said
to her: "What will you give me for ferrying you
across to the Island-in-the-Midst?" Isis said to him:
"I will give you this cake." He said to her: "What
is it to me, your cake? Shall I ferry you across to
the Island-in-the-Midst when I was told, 'Ferry no
woman across,' in exchange for your cake?" Then
she said to him: "I will give you the signet ring of
gold that is on my hand." He said to her: "Give me
the signet ring of gold." She gave it to him, and he
ferried her across to the Island-in-the-Midst.

Now as she walked under the trees, she looked
and saw the Ennead as they sat eating bread
before the All-Lord in his pavilion. And Seth
looked and saw her coming from afar. Thereupon

she pronounced a spell of hers and changed herself into a young girl of beautiful body, the like of
which did not exist in the whole land. Then he
desired her very much.

Seth got up from sitting and eating bread with
the great Ennead and went to meet her, while no
one but himself had seen her. He stood behind a
sycamore, called to her, and said to her: "I am here
with you, handsome girl!" She said to him: "Let
me tell, my great lord: As for me, I was the wife
of a herdsman and I bore him a son. My husband
died, and the boy began to tend the cattle of his
father. But then a stranger came. He sat down in
my stable and spoke thus to my child: 'I shall beat
you, I shall take your father's cattle, and I shall
throw you out!' So he spoke to him. Now I wish
to make you his defender." Then Seth said to her:
"Shall one give the cattle to the stranger while
the man's son is here?" Thereupon Isis changed
herself into a kite, flew up, and sat on top of an
acacia. She called to Seth and said to him: "Weep
for yourself! Your own mouth has said it. Your own
cleverness has judged you! What do you want?"[2]

Then he began to weep; and he went to where
Re-Harakhti was and wept. Re-Harakhti said to
him: "What do you want?" Seth said to him: "That
evil woman came to me again. She has cheated
me again. She had changed herself into a beautiful girl before me, and she said to me: 'I was the
wife of a herdsman who is dead. I had born him
a son; he tended the cattle of his father. Then a
stranger intruded in my stable to be with my son,
and I gave him food. And many days after this the
intruder said to my son: "I shall beat you; I shall
take your father's cattle; it shall be mine." Thus
he spoke to my son.' So she said to me." Then
Re-Harakhti said to him: "What did you say to
her?" And Seth told him: "I said to her: 'Shall
one give the cattle to the stranger while the man's
son is there?' So I said to her: 'One must beat the
intruder with a stick, and throw him out, and set
the son in the place of his father.' So I said to her."

Then Re-Harakhti said to him: "Now look, you
yourself have judged yourself. What do you want?"
Seth said to him: "Let Nemty, the ferryman, be
brought, and let a great punishment be done to
him, saying: 'Why did you ferry her across?' So

---

[1] A solar deity, depicted as a scarab beetle.

[2] For similar uses of a fictional case to elicit a verdict against the
judge, see 2 Samuel 12:1–7; 14:1–24.

one shall say to him." Then Nemty, the ferryman, was brought before the Ennead, and they removed his toes. And Nemty forswore gold to this day before the great Ennead, saying: "Gold shall be an abomination to me in my town!"

The Ennead crossed over to the western shore and sat on the mountain. Now when evening had come, Re-Harakhti and Atum, Lord of the Two Lands, the Heliopolitan, wrote to the Ennead, saying: "Why are you sitting here again? Are you going to make the two youths spend their lifetime in court? When my letter reaches you, you shall place the White Crown on the Head of Horus, son of Isis, and appoint him to the position of his father Osiris."

Thereupon Seth became exceedingly angry, and the Ennead said to him: "Why are you angry? Should one not act according to the word of Atum, Lord of the Two Lands, the Heliopolitan, and Re-Harakhti?" Then the White Crown was placed on the head of Horus, son of Isis. And Seth cried out aloud to the Ennead in anger and said: "Shall the office be given to my younger brother while I, his elder brother, am here?" And he took an oath, saying: "The White Crown shall be removed from the head of Horus, son of Isis, and he shall be thrown into the water! I shall yet contend with him for the office of ruler!" Then Re-Harakhti acted accordingly.

Seth said to Horus: "Come, let us change ourselves into two hippopotamuses and plunge into the depth in the midst of the sea. And he who emerges in the course of three whole months, he shall not receive the office." So they plunged together. Then Isis sat down weeping and said: "Seth will kill Horus, my son!" She took a quantity of yarn and made a rope. She took a *deben*[1] of copper and cast it into a harpoon. She tied the rope to it and threw it into the water at the spot where Horus and Seth had plunged. Then the weapon bit into the body of her son Horus. And Horus cried out aloud, saying: "Come to me, mother Isis, my mother! Tell your weapon to let go of me! I am Horus, son of Isis!" Then Isis cried aloud and said to her weapon: "Let go of him! He is Horus my son." And the weapon let go of him.

Then she threw it again into the water, and it bit into the body of Seth. And Seth cried out

aloud, saying: "What have I done to you, my sister Isis? Call to your weapon to let go of me! I am your maternal brother, O Isis!" Then she felt very sorry for him. And Seth called to her, saying: "Do you love the stranger more than your maternal brother Seth?" Then Isis called to her weapon, saying: "Let go of him! It is the maternal brother of Isis whom you are biting." And the weapon let go of him.

Thereupon Horus, son of Isis, was angry with his mother Isis. He came out, his face fierce like that of a leopard and his knife of 16 *deben* in his hand. He cut off the head of his mother Isis, took it in his arms, and went up the mountain. Then Isis changed herself into a statue of flint without a head. And Re-Harakhti said to Thoth: "Who is she who is coming and has no head?" Thoth said to Re-Harakhti: "My good lord, she is Isis the Great, the divine mother. Her son Horus has cut off her head." The Re-Harakhti cried out aloud and said to the Ennead: "Let us go and punish him severely!" So the Ennead went up into the mountains to search for Horus, son of Isis.

As for Horus, he was lying under a *shenusha*-tree in the oasis country. Then Seth found him, seized him, and threw him on his back on the mountain. He removed his two eyes from their places and buried them on the mountain. Toward morning his two eyeballs became two bulbs, and they grew into lotuses. And Seth came and told Re-Harakhti falsely: "I did not find Horus," although he had found him. Then Hathor, Mistress of the southern sycamore, went and found Horus as he lay weeping in the desert. Thereupon she caught a gazelle, milked it, and said to Horus: "Open your eyes, that I may put this milk in." He opened his eyes and she put the milk in. She put it in the right eye; she put it in the left eye; she said to him: "Open your eyes!" He opened his eyes. She looked at them; she found them healed. Then she went to tell Re-Harakhti: "I found Horus deprived of his eyes by Seth, but I restored him. Now here he comes."

Then the Ennead said: "Horus and Seth shall be summoned and judged!" So they were brought before the Ennead. The All-Lord spoke before the great Ennead to Horus and Seth: "Go and heed what I tell you: Eat, drink, and leave us in peace! Stop quarreling here every day!"

Then Seth said to Horus: "Come, let us have a feast day at my house." And Horus said to him: "I will, I will." Now when evening had come, a bed

---

[1]A measure of weight, equivalent to ca. 3 ounces (85 grams) when the text was copied.

was prepared for them, and they lay down together. At night, Seth let his member come stiff and he inserted it between the thighs of Horus. And Horus placed his hands between his thighs and caught the semen of Seth. Then Horus went to tell his mother Isis: "Come, Isis my mother, come and see what Seth did to me." He opened his hand, and let her see the semen of Seth. She cried out aloud, took her knife, cut off his hand, and threw it in the water. Then she made a new hand for him. And she took a dab of sweet ointment and put it on the member of Horus. She made it become stiff, placed it over a pot, and let his semen drop into it.

In the morning Isis went with the semen of Horus to the garden of Seth and said to the gardener of Seth: "What plants does Seth eat here with you?" The gardener said to her: "The only plant Seth eats here with me is lettuce." Then Isis placed the semen of Horus on them. Seth came according to his daily custom and ate the lettuces which he usually ate. Thereupon he became pregnant with the semen of Horus.

Then Seth went and said to Horus: "Come, let us go, that I may contend with you in court." And Horus said to him: "I will, I will." So they went to the court together. They stood before the great Ennead, and they were told: "Speak!" Then Seth said: "Let the office of ruler be given to me, for as regards Horus who stands here, I have done a man's deed to him." Then the Ennead cried aloud, and they spat out before Horus. And Horus laughed at them; and Horus took an oath by the god, saying: "What Seth has said is false. Let the semen of Seth be called, and let us see from where it will answer. Then let mine be called, and let us see from where it will answer."

Thoth, lord of writing, true scribe of the Ennead, laid his hand on the arm of Horus and said: "Come out, semen of Seth!" And it answered him from the water in the midst of the marsh. Then Thoth laid his hand on the arm of Seth and said: "Come out, semen of Horus!" And it said to him: "Where shall I come out?" Thoth said to it: "Come out of his ear." It said to him: "Should I come out of his ear? I who am a divine seed?" Then Thoth said to it: "Come out from the top of his head." Then it came out as a golden sun-disk on the head of Seth. Seth became very angry, and he stretched out his hand to seize the golden sun-

disk. Thereupon Thoth took it away from him and placed it as a crown upon his own head. And the Ennead said: "Horus is right, Seth is wrong." Then Seth became very angry and cried out because they had said: "Horus is right, Seth is wrong."

Seth took a great oath by the god, saying: "He shall not be given the office until he has been dismissed with me, and we shall build ships of stone and race each other. He who wins over his rival, he shall be given the office of ruler." Then Horus built himself a ship of pine, plastered it all over with gypsum, and launched it on the water in the evening, while no one in the whole land saw it. And Seth looked at the ship of Horus and thought it was of stone. He went to the mountain, cut off a mountain peak, and built himself a ship of stone of 138 cubits.[1] Then they went into their ships in the presence of the Ennead. Thereupon the ship of Seth sank in the water. Seth changed himself into a hippopotamus and wrecked the ship of Horus. Then Horus seized his weapon and hit the body of Seth. Then the Ennead said to him: "Do not hit him."

So he took his sailing gear, placed it in his boat, and journeyed downstream to Sais to tell Neith the Great, the divine mother: "Let me be judged with Seth! For it is now eighty years that we are in court, but they don't know how to judge between us. He has not been vindicated against me; and a thousand times now I have been in the right against him day after day. But he pays no attention to what the Ennead says. I have contended with him in the hall 'Way-of-Truth.' I was found right against him. I have contended with him in the hall 'Horned-Horus.' I was found right against him. I have contended with him in the hall 'Field-of-Rushes.' I was found right against him. I have contended with him in the hall 'Field-Pool.' I was found right against him. The Ennead has said to Shu, son of Re: 'Horus, son of Isis, is right in all that he has said.'"

Thoth spoke to the All-Lord: "Have a letter sent to Osiris, that he may judge between the two youths." And Shu, son of Re, said: "Right a million times is what Thoth has said to the Ennead." Then the All-Lord said to Thoth: "Sit down and write a letter to Osiris, that we may hear what he has to say." So Thoth sat down to compose a letter to

---

[1]A cubit was ca. 18 inches (44 cm).

Osiris as follows: "The Bull: Hunting Lion; Two Ladies: Protector of gods, Curber of the Two Lands; Gold Horus: Inventor of mankind in the beginning; King of Upper and Lower Egypt: Bull who dwells in On; Son of Ptah: Benefactor of the Two Shores, who arose as father of his Ennead, who lives on gold and all precious glazes: Life, prosperity, health! Write us what we should do about Horus and Seth, so that we do not take action in ignorance!"

Many days after this, the letter reached the King, the son of Re, Great in Bounty, Lord of Sustenance. He cried out aloud when the letter was read before him. He replied in great haste to where the All-Lord was with the Ennead, saying: "Why is my son Horus being defrauded when it was I who made you strong? It was I who made barley and emmer to nourish the gods, and the cattle after the gods, while no god or goddess was able to do it!"

The letter of Osiris arrived at the place where Re-Harakhti was, as he sat with the Ennead in the White Field at Xois. It was read to him and the Ennead, and Re-Harakhti said: "Answer this letter of Osiris quickly, and tell him concerning his letter: 'If you had not existed, if you had not been born, barley and emmer would yet exist!' "

The letter of the All-Lord reached Osiris and was read before him. Then he wrote to Re-Harakhti again, saying: "Very good is all you have done and what the Ennead has found to do! Maat[1] has been made to sink into the netherworld! Now you pay attention to this matter! The land in which I am is full of savage-looking messengers who fear no god or goddess. If I send them out, they will bring me the heart of every evildoer, and they will be here with me! What good is my being here, resting in the West, while all of you are outside? Who among you is mightier than I? But they have invented wrongdoing! When Ptah the Great, South-of-his-Wall, Lord of Memphis, created the sky, did he not say to the stars in it: 'You shall go to rest in the West every night, in the place where King Osiris is? And after the gods all mankind shall also go to rest where you are!' So he said to me."

Many days after this, the letter of Osiris arrived at the place where the All-Lord was with the Ennead. Thoth received the letter and read it to Re-Harakhti and the Ennead. Then they said:

"He is right, he is right in all he says, the Great in Bounty, the Lord of Sustenance!" Then Seth said: "Let us be taken to the Island-in-the-Midst, that I may contend with him!" And he went to the Island-in-the-Midst. But Horus was declared in the right against him.

Then Atum, Lord of the Two Lands, the Heliopolitan, sent to Isis, saying: "Bring Seth bound in fetters." So Isis brought Seth bound in fetters as a prisoner. Atum said to him: "Why have you resisted being judged and have taken for yourself the office of Horus?" Seth said to him: "Not so, my good lord. Let Horus, son of Isis, be summoned, and let him be given the office of his father Osiris!"

They brought Horus, son of Isis. They placed the White Crown on his head. They placed him on the seat of his father Osiris and said to him: "You are the good King of Egypt! You are the good lord of all lands for ever and ever!" Then Isis uttered a loud shout to her son Horus, saying: "You are the good King! My heart rejoices that you will brighten the earth with your luster!" Then said Ptah the Great, South-of-his-Wall, Lord of Memphis: "What shall we do for Seth, now that Horus has been placed on the seat of his father?" Then Re-Harakhti said: "Let Seth, son of Nut, be given to me to dwell with me and be my son. And he shall thunder in the sky and be feared."

They came to say to Re-Harakhti: "Horus, son of Isis, has risen as Ruler." Then Re rejoiced greatly and said to the Ennead: "Jubilate throughout the land, jubilate throughout the land for Horus, son of Isis!" And Isis said:

"Horus has risen as ruler, life, prosperity,
    health!
The Ennead is in feast, heaven in joy!
They take garlands seeing Horus, son of Isis
risen as great Ruler of Egypt.
The hearts of the Ennead exult,
    the entire land rejoices
as they see Horus, son of Isis,
    given the office of his father,
    Osiris, lord of Busiris."

It has come to a good ending in Thebes, the place of truth.[2]

---

[1]The goddess of truth and justice.

[2]A concluding note by the scribe.

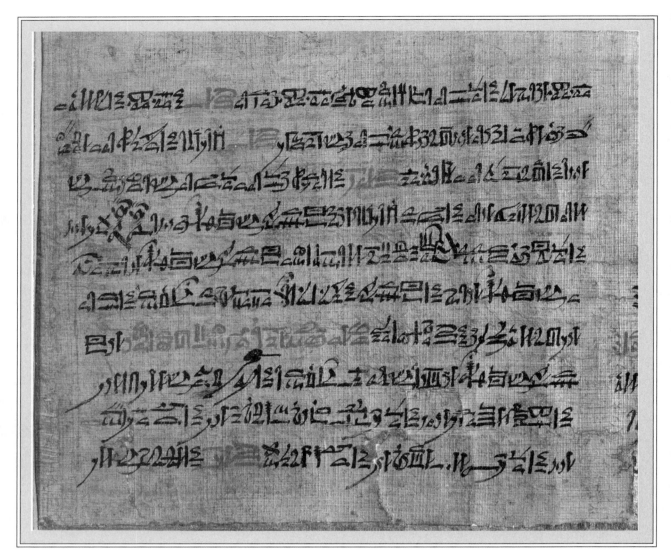

The Tale of Two Brothers

The Tale of Two Brothers (see Text 19) was written in Egyptian hieroglyphics in red and black ink on a papyrus dating to the early twelfth century BCE. This column is ca. 8 inches (20 cm) high.

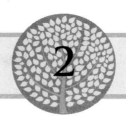

2

EPICS

MESOPOTAMIA

13. GILGAMESH

One of the most popular works of literature in the ancient Near East, *Gilgamesh* is named for its hero, a legendary king of the city of Uruk in southern Mesopotamia.[1] Versions of and references to the epic date from the third millennium BCE into the Common Era, and copies of it have been found at many sites. The version excerpted here is the "Standard Babylonian Version," dating to the late second millennium BCE.[2]

TABLET 1

Of him who found out all things, I shall tell
    the land,
of him who experienced everything, I shall
    teach the whole.
He searched lands everywhere.
He who experienced the whole gained
    complete wisdom.
He found out what was secret and uncovered
    what was hidden,
he brought back a tale of times before the
    Flood.

He had journeyed far and wide, weary and at
    last resigned.
He had engraved all toils on a memorial
    monument of stone.
He had the wall of Uruk built, the sheepfold
    of holiest Eanna,[3] the pure treasury.
See its wall, which is like a copper band,
survey its battlements, which nobody else can
    match,
take the threshold, which is from time
    immemorial,
approach Eanna, the home of Ishtar,
which no future king nor any man will ever
    match!
Go up to the wall of Uruk and walk around!
Inspect the foundation platform and
    scrutinize the brickwork!
Testify that its bricks are baked bricks,
and that the Seven Counselors[4] must have
    laid its foundations!
One square mile is the city, one square mile is
    orchards, one square mile is claypits,
    as well as the open ground of Ishtar's
      temple.

---

[1] See Text 20, page 66.
[2] Translation by Stephanie Dalley, *Myths from Mesopotamia: Creation, the Flood, Gilgamesh, and Others* (Oxford: Oxford University Press, rev. ed., 2000), 50–120.

[3] The name of the main temple of the goddess Ishtar in the city of Uruk.
[4] The seven sages, the legendary bringers of elements of civilization from the gods to humans.

Three square miles and the open ground
    comprise Uruk.
Look for the copper tablet-box,
undo its bronze lock,
open the door to its secret, lift out the lapis
    lazuli tablet and read it,
the story of that man, Gilgamesh, who went
    through all kinds of sufferings.
He was superior to other kings, a warrior lord
    of great stature,
a hero born of Uruk, a goring wild bull.
He marches at the front as a leader,
he goes behind, the support of his brothers,
a strong net, the protection of his men,
the raging flood-wave, which can destroy even
    a stone wall.
Son of Lugalbanda, Gilgamesh, perfect in
    strength,
son of the lofty cow, the wild cow Ninsun.[1]
He is Gilgamesh, perfect in splendor,
who opened up passes in the mountains,
who could dig pits even in the
    mountainside,
who crossed the ocean, the broad seas, as far
    as the sunrise,
who inspected the edges of the world, kept
    searching for eternal life,
who reached Utnapishtim the far distant, by
    force,[2]
who restored to their rightful place cult
    centers which the Flood had ruined.
There is nobody among the kings of teeming
    humanity
who can compare with him,
who can say "I am king" beside Gilgamesh.
Gilgamesh was named from birth for fame.
Two-thirds of him was divine, and one-third
    mortal....
In Uruk the Sheepfold he would walk about,
show himself superior, his head held high like
    a wild bull....
The young men of Uruk became dejected in
    their private quarters.
Gilgamesh would not leave any son alone for
    his father

Day and night his behavior was overbearing....
Gilgamesh would not leave young girls alone,
the daughters of warriors, the brides of young
    men.
The gods often heard their complaints....
They called upon great Aruru:[3]
"You, Aruru, you created mankind![4]
Now create someone for him, to match the
    ardor of his energies!
Let them be regular rivals, and let Uruk be
    allowed peace!"
When Aruru heard this, she created inside
    herself the word of Anu.[5]
Aruru washed her hands, pinched off a piece
    of clay, cast it out into the open country.
She created a primitive man, Enkidu the
    warrior: offspring of silence, sky-bolt of
    Ninurta.
His whole body was shaggy with hair, he was
    furnished with tresses like a woman,
his locks of hair grew luxuriant like grain.
He knew neither people nor country: he was
    dressed as cattle are.
With gazelles he eats vegetation,
with cattle he quenches his thirst at the
    watering place,
with wild beasts he presses forward for water.
A hunter, a brigand,
came face to face with him beside the
    watering place.
He saw him on three successive days beside
    the watering place.
The hunter looked at him, and was
    dumbstruck to see him.
In perplexity he went back to his house
and was afraid, stayed mute, was silent,
and was ill at ease, his face worried....
The hunter made his voice heard and spoke,
    he said to his father,
"Father, there was a young man who came
    from the mountain,
on the land he was strong, he was powerful.
His strength was very hard, like a sky-bolt of
    Anu.
He walks about on the mountain all the time,

---

[1]Gilgamesh's parents were Lugalbanda, the king of Uruk, and the
goddess Ninsun.
[2]See page 42.

[3]The mother goddess.
[4]Cf. Text 14, page 46.
[5]The sky god.

all the time he eats vegetation with cattle,
all the time he puts his feet in the water at
    the watering place.
I am too frightened to approach him.
He kept filling in the pots that I dug,
he kept pulling out the traps that I laid.
He kept helping cattle, wild beasts of open
    country, to escape my grasp.
He will not allow me to work in open country."

*[In broken lines, the hunter's father advises his son to
have Gilgamesh send a prostitute to seduce Enkidu:]*

"When he approaches the cattle at the
    watering place,
she must take off her clothes and reveal her
    attractions.
He will see her and go close to her.
Then his cattle, who have grown up in the
    open country with him, will become alien
    to him."

*[The hunter follows his father's advice, and Gilgamesh
sends the prostitute Shamhat back with the hunter.]*

The hunter went; he led forth the harlot
    Shamhat with him,
and they took the road, they made the
    journey.
In three days they reached the appointed
    place.
Hunter and harlot sat down in their hiding
    place.
For one day, then a second, they sat at the
    watering place.
Then cattle arrived at the watering place;
    they drank.
Then wild beasts arrived at the water; they
    satisfied their need.
And he, Enkidu, whose origin is the mountain,
who eats vegetation with gazelles,
drinks at the watering place with cattle,
satisfied his need for water with wild beasts.
Shamhat looked at the primitive man,
the murderous youth from the depths of open
    country.
"Here he is, Shamhat, bare your bosom,
open your legs and let him take in your
    attractions!

Do not pull away, take wind of him!
He will see you and come close to you.
Spread open your garments, and let him lie
    upon you,
do for him, the primitive man, as women do.
Then his cattle, who have grown up in
    open country with him, will become alien
    to him.
His love-making he will lavish upon you!"
Shamhat loosened her undergarments,
    opened her legs and he took in her
    attractions.
She did not pull away. She took wind of him,
spread open her garments, and he lay upon
    her.
She did for him, the primitive man, as
    women do.
His lovemaking he lavished upon her.
For six days and seven nights Enkidu was
    aroused and poured himself into Shamhat.
When he was sated with her charms,
he set his face toward the open country of his
    cattle.
The gazelles saw Enkidu and scattered,
the cattle of the open country kept away from
    his body.
For Enkidu had stripped; his body was too
    clean.
His legs, which used to keep pace with his
    cattle, were at a standstill.
Enkidu had been diminished, he could not
    run as before.
Yet he had acquired judgment, had become
    wiser.
He turned back, he sat at the harlot's feet.
The harlot was looking at his expression,
and he listened attentively to what the harlot
    said.
The harlot spoke to him, to Enkidu,
"You have become profound, Enkidu, you
    have become like a god.[1]
Why should you roam open country with wild
    beasts?
Come, let me take you to Uruk the Sheepfold,
to the pure house, the dwelling of Anu and
    Ishtar,
where Gilgamesh is perfect in strength,

---

[1]Cf. Genesis 3:5, 22.

and is like a wild bull, more powerful than
    any of the people."

[*Enkidu agreed, and Shamhat told him of a series of
dreams that Gilgamesh had had, in which he would
meet a powerful friend whom he would love as a wife.*]

[*Tablet 2 is incomplete; in it Shamhat clothes Enkidu
with part of her own clothing,[1] and together they go
to Uruk. There they meet Gilgamesh as he is about
to enter the house of a new bride to sleep with her.
Enkidu blocks the door; they get into a fight and then
form a friendship. Together they set off on a series of
adventures. In Tablets 3–5 they travel to the great
cedar forest in Lebanon and defeat its guardian, the
fire-breathing monster Humbaba. In Tablet 6, the goddess Ishtar tries to get Gilgamesh to be her lover, but he
rejects her in less than diplomatic language, reminding
her of the fate of her other lovers:*]

    (You would be) a drafty door that can't keep
        out winds and gusts...
    a waterskin which soaks its carrier...
    a shoe which bites into the foot of its wearer.
    Which of your lovers lasted forever?
    Which of your masterful paramours went to
        heaven?
    Come, let me describe your lovers to you!...
    For Dumuzi[2] the lover of your youth
    you decreed that he should keep weeping year
        after year.
    You loved the colorful *allallu*-bird,
    but you hit him and broke his wing.
    He stays in the woods crying, "My wing!"
    You loved the lion, whose strength is
        complete,
    but you dug seven and seven pits for him.
    You loved the horse, so trustworthy in battle,
    but you decreed the whip, goad, and lash for
        him,
    you decreed that he should gallop seven
        leagues nonstop,
    you decreed that he be overwrought and thirsty,
    you decreed endless weeping for his mother
        Sililu.

You loved the shepherd, herdsman, and chief
    shepherd
who was always heaping up the glowing ashes
    for you,
and cooked ewe-lambs for you every day.
But you hit him and turned him into a wolf,
his own herd-boys hunt him down
and his dogs tear at his haunches....
And how about me? You will love me and
    then treat me just like them!"

[*Enraged at this rejection, Ishtar complained to her
father Anu, who agreed to give her the Bull of Heaven
to kill Gilgamesh. But Enkidu and Gilgamesh killed it,
and at the end of Tablet 7, Enkidu dies as a punishment for their having done so. In Tablet 8, Gilgamesh
mourns his friend. In Tablets 9 and 10, now painfully
aware of his own mortality, Gilgamesh sets out on a
quest for immortality. This leads him to Utnapishtim,
whose name means "he found life," and who, together
with his wife, are the only humans to whom the gods
have given immortality. In Tablet 11, probably a later
addition to the epic (note the parallel in Atrahasis
[Text 14]), Utnapishtim explains why this happened.*]

TABLET 11

Gilgamesh spoke to him, to Utnapishtim the
    far distant,
"I look at you, Utnapishtim
and your limbs are no different—you are just
    like me.
Indeed, you are not at all different—you are
    just like me...
how you came to stand in the gods' assembly
    and sought eternal life?"
Utnapishtim spoke to him, to Gilgamesh,
"Let me reveal to you a closely guarded
    matter, Gilgamesh,
and let me tell you the secret of the gods.
Shuruppak is a city that you yourself know,
situated on the bank of the Euphrates.
That city was already old when the gods
    within it
decided that the great gods should make a flood.
There was Anu their father,
warrior Enlil their counselor,
Ninurta was their chamberlain,
Ennugi their canal-controller.

---

[1] Cf. Genesis 3:7, 21.

[2] A fertility god, the husband of Ishtar, whom she condemned to
live in the underworld for half the year; later called Tammuz (see
Ezekiel 8:14); see Text 4.

Far-sighted Ea[1] swore the oath (of secrecy)
    with them,
so he repeated their speech to a reed hut,[2]
'Reed hut, reed hut, brick wall, brick wall.
Listen, reed hut, and pay attention, brick wall:
(This is the message):
Man of Shuruppak,[3] son of Ubaru-Tutu,
dismantle your house, build a boat.
Leave possessions, search out living things.
Reject chattels and save lives!
Put aboard the seed of all living things, into
    the boat.
The boat that you are about to build
shall have her dimensions in proportion,
her width and length shall be in harmony,
roof her like the Apsu.'[4]
I realized and spoke to my master Ea,
'I have paid attention to the words that you
    spoke in this way,
my master, and I shall act upon them.'

• • •

"When the first light of dawn appeared
the country gathered about me.
The carpenter brought his axe,
the reed-worker brought his stone....
Children carried the bitumen,
the poor fetched what was needed.
On the fifth day I laid down her form.
One acre was her circumference, ten poles
    each the height of her walls,
her top edge was likewise ten poles all round.
I laid down her structure, drew it out,
gave her six decks,
divided her into seven.
Her middle I divided into nine,
drove the water pegs into her middle.
I saw to the paddles and put down what was
    needed:
three *sar*[5] of bitumen I poured into the kiln,
three *sar* of pitch I poured into the inside.

[*After a sacrifice, the boat is launched.*]

"I loaded her with everything there was,
loaded her with all the silver,
loaded her with all the gold,
loaded her with all the seed of living things,
    all of them.
I put on board the boat all my kith and kin,
put on board cattle from the open country,
    wild beasts from open country, all kinds of
    craftsmen.
Shamash[6] had fixed the hour....
When the first light of dawn appeared,
a black cloud came up from the base of the sky.
Adad[7] kept rumbling inside it....
The Anunnaki[8] had to carry torches,
they lit up the land with their brightness.
The calm before the Storm God came over
    the sky,
everything light turned to darkness.

• • •

"On the first day the tempest rose up....
No man could see his fellow,
nor could people be distinguished from the sky.
Even the gods were afraid of the flood-weapon.
They withdrew; they went up to the heaven
    of Anu.[9]
The gods cowered, like dogs crouched by an
    outside wall.
Ishtar screamed like a woman giving birth.

• • •

"For six days and [seven] nights
the wind blew, flood and tempest
    overwhelmed the land;
when the seventh day arrived, flood and
    onslaught
which had struggled like a woman in labor,
    blew themselves out.

---

[1] The god of wisdom and helper of humans.
[2] Apparently the gods' plan is a secret, which Ea has sworn not to reveal to anyone. But he does repeat it to the reed hut and the brick wall, while Utnapishtim overhears.
[3] I.e., Utnapishtim.
[4] The subterranean fresh waters over which the god Ea ruled.
[5] A *sar* was ca. 8,000 gallons.

[6] The sun god.
[7] The storm god.
[8] The assembly of the gods.
[9] The uppermost part of heaven.

The sea became calm, the *imhullu*-wind[1] grew
    quiet, the flood held back.
I looked at the weather; silence reigned,
for all mankind had returned to clay.
The flood-plain was flat as a roof.
I opened a porthole, and light fell on my
    cheeks.
I bent down, then sat. I wept.
My tears ran down my cheeks.
I looked for banks, for limits to the sea.
Areas of land were emerging everywhere.
The boat had come to rest on Mount
    Nimush.[2]
The mountain Nimush held the boat fast and
    did not let it budge.
The first and second day the mountain
    Nimush held the boat fast and did not let
    it budge.
The third and fourth day the mountain
    Nimush held the boat fast and did not let
    it budge.
The fifth and sixth day the mountain Nimush
    held the boat fast and did not let it budge.
When the seventh day arrived,
I put out and released a dove.
The dove went; it came back,
for no perching place was visible to it, and it
    turned round.
I put out and released a swallow.
The swallow went; it came back,
for no perching place was visible to it, and it
    turned round.
I put out and released a raven.
The raven went, and saw the waters receding.
And it ate, preened, lifted its tail, and did not
    turn round.[3]
Then I put everything out to the four winds,
    and I made a sacrifice,
set out a *surqinnu*[4]-offering upon the
    mountain peak,
arranged the jars seven and seven;
into the bottom of them I poured essences of
    reeds, pine, and myrtle.
The gods smelled the fragrance,

the gods smelled the pleasing fragrance,
the gods like flies gathered over the sacrifice."[5]

[*Utnapishtim then tells how the god Enlil then bestowed immortality upon him and his wife. Utnapishtim concludes by challenging Gilgamesh to go without sleep for seven days. When he is unable to do so, he is washed and given new clothing for his journey back to Uruk. At his wife's suggestion, Utnapishtim speaks to Gilgamesh.*]

"Gilgamesh, you came, weary, striving,
What can I give you to take back to your
    country?
Let me reveal a closely guarded matter,
    Gilgamesh,
and let me tell you the secret of the gods.
There is a plant whose root is like camel-
    thorn,
whose thorn, like a rose's, will spike your
    hands.
If you yourself can win that plant, you will
    find rejuvenation."

[*Gilgamesh dives to the bottom of the sea and retrieves the plant, which he names "An old man grows into a young man." On his journey home, he and the boatman Urshanabi stopped for the night.*]

Gilgamesh saw a pool whose water was cool,
and went down into the water and washed.
A snake smelled the fragrance of the plant.
It came up silently and carried off the plant.
As it took it away, it shed its scaly skin.
Thereupon Gilgamesh sat down and wept.
His tears flowed over his cheeks.

[*Gilgamesh then returns to Uruk. Tablet 12 is generally considered an addition to the main text.*]

14. ATRAHASIS

The tale of *Atrahasis* combines plot elements from *Enuma Elish* (Text 1) and *Gilgamesh* (Text 13). The version given here is the oldest, dating to the Old Babylonian Period (ca. 1850–1500 BCE), which is

---

[1] The evil wind.
[2] Cf. Genesis 8:4.
[3] Cf. Genesis 8:6–12.
[4] An incense offering.

[5] Cf. Genesis 8:20–22.

probably its time of composition. Several other versions are known, but none is a complete text. The epic is named for its hero, Atrahasis, whose name means "exceedingly wise." Repetitions in it, characteristic of many ancient texts, are omitted here after the first episode.[1]

TABLET 1

When the gods instead of man
did the work, bore the loads,
the gods' load was too great,
the work too hard, the trouble too much.
the great Anunnaki[2] made the Igigi[3]
carry the workload sevenfold.
Anu their father was king,
their counselor warrior Enlil,
their chamberlain was Ninurta,
their canal-controller Ennugi....
When Anu had gone up to the sky,
and the gods of the Apsu[4] had gone below,
the Anunnaki of the sky
made the Igigi bear the workload.
The gods had to dig out canals,
had to clear the channels, the lifelines of the
    land,
the Igigi had to dig out canals,
had to clear channels, the lifelines of the land.
The gods dug out the Tigris river bed
and then dug out the Euphrates....
They were counting the years of loads.
For 3,600 years they bore the excess,
hard work, night and day.
They groaned and blamed each other,
grumbled over the masses of excavated soil:
"Let us confront...the chamberlain,
and get him to relieve us of our hard work!
Come, let us carry the lord,
the counselor of the gods, the warrior from
    his dwelling.
Come, let us carry Enlil,
the counselor of the gods, the warrior from
    his dwelling."
Then [a god] made his voice heard

and spoke to the gods his brothers...:
"Come! Let us carry
the counselor of gods, the warrior, from his
    dwelling.
Come! Let us carry Enlil,
the counselor of gods, the warrior, from his
    dwelling.
Now, cry battle!
Let us mix fight with battle!"
The gods listened to his speech,
set fire to their tools,
put aside their spades for fire,
their loads for the fire god,
they flared up. When they reached
the gate of warrior Enlil's dwelling,
it was night, the middle watch,
the house was surrounded, the god had not
    realized.
It was night, the middle watch,
Ekur[5] was surrounded, Enlil had not realized.
Yet Kalkal[6] was attentive, and had it closed,
he held the lock and watched the gate.
Kalkal roused Nusku.[7]
They listened to the noise of the Igigi.
Then Nusku roused his master,
made him get out of bed:
"My lord, your house is surrounded,
a rabble is running around your door!"
Enlil had weapons brought to his dwelling.
Enlil made his voice heard
and spoke to the vizier Nusku,
"Nusku, bar your door,
take up your weapons and stand in front
    of me."
Nusku barred his door,
took up his weapons and stood in front of
    Enlil.
Nusku made his voice heard
and spoke to the warrior Enlil,
"O my lord, your face is sallow as tamarisk!
Why do you fear your own sons?
O Enlil, your face is sallow as tamarisk!
Why do you fear your own sons?
Send for Anu to be brought down to you,

---

[1]Translation by Stephanie Dalley, *Myths from Mesopotamia: Creation, the Flood, Gilgamesh, and Others* (Oxford: Oxford University Press, rev. ed., 2000), 9–35.
[2]The assembly of the gods.
[3]The younger generation of gods, a subset of the Anunnaki.
[4]The subterranean fresh waters.

[5]The "mountain house," Enlil's home and the name of his temple at Nippur.
[6]Enlil's gatekeeper.
[7]God of light, Enlil's chief of staff.

have Enki[1] fetched into your presence."
He sent for Anu to be brought down to him,
Enki was fetched into his presence,
Anu king of the sky was present,
Enki king of the Apsu attended.
The great Anunnaki were present.
Enlil got up and the case was put.
Enlil made his voice heard
and spoke to the great gods,
"Is it against me that they have risen?
Shall I do battle?...
What did I see with my own eyes?
A rabble was running around my door!"
Anu made his voice heard
and spoke to the warrior Enlil,
"Let Nusku go out
and find out the word of the Igigi
who have surrounded your door."...
Nusku opened his door,
took up his weapons....
In the assembly of all the gods
he bowed, then stood and told the message:
"Your father Anu,
your counselor warrior Enlil,
your chamberlain Ninurta,
and your canal controller Ennugi
have sent me to say,
'Who is in charge of the rabble?
Who is in charge of the fighting?
Who declared war?
Who ran to the door of Enlil?'"...
"Every single one of us gods declared war!
We have put a stop to the digging.
The load is excessive, it is killing us!
Our work is too hard, the trouble too much!
So every one of us gods
has agreed to complain to Enlil."...
Enlil listened to that speech.
His tears flowed.
Enlil spoke guardedly,
addressed the warrior Anu,
"Noble one, take a decree
with you to the sky, show your strength—
while the Anunnaki are sitting before you
call up one god and let them cast him for
    destruction!"
Anu made his voice heard

and spoke to the gods, his brothers,
"What are we complaining of?
Their work was indeed too hard, their trouble
    was too much.
Every day the earth resounded.
The warning signal was loud enough, we kept
    hearing the noise...."
Belet-ili the womb goddess[2] is present,
let the womb goddess create offspring,
and let man bear the yoke of the gods."...
Nintu[3] made her voice heard
and spoke to the great gods,
"It is not proper for me to make him.
The work is Enki's;
he makes everything pure!
If he gives me clay, then I will do it."
Enki made his voice heard
and spoke to the great gods,
"On the first, seventh, and fifteenth of the
    month
I shall make a purification by washing.
Then one god should be slaughtered.
And the gods can be purified by immersion.
Nintu shall mix clay
with his flesh and his blood.
Then a god and a man
will be mixed together in clay.
Let us hear the drumbeat forever after,
let a ghost come into existence from the god's
    flesh,
let her proclaim it as his living sign,
and let the ghost exist so as not to forget the
    slain god."[4]
They answered "Yes" in the assembly,
the great Anunnaki who assign the fates.

On the first, seventh, and fifteenth of the
    month
he made a purification by washing.
Ilawela who had intelligence,
they slaughtered in their assembly.
Nintu mixed clay
with his flesh and blood.[5]

---

[1] The god of wisdom; also known as Ea.

[2] The divine midwife.
[3] Another name of Belet-ili.
[4] The drumbeat may be the heartbeat or pulse, a sign of the ghost of the slain god.
[5] Cf. the slaughter of a god or gods in creating humans on pages 13 and 16.

They heard the drumbeat forever after.
A ghost came into existence from the god's
    flesh,
and she proclaimed it as his living sign.
The ghost existed so as not to forget the slain
    god.
After she had mixed that clay,
she called up the Anunnaki, the great
    gods,
spat spittle upon the clay.
Mami[1] made her voice heard
and spoke to the great gods,
"I have carried out perfectly
the work that you ordered of me.
You have slaughtered a god together with his
    intelligence.
I have relieved you of your hard work,
I have imposed your load upon man.
You have bestowed noise on mankind.
I have undone the fetter and granted
    freedom."
They listened to this speech of hers,
and were freed from anxiety, and kissed her
    feet:
"We used to call you Mami
but now your name shall be Mistress of All
    Gods."
Far-sighted Enki and wise Mami
went into the room of fate.
The womb goddesses were assembled.
He trod the clay in her presence;
she kept reciting an incantation,
for Enki, staying in her presence, made her
    recite it.
When she had finished her incantation,
she pinched off fourteen pieces of clay,
and set seven pieces on the right,
seven on the left.
Between them she put down a mud brick.
She made use of a reed, opened it to cut the
    umbilical cord,
called up the wise and knowledgeable
womb goddesses, seven and seven.
Seven created males,
seven created females,
for the womb goddess is creator of fate....
The womb goddesses were assembled,

and Nintu was present. They counted the
    months,
called up the tenth month as the term of
    fates.
When the tenth month came,
she slipped in a staff and opened the womb.
Her face was glad and joyful.
She covered her head,
performed the midwifery,
put on her belt, said a blessing....

[*After a gap in the text, the now-mature humans have
begun their work.*]

They made new picks and spades,
made big canals
to feed people and sustain the gods....
600 years, less than 600, passed,[2]
and the country became too wide, the people
    too numerous.
The country was as noisy as a bellowing bull.
The god grew restless at their racket,
Enlil had to listen to their noise.
He addressed the great gods,
"The noise of mankind has become too much,
I am losing sleep over their racket.[3]
Give the order that *shuruppu*-disease[4] shall
    break out...."
Now there was one Atrahasis
whose ear was open to his god Enki.
He would speak with his god
and his god would speak with him.
Atrahasis made his voice heard
and spoke to his lord,
"How long will the gods make us suffer?
Will they make us suffer illness forever?"

[*Enki instructs Atrahasis to have his countrymen offer
a sacrifice to the god Namtara, a god of the underworld.
The offering is accepted, and the disease stopped. This
pattern repeats itself: the population increases, and the
gods send a drought that causes famine. At this point
the text is badly damaged, but it is clear that divine
efforts to control human overpopulation continue,
and humans are reduced to cannibalism to survive.*

---

[1]Another name of the birth goddess.

[2]I.e., a little less than twelve hundred years.
[3]Compare pages 9–10.
[4]Chills and fever.

But these divine efforts fail, because Enki continues to advise Atrahasis on how to appease the gods. Finally, Enlil decides to send a Flood to wipe out the humans (compare pages 42–43). Enki then advises Atrahasis.]

"Dismantle the house, build a boat,
    reject possessions, and save living things....
Make upper and lower decks.
The tackle must be very strong,
    the bitumen strong, to give strength...."

[The boat is built, Atrahasis brings on board animals and his family, and the Flood comes.]

No one could see anyone else,
    they could not be recognized in the
        catastrophe.
The Flood roared like a bull,
    like a wild ass screaming the winds
        howled.
The darkness was total, there was no sun.

[Without humans to feed them, the gods themselves suffered starvation, and they blame Enlil and Anu. After a long gap, it is clear that the Flood had ended, and Atrahasis has offered a sacrifice to the gods.]

The gods smelled the fragrance,
    gathered like flies over the offering....
The warrior Enlil spotted the boat
    and was furious with the Igigi.
"We, the great Anunnaki, all of us,
    agreed together on an oath!
No form of life should have escaped!
    How did any man survive the catastrophe?"
Anu made his voice heard
    and spoke to the warrior Enlil,
"Who but Enki would do this?..."
Enki made his voice heard
    and spoke to the great gods,
"I did it in defiance of you!
    I made sure life was preserved!"

[The text is damaged here, but the gods now agree to control human population by making some women infertile or suffer miscarriage or the death of their newborns. The epic concludes with the gods praising Enki.]

"...how we sent the Flood.
But a man survived the catastrophe.
You are the counselor of the gods....
Let the Igigi listen to this song
    in order to praise you,
    and let them record your greatness.
I shall sing of the Flood to all people:
Listen!"

UGARIT

15. KIRTA

This is part of the tale of Kirta, the legendary founder of the dynasty of Ugarit. It is preserved on three tablets, but the beginning and end of the tale are missing, and the surviving tablets are incomplete. Dating to the mid-second millennium BCE, its themes of a childless patriarch and the succession to a sick king have many biblical parallels.[1]

Belonging to *Kirta*[2]
Perished was the house of the king,
    which had had seven brothers,
        eight sons of one mother.
Kirta our patriarch was destroyed,
    Kirta's dynasty was finished.
A legal wife he had found for himself,
    his lawfully wedded spouse;
        he had wed a wife, but she passed away.
She had had a mother's clan:
    one-third died in childbirth,
        one-fourth by disease,
        one-fifth was gathered by Resheph,[3]
        one-sixth was lost at sea,
        one-seventh fell in a water channel.
Kirta saw his offspring,
    he saw his offspring destroyed,
        his royal house completely finished.
So all his offspring had perished,
    his line in its entirety.
He entered his room and wept,
    he continued his moans and shed tears;
his tears poured out

---

[1] Translation by Michael D. Coogan and Mark S. Smith, *Stories from Ancient Canaan* (Louisville, KY: Westminster John Knox, 2d ed., 2012), 72–95.
[2] A scribal title, meaning "belonging to (the work called) *Kirta*."
[3] A god of plague.

like shekel-weights to the ground,
   like five-pieces on his bed.
As he wept, he fell asleep,
   as he shed tears, there was slumber;
sleep overpowered him as he lay down,
   slumber, as he curled up.
In his dream El[1] came down,
   in his vision the Father of Humanity.
He approached Kirta, asking:
   "Why are you weeping, Kirta?
   why does the Graceful Lad of El shed tears?
Is it kingship like his Father's that he desires,
   or dominion like that of the Father of
      Humanity?"

[*In missing lines, El offers power and wealth to Kirta.
He instead asks that he have sons:*]

   "Why should I want silver or gleaming gold,
      along with its land,
   or perpetual slaves,
      three horses,
   chariots in a courtyard,
      a slave woman's sons?
   Give me sons that I may be established,
      give me a clan that I may be magnified!"
And the Bull, his father El, replied:
   "Enough of your weeping, Kirta,
      of shedding tears, Graceful Lad of El.
   Wash yourself and put on rouge,
      wash your forearms to the elbow,
      from your fingers to your shoulder.
   Enter the shade of your tent;
   take a lamb in your hand,
      a sacrificial lamb in your right hand,
      a young animal in both your hands,
   the measure of your food that can be
         poured out.
   Take the proper sacrificial bird,
      pour wine into a silver goblet,
      honey into a golden bowl,
   and go up to the top of the tower,
      climb to the height of the wall;
   raise your hands to heaven,
      sacrifice to the Bull, your father El;
   serve Baal with your sacrifice,
      the son of Dagan with your game.

Then let Kirta come down from the roof;
   and prepare food for the city,
      grain for Bit-Hubur;
let him bake enough bread for five months,
   enough provisions for six.
Let the force be supplied and go forth,
   let the mighty army be supplied
   and let the force go forth.
Your army will be powerful indeed,
   three million strong,
soldiers beyond counting,
   archers beyond reckoning.
They will go in thousands, like a downpour,
   and in ten thousands, like the early rain;
they will go two by two,
   three by three, all together.
The only son will close up his house;
   the widow will hire a substitute;
the invalid will carry his own bed;
   the blind will run quickly;
even the newlywed will go forth:
   he will entrust his wife to another,
   his beloved to a stranger.
Like locusts that live in the field,
   like grasshoppers at the edge of the desert,
go one day, and a second,
   a third, then a fourth day,
   a fifth, then a sixth day.
Then, at sunset on the seventh,
   you will arrive at Udm the great,
   Udm the powerful;
and attack the towns,
   raid the villages;
let the woodcutters be swept from the fields,
   the women gathering straw from the
         threshing floors;
let the women drawing water be swept from
      the well,
   the women filling their jars from the
         spring.
Stop for a day, and a second,
   a third, then a fourth day,
   a fifth, then a sixth day:
don't shoot your arrows into the city,
   your slingstones into the fortress.
Then, by sunset on the seventh,
   King Pabil will be unable to sleep
because of the noise of his horses neighing,
   because of the sound of his asses braying,

---

[1]The head of the gods.

because of the lowing of the plow oxen,
    because of the howling of the hunting dogs.
And he will send messengers to you,
    to Kirta at his headquarters:
'Message of King Pabil:
Accept silver and gleaming gold,
    along with its land,
and perpetual slaves,
    three horses,
chariots in a courtyard,
    a slave woman's sons.
Kirta, accept these as peace offerings,
    and leave my house, king,
    go away from my court, Kirta.
Do not lay siege to Udm the great,
    Udm the powerful.
For Udm is a gift of El,
    a present from the Father of Humanity.'
Then you are to send messengers back to him:
'Why should I want silver or gleaming gold,
    along with its land,
or perpetual slaves,
    three horses,
chariots in a courtyard,
    a slave woman's sons?
You must give me rather what is not in my
        house:
    give me Lady Hurriya,
    the loveliest of your first-born offspring:
her loveliness is like Anat's,[1]
    her beauty is like Astarte's,[2]
her pupils are lapis lazuli,
    her eyes are gleaming alabaster.
    . . . I will rest in the gaze of her eyes.
This in my dream El granted,
    in my vision the Father of Humanity,
to bear offspring for Kirta,
    a boy for El's servant.'"
Kirta awoke—it was a dream,
    El's servant had had a vision.

[In the repetition characteristic of much ancient literature, Kirta carries out the instructions El had given him. On his journey to Udm, he stops at a shrine of Asherah, El's goddess wife:]

Like locusts that live in the field,
    like grasshoppers at the edge of the desert,
they went one day, and a second,
    then at sunset on the third,
they arrived at the shrine of Asherah of Tyre,
    of the goddess of Sidon.
There Kirta the Noble made a vow:
"As Asherah of Tyre lives,
    Goddess of Sidon,
if I take Hurriya to my house,
    if I bring the maiden to my court,
then I will give double her price in silver,
    and triple her price in gold."
He went one day, and a second,
    a third, then a fourth day,
then, at sunset on the fourth,
    he arrived at Udm the great,
    Udm the powerful. . . .

[As promised in the dream, Kirta's siege of Udm is successful, and he is given the king's daughter Hurriya as a wife. In the broken second tablet, the gods come to the wedding to bless the couple:]

    . . . Baal the Conqueror,[3]
        . . . Prince Moon,
    . . . Kothar-wa-Hasis,[4]
    . . . the Maiden,[5]
    Prince Resheph,
    the congregation of the gods,
        three by three.
Then Kirta the Noble
    placed a doorman at his palace.
Entry into the house he allowed,
    exit he did not allow.
The Assembly of the gods arrived,
    and Baal the Conqueror said:
"Do not depart, El the Kind, the
        Compassionate;
    bless Kirta the Noble,
    strengthen the Graceful Lad of El."
El took a cup in his hand,
    a goblet in his right hand;
he pronounced a blessing over his servant,
    El blessed Kirta the Noble,

---

[1] The goddess of love and the hunt; she is the storm god Baal's sister.
[2] Another goddess of love, also connected with Baal.

[3] The storm god; see Text 5.
[4] The craftsman of the gods.
[5] The goddess Anat.

strengthened the Gracious Lad of El:
"The wife you have taken, Kirta,
   the wife you have taken into your house,
   the maiden you brought into your court,
she will bear you seven sons and daughters,
   she will produce eight for you;
she will bear Yassub the Lad,
   who will nurse on the milk of Astarte,
suck the breasts of Maiden Anat,
   the two wet nurses of the gods....
May Kirta be highly praised,
   in the midst of the Rephaim[1] of the
      underworld,
   in the assembly of Ditan's[2] company.
She will soon bear you daughters:
   she will bear the girl...
   she will bear the girl...
   she will bear the girl...
   she will bear the girl...
   she will bear the girl...
   she will bear the girl....
May Kirta be highly praised,
   in the midst of the Rephaim of the
      underworld,
   in the assembly of Ditan's company.
The youngest of these I declare the first-
   born!"
The gods pronounced their blessing and went,
   the gods went to their tents,
   the Council of El to their homes.
And she soon bore him a son,
   she soon bore him two sons.
Then, after seven years,
   the sons of Kirta were as many as had been
      promised;
   so, too, were the daughters of Hurriya.
But Asherah remembered his vow....

[In the broken text that follows, Kirta is stricken by an
apparently fatal illness for his failure to fulfill his vow.
Eventually, in the third tablet, his son Ilihu comes to
visit him on his sickbed:]

   He entered his father's presence;
      he wept, bitterly so;
      he spoke as he wept:

---

[1]The deified dead; see Text 127.
[2]Ditan was an ancestor of Kirta.

"Our father, I rejoice in your living,
   we exult in your not-dying;
but like a dog that has passed from your
      house,
   like a hound also from your grave,
so you, too, father, are dying like a mortal;
   your grave will become a place of mourning,
   with women's laments, glorious father.
How can Kirta be called El's son,
   the offspring of the Kind and Holy One?
Or do gods die?
   Will the Kind One's offspring not live on?"
But Kirta the Noble replied:
"My son, don't weep,
   don't grieve for me;
my son, don't drain the well of your eyes,
   your head's springs of tears."

[One of Kirta's daughters then also visits him. After a
long break in the text, someone gives orders to investi-
gate the drought caused by the king's illness:]

"Look, go about earth and heaven,
   travel to the far reaches of the earth,
   for emmer in watered fields.
Look to the earth for Baal's rain,
   to the field for the rain of the Most High;
for Baal's rain benefits the earth,
   and the rain of the Most High the field;
it benefits the wheat in the furrow,
   the emmer in the tilled ground...."
The plowmen lifted their heads,
   upward, the workers of grain:
used up was the food from their bins,
   used up was the wine from their skins,
   used up was the oil from their vats.

[After another break in the text, El proceeds to create a healing goddess, Shataqat ("Expeller"), who then
tends to Kirta:]

"Who among the gods can expel the sickness,
   drive out the disease?"
But none of the gods answered him.
Then El the Kind, the Compassionate,
   replied:
"My sons, sit down upon your thrones,
   upon your princely seats.
I will fashion and establish,

I will establish one to expel the sickness,
   to drive out the disease."
He filled his palms with dirt,
   his fingers with the best dirt.
He pinched off some clay....[1]
She turned and washed off his sweat;
   she restored his appetite for food,
   his desire for a meal.
Death was broken!
   Expeller was strong!
Then Kirta the Noble gave a command,
   he raised his voice and declared:
"Listen, Lady Hurriya:
slaughter a lamb so that I may eat,
   some mutton for my meal."
Lady Hurriya obeyed:
   she slaughtered a lamb and he ate,
   some mutton for his meal.
One day ended, and on the second
Kirta returned to his throne-room;
   he sat on the royal throne,
   on the resting place, the seat of dominion.
Now Yassub[2] too lived in the palace,
   and his heart instructed him:
"Go to your father, Yassub,
   go to your father and speak,
   recite to Kirta your lord:
'Listen closely and pay attention:
   when raiders raid, you talk;
   when there are invaders, you are idle.
You have let your power become feeble:
   you do not judge the cases of widows,
   you do not preside over the hearings of the
      oppressed;
for you have taken to a sick bed,
   you languish on a bed of disease.
Step down from the kingship—let me be king,
   from your dominion—let me be
      enthroned.'"
Yassub the Lad left;
   he entered his father's presence;
He raised his voice and declared:
"Listen, Kirta the Noble,
   listen closely and pay attention:
when raiders raid, you talk,
   when there are invaders, you are idle.

You have let your power become feeble:
   you do not judge the cases of widows,
   you do not preside over the hearings of the
      oppressed;
you do not drive out those who burden the
      yoke of the poor,
   you do not feed the orphan before you,
   nor the widow at your back;
for you have taken to a sick bed,
   you have languished on a bed of disease.
Step down from the kingship—let me be
      king,
   from your dominion—let me be
      enthroned."
But Kirta the Noble replied:
"My son, may Horon[3] smash,
   may Horon smash your head,
   Astarte, Baal's other self, your skull.
May you fall at the peak of your years,
   in your prime may you be humbled."

[*The tablet ends here, so there must have been a
sequel.*]

16. AQHAT

**Partially preserved on three tablets, this mid-second-
millennium-BCE epic, like Text 15, concerns a childless
patriarch, Danel, who eventually has a son, Aqhat,
and goes on to describe how the son is killed by the
goddess Anat and is eventually avenged by his sister. Danel is mentioned in Ezekiel 14:14, 20; 28:3.[4]**

Then Danel, the man of Rapau,
   the Hero, the man of the Harnamite,[5]
girded, he gave the gods food,
   girded, he gave the holy ones drink.
He cast off his cloak and lay down,
   put off his garment and spent the night....
Then, on the seventh day,
Baal approached with his compassion:[6]
"Danel, the man of Rapau, laments,

---

[1]Cf. pages 40 and 47.
[2]Another of Kirta's sons.

[3]A god of the underworld
[4]Translation by Michael D. Coogan and Mark S. Smith, *Stories
from Ancient Canaan* (Louisville, KY: Westminster John Knox, 2d
ed., 2012), 34–55.
[5]Danel's titles are not fully understood.
[6]The hero's divine patron, the storm god Baal, approaches El, the
head of the pantheon.

the Hero, the man of the Harnamite,
    moans:
For he has no son as his brothers do,
    no heir like his kinsmen;
unlike his brothers, he has no son,
    nor an heir, like his kinsmen.
Girded, he has given the gods food,
    girded, he has given the holy ones drink.
So, my father, El the Bull, bless him,
    Creator of Creatures, show him your favor.
Let him have a son in his house,
    an heir inside his palace,
to set up a stela for his divine ancestor,
    a votive marker for his clan in the sanctuary;
to send his incense up from the earth,
    the song of his burial place from the dust;
to shut the jaws of his abusers,
    to drive off his oppressors;
to hold his hand when he is drunk,
    to support him when he is full of wine;
to eat his grain-offering in the temple of Baal,
    his portion in the temple of El;
to patch his roof when it gets muddy,
    to wash his clothes when they get dirty."
El took care of his servant,
    he blessed Danel, the man of Rapau,
    he showed favor to the Hero, the man of
        the Harnamite:
"With passion may Danel, the man of Rapau,
    live,
    with desire the Hero, the man of the
        Harnamite.
Let him go up to his bed:
    as he kisses his wife, she'll become pregnant,
    as he embraces her, she'll conceive;
She will become pregnant,
    she will conceive;
and there will be a son in his house,
    an heir inside his palace...."

[*The text is broken here, but the news is apparently given to Danel. After the birth goddesses visit him, his wife conceives, and a son is born, named Aqhat. After a long break, the craftsman of the gods, Kothar-wa-Hasis, visits Danel bringing a marvelous bow and arrows:*]

And then, on the seventh day,
    Danel, the man of Rapau,

the Hero, the man of the Harnamite,
    got up and sat at the entrance to the gate,
    among the leaders on the threshing floor.
He judged the cases of widows,
    presided over orphans' hearings.
Then he raised his eyes and looked:
    a thousand fields, ten thousand acres at
        each step,
he saw Kothar coming,
    he saw Hasis approaching.
Look!—he was bringing a bow,
    look!—he was bearing arrows.
Then Danel, the man of Rapau,
    the Hero, the man of the Harnamite,
    called to his wife:
"Listen, Lady Danataya:
    prepare a lamb from the flock
for Kothar-wa-Hasis's appetite,
    for the desire of the Skillful Craftsman.
Give food and drink to the god;
    serve and honor him,
    the lord of Egypt, the god of it all."

[*After the meal Kothar departs, and then there is a break in the text. When it resumes, the goddess Anat is speaking with Aqhat:*]

She poured her cup on the ground,
    she raised her voice and declared:
"Listen, Aqhat the Hero:
    ask for silver, and I'll give it to you,
    for gold—I'll make it yours.
But give your bow to Anat,
    let the Mistress of the Peoples have your
        arrows."
But Aqhat the Hero replied:
"The strongest ash trees from the Lebanon,
    the strongest sinews from wild oxen,
the strongest horns from mountain goats,
    the strongest tendons from the hocks of a
        bull,
    the strongest reeds from the vast marshes:
give them to Kothar-wa-Hasis,
    so he can make a bow for Anat,
    arrows for the Mistress of the Peoples."
But Maiden Anat replied:
"Ask for eternal life, Aqhat the Hero;
    ask for eternal life, and I'll give it to you,
    immortality—I'll make it yours.

I'll make you able to match years with Baal,
    months with the sons of El.
For Baal, when he gives life, makes a feast,
    he makes a feast for the life-given, and
        gives him drink;
he sings a song in his honor,
    a pleasant refrain for him.
So will I give life to Aqhat the Hero."
But Aqhat the Hero replied:
"Don't lie to me, Maiden;
    for to a hero your lies are filth.
A mortal—what does he get in the end?
    what does a mortal finally get?
Glaze poured on his head,
    lime on top of his skull.
As every man dies, I will die;
    yes, I too will surely die.
And I have something else to tell you:
Bows are for warriors—
    do women ever hunt?"
Anat laughed aloud,
    but in her heart she plotted:
"Listen to me, Aqhat the Hero,
    listen to me while I speak:
If I meet you on the path of rebellion,
    ...on the proud path,
I'll make you fall under my feet,
    you pretty-boy, he-man."
She stamped her feet and left the earth;
    then she headed for El,
at the source of the two rivers,
    in the midst of the channels of the
        two seas.
She came to the encampment of El and
        entered
    the tent of the King, the Father of Time.
At El's feet she bowed and lowered herself,
    she prostrated herself and honored him.
Then she maligned Aqhat, the Hero,
    she slandered the child of Danel, the man
        of Rapau....

[*Again the text is poorly preserved. As the second tablet becomes legible, Anat is threatening El:*]

    "Don't rejoice in your well-built house,
        in your well-built house, El,
    don't rejoice in the height of your palace:
        don't rely on them!

I'll smash your head,
    I'll make your gray hair run with blood,
    your gray beard with gore;
then you may call to Aqhat—he can save you;
    to the son of Danel—he can save you
        from the hand of Maiden Anat!"
But El the Kind, the Compassionate, replied:
"1 know you, daughter, how angry you can be;
    among goddesses there is no restraining you.
Leave, my unscrupulous daughter;
    you will store it up inside you,
set your heart on whatever you desire;
    whoever resists you will be crushed."
Maiden Anat left;
    she headed to Aqhat the Hero,
    a thousand fields, ten thousand acres at
        each step.
And Maiden Anat laughed;
    she raised her voice and declared:
"Listen, Aqhat the Hero:
    you are my brother and I..."

[*After a long break in the text, Anat in the form of a vulture prepares to attack Aqhat:*]

    As Aqhat sat down to eat,
        the son of Danel to his meal,
        vultures hovered over him,
        a flock of birds watched.
    Among the vultures hovered Anat;
        she set him[1] over Aqhat.
    He struck him twice on the skull,
        three times over the ear;
    he made his blood run like a slaughterer,
        run to his knees like a butcher.
    His breath went out like wind,
        his spirit like a breeze,
        like smoke, from his nostrils....

[*As the third tablet opens, Anat apparently regrets what she has done. Meanwhile, Danel and his daughter Pugat realize that something is amiss:*]

    Then Danel, the man of Rapau,
        the Hero, the man of the Harnamite,
        got up and sat at the entrance to the gate,

---

[1]One of her attendants, called Yatpan, also in the form of a vulture.

among the leaders on the threshing floor.
He judged the cases of widows,
   presided over orphans' hearings....
She raised her eyes and looked:
   on the threshing floor the greenery had
      dried,
      it drooped, it had withered.
Over her father's house vultures hovered,
   a flock of birds watched.
Pugat wept in her heart,
   she cried inwardly.
She tore the clothes of Danel, the man of
      Rapau,
   the garment of the Hero, the man of the
      Harnamite.[1]
Then Danel, the man of Rapau,
cursed the clouds in the awful heat,
   the rain of the clouds that falls in late
      summer,
   the dew that drops on the grapes:
"For seven years let Baal fail,
   eight, the Rider on the Clouds:
No dew, no showers,
   no surging of the two seas,
   no benefit of Baal's voice.
For the clothes of Danel, the man of Rapau,
      have been torn,
   the garment of the Hero, the man of the
      Harnamite."...
Danel went around his dried land;
   he saw a stalk in the dried land,
   he saw a stalk in the languishing land.
He embraced the stalk and kissed it:
"I pray the stalk could grow
   in the dried land the stalk could grow,
   the plant in the languishing land;
   the hand of Aqhat the Hero would harvest
      you,
      place you in the granary."

[*Danel realizes what has happened, and begins seven
years of mourning:*]

Danel arrived at his house,
   Danel reached his palace.
The weepers entered his house,

the mourners his palace,
   those who gash their skin his court.[2]
They wept for Aqhat the Hero,
   shed tears for the child of Danel, the man
      of Rapau.
The days became months,
   the months became years,
   up to seven years,
they wept for Aqhat the Hero,
   shed tears for the child of Danel, the man
      of Rapau.
Then, in the seventh year,
   Danel, the man of Rapau man, spoke;
the Hero, the man of the Harnamite,
   raised his voice and declared:
"Leave my house, weepers,
   leave my palace, mourners,
   leave my court, you who gash your skin."
He made a sacrifice to the gods,
   he sent incense up to heaven....
Pugat who carries water spoke:
"My father, you have made a sacrifice to the
      gods,
   you have sent incense up to heaven,
   incense of the Harnamite to the stars.
Now bless me, that I may go with your
      blessing;
   favor me, that I may go with your favor.
I will kill my brother's killer,
   put an end to whoever put an end to my
      mother's son."
Danel, the man of Rapau, replied:
"Pugat, with passion may you live—
you who carry water,
   you who collect dew on your hair,
   you who know the course of the stars....
May you kill your brother's killer,
   put an end to whoever put an end to your
      mother's son."
...She washed and put on rouge,
   she put on rouge of sea-dye,
   from a thousand fathoms in the vast
      expanse of the sea.
She put on a hero's clothes,
   she placed a knife in her sheath,
   she placed a sword in her scabbard;
and on top she put on women's clothes.

---

[1]Tearing clothing was a traditioal act of mourning; cf., e.g., Genesis 37:29, 34; 2 Samuel 13:19.

[2]Cf. Leviticus 19:28; Deuteronomy 14:1.

As Sun, the gods' torch, went down,
　Pugat entered the fields;
As Sun, the gods' torch, set,
　Pugat arrived at the tents.
Word was brought to Yatpan:
"The woman we hired has come to your
　　encampment,
　she has come to the tents."
And Yatpan, the Lady's Warrior, replied:
"Receive her: she'll give me wine to drink;
　she'll take the cup from my hand,
　the mug from my right hand."
Pugat was received; she gave him a drink;
　she took the cup from his hand,
　the mug from his right hand.
Then Yatpan, the Lady's Warrior, said:
"...May the hand that killed Aqhat
　　the Hero,
　kill enemies by the thousands...."
Twice she gave him wine to drink,
　she gave him wine to drink.

[The text ends here. One or more tablets must have related how Pugat killed Yatpan, and perhaps how Aqhat was restored to life.]

HITTITE
17. KANESH AND ZALPA

Often called "a tale of two cities," this incomplete text is apparently a legendary account of the origins of a relationship between the Hittite city of Kanesh in central Asia Minor and a city on the Black Sea called Zalpa. It probably originated in the early second millennium BCE.[1]

The Queen of Kanesh once bore thirty sons[2] in a single year. She said: "What a horde is this which I have borne!" She filled the cracks of baskets with grease, put her sons in them, and launched them in the river. The river carried them down to the sea[3] at the land of Zalpa. But the gods took them up out of the sea and reared them.[4]

When some years had passed, the queen again gave birth, this time to thirty daughters. This time she herself reared them. Now the sons were on their way back to Kanesh, driving a donkey. When they reached the city of Tamarmara, they said, "Heat up a bedroom, and our donkey will climb up a staircase!" At this the men of the city replied: "What have we come to, that a donkey can climb a staircase?" The boys countered: "What have we come to, that a woman can give birth to thirty children in a single year? Yet one did give birth to us all in one pregnancy!" Not to be outdone, the men of the city retorted: "Our Queen of Kanesh also gave birth to thirty daughters in one pregnancy. Her sons born earlier have vanished." The boys said to each other: "We have found our mother, whom we were seeking! Come, let us go to Kanesh!" Now when they had gone to Kanesh, the gods put another... in them, so that their mother didn't recognize them. She wanted to give her daughters in marriage to her sons. The older sons didn't recognize their sisters. But the youngest objected: "Should we take our own sisters in marriage? Don't do such an impious thing! It is surely not right that we should sleep with them."

[The rest of the text is badly broken. It seems to describe the later history of the Hittites and the region of Zalpa.]

18. APPU AND HIS TWO SONS

Like other biblical and nonbiblical texts, this fragmentary tale features a childless patriarch and rival brothers. It originally dates to the early second millennium BCE and begins with a moral.[5]

[Some deity] it is who always exonerates just men, but chops down evil men like trees, repeatedly striking evil men on their skulls...until [the deity] destroys them.

[1]Translation by Harry A. Hoffner, Jr., *Hittite Myths* (Writings from the Ancient World 2; Atlanta, GA: Scholars Press, 2d ed., 1998), 81–82.
[2]Cf. Judges 10:4.
[3]The Black Sea.
[4]Cf. Exodus 2:1–10. See also Text 21.
[5]Translation by Harry A. Hoffner, Jr., *Hittite Myths* (Writings from the Ancient World 2; Atlanta, GA: Scholars Press, 2d ed., 1998), 83–85.

There was a city named Shudul. It was situated on the seacoast in the land of Lulluwa.[1] Up there lived a man called Appu. He was the richest man in the land. He had many cattle and sheep. He had accumulated silver, gold, and lapis lazuli like a whole heap of threshed grain.

There was nothing which he lacked but one thing: he had neither son nor daughter. The elders of Shudul sat eating in his presence. One gave bread and a piece of grilled meat to his son; another gave his son a drink. But Appu had no one to whom to give bread.

The table was covered with a linen cloth and stood in front of the altar. Appu arose, went home, and lay on his bed with his shoes on. Appu's wife questioned their servants: "He has never had success before. You don't think he has now had success, do you?" The woman went and lay with Appu with her clothes on.

Then Appu awoke from his sleep, and his wife questioned him: "You have never had success before. Have you now been successful?" When Appu heard this, he replied: "You are a woman and think like one. You know nothing at all."

Appu rose from his bed, took a white lamb, and set out to meet the Sun God. The Sun God looked down from the sky, changed himself into a young man, came to him, and questioned him: "What is your problem, that I may solve it for you?" When Appu heard this, he replied to him: "The gods have given me wealth. They have given me cattle and sheep. I lack only one thing: I have neither son nor daughter." When the Sun God heard this, he said: "Go get drunk, go home, and have good sexual intercourse with your wife. The gods will give you one son."

When Appu heard this, he went back home, but the Sun God went back up to the sky. Now Teshub[2] saw the Sun God coming three miles distant, and said to his vizier: "Look who's coming: the Sun God, Shepherd of the Lands! You don't suppose that somewhere the land is laid waste? Might not cities somewhere be devastated? Might not troops be put to rout? Instruct the cook and cupbearer to provide him with food and drink."

The Sun God came,...and Teshub...began to question him: "Why have you come, O Sun God of the Sky?..."

[*The text is broken here.*]

Appu's wife became pregnant. The first month, the second month, the third month, the fourth month, the fifth month, the sixth month, the seventh month, the eighth month, the ninth month passed, and the tenth month arrived. Appu's wife bore a son. The nurse lifted the boy, and put him on Appu's knees. Appu began to amuse the boy and to clean him off. He put a fitting name upon him: "Since my paternal gods didn't take the right way for him, but kept to a wrong way, let his name be Wrong."

Again, a second time, Appu's wife became pregnant. The tenth month arrived, and the woman bore a son. The nurse lifted the boy, and Appu put the right name upon him: "Let them call him the right name. Since my paternal gods took the right way for him, let his name be Right." Appu's boys grew up and matured and came into manhood.

When Appu's boys had grown up and matured and come into manhood, they parted from Appu, and divided up the estate. Brother Wrong said to Brother Right: "Let us part and settle down in different places."[3]...Brother Wrong said to Brother Right: "Since the mountains dwell separately, since the rivers flow in separate courses, as the very gods dwell separately, I say these things to you: The Sun God dwells in Sippar. The Moon God dwells in Kuzina. Teshub dwells in Kummiya. And Shaushga[4] dwells in Nineveh. Nanaya dwells in Kissina. And Marduk dwells in Babylon. As the gods dwell separately, so let us settle in different places."

Wrong and Right began to divide up the estate, while the Sun God looked down from heaven. Brother Wrong took a half and gave the other half to his brother Right....There was one plow ox and one cow. Wrong took the good plow ox, and gave the bad cow to his brother Right. The Sun God

---

[1]The locales cannot be identified and are probably fictional.
[2]The storm god.

[3]Cf. Genesis 13:8–12.
[4]The Hittite name of Ishtar, the principal goddess of Nineveh.

looked down from heaven and said: "Let Right's bad cow become good, and let her bear...."

[*Another fragment describes a judgment by the Sun God in favor of Right, and then an appeal to Shaushga, whose decision is not preserved.*]

EGYPT

19. THE TALE OF TWO BROTHERS

This well-preserved narrative dates to the late second millennium BCE. It includes mythological elements, as is clear from the names of the two brothers, Anubis and Bata, which are also the names of deities.[1] The dismemberment and repeated death and restoration to life of the younger brother resembles elements of the myth of Osiris, known best from late classical sources (see page 60, n. 1). It may also have a historical basis, perhaps explaining the complicated succession to the Pharaoh Merneptah in the late thirteenth century BCE. It shares with biblical literature the attempted seduction of a man by the wife of another, like Joseph and Potiphar's wife in Genesis 39, and the account of the rise to kingship of a shepherd, like David.[2]

Once upon a time there were two brothers of one father and one mother. Anubis was the name of the older; Bata was the name of the younger. Now Anubis had a house and a wife, his younger brother being with him in the manner of a son. He used to make clothes for him, and he used to follow after his herd to the fields. It was he who did the plowing, and it was he who harvested, and it was he who used to do all the affairs of the fields. Indeed, his younger brother was a beautiful young man, there being none of his form in the whole land. Indeed the strength of a god was in him.

Now many days after this, his younger brother followed his cattle in his daily custom, and he returned to his house every evening, and he was loaded with every plant of the field, with milk, with wood, with every good thing of the field, and he laid it before his older brother, he being seated with his wife. He used to drink, he used to eat, and he used to sleep in his stable in the midst of his cattle.

Now after the land was light and a second day dawned, he took foods which were cooked and he placed them before his older brother, and he gave him loaves for the field, and he drove his cattle to allow them to eat in the fields, he going after the cattle, they telling him, "The herbage is good in such-and-such place." And he used to hear all which they said, and he took them to the good place of herbage which they desired, the cattle before him becoming very beautiful. They multiplied their offspring very much.

Now at the time of plowing, his older brother said to him, "Have ready for us a span of oxen for the plowing because the high land has gone forth, it being good to plow it. Likewise go to the field carrying seed because we will begin to plow tomorrow." And then his younger brother did all the things which his older brother said to him, "Do them."

Now after the land became light and a second day dawned, they went to the field carrying their seed and they began to plow. Their hearts were very pleased because of their work at the beginning of their work.

Now after many days, they being in the field and waiting for seed, then he sent his younger brother saying, "Hurry, bring us seed from the town." And this younger brother found the wife of his older brother with one sitting braiding her. And then he said to her, "Stand, get for me seed that I may hasten to the field because my older brother waits for me. Do not make a delay." Then she said to him, "Go, open the storehouse and bring yourself what you want. Do not make me abandon my hair dressing."

And then the young man entered his barn and he brought one of the large jars, he desiring to take much seed, and he loaded himself with barley and emmer and he went forth carrying them. Then she said to him, "How much weight is what is on your shoulder?" And he said to her,

---

[1] Anubis is the jackal god, a god of cemeteries and the afterlife; Bata is a bull god.
[2] Translated by Susan Tower Hollis, *The Ancient Egyptian "Tale of Two Brothers": A Mythological, Religious, Literary, and Historico-Political Study* (Oakville, CT: Bannerstone, 2d ed., 2008), 1–9.

"Three sacks of emmer and two sacks of barley, five in all are those which are on my shoulder." He said thus to her. And then she spoke with him saying, "Strength is great in you, for I see your strength daily." And she desired to know him as to know a young man. And then she stood, and she seized him, and she said to him, "Come, let us spend an hour lying down. It will be beneficial for you. Then I will make beautiful clothes for you." Then the young man became angry like an Upper Egyptian leopard because of the evil word which she said to him, and she was very frightened. And then he spoke with her saying, "Now see, you are like a mother to me. Further, your husband is like a father to me. Now the one older than I, he has raised me. What is the great wrong which you said to me? Do not say it to me again. Further I will not speak of it to anyone, and I will not cause it to go forth from my mouth to any people." And lifting his load, he went to the field. And then he reached his older brother, and they started to work again in their work.

Now when it was evening, his older brother returned to his house, his younger brother being behind his cattle, and he was loaded with everything of the field, and he brought his cattle before him to have them spend the night in their barn in the village.

Now the wife of the older brother was afraid of the word which she said. And then she brought fat and grease, and she became like one who was beaten, saying to her husband, "It was your young brother who beat me." When her husband returned in the evening in his daily fashion, he found his wife lying ill of guilt, and she did not put water over his hand in his daily fashion. And she did not make a light before him, his house being in darkness, because she was lying down vomiting. And her husband said to her, "Who had words with you?" Then she said to him, "No one spoke to me except your young brother. When he came to fetch seed for you, he found me sitting alone, and he said to me, 'Come, let us spend an hour lying down. Loosen your hair.' Thus he said to me. I did not listen to him. He was afraid. He beat me in order that I not give you a report. Now if you let him live, I will die. See, when he comes do not let him live because I suffer the evil thing which he did yesterday."

And then his older brother became like a leopard of Upper Egypt, and he had his spear sharpened, and he put it in his hand. And then his older brother stood behind the door of his stable to kill his young brother in his coming in the evening to have his cattle enter the stable.

When the sun came to rest, he loaded himself with all the herbage of the fields in his fashion of every day, and he came, and the foremost cow entered the stable. And she said to her shepherd, "Behold, your older brother stands before you carrying his spear to kill you. Flee before him." And then he heard the speaking of his lead cattle and another entered and she said the same. And he looked under the door of his stable, and he saw the feet of his older brother as he stood behind the door with his spear in his hand. And he put his load down, and he raised himself to run in order to flee, and his older brother went after him, carrying his spear.

And then his younger brother prayed to Re-Harakhti,[1] saying, "My good Lord, it is you who judges between the guilty and the innocent." Re heard his whole petition, and Re caused a great water to come between them, to separate him from his older brother, it being filled with crocodiles. And one of them was on the one side and the other on the other, and his older brother struck his hand twice for not killing him.

And then his younger brother called to him on the side, saying, "Stand here until the dawn. When the disk shines, I will contend with you before him in order that he give the guilty to the just, because I will not be with you forever, and I will not be in the place in which you are. And I will go to the Valley of the Pine."

Now when the land was light and a second day became, Re-Harakhti arose and one saw the other. And then the young man spoke to his older brother, saying, "What is your coming after me to kill me falsely, not hearing my mouth speak on the matter? And further I am still your young brother, and also you are with me in the manner of a father and also your wife is with me in the manner of a mother. Is it not so when you sent to bring seed for us, your wife said to me, 'Come, let us spend an hour

[1]The sun god and head of the pantheon.

lying together.' Further, see, she turned it about for you into another thing." And then he swore to Re-Harakhti, saying, "As for your coming to kill me wrongfully, carrying your spear on the word of a filthy whore," and he brought a reed knife and he cut off his phallus, and he threw it to the water, and the catfish fish swallowed it.[1] And he was weak and he became feeble. And his older brother was very sorrowing in his heart, and he stood and wept loudly for him, and he was not able to be where his young brother was because of the crocodiles.

And then his young brother called to him, saying, "Indeed, if you recall an evil, do you not also recall a good or something I did for you? Now go to your house and care for your cattle because I will not stand in the place in which you are. And I will go to the Valley of the Pine. Now as to what you will do for me, it is your coming to care for me when you know that something has happened to me. I will have cut out my heart and placed it on the top of the blossom of the pine. When the pine is cut and it falls to the ground, you will come to seek it. If you spend seven years seeking it, do not let your heart show dislike, and when you find it, put it in a bowl of cool water and I will live and I shall avenge the transgressions against me. Further, you will know something has happened to me when you are given a jug of beer to your hand and it foams. Do not wait, for already it has happened with you."

And then he went to the Valley of the Pine and his older brother went to his house, his hands on his head, he being covered with dirt. He reached his house and killed his wife, and he threw her to the dogs[2] and he sat mourning for his young brother.

Now many days after this, his young brother was in the Valley of the Pine, no one being with him and he spending the day hunting small game in the hills, and he came to spend the night under the pine on top of whose blossom was his heart.

Now many days after this, he built himself a house with his hands in the Valley of the Pine,

and he filled it with every good thing of his desire to furnish for himself a house. He went out from his house and he met the Ennead[3] as they were going out to administer the whole land. And then the Ennead spoke, one of them to another, saying to him, "Ho, Bata, bull of the Ennead, are you here alone, you having escaped your town because of the wife of Anubis, your older brother? See, he killed his wife. Now you are avenged by him upon all the transgressions against you."

Their heart was very sore for him, and Re-Harakhti said to Khnum,[4] "Now make a wife for Bata that he not live alone." And then Khnum made for him a companion.[5] She was more beautiful of body than any woman in the whole land, the fluid of every god being in her. And then the Seven Hathors[6] came to see her, and they spoke as one, "She will die of a knife." And then he desired her very very much, and she sat in his house while he spent the day hunting small animals in the hills and bringing them to lay before her. And he said to her, "Do not go out lest the sea seize you because I will not be able to save you from it because I am a woman like you. Further my heart is placed on the top of the flower of the pine. When another finds it, I will fight with him." And then he reported his heart to her in its entirety.

Now many days after that when Bata went out to hunt as customary, the young woman went forth to stroll under the pine beside her house. She saw the sea surge up after her, and she rose up to run before it, and she entered her house. And then the sea called to the pine, saying, "Catch her for me." And the pine brought one plait of her hair. And then the sea brought it to Egypt, and he put it in the place of the washer men of the pharaoh. And then the odor of the plait of hair happened into the clothing of the pharaoh, and the king fought with the washer men of the house, saying, "The odor of tallow is in the clothes of the pharaoh." And the king became quarrelsome with them daily, and they did not know what to do. And the head washer man of the pharaoh went

---

[1] This resembles the story of Osiris, alluded to in other Egyptian sources, and most fully described in the first- to second-century CE Roman writer Plutarch's *Isis and Osiris,* Chap. 18. Osiris's dismembered body was recovered by his wife Isis, except for his phallus, which fish had eaten; see also page 32.

[2] Cf. 2 Kings 9:30–37.

[3] The nine principal gods of Egypt.

[4] A potter god who formed humans from clay.

[5] Cf. Genesis 2:18–22.

[6] Goddesses of fate.

to his bank, his heart being very pained after the quarreling with him daily. And then he determined for himself he was standing on the land opposite the plait of hair which was in the water, and he had one go down, and it was brought to him. And an extremely sweet odor was found, and he took it to the pharaoh.

And then the scribes-who-knew-things of the king were brought, and then they said to the pharaoh, "As for the plait of hair, it belongs to a daughter of Re-Harakhti with the fluid of all the gods in her. Now it is a greeting of another land. Cause messengers to go to every land to seek her. As for the messenger who is for the Valley of the Pine, have many people go with him to bring her." Then his majesty said, "What you have said is very good." And they were caused to hurry.

Now many days after this, the people who went to the foreign land came to tell reports to his majesty while the ones who went to the Valley of the Pine did not come because Bata killed them. And he left one of them to report to his majesty. And then his majesty had people, many bowmen, go, likewise chariotry, to bring her back, and a woman was with them, and every beautiful ornament was put in her hand. And then the young woman came to Egypt with her, and there was shouting for her in the whole land. And then his majesty loved her very much and he appointed her to the position of Great Noble Lady. And then he spoke with her to make her tell the manner of her husband, and she spoke to his majesty, "Have the pine cut and have it destroyed." And the people were made to go, carrying their weapons to cut the tree, and they reached the pine, and they cut the blossom upon which was the heart of Bata. And he fell dead in the evil hour.

Now after the land was light and a second day began, when the pine was cut, Anubis, the elder brother of Bata, entered his house, and he was given a jug of beer, and it foamed, and he was given another of wine, and it made an offensive smell. And then he took his staff and his sandals, likewise his clothes and his weapons of combat, and he rose up to make an expedition to the Valley of the Pine, and he entered the mansion of his young brother. And he found his young brother lying dead upon his bed, and

he wept when he saw his young brother lying in death. And he went to seek the heart of his young brother under the pine under which his young brother lay in the evening. And he spent three years seeking it without finding it. When he began the fourth year, his heart wished to go to Egypt, and he said, "I will go tomorrow." Thus he said in his heart.

Now after the land was bright and another day began, he began and went under the pine and he spent the day seeking it again, and he returned in the evening, and he spent time to seek it again. And he found a bunch of grapes, and he returned carrying it, and there was the heart of his young brother. And he brought a bowl of cool water and he put it in it, and he sat as was his custom.

Now when evening came, his heart swallowed the water, and Bata trembled in every limb, and he began to look at his older brother, his heart being in the bowl. And Anubis, his older brother, took the bowl of cool water with the heart of his young brother in it, and he caused him to drink it, and his heart stood in its place, and he became like he had been. And then one embraced the other, and one spoke with his companion. And then Bata spoke to his older brother, "See, I will become a great bull with every beautiful color and none knows his nature, and you will sit on my back. By the time the sun rises, we will be in the place where my wife is in order that I avenge myself. And you will take me to where the king is because he will do for you every good thing. Then he will raise you with silver and gold because you brought me to the pharaoh because I shall be a great marvel and I will be raised in the whole land and you will go to your village."

Now when the land was light and another day began, and Bata became in the form which he told his older brother. And then Anubis, his older brother, sat on his back. At dawn he reached where the king was, and his majesty was made to know of him, and he saw him, and he became very joyful because of him. And he made him great offerings, saying, "A great miracle has happened." And there was rejoicing because of him in the whole land. And then he was raised, rewarded with silver and gold for his older brother, and he lived in his town. And the king gave to him many people and many things, and the pharaoh loved him very much, more than any people in the whole land.

Now many days after this, he entered the kitchen, and he stood where the noble lady was and he began to speak with her, saying, "See, I am alive again." And she said to him, "Who then are you?" And he said to her, "I am Bata. I noticed when you had one destroy the pine for the pharaoh on account of me that I not live. See, I have been made alive again. I am a bull." And then the noble lady was very afraid of the word her husband told to her. And then he went out from the kitchen.

And his majesty sat and made a feast day with her and she poured for his majesty and the king was very happy with her. And she said to his majesty, "Come, swear an oath by the god, saying, 'As for what I say, I will hear it because of her.'" And he heard all which she said. "Allow me to eat from the liver of the bull because he will not do anything." Thus she said to him. And he suffered very much because of what she said, and the heart of the king was very, very ill.[1]

Now when the land was light and a second day became, the king invoked a great offering in the offering of the bull. The king had one of the head royal butlers of his majesty go to make ready the bull. When he had been slaughtered, when he was upon the shoulder of the people, he quivered in his neck and he made fall two drops of blood beside the two doorposts of his majesty, the one happening on the one side of the great door and the other upon the other side. And they grew into two great persea trees, each one being outstanding. And then one went to tell his majesty, "Two great perseas are grown as a great marvel for his majesty in the night beside the great portal of his majesty." And there was shouting because of them in the whole land, and the king made offerings to them.

Now many days after this, his majesty appeared in the window of lapis lazuli, a wreath of every flower at his neck, and he was upon a chariot of fine gold, and he went forth from the royal house

to see the perseas. And then the noble lady went forth upon a team after the pharaoh. And then his majesty sat under one of the perseas and the noblewoman under the other persea. And then Bata spoke with his wife, "Ha, traitor, I am Bata. I am living despite you. I noticed that one was caused to cut the pine for the pharaoh, it was because of me, and I became a bull. And you caused me to be killed."

Now many days after this, the noblewoman stood to pour for his majesty, he being happy with her, and she said to his majesty, "Make an oath to me by the god, saying, 'As for what the noblewoman says to me, I will hear it for her,' you shall say." And he heard all which she said, and she said, "Have the two perseas cut and have one make them into beautiful furniture." And then all that she said was heard.

And now, after a small moment, his majesty had skilled craftsmen go and the perseas of the pharaoh were cut while the royal wife, the noblewoman, watched it. And then a splinter flew and it entered the mouth of the noblewoman. And then she swallowed it, and she became pregnant. In the completion of a short while, the king had made all that she desired from them.

Now many days after this, she gave birth to a son, and one sent to say to his majesty, "A son has been born for you." And he was brought, and he was given a *mn't*-nurse and *hmnw*-nurses, and there was rejoicing for him in the whole land. And the king sat and made a feast, and he began to be caressed, and his majesty loved him very, very much from the hour. And the king appointed him Royal Son of Kush. Now many days after this, his majesty made him as *iry-p't*[2] of the whole land.

Now many days after this, when he completed many years as *iry-p't* in the whole land, then his majesty flew to heaven.[3] And then the king[4] said, "Have brought to me my great officers of his majesty so that I can make known all the past affairs with me." And then his wife was brought and he judged her before them

---

[1] Cf. Esther 5:1–8; 7:2–10; Mark 6:17–29.

[2] Crown prince.
[3] I.e., died.
[4] I.e., the new king, Bata.

and a "yes" was made from them,[1] and his older brother was brought to him and he made him *iry-p't* in the whole land. And he was thirty years as king of Egypt, and he went out to life, and his older brother stood in his place the day of his death.

Colophon: It has come well to a conclusion by the spirit of the scribe of the treasury, Ka-geb of the treasury of the pharaoh and the scribe Heri-Merimipet. Made by the scribe In-na, the lord of the papyrus roll. Whoever speaks against this papyrus roll, to him will Thoth[2] be a hostile adversary.

---

[1] I.e., she was found guilty and apparently executed, as the Seven Hathors had earlier predicted.

[2] The scribe god and patron of scribes.

Black Obelisk of Shalmaneser III
A diorite monument dating toward the end of the reign of the Assyrian King Shalmaneser III (ruled 858–824 BCE), and celebrating his victories and the tributes he received. The second panel from the top shows Jehu, king of Israel, bowing in submission before Shalmaneser (see Text 29); it is the earliest contemporaneous depiction of an Israelite king. The monument is nearly 6.5 feet (2 m) high.

HISTORIOGRAPHIC TEXTS

MANY OF THE texts in this chapter concern individuals or events mentioned in the Bible. They are presented in rough chronological order rather than by language or place of origin.

20. THE SUMERIAN KING LIST

Written in Sumerian, this chronicle of the early history of kingship in Mesopotamia probably originally dates to the late third millennium BCE; it survives in more than a dozen copies from later centuries. History is divided into two eras, before and after the Flood. In the first, kings had reigns of tens of thousands of years; after the Flood, the reigns were considerably shorter, although still impossibly long, until Gilgamesh (see Text 13), after whom normal spans of rule began to occur. A similar pattern is found in genealogies in Genesis 5 and 11.[1]

When kingship had come down from heaven, kingship was at Eridu. Alulim was king; he reigned 28,800 years; Alalgar reigned 36,000 years; two kings reigned 64,800 years. Eridu was abandoned; its kingship was taken to Bad-tibira.

At Bad-tibira, Enmen-lu-ana reigned 43,200 years; Enmen-gal-ana reigned 28,800 years; the divine Dumuzi,[2] the shepherd, reigned 36,000 years; three kings reigned 108,000 years. I abandon Bad-tibira; its kingship was taken to Larak.

At Larak, En-sipazi-ana reigned 28,800 years; one king reigned 28,800 years. I abandon Larak; its kingship was taken to Sippar.

At Sippar, Enmen-dur-ana was king; he reigned 21,000 years; one king reigned 21,000 years. I abandon Sippar; its kingship was taken to Shuruppak.

At Shuruppak, Ubar-Tutu was king; he reigned 18,600 years; one king reigned 18,600 years.

Five cities; eight kings ruled 385,200 years.[3] The Flood swept over. After the Flood had swept over, when kingship had come down from heaven, kingship was at Kish.

At Kish, Gishur was king; he reigned 1,200 years; Kullassina-bel reigned 900 years; Nan-gish-lishma reigned 1,200 years; En-dara-ana reigned 420 years, 3 months, and $\frac{1}{2}$ days; Babum reigned 300 years; Puannum reigned 840 years; Kalibum reigned 900 years; Kalumum reigned 840 years; Zuqapip reigned 900 years; Atab reigned 600 years; Mashda, son of Atab, reigned 840 years; Arwium, son of Mashda, reigned 720 years; Etana the shepherd, the one who went up to heaven,[4] who

---

[1]Translation by Jean-Jacques Glassner, *Mesopotamian Chronicles* (Writings from the Ancient World; Atlanta, GA: Society of Biblical Literature, 2004), 119–123.

[2]See Text 4.

[3]The total is wrong, probably because of scribal error.

[4]A reference to a now fragmentary legend in which Etana goes to heaven on the back of an eagle.

put all countries in order, was king; he reigned 1,500 years; Balih, son of Etana, reigned 400 years; Enme-nuna reigned 660 years; Melam-Kish, son of Enmenuna, reigned 900 years; Barsal-nuna, son of Enme-nuna, reigned 1,200 years; Samug, son of Barsal-nuna, reigned 140 years; Tizkar, son of Samug, reigned 305 years; Ilkuu reigned 900 years; Ilta-sadum reigned 1,200 years; Enmen-baragesi, the one who destroyed Elam's weapons,[1] was king; he reigned 900 years; Aka, son of Enmen-baragesi, reigned 625 years. Twenty-three kings reigned 23,310 years, 3 months, and $\frac{1}{2}$ days. Kish was defeated; its kingship was taken to Eanna.

In Eanna, Mes-kiag-gasher, son of Utu,[2] was lord and was king; he reigned 324 years; Mes-kiag-gasher entered into the sea and disappeared;[3] Enmekar, son of Mes-kiag-gasher, the king of Uruk, the one who founded Uruk, was king; he reigned 420 years; the divine Lugalbanda, the shepherd, reigned 1,200 years;[4] the divine Dumuzi, the fisherman,[5] whose city was Kuara, reigned 100 years; the divine Gilgamesh[6]—his father was an invisible being— the lord of Kulaba, reigned 126 years; Ur-Nungal, son of the divine Gilgamesh, reigned 30 years; Udul-kalama, son of Ur-Nungal, reigned 15 years; La-basher reigned 9 years; Ennun-dara-ana reigned 7 years; Meshe, the metalworker, reigned 36 years; Melam-ana reigned 6 years; Lugal-ki-gin reigned 36 years; twelve kings reigned 2,310 years. Uruk was defeated; its kingship was taken to Ur.

[*Lists of rulers of several other cities follow, apparently reflecting shifting political power among the Mesopotamian city-states. Toward the end, we find the following:*]

At Akkad, Sargon—his father was a gardener[7]—the cupbearer of Ur-Zababa, the king of Akkad, the one who founded Akkad, was king; he reigned 56 years.

---

[1]Elam was a region east of Mesopotamia.

[2]Probably the sun god.

[3]A reference to an otherwise unknown legend.

[4]The father of Gilgamesh, like some other kings, deified after his death.

[5]Perhaps a different person or deity than Dumuzi the shepherd, named previously.

[6]See Text 13.

[7]See Text 21.

21. THE BIRTH LEGEND OF SARGON

This Akkadian text purports to be an autobiographical account of the humble origins of Sargon of Akkad (ruled ca. 2340–2284 BCE), but it may have been written by Sargon II of Assyria (721–705 BCE) to glorify his namesake. It is similar to the birth story of Moses (Exodus 2:1–10).[8]

I am Sargon, the great king, king of Akkad.
My mother was a high priestess; I did not
    know my father.
My father's brother dwells in the uplands.
My city is Azupiranu, which lies on the
    Euphrates bank.
My mother, the high priestess, conceived me;
    she bore me in secret.
She placed me in a reed basket; she sealed my
    hatch with pitch.
She left me to the river, whence I could not
    come up.
The river carried me off; it brought me to
    Aqqi, drawer of water.
Aqqi, drawer of water, brought me up as he
    dipped his bucket.
Aqqi, drawer of water, raised me as his
    adopted son.
Aqqi, drawer of water, set me to his orchard
    work.
During my orchard work, Ishtar[9] loved me.
Fifty-four years I ruled as king.
I became lord over and ruled the people of
    this land.
I cut through hard mountains with picks of
    copper;
I ascended high mountains, one after another;
I crossed over low mountains, one after
    another.
The land of the sea I sieged three times;
    Dilmun[10] knelt before me.
I went against the greatest walls in the
    universe....
Whatsoever king shall arise after me,
let him rule as king fifty-four years;

---

[8]Translation by Benjamin R. Foster, *Before the Muses: An Anthology of Akkadian Literature* (Bethesda, MD: CDL Press, 3d ed., 2005), 912–913.

[9]The goddess of love and war.

[10]A far-off place, probably somewhere in the Persian Gulf.

let him become lord over and rule the people
of this land.
Let him cut through hard mountains with
picks of copper;
let him ascend high mountains, one after
another;
let him cross over low mountains, one after
another.
Let him siege the land of the sea three times;
let Dilmun kneel before him.
Let him go against the greatest walls in the
universe. . . .

[*The rest of the text is broken.*]

22. THE CURSE OF AKKAD

This poetic narrative probably served as a model for
the Sumerian city laments (see Texts 107 and 108).
Written in Sumerian some time after the events it
describes, it tells how Enlil and the other gods allowed
the city of Akkad in central Mesopotamia to be destroyed and how dominance passed to the southern
city of Ur about 2100 BCE in the Third Dynasty of Ur.
Naram-Sin, the king of Akkad, planned to demolish and then rebuild the temple of Enlil at Nippur,
but ignoring a dream omen not to do so, he proceeded with his plan, and as a punishment Akkad was
defeated by Gutian invaders from the northeast. The
text thus serves to legitimate the rise of the southern
cities after the divinely inflicted fall of Akkad.[1]

When Enlil's frowning brow had killed Kish,[2]
as were it the bull of heaven,
had felled the house of Uruk[3] land down in
the dust, as one would a great ox,
and Enlil then and there had given Sargon,
king of Akkad,[4] lordship and kingship,
from south to north—
in those days holy Inanna[5] was building
Akkad's temple close to be her august
home,

set up the throne in Ulmash;[6]
like a young married man building a house for
the first time,
like a young daughter setting up a home,
holy Inanna went without sleep
to provision the storehouse with things,
furnish that city with dwellings and building
plots,
feed its people superb food,
give its people superb water to drink,
have the courtyard joyful with celebrants
with rinsed heads,
have the people sit down in festival grounds,
have acquaintances eat together and outsiders
circle around like strange birds in the sky,
have Marhashi put back in the rolls,[7]
have monkeys, huge elephants, water
buffaloes, beasts of faraway places, jostle
each other in the wide streets,
and dogs, panthers, mountain goats, and
alum-sheep full of long wool.

In those days she filled Akkad's stores for
emmer wheat with gold,
filled its stores for white emmer wheat with
silver,
had copper, tin, and slabs of lapis lazuli
regularly delivered into its barns for grain,
while she plastered its grain piles over with
mud plaster outside.
She gave its old women the gift of counsel,
gave its old men the gift of just testimony,
to its maidens she gave playgrounds,
to its young men she gave arms worthy of
weapons,
to its little ones she gave a merry heart.
Handholding nursing mothers, daughters of
generals,
were dancing to the *algasur*-lyre;
the heart of the city was one of *tigi*-harps;
its outskirts of reed pipes and tambourines;
its quay, where the boats moored, was
resounding with jocund shouts.
All lands lay in safe pastures, its people
looked out over pleasant tracts,

---

[1]Translation by Thorkild Jacobsen, *The Harps That Once. . .:
Sumerian Poetry in Translation* (New Haven, CT: Yale University
Press, 1987), 360–374.
[2]A Sumerian city in central Mesopotamia.
[3]A Sumerian city in southern Mesopotamia.
[4]See Texts 20 (end) and 21.
[5]The Sumerian goddess of love and war (Akkadian Ishtar).

[6]The name of Inanna's temple.
[7]Probably meaning that even the distant land of Marhashi would
resume paying tribute.

its king, the shepherd Naram-Sin, radiated
    light flamelike on Akkad's holy throne dais.
Its city wall—like a great mountain range—
    abutted heaven;
in its city-gates—like unto the Tigris going to
    the sea—Inanna opened up the gateways.
From Sumer's own stores barges were towed
    upstream.
The Amorites[1] of the highland, men who
    knew not grain,
were coming in to her with perfect bulls,
    perfect kids;
the Meluhhans,[2] men of the black mountains,
were bringing down strange goods to her from
    them;
the Elamites and Subareans[3] were toting
    things to her as were they packasses.
All the city-rulers, the heads of temples, and
    the surveyors of the desert fringe,
were bringing in punctually their monthly
    and new year food offerings.
O how it caused vexation in Akkad's city
    gate!
Holy Inanna just didn't know how to receive
    all those food portions,
but like the citizens, she did not tire of the
    pleasure of finding storehouses and storage
    plots to keep up with them.

Upon this fell—as an ominous silence—the
    matter of Ekur.[4]
Akkad became to her fraught with
    shuddering,
fear befell her in Ulmash,
she took her seat out of the city.
Like a maiden who decides to abandon home
holy Inanna abandoned Akkad's temple close,
like a warrior going up against armed might,
she brought the forces for fight and battle
    out of the city, confronted with them
    murderous foes.

Not five days it was, not ten days it was,
before Ninurta had the ornament of lordship,
    the crown of kingship, the podium, and
    the throne granted to kingship
fetched into his temple Eshumesha.[5]
Utu[6] took advancement away from the city;
Enki[7] took away its wits.
Its halo, that abutted heaven, An[8] drew up
    into heaven's inside.
Its holy mooring stakes, that were firmly
    driven in, Enki pulled down into the
    Apsu.
Its weapons Inanna had carried off.
Akkad's temple close ended its life as were it
    but a little carp in the deep.
The city's enemies appeared in front of it;
like a huge elephant it put its neck down,
like a huge bull it lifted the horns,
like a raging basilisk it slithered the head from
    side to side,
and, heavyweight that it was, it went pillaging
    instead of in combat.

That Akkad's royalty was not to occupy a
    good steady seat,
that nothing whatever that was in store for it
    was propitious,
that the house would be shaken, its treasures
    dispersed,
which Naram-Sin had seen in a dream-vision,
he let only his heart know, put it not on his
    tongue, spoke of it with no man.
Because of Ekur he dressed in mourning,
covered his chariot over with a cargo mat,
took down the cabin from his barge,
cut down on his royal requirements.
For all of seven years Naram-Sin persevered,
—who ever saw a king holding his head in his
    hands for all of seven years?
When in his seeking an omen about the
    temple,
building the temple was not in the omen;

---

[1]Literally "Westerners," the Amorites were a rural, perhaps semi-nomadic Semitic group that at times threatened the cities of Mesopotamia and at times succeeded in controlling some of it.
[2]Meluhha may be the Indus Valley, with which the Sumerians had contact.
[3]Elam was east of Mesopotamia; the Subareans were from north-western Mesopotamia.
[4]Enlil's temple in the city of Nippur.

---

[5]Ninurta was the chief god of the southern city of Lagash, which prospered after the collapse of Akkad.
[6]The sun god.
[7]The god of the subterranean fresh waters (the Apsu) and wisdom (Akkadian Ea).
[8]The king of the gods, called Anu in Akkadian.

and a second time seeking an omen about the
    temple,
building the temple was not in the omen:
he, to change what had been entrusted to him,
denied, O Enlil, what had been told him,
scattered what had been put together for him.
He called up his troops
and like a bruiser entering the main
    courtyard, he balled the hands at Ekur;
like one having strong knees bending down
    to wrestle, he counted the *gigunu*[1] worth
    but thirty shekels;
like a marauder raiding a town, he set up big
    storm ladders against the house.
To dismantle Ekur as were it a great ship,
to remove the earth from it like one mining a
    silver mountain,
to cleave it as were it a lapis lazuli range,
to make it collapse like a city Ishkur[2] has
    flooded,
he had great copper axes cast for the temple.
Though verily it was not the cedar
    mountains,
both edges he sharpened on the *agasiliqqu* axes.
To its socle he put copper mattocks
—and the ground settled in the country's
    foundations;
to its top he put copper axes
—and with that the temple let the neck sink
    to the ground,
like a young man who is killed,
and with it the necks of all lands were let sink
    to the ground.
Its rain gutters he peeled off
—and the rains vanished in the sky.
Its doorsills he took down
—and the decorum of the country changed.
In its "gate in which the grain is not to be
    cut" he cut the grain
—and with that, grain was cut off from the
    country's lands.
Into its "gate of peace" he had pickaxes strike
—and for all lands their peace became
    hostility.
In the "grand arch," like a heavy spring flood,

he made Ekur's wooden posts into splinters
    like firewood.
Into its holy of holies, the house not knowing
    daylight, looked the nation,
and upon the gods' holy bath vessels looked
    the men of Uri.[3]
Its *lahamu* figures[4] standing along the great
    supporting terrace and the house,
although they were not men who had
    committed sacrilege,
Naram-Sin threw into the fire;
and for the cedars, cypresses, *supalus*, and
    boxwoods,
its trees of the *gigunu* he cast lots.
Its gold he did up in crates;
its silver he did up in leather packs;
with its copper he filled the harbor quay, like
    grain brought en masse.
Its silver the silversmith was reshaping;
its precious stones the jeweler was reshaping;
its copper the metal-caster was pounding into
    scrap.
Though it was not the goods of a sacked city,
he had big boats moor at the quay by the
    house;
he had big boats moor at the quay toward
    Enlil's temple, and the goods leave the city.
As he made the goods leave the city, Akkad's
    sense left it.
He was letting the boats pitch in taking off,
    and Akkad's judgment wavered.
The roaring storm, hushing the people one
    and all,
the risen floodstorm, having none that could
    oppose,
Enlil, in considering what he would lay waste
because his beloved Ekur had been laid waste,
decided to lift his eyes unto the mountains of
    Gubin,[5]
decided to bring down from it as one the
    widespread foothill tribes.
No likes of the nation, not counted with the
    country,
the Gutians, knowing no restraints,

---

[1] The temple on top of the ziggurat.
[2] The Sumerian storm god.

[3] I.e., Akkad.
[4] Statues of guardian deities.
[5] Probably the mountainous home of the Gutians.

of human face, dogs' cunning, monkeys' build,
Enlil decided to bring out of the mountains.
Numerous like locusts they came striding;
stretched out their arms in the desert for him
    like gazelle and wild-ass snares;
nothing escaped their arms; nobody did their
    arms leave.
No envoy traveled the road. No ambassador's
    boat was passing by on the river.
Enlil's yellow goats had been driven as spoil
    from the fold, their herdsmen made to
    follow them.
The cows had been driven as spoil from their
    pen, their cow herders made to follow them.
The watch were put in neck-stocks; footpads
    sat in ambush on the roads;
in the country's city gates the door leaves
    were stuck in the mud;
in all lands on the walls of their cities they
    were crying sore cries;
inside the city, not in the wide desert outside,
    they had the gardens.
It being like the days when cities were first built,
the great fields carried no grain,
the flooded tracts carried no fish,
the gardens' irrigation beds carried no syrup
    and wine,
for long days rain rained not, no underbrush
    grew up.
In those days oil for one silver shekel was half
    a quart,
barley for one shekel was half a quart,
wool for one shekel was half a mina,
fish for one shekel filled a ten-quart measure.
Thus they bought at the market rate of their
    cities.[1]
He who lay down ill on the roof died on the
    roof.
He who lay down ill in the house was not
    buried.
The people from their hunger were coming to
    blows among themselves.
At Kiur, Enlil's great place,
dogs banded together in the silent streets;
in these dogs would devour men walking by
    twos,

dogs would devour men walking by threes;
numerous teeth were strewn about, numerous
    heads tossed around;
teeth were strewn, heads sown as seed corn;
decent heads were exchanged for crooked
    heads;
men lay on top of men, crooks bled from
    above on blood of decent men.
In those days Enlil built out of scraps from his
    great sanctuaries a small reed sanctuary;
between sunrise and sunset its stores
    dwindled.
Old women who were left over from
    that day,
old men who were left over from that day,
and the chief elegist who was left over from
    that year,
set up, for seven days and seven nights,
seven harps toward him on the ground, like
    the firm base of heaven,
and played within them also tambourine,
    sistron, and kettledrum for him,
thunderously like Ishkur.
The old women held not back cries of: "Woe,
    my city!"
The old men held not back cries of: "Woe, its
    men!"
The elegist held not back cries of: "Woe,
    Ekur!"
Its maidens held not back from pulling out
    their hair,
its lads held not back the pointed knives
    lacerating themselves.[2]
Weeping, Enlil's ancestors were placing their
    supplications
on Enlil's holy knees, in Duku,[3] laden with
    holy dread;
and so Enlil entered the holy "holy of holies"
    and lay down, eschewing food.

At that time Sin, Enki, Inanna, Ninurta,
    Ishkur, Utu, Nusku, Nidaba, and the great
    gods,
were trying to calm Enlil's heart, were making
    pleas saying:

---

[1] I.e., prices were exorbitant; cf. 2 Kings 6:25.

[2] Cf. Leviticus 19:28; Deuteronomy 14:1.
[3] A shrine within the temple.

"Enlil, may the city that sacked your city be
   done to as your city was,
that defiled your *gigunu* be done to as Nippur
   was.
May the one who knew the city turn the head
   unto the clay-pit left of it,
and may the men who knew men there not
   find them in it;
may a brother not recognize his brother;
may its maiden be wickedly killed in her
   home;
may its father cry out bitterly in his house
   where the wife was killed;
may its doves mourn in their crannies;
may things be thrown at its sparrows in their
   hiding places;
may it be wary like a frightened dove!"
A second time Sin, Enki, Inanna, Ninurta,
   Ishkur, Utu, Nusku, and heavenly Nidaba,
verily spoke, set their face toward the city,
   and were bitterly cursing Akkad saying:
"O city, you rushed at Ekur"
—O Enlil, may it come to be!—
"Akkad, you rushed at Ekur"
—O Enlil, may it come to be!—
"May at your holy city wall, as high as it is,
   laments be set up;
may your *gigunus* be heaped up like dust;
may the standing *lahamus* of the upper terrace
pitch from it to earth like huge lands drunk
   with wine!
May your clay return to its Apsu, be clay
   cursed by Enki!
May your grain return to its furrow, be grain
   cursed by the grain goddess!
May your wood return to its forests, be wood
   cursed by the carpenter god!
May the bull-butcher butcher the spouse!
May your sheep-slaughterer slaughter the son!
May the waters wash away your pauper as he
   finds children to sell for money!
May your harlot hang herself in the gate of
   her hostel!
May your hierodule who is a mother, and your
   courtesan who is a mother, stab the child!
May your gold have the purchasing power of
   silver;
may your silver be priced as...;

may your copper be priced as lead!
Akkad, may your strong one be cut off from
   his strength;
may he not manage to lift the provision sack
   onto his saddle;
may his arms not enjoy controlling your
   choice chariot donkeys;
may he lie ill until evening.
May the city die in famine;
may your patrician, who eats finest bread, lie
   down hungry;
may your man who used to get up from first
   fruits eat cutting from his beams;[1]
may he grind with his teeth the leather
   fittings of "the great door of the leather
   fittings" of his father's house;
into your palace built in joy of heart may
   anguish be cast;
may the "bad men" of the deserts of silent
   tracts howl, howl, and howl from it.
Over your consecrated grounds where ritual
   hand-washings are established,
may the fox of the ruined mounds sweep its
   tail;[2]
in your "gate of the country" that was
   established,
may the sleeper-bird, the bird foreboder of
   anguish, place its nest.
In your city that, celebrating with *tigi*-harps,
   does not sleep,
that for merriness of heart lies not down,
may Nanna's bull Turesi[3] bellow as were it
   roaming a desert of silent tracts.
May long grass grow on your canal banks
   where boats were hauled,
and may grass, lamentably, grow on your road
   laid down for chariots.
Moreover, may no man pass along your canal
   banks where boats are hauled,
places where in future water is to be drawn by
   splay-horned mouflons and fleet snakes of
   the mountains only.
May your central plain growing fine grass
   grow reeds for lament.

---

[1]Probably thatch.
[2]Cf. Lamentations 5:18.
[3]Nanna was the moon god; his bull is otherwise unknown.

Akkad, may your waters pouring sweet pour
    as saline waters.
May one who has said: 'Let me settle in that
    city!' not have pleasant residence there,
who has said: 'Let me lie down in Akkad!' not
    have pleasant resting place there."

Presently under the sun of that day thus verily
    it came to be,
long grass grew up on its canal banks where
    the boats were hauled;
grass, lamentably, grew up on its road laid
    down for chariots;
moreover, no man passed along on its canal
    banks where boats were hauled,
places where water was now drawn by splay-
    horned mouflons and fleet snakes of the
    mountains only.
Its central plain growing fine grass grew reeds
    of lament;
Akkad's water flowing sweet flowed as saline
    waters.
For him who had said "Let me settle in that
    city!" residence was not pleasant;
for him who had said: "Let me lie down in
    Akkad!" the resting place was not pleasant;
Akkad was destroyed.
A praise hymn for Inanna.[1]

23. THE APOLOGY OF HATTUSILI III

**Found in multiple copies, this long Hittite text is a
rationalization of Hattusili's taking the throne from
his nephew Mursili III in the early thirteenth century
BCE. It has been compared to the account in 1–2
Samuel of David assuming the throne after Saul;
it also has some similarities to the rivalry among
David's sons to succeed him in 1 Kings 1–2.[2]**

Thus speaks King Hattusili, the Great King, king
of the land of Hatti, son of Mursili, the Great King,
king of the land of Hatti, grandson of Suppiluliuma,
the Great King, king of the land of Hatti, descendant of Hattusili, king of the city of Kussar.

I tell of Ishtar's divine power: let mankind
hear it. And in the future among the gods of
My Majesty, of his son, of his grandson, of the
descendants of my majesty, let there be reverence
to Ishtar.[3]

My father Mursili[4] begot us four children, Halpasulupi, Muwatalli, Hattusili, and
Massanauzzi, a daughter. Now of them all I was
the last child.[5] And while I was still a child and
was groom, My Lady Ishtar by means of a dream
sent to my father Mursili my brother Muwatalli
with this message: "For Hattusili the years are
short; he is not to live. Now give him to me and
let him be my priest. Then he shall be alive." And
my father took me, still a child, and gave me to
the goddess for service.[6] And, serving as priest
to the goddess, I poured libations. And so at the
hand of My Lady Ishtar I saw prosperity. And My
Lady Ishtar took me by the hand; and she
guided me.

But when my father Mursili became a god,[7]
and my brother Muwatalli sat upon the throne of
his father, I became a general in the presence of
my brother, and then my brother appointed me
to the office of chief of the Meshedi,[8] and gave
me the Upper Country to rule. Then I governed
the Upper Country. Before me, however, Arma-
Tarhunda, son of Zida, had been ruling it. Now
because My Lady Ishtar had favored me and my
brother Muwatalli was well disposed toward me,
when people saw My Lady Ishtar's favor toward me
and my brother's kindness, they envied me. And
Arma-Tarhunda, son of Zida, and other men too
began to stir up ill will against me. They brought
malice against me, and I had bad luck; and my
brother Muwatalli named me for the wheel.[9] My
Lady Ishtar, however, appeared to me in a dream,
and by means of the dream said this to me: "Shall
I abandon you to a hostile deity? Fear not." And
I was cleared from the hostile deity. And since
the goddess, My Lady, held me by the hand, she

---

[1] A concluding note by the scribe.
[2] Translation by Edgar H. Sturtevant and George Bechtel, *A Hittite Chrestomathy* (Philadelphia, PA: Linguistic Society of America, University of Pennsylvania, 1935), 65–83.

---

[3] The originally Mesopotamian goddess of love and war.
[4] Mursili II.
[5] Cf. 1 Samuel 16:6–13.
[6] Cf. 1 Samuel 1:28.
[7] I.e., died.
[8] The royal bodyguard.
[9] Perhaps a judicial procedure.

did not ever abandon me to the hostile deity, the hostile court; and the weapon of my enemy never overthrew me. My Lady Ishtar always rescued me. If ever ill health befell me, even while ill I observed the goddess's divine power. The goddess, My Lady, always held me by the hand. Because I, for my part, was an obedient man, and because I walked before the gods in obedience, I never pursued the evil course of mankind. You, goddess, My Lady, always rescue me. Has it not been so? In fact, the goddess, My Lady, did not ever in time of danger pass me by; to an enemy she did not ever abandon me, and no more to my opponents in court, my enviers, did she abandon me. If it was a plot of an enemy, if it was a plot of an opponent at law, if it was a plot of the palace, My Lady Ishtar always held over me protection. She always rescued me. Envious enemies My Lady Ishtar put into my hand; and I destroyed them utterly.

When, however, my brother Muwatalli came to understand the matter, and there remained no ill repute against me, he took me back; and he put the infantry and charioteers of the land of Hatti into my hand, and I commanded all the infantry and charioteers of the land of Hatti. And my brother Muwatalli used to send me on expeditions. And as My Lady Ishtar had granted me her favor, wherever among the countries of the enemy I turned my eyes, not an enemy turned back his eyes upon me. And I kept conquering the countries of the enemy. The favor of My Lady Ishtar, as ever, was mine. And whatever enemy there was within the lands of Hatti, I drove him clear out of the lands of Hatti. However, what countries of the enemy I conquered while I was still a minor, that I shall make into a tablet separately; and I shall set it up before the goddess.

[The next sections describe how Muwatalli moved the capital south, leaving Hattusili in charge of the north, where he was repeatedly victorious. The text then moves to an account of the battle with Egypt at Qadesh in 1275 BCE:]

When once my brother came and marched against the land of Egypt, these countries which I had caused to be inhabited again—the army and the charioteers of this country I led for my brother's campaign against the land of Egypt. Now because, in the presence of my brother, infantry and charioteers of the land of Hatti were in my hands, I commanded them. Now when Arma-Tarhunda, son of Zida, saw the kindness to me of My Lady Ishtar and of my brother, he nevertheless did not in any respect show them any reverence; and thereupon with his wife and his sons tried to bewitch me. And he filled Samuhas, the city of the goddess, with witchcraft. When, however, I was on my way back from the land of Egypt, I journeyed to Lawazantiya to pour libations to the goddess; and I worshipped the goddess. And at the command of the goddess I took in marriage Pudu-Heba, the daughter of Pentipsarri, the priest. And we founded a family, and the goddess gave us the love of husband and wife. And we got us sons and daughters. Furthermore, the goddess, My Lady, said to me: "Do you with your house be subject to me." And with my house I was true to the goddess.

[The text goes on to relate how Arma-Tarhunda was found guilty of witchcraft, but Hattusili had mercy on him and sent him into exile on Cyprus. It continues with an account of how Hattusili came to the throne:]

And my brother died.[1] I, however, firm in my respect for my brother, did not act selfishly; but, as at this time my brother did not yet have a legitimate son, I took Urhi-Teshub, the son of a secondary wife, and set him in authority in the land of Hatti.[2] And I put all the army in his hands. And in the lands of Hatti he was Great King. I, however, was king in Hakpis. And with army and charioteers I took the field. And, since Nerik had been in ruins since the days of Hantili,[3] I took it and rebuilt it. And the countries which were near Nerik and had made Nera and Hassura their boundary, all these I subjected and made tributaries.

Now when Urhi-Teshub thus observed the kindness of the goddess to me, he envied me, and

---

[1] Literally, "became a god."
[2] As Hittite law required. Probably disrespectfully, Hattusili refers to his nephew by his birth name instead of his throne name, Mursili (III).
[3] Probably Hantili II, who ruled in the fifteenth century BCE.

he brought ill will upon me. He took away from me all my subjects; Samuha also he took away from me; the depopulated lands also that I had settled again, all those too he took away from me, and he made me weak. Hakpis, however, according to the command of a god he did not take away from me. Because I was a priest of the storm god of Nerik, for that reason he did not take it away from me. And, firm in my respect for my brother, I did not act selfishly. And for seven years I submitted. But he at the command of a god and the suggestion of man tried to destroy me. And he took Hakpis and Nerik away from me. And I did not submit any longer. And I made war upon him. But when I made war upon him, I did not do it as a crime. Did I rebel against him in the chariot or rebel against him within the palace? I sent him a declaration of war as an open enemy: "You started hostilities with me. Now you are Great King; but as for me, the one fortress that you have left me—of that one I am king. Come! Ishtar of Samuha and the storm god of Nerik shall decide the case for us."

Now whereas I wrote Urhi-Teshub thus, if anyone speaks as follows: "Why did you formerly establish him on the throne? And why are you now declaring war upon him?" I answer: "Very well, if he had never started hostilities with me." Would the gods have subjected a Great King who was upright to a small king? Now because he started hostilities with me, they subjected him to me in the trial. Now when I communicated these words to him saying "Come on" to him, he marched out from Marassantiya, and came to the Upper Country. And Sippaziti, the son of Arma-Tarhunda, was with him. And he appointed him to gather the troops of the Upper Country. But because Sippaziti was hostile to me, he did not succeed against me.

Now, while My Lady Ishtar had even before this been promising me the kingship, at that time My Lady Ishtar appeared to my wife in a dream: "I shall march before your husband. And all Hattusa shall be led with your husband. Since I thought highly of him, I did not—no, not ever—abandon him to the hostile trial, the hostile deity. Now also I will exalt him, and make him priest of the sun goddess of Arinna. Do you

also make me, Ishtar, your patron deity." And My Lady Ishtar stood behind me; and whatever she promised occurred. And My Lady Ishtar then also showed me her divine power abundantly. To whatever nobles Urhi-Teshub had ever banished, My Lady Ishtar appeared in a dream: "...I, Ishtar, have turned all the lands of Hatti to the side of Hattusili." And then also I saw the divine power of Ishtar abundantly. Whereas she did not ever at another time abandon Urhi-Teshub, she shut him up in Samuha like a pig in a sty. As for me, however, the Kaska men who had been hostile supported me; and all Hattusa supported me. But firm in my respect for my brother, I did not act selfishly. And I marched back to Samuhas to be with Urhi-Teshub and I brought him down like a captive. And I gave him fortified towns in the land of Nuhashshi,[1] and he dwelt there. He would have planned another plan, and would have proceeded into the land of Karaduniya;[2] but when I heard of the matter, I arrested him and banished him across the sea. And they sent Sippaziti across the border, but I took his house from him and gave it to My Lady Ishtar. Now I gave that to My Lady Ishtar, and My Lady Ishtar thereafter granted me desire after desire.

Now I was a prince, and became chief of the Meshedi. Again I, chief of the Meshedi, became king of Hakpis. Again I, king of Hakpis, later became Great King. Thereupon My Lady Ishtar put into my hands my enviers, enemies, and opponents at law. And some of them died by the weapon, but others died on the appointed day; and I completely got rid of them all. And My Lady Ishtar gave me the kingship of the land of Hatti also, and I became Great King. My Lady Ishtar took me as a prince and placed me on the throne. And those who had been well disposed toward the kings, my predecessors, became well disposed toward me. And they began to send me messengers, and they began to send me gifts as well. But such gifts as they kept sending me, they had not sent to any of my fathers and forefathers. On the other hand, whatever king owed me homage paid me homage. But the lands that were hostile to

---

[1]Northwestern Syria.
[2]Babylonia.

me I conquered; I annexed district after district to the lands of Hatti. And those who had been hostile in the time of my fathers and my forefathers made peace with me. And since the goddess, My Lady, had thus favored me, being firm in my loyalty to my brother, I did not act selfishly. And I took my brother's son Kurunta, and set him upon a throne in the very spot, namely Tarhuntassa, which my brother Muwatalli used for his palace. Insignificant as I was when you, My Lady Ishtar, took me, you set me in the high place in the land of Hatti, upon the throne. For my part, I gave My Lady Ishtar the house of Arma-Tarhunda. I consecrated it and gave it to her. What was there previously, I gave her; and what I had, that also I gave. I consecrated it and gave it to the goddess. Furthermore, as to the house of Arma-Tarhunda that I gave her, and the cities that belonged to Arma-Tarhunda, behind every one they are again setting up her statue, and distributing libation cups. Ishtar is my goddess, and for themselves, men pour libations to Ishtar, the Highest. Whatever mausoleum I have built, that I have given to the goddess. And my son Tudhaliya I gave for your service; may my son Tudhaliya rule the house of Ishtar. I am the servant of the goddess; let him also be the servant of the goddess....

Now, whoever, in the future takes a descendant of Hattusili and Pudu-Heba away from the service of Ishtar or covets the...granary of Ishtar of Samuha, let him be an opponent at law of Ishtar of Samuha. Let no one assess feudal services or taxes upon them.

In the future whatever son, grandson, or future descendant of Hattusili and Pudu-Heba ascends the throne, let him be reverent toward Ishtar of Samuha among the gods.

24. THE MERNEPTAH STELA

In a long victory poem on a large stela, the Egyptian Pharaoh Merneptah (ruled 1213–1203 BCE) celebrates a victory over the Libyans. It concludes as follows, with the earliest mention of Israel in a nonbiblical source.[1]

The princes are prostrate saying: "Shalom!"[2]
Not one of the Nine Bows[3] lifts his head:
Tehenu[4] is pacified, Hatti[5] at peace,
Canaan is captive with all woe.
Ashkelon is conquered, Gezer seized,
Yanoam[6] made nonexistent;
Israel is wasted, bare of seed,
Hurru[7] is become a widow for Egypt.
All who roamed have been subdued
by the King of Upper and Lower Egypt,
    Banere-meramun,
son of Re, Merneptah, Content with Maat,
given life like Re every day.

25. THE BATTLE OF QARQAR

This excerpt from the annals of the Assyrian king Shalmaneser III (858–824 BCE) describes a battle in 853 between the Assyrians and a coalition of Levantine states, at Qarqar on the Orontes River in northwestern Syria. The battle is not reported in the Bible.[8]

I set out from Aleppo and approached the cities of Irhuleni of Hamath. I captured the cities Adennu, Parga, and Argana, his royal cities; I took his booty, his property, the possessions in his palaces, and set fire to his palaces. I set out from Argana and approached Qarqar. Qarqar, his royal city, I demolished, tore down, and burned. He took as his allies these twelve kings:

1,200 chariots, 1,200 horsemen, 20,000 soldiers of
    Hadad-ezer of Damascus;
700 chariots, 700 horsemen, 10,000 soldiers of
    Irhuleni of Hamath;
2,000 chariots, 10,000 soldiers of Ahab of Israel;[9]
500 soldiers of Byblos;
1,000 soldiers of Egypt;

---

[1]Translation by Miriam Lichtheim, *Ancient Egyptian Literature* (Berkeley, CA: University of California Press, 1976; 2006), 2.77.

[2]Meaning "peace."
[3]The traditional enemies of Egypt.
[4]Libya.
[5]The country of the Hittites.
[6]Like Ashkelon and Gezer, a city in Canaan.
[7]The country of the Hurrians, here meaning Syria.
[8]Translation by Mordechai Cogan, *The Raging Torrent: Historical Inscriptions from Assyria and Babylonia Relating to Ancient Israel* (Jerusalem: Carta, 2008), 14–15.
[9]Ruled 873–852 BCE.

10 chariots, 10,000 soldiers of Irqatu;
200 soldiers of Matinu-Baal of Arvad;
200 soldiers of Usanatu;
30 chariots, [],000 soldiers of Adunu-Baal of
Siannu;
1,000 camels of Gindibu, the Arab;
[ ]00 soldiers of Baasha, son of Rehob, from Mount
Amanus.

They attacked me, waging battle and war.

I fought with them with the exalted strength that Ashur,[1] my lord, had granted me, and with the mighty weapons that Nergal,[2] who goes before me, had granted me. I defeated them from Qarqar up to Gilzau. I felled with the sword 14,000 of his fighting men, and like the god Adad,[3] I rained down on them a flood. I scattered their corpses and filled the plain with them.... I blocked the River Orontes with their bodies like a bridge. In the midst of this battle I took from them their chariots, their horsemen, and their horse-teams.

26. KILAMUWA

Several well-preserved inscriptions have been found at the important Neo-Hittite city of Samal, modern Zincirli in southern Turkey, which was the capital of the kingdom of Yaudi. The texts are written in various languages, including Phoenician, Aramaic, and Luwian (a language related to Hittite), and, as is this text, in a version of the local dialect related to Aramaic. (See also Texts 35, 133, 140, and 144.) In this text, which dates to the mid-ninth century BCE, King Kilamuwa memorializes his accomplishments.

I am Kilamuwa, son of Hayya. Gabbar ruled over Yaudi and he did nothing. There was Bamah and he did nothing. And there was my father Hayya and he did nothing. And there was my brother Shail and he did nothing. But I am Kilamuwa, son of Tam[ ]:[4] whatever I did, those

before me did not do. My father's house was in the midst of powerful kings, and each stretched out his hand to fight. And I was in the hands of kings as when fire eats a beard or as when fire eats a hand. And the king of the Danunians[5] held power over me, and I hired against him the king of Assyria.[6] A young woman was given for a sheep, and a man for a robe.[7]

I, Kilamuwa, son of Hayya, sat on the throne of my father. Before the kings who were before me, the Mushkabim[8] writhed like dogs. But as for me, to some I was a father and to some I was a mother and to some I was a brother. And whoever had not seen the face of a sheep, I made him owner of a flock, and whoever had not seen the face of an ox, I made him owner of a herd, and owner of silver and owner of gold. And whoever had not seen a tunic since his youth, in my days fine linen covered him. And I took the Mushkabim by the hand, and they felt about me as an orphan feels for his mother.

As for any one of my sons who sits in my place and damages this inscription, may the Mushkabim not honor the Baririm,[9] and may the Baririm not honor the Mushkabim. And whoever destroys this inscription, may Baal-samad, who belongs to Gabbar, destroy his head, and may Baal-hammon, who belongs to Bamah, destroy his head, along with Rakib-El,[10] lord of the dynasty.

27. THE MESHA STELA (ALSO CALLED THE MOABITE STONE)

Discovered in 1868, this monument dates to the mid-ninth century BCE. The Moabite king Mesha is mentioned in the Bible (2 Kings 3). It is written in Moabite, a language closely related to Hebrew; the

---

[1]The principal god of Assyria.
[2]A god of war, plague, and the underworld.
[3]The storm god.
[4]Probably his mother's name (the text is broken), since his father's name was Hayya. Perhaps he and his brother had different mothers.

[5]A nearby people; see Text 35.
[6]Shalmaneser III (858–824 BCE). For a similar situation, see 2 Kings 16:5–9.
[7]The meaning of this phrase is unclear. After it the text is divided by a double line.
[8]The vocalization and meaning of this term are uncertain.
[9]Another group whose vocalization and identity are uncertain. The phrase implies that social upheaval will be the punishment for Kilamuwa's successor's action.
[10]Probably a title of Baal, meaning "the divine rider"; cf. the epithet "rider on the clouds," page 19, and Psalm 68:4, 33.

role of the national deity and the practice of the "ban" in this text are similar to those found in the Bible.

I am Mesha, son of Chemosh-yat, king of Moab, the Dibonite.[1] My father ruled over Moab for thirty years, and I ruled after my father. And I made this high place for Chemosh[2] in Qarhoh...because he rescued me from all the kings and made me gloat over all my enemies.

When Omri was king of Israel,[3] he oppressed Moab for many days because Chemosh was angry with his land. When his son succeeded him, he also said, "I will oppress Moab in my days." That is what he said, but I gloated over him and his house, and Israel has perished forever.

Now Omri had taken possession of the land of Medeba,[4] and he lived there in his days and half the days of his son, forty years. But Chemosh restored it in my days, and I built Baal-meon,[5] and I made the reservoir in it, and I built Kiriathaim.[6]

Now the men of Gad[7] had lived in the land of Ataroth[8] from of old, and the king of Israel had built Ataroth for them. But I attacked the city and I took it and I killed all the people of the city as satisfaction for Chemosh and for Moab. And I brought back from there the altar of its beloved (god) and I dragged it before Chemosh in Kerioth.[9] And I settled in it the men of Sharon and the men of Maharith.

And Chemosh said to me, "Go, take Nebo[10] from Israel!" So I went by night and attacked it from daybreak until noon, and I took it. And I killed everyone in it, seven thousand men, male resident aliens, women, female resident aliens

(?), and slave-girls. For I had put it to the ban[11] for Ashtar-Chemosh. And I took from there the vessels of Yahweh, and I dragged them before Chemosh.

Now the king of Israel had built Jahaz[12] and he lived in it when he was attacking me. But Chemosh drove him out before me: I took two hundred men from Moab, all its elite (troops), and I brought them up to Jahaz, and I took it, in order to add it to Dibon. I built Qarhoh, the wall of the woods and the wall of the Ophel;[13] and I built its gates; and I built its towers; and I built the house of the king; and I made the retaining walls of the reservoir for the spring in the middle of the city. Now there was no cistern in the middle of city, in Qarhoh, and I said to all the people, "Let every man make a cistern for himself in his own house." And I cut the channels for Qarhoh using captives from Israel.

I built Aroer[14] and I made the highway in the Arnon (Valley).[15] I built Beth-bamoth,[16] for it had been destroyed. I built Bezer,[17] for it was in ruins.

[In the rest of the text, which is fragmentary, Mesha describes more victories and building projects.]

28. THE TEL DAN STELA

Found at Tel Dan in northern Israel in three fragments in 1993 and 1994, this incomplete Aramaic text dates to the mid-ninth century BCE. It commemorates a victory by an Aramean king, perhaps Hazael (ruled ca. 844–800 BCE; see 1 Kings 19:15; 2 Kings 8:7–15, 28–29). It contains the earliest nonbiblical mention of David, the second king of Israel, and the dynasty that he founded.

... my father lay down; he went to [his fathers]. And the king of [Is]rael formerly went up to my

---

[1]Dibon was the capital of the kingdom of Moab; it is mentioned several times in the Bible. The Mesha Stela was found not far from it.
[2]The national god of Moab (see Numbers 21:29; 1 Kings 11:33; Jeremiah 48:46); later in the text he is called by the fuller name Ashtar-Chemosh.
[3]882–871 BCE. His son Ahab succeeded him (873–852 BCE).
[4]A city in northern Moab (Joshua 13:9).
[5]A city in northern Moab (Numbers 32:38).
[6]A city in northern Moab (Numbers 32:37).
[7]The Israelite tribe that at times had territory in Transjordan.
[8]A city in northern Moab (Numbers 32:34).
[9]A city in northern Moab (Jeremiah 48:24).
[10]A city in northern Moab (Jeremiah 48:22).

[11]The dedication of spoils of war, including human beings, to a deity, as in the Bible (e.g., Deuteronomy 20:16–17; Joshua 6:17–21).
[12]A city in northern Moab (Jeremiah 38:44).
[13]The citadel; cf. 2 Kings 5:24; Micah 4:8.
[14]A city in central Moab (Deuteronomy 2:36).
[15]A major valley in central Moab (Numbers 21:13; Deuteronomy 2:36).
[16]Perhaps biblical Bamoth (Numbers 21:19–20).
[17]A city in northern Moab (Deuteronomy 4:43).

father's land. And as for me, Hadad[1] made me king. And Hadad went before me and I went out from the seven…of my kingdom; and I killed seventy kings, who harnessed thou[sands of cha]riots and thousands of horsemen. [And I killed Jo]ram,[2] the son of A[hab], king of Israel, and [I] killed [Ahaz]iah,[3] the son of [Joram, kin]g of the house of David. And I set [ ] their land into desolation… [r]uled over Israel.…

29. OBELISK OF SHALMANESER III, KING OF ASSYRIA (858–824 BCE).

This is the text under the picture of King Jehu of Israel paying tribute in 841 BCE (see page 64).[4]

I received the tribute of Jehu,[5] son of Omri,[6] silver, gold, a gold bowl, a gold vase, gold goblets, gold buckets, tin, a royal scepter, and javelins.

30. STELA OF ADAD-NIRARI III, KING OF ASSYRIA (811–783 BCE).

This Assyrian text dates to ca. 796 BCE.[7]

He received 2,000 talents of silver, 1,000 talents of bronze, 2,000 talents of iron, 3,000 multicolored linen garments as tribute from Mari[8] of Damascus. He received the tribute of Joash[9] of Samaria, of the people of Tyre and Sidon.

31. ANNALS OF TIGLATH-PILESER III, KING OF ASSYRIA (745–727 BCE)

a. This text dates to ca. 738 BCE.[10]

I received the tribute of Kushtashpi of Kummuh, Rezin of Damascus,[11] Menahem of Samaria,[12] Hiram of Tyre, Sibitti-Biil of Byblos, Urikki of Que, Pisiris of Carchemish, Eni-il of Hamath, Panammu of Samal,[13] Tarhulara of Gurgum, Sulumal of Melid, Dadi-ilu of Kaska, Uassurme of Tabal, Ushhitti of Tuna, Urballa of Tuhana, Tuhamme of Ishtunda, Urimmi of Hubishna, Zabibe, queen of the Arabs: gold, silver, tin, iron, elephant hides, ivory, multicolored garments, linen garments, blue-purple and red-purple wool, ebony, boxwood, all kinds of precious things from the royal treasure, live sheep whose wool is dyed red-purple, birds of the heavens whose wings are dyed blue-purple, horses, mules, cattle and sheep, she-camels together with their young.

b. Summary inscription, dated to 734 BCE.[14]

[The tribute] of…Matanbiil of Arvad, Sanipu of Beth-Ammon, Salamanu of Moab…Mitiniti of Ashkelon, Jehoahaz[15] of Judah, Qaus-malaka of Edom,…Hanunu of Gaza: gold, silver, tin, iron, lead, multicolored garments, linen garments, red-purple garments of their lands, all kinds of costly items, the produce of sea and land, the commodities of their lands, royal treasures, mules broken to the yoke…I received.

c. Summary inscription, dated to 729 BCE.[16]

The land of Bit-Humria[17]…all of its people…[to] Assyria I carried off. Pekah, their king…and

---

[1]The storm god Baal-hadad, the chief god of Aram.

[2]Joram (Jehoram), son of Ahab, ruled the northern kingdom of Israel 851–842 BCE.

[3]Ahaziah ruled the southern kingdom of Judah 843–842 BCE; his father J(eh)oram was not the same person as Joram the son of Ahab just mentioned.

[4]Translation by Mordechai Cogan, *The Raging Torrent: Historical Inscriptions from Assyria and Babylonia Relating to Ancient Israel* (Jerusalem: Carta, 2008), 23.

[5]King of the northern kingdom of Israel, 842–814 BCE.

[6]King of the northern kingdom of Israel, 882–871 BCE. Jehu was not his son, but the title "son of Omri" was used by the Assyrians as a generic term for the kings of the northern kingdom.

[7]Translation by Mordechai Cogan, *The Raging Torrent: Historical Inscriptions from Assyria and Babylonia Relating to Ancient Israel* (Jerusalem: Carta, 2008), 39–40.

[8]Probably Ben-Hadad, son of Hazael.

[9]King of the northern kingdom of Israel, 800–784 BCE.

[10]Translation by Mordechai Cogan, *The Raging Torrent: Historical Inscriptions from Assyria and Babylonia Relating to Ancient Israel* (Jerusalem: Carta, 2008), 51.

[11]2 Kings 16:5–9; Isaiah 7:1, 8.

[12]King of the northern kingdom of Israel, 747–737 BCE.

[13]See Text 144.

[14]Translation by Mordechai Cogan, *The Raging Torrent: Historical Inscriptions from Assyria and Babylonia Relating to Ancient Israel* (Jerusalem: Carta, 2008), 58.

[15]I.e., Ahaz, who ruled 735–715 BCE.

[16]Translation by Mordechai Cogan, *The Raging Torrent: Historical Inscriptions from Assyria and Babylonia Relating to Ancient Israel* (Jerusalem: Carta, 2008), 65–66.

[17]The house of Omri, i.e., the northern kingdom of Israel.

Hoshea as king I appointed over them.[1] 10 talents of gold, [ ] talents of silver, with their property I received from them and to Assyria I carried them off.

32. SUMMARY INSCRIPTION OF SARGON II, KING OF ASSYRIA (722–705 BCE)

This Assyrian text, which describes the fall of Samaria, the capital of the northern kingdom of Israel, in 722 BCE (see 2 Kings 17:1–6), dates to 707 BCE.[2]

From accession year to the fifteenth year of my reign, I defeated Humbanigash, king of Elam.[3] I besieged and captured Samaria. I took as spoil 27,290 people who live there; I organized a contingent of 50 of their chariots and I instructed the rest of them in correct conduct. I appointed my eunuch[4] over them and imposed on them the tribute of the former king.

Hanunu, king of Gaza, and Re'e, the commander-in-chief of Egypt, marched against me to wage war and battle at Raphia.[5] I defeated them. Re'e was frightened by the sound of my weapons and he fled, and his place is undisclosed. I captured with my own hand Hanunu of Gaza. I received the tribute of Pharaoh, the king of Egypt, Samsi, queen of the Arabs, Itamara, the Sabean: gold, dust of the mountains, horses, and camels.

Yaubidi of Hamath, a low-class person, with no right to the throne, an evil Hittite, schemed to become king of Hamath. He caused Arpad, Simirra, Damascus, and Samaria to rebel against me, and he came to an agreement with them and prepared for battle. I mobilized the numerous troops of Assyria; at Qarqar,[6] his beloved city, I besieged him and his troops, and I captured him. I set fire to Qarqar. I flayed him. I killed the rebels of those cities and established order. I organized a

contingent of 200 chariots and 600 riding horses from among the people of Hamath, and added them to my royal corps.

Azuri, king of Ashdod, plotted not to deliver tribute and sent seditious words concerning Assyria to the kings in his neighborhood. Because of the crimes he committed against the people of his land, I abolished his rule. I appointed Ahimiti, his favorite brother, as king. But the people of Hatti,[7] speakers of lies, disliked his kingship and they elevated Yamani, who had no right to the throne, and like them, did not respect my authority. In my fury, I did not gather my numerous troops and did not mobilize my soldiers; with only my warriors, who even in friendly areas do not leave my side, I marched to Ashdod. And he, Yamani, heard from afar the approach of my campaign, and he fled to the border of Egypt in the district of Meluhha,[8] and his place is undisclosed. I besieged Ashdod, Gath, and Ashdod-yam, and captured them.[9] I counted as spoil his gods, his wives, his sons and his daughters, property and possessions, the treasures of his palace, together with the people of his land. I reorganized these cities. People from the lands that I had conquered with my own hand, that were in the eastern [district], I settled in them, and I appointed my eunuch as governor over them. I counted them with the people of Assyria and they bear my yoke.

The king of Meluhha…heard from afar of the might of the gods Ashur, Nabu, and Marduk; the awesome splendor of my kingship overwhelmed him and he was seized by panic. He put him (Yamani) in manacles and iron fetters and they brought him before me to Assyria after a long journey.

33. CHRONICLES OF MERODACH-BALADAN, KING OF BABYLON (721–710; 703 BCE)

This excerpt from the Neo-Babylonian Chronicles mentions Merodach-baladan (Marduk-apla-iddina),

---

[1]2 Kings 15:30; the year is 732 BCE. Hoshea ruled until 722 BCE.
[2]Translation by Mordechai Cogan, *The Raging Torrent: Historical Inscriptions from Assyria and Babylonia Relating to Ancient Israel* (Jerusalem: Carta, 2008), 82–83.
[3]A region east of Mesopotamia.
[4]A high-ranking Assyrian official.
[5]Raphia was near the northeastern border of Egypt. The battle took place in 720 BCE.
[6]On the Orontes River in northwestern Syria; cf. Text 25.

[7]In this period, north Syria.
[8]I.e., Cush, south of Egypt.
[9]In 713–712 BCE.

who revolted briefly against Assyria in the late eighth century BCE; see 2 Kings 20:12–19 (= Isaiah 39).[1]

Year 2.[2] Merodach-baladan. Ummanigash, king of Elam,[3] in the district of Der, engaged Sargon, king of Assyria, in battle and caused the Assyrians to retreat; he inflicted a great defeat upon them. Merodach-baladan and his troops, who to the aid of the king of Elam had marched, did not reach the battle in time, and he withdrew.

Year 12. Merodach-baladan. Sargon went down to Akkad and engaged Merodach-baladan in battle. Merodach-baladan retreated before him; he escaped to Elam. Twelve years Merodach-baladan ruled Babylon. Sargon ascended the throne in Babylon.

34. CAMPAIGN OF SENNACHERIB, KING OF ASSYRIA (705–681 BCE)

This is the earliest of several accounts of Sennacherib's campaign to the west in 701 BCE; compare 2 Kings 18:13–19:37.[4]

In my third campaign, I marched to Hatti.[5] The awesome splendor of my lordship overwhelmed Luli, king of Sidon, and he fled overseas far-off. The terrifying nature of the weapon of the god Ashur my lord overwhelmed his strong cities, Greater Sidon, Little Sidon, Bit-zitti, Zarephath, Mahaliba, Ushu,[6] Achzib, Acco, walled cities provided with food and water for his garrisons, and they bowed in submission at my feet. I installed Tubalu on his royal throne over them and imposed upon him tribute and dues for my lordship payable annually without interruption.

The kings of Amurru, all of them— Minuhimmu of Samsimuruna, Tubalu of Sidon,

Abdiliti of Arvad, Urumilki of Byblos, Mitinti of Ashdod, Puduilu of Beth-Ammon, Chemosh-nadbi of Moab, Ayarammu of Edom—brought me sumptuous presents as their abundant audience-gift, fourfold, and kissed my feet.

As for Sidqa, king of Ashkelon, who had not submitted to my yoke—his family gods, he himself, his wife, his sons, his daughters, his brothers, and all the rest of his descendants, I deported and brought him to Assyria. I set Sharru-lu-dari, son of Rukibi, their former king, over the people of Ashkelon and imposed upon him payment of tribute and presents to my lordship; he now bears my yoke. In the course of my campaign, I surrounded and conquered Beth-dagon, Joppa, Bene-barak, Azor, cities belonging to Sidqa, who did not submit quickly, and I carried off their spoil.

The officials, the nobles, and the people of Ekron who had thrown Padi, their king, who was under oath and obligation to Assyria, into iron fetters and handed him over in a hostile manner to Hezekiah, the Judean, took fright because of the offense they had committed. The kings of Egypt, and the bowmen, chariot corps, and cavalry of the king of Cush, assembled a countless force and came to their aid. In the plain of Eltekeh, they drew up their ranks against me and sharpened their weapons. Trusting in the god Ashur, my lord, I fought with them and inflicted a defeat upon them. The Egyptian charioteers and princes, together with the charioteers of the Cushites, I personally took alive in the midst of the battle. I besieged and conquered Eltekeh and Timnah and carried off their spoil. I advanced to Ekron and slew its officials and nobles who had stirred up rebellion and hung their bodies on watchtowers all about the city. The citizens who committed sinful acts I counted as spoil, and I ordered the release of the rest of them, who had not sinned. I freed Padi, their king, from Jerusalem, and set him on the throne as king over them, and imposed tribute for my lordship over him.

As for Hezekiah, the Judean,[7] I besieged 46 of his fortified walled cities and surrounding smaller towns, which were without number. Using packed-down ramps and applying battering

[1]Translation by Mordechai Cogan, *The Raging Torrent: Historical Inscriptions from Assyria and Babylonia Relating to Ancient Israel* (Jerusalem: Carta, 2008), 178–179.

[2]I.e., 720 BCE.

[3]A region east of Mesopotamia.

[4]Translation by Mordechai Cogan, *The Raging Torrent: Historical Inscriptions from Assyria and Babylonia Relating to Ancient Israel* (Jerusalem: Carta, 2008), 112–115, with minor correction supplied by Prof. Cogan.

[5]In this period, north Syria.

[6]Mainland Tyre.

[7]King Hezekiah of Judah ruled 715–687 BCE.

rams, infantry attacks by mines, breeches, and siege machines, I conquered them. I took out 200,150 people, young and old, male and female, horses, mules, donkeys, camels, cattle, and sheep, without number, and counted them as spoil. He himself I locked up within Jerusalem, his royal city, like a bird in a cage. I surrounded him with armed posts, and made it unthinkable for him to exit by the city gate. His cities which I had despoiled I cut off from his land and gave them to Mitinti, king of Ashdod, Padi, king of Ekron, and Silli-Bel, king of Gaza, and thus diminished his land. I imposed dues and gifts for my lordship upon him, in addition to the former tribute, their yearly payment.

He, Hezekiah, was overwhelmed by the awesome splendor of my lordship, and he sent me after my departure to Nineveh, my royal city, his elite troops and his best soldiers, which he had brought in as reinforcements to strengthen Jerusalem, his royal city, with 30 talents of gold, 800 talents of silver, choice antimony, large blocks of carnelian, beds inlaid with ivory, armchairs inlaid with ivory, elephant hides, ivory, ebony-wood, box-wood, multicolored garments, garments of linen, wool dyed red-purple and blue-purple, vessels of copper, iron, bronze and tin, iron, chariots, siege shields, lances, armor, daggers for the belt, bows and arrows, countless trappings and implements of war, together with his daughters, his palace women, his male and female singers. He also dispatched his messenger to deliver the tribute and to do obeisance.[1]

35. KARATEPE

Not far west of Samal (see introduction to Text 26) was another small kingdom, that of the Danunians. In their capital, the modern site of Karatepe in southern Turkey, large inscribed stones contained this late-eighth-century-BCE bilingual inscription, one copy in Luwian (a language closely related to Hittite) and three copies in Phoenician. This is the longest Phoenician inscription known, although there is a great deal of repetition, and that version is excerpted here. Little is known of the history of this kingdom, so the background of this text is unclear, especially the relationship of Azitawada to Awarku.

I am Azatiwada, blessed of Baal, servant of Baal, whom Awarku, king of the Danunians, made mighty. Baal made me a father and a mother to the Danunians. I revived the Danunians. I extended the land of the valley of Adana from the rising of the sun to its setting. And in my days the Danunians had everything pleasant and abundance and delicacies. And I filled the granaries of Pahar. And I acquired horse upon horse and shield upon shield and army upon army, because of Baal and the gods. And I smashed the rebels, and I drove out every evildoer who was in the land. And I established the house of my lord in pleasantness; and I acted kindly toward the offspring of my lord, and I seated him on his father's throne. And I made peace with every king, and every king also treated me as a father because of my righteousness, and because of my wisdom, and because of the beneficence of my heart. And I built strong fortresses in all border regions, in the places where there had been evil men, leaders of gangs, no one of whom had been a servant to the house of Mopsos.[2] And I, Azatiwada, placed them under my feet.[3] And I built fortresses in those places so that the Danunians might dwell in them with their hearts at rest. And I humbled strong lands at the setting of the sun, which all the kings before had not humbled; but I, Azatiwada, humbled them. I subdued them. I made them dwell in my border regions at the rising of the sun, and I made the Danunians dwell there.

So in my days they were in all the borders of the valley of Adana, from the rising of the sun to its setting, even in the places which were formerly fearsome, where a man feared to walk on a road—but in my days a woman could go alone with her spindles, because of Baal and the gods. And in all my days there was abundance and pleasant things and a pleasant life and peace of heart for the Danunians and for all the valley of Adana.

---

[1]For Sennacherib's attack on Judah and Jerusalem, and Hezekiah's surrender, see especially 2 Kings 18:13–16.

[2]Probably the legendary founder of the royal house of Azitawada.
[3]Cf. Joshua 10:24; 1 Kings 5:3; Psalms 8:6; 110:2.

And I built this city, and I named it
Azatiwadiya; for Baal and Resheph of the goats[1]
had sent me to build it. And I built it, because
of Baal and because of Resheph of the goats,
with abundance and a pleasant life and peace
of heart, so that it might be a guard post for the
valley of Adana and for the house of Mopsos.
For in my days there was for the land of the valley of Adana abundance and pleasant
things, and there was never any night for
the Danunians in my days. And I built this
city; I named it Azatiwadiya; I made Baal
KRNTRYSH[2] dwell in it.

Now let them bring a sacrifice to all the cast
images: a yearly sacrifice, 1 ox; and at plowing
time, 1 sheep; and at harvest time, 1 sheep. And
may Baal KRNTRYSH bless Azatiwada with life
and peace and great strength over every king.
May Baal KRNTRYSH and all the gods of the
city give to Azatiwada length of days and many
years and a pleasant rule and great strength over
every king. And may this city be owner of abundant grain and new wine; and may this people
who dwell in it be owners of oxen and owners of
sheep and owners of abundant grain and
new wine. And may they bear many children,
and as they increase may they be powerful and
as they increase may they serve Azatiwada
and the house of Mopsos, because of Baal and
the gods.

And if a king among kings or a prince among
princes or any man who is a man of renown
erases the name of Azatiwada from this gate
and places his own name, or especially if he
covets this city and pulls down this gate which
Azatiwada made, and makes a different gate for
it and puts his name on it, whether he pulls it
down in covetousness or he pulls down this gate
in hatred and in evil, then may Baal-shamem[3]
and El, creator of the earth,[4] and the eternal
Sun, and all the generations of the sons of the
gods erase that kingdom and that king and that

man who is a man of renown. But may the name
of Azatiwada be forever, like the name of the sun
and the moon![5]

[*The rest of the text repeats earlier ideas.*]

36. SUMMARY INSCRIPTION OF ESAR-HADDON, KING OF AS-SYRIA (681–669 BCE)

Esar-haddon requires building materials from vari-ous kings for his palace.[6]

I mobilized the kings of Hatti[7] and "Beyond
the River":[8] Baal, king of Tyre; Manasseh, king of
Judah;[9] Qaus-gabri, king of Edom; Musuri, king
of Moab; Silli-Bel, king of Gaza; Mitinti, king
of Ashkelon; Ikausu,[10] king of Ekron; Milki-ashapa,
king of Byblos; Mattan-baal, king of Arvad;
Abibaal, king of Samsimuruna; Puduilu, king of
Beth-Ammon; Ahimilki, king of Ashdod—twelve
kings of the seacoast;. . .—ten kings of Cyprus, in
the midst of the sea—a total of twenty-two kings
of Hatti, the seacoast, and the midst of the sea.
I gave orders for all of them to drag to Nineveh,
my lordly city, with exertion and difficulty, large
timbers, long beams, and thin boards of cedar and
cypress, the product of Mount Sirara and Mount
Lebanon, that from older days grew exceedingly
thick and long; also bull colossi of granite, *lamassu*
and *apsasatu* figures,[11] thresholds and building
stone of alabaster and granite, colored marble,
alallu and *girinhiliba* stone,[12] the products of the
mountains.

---

[1]An unknown title whose translation is uncertain. Resheph was a god of plague and death.
[2]Probably a Luwian place-name; location and vocalization unknown.
[3]Literally, "lord of the heavens."
[4]Cf. Genesis 14:19, 22; and see Text 6.

[5]Cf. Psalms 72:5; 89:36–37.
[6]Translation by Mordechai Cogan, *The Raging Torrent: Historical Inscriptions from Assyria and Babylonia Relating to Ancient Israel* (Jerusalem: Carta, 2008), 133.
[7]In this period, north Syria.
[8]The Assyrian province comprising the Levant west of the Euphrates River.
[9]Ruled 687–642 BCE.
[10]See Text 151.
[11]Statues of composite human and animal figures.
[12]Types of limestone.

37. CHRONICLE OF NEBUCHADREZZAR II,[1] KING OF BABYLON (605–562 BCE)

This fragmentary text mentions Nebuchadrezzar's attack on Ashkelon in 604 and on Jerusalem in 597 BCE; see also Text 82 and 2 Kings 24:1–17.[2]

Year 1. Nebuchadrezzar, in the month Sivan,[3] mobilized his troops and marched to Hatti.[4] Until the month Kislev[5] he marched about Hatti victoriously. All the kings of Hatti came before him and he received their rich tribute. He marched to Ashkelon and in the month Kislev, he captured it. He seized its king, took its prisoners, and carried off its spoil. He turned the city into a ruin heap. In the month Shebat,[6] he marched to Babylon.

Year 7. The month Kislev. The king of Akkad mobilized his troops and marched to Hatti. He encamped against the city of Judah and in the month Adar,[7] day 2, he captured the city; he seized the king.[8] He appointed a king of his choice;[9] he took its rich spoil and brought it into Babylon.

38. ADMINISTRATIVE TEXT OF NEBUCHADREZZAR II

Several fragmentary Babylonian records mention delivery of rations to Jehoiachin, the king of Judah who had been taken captive to Babylon in 597 BCE (2 Kings 24:12; see Text 37), and his sons, as well as to captives from other regions in the Neo-Babylonian empire. One is dated to the thirteenth year of Nebuchadrezzar (593 BCE).

$\frac{1}{2}$ PI[10] for Jehoiachin king of Judah

$2\frac{1}{2}$ sila[11] for the 5 sons of the king of Judah by the hand of Qanama.

39. CHRONICLES OF NABONIDUS, KING OF BABYLON (556–539 BCE)

This fragmentary text records events in the reign of Nabonidus, the last king of Babylon, including his absence in the north Arabian city of Tema and Babylon's capture by the Persian king Cyrus. (See also Texts 40, 104, and 105.)[12]

YEAR 7

The king was in Tema; the crown prince, his nobles, his troops in Akkad. The king, in the month Nisan, did not go to Babylon, (the god) Nabu did not go to Babylon. (The god) Bel did not come out. The Akitu festival[13] was cancelled. The offerings in Esagila and Ezida to the gods of Babylon and Borsippa as in normal times were presented. The high priest made a libation and inspected the temple.[14]

YEAR 17

…In the month of Tishri, when Cyrus made an attack on Opis, which is on the bank of the Tigris, against the troops of Akkad, the men of Akkad retreated; he took spoil and killed the men. Day 14, Sippar was taken without a battle. Nabonidus fled. Day 16, Ugbaru, governor of Gutium, and the troops of Cyrus without a battle entered Babylon. Afterward, after Nabonidus retreated, he was captured in Babylon. Until the end of the month, the shield-bearers of Gutium surrounded the gates of Esagila. There was no interruption of anything in Esagila or other temples and no date was missed. The month Marheshwan, day 3, Cyrus entered Babylon. The wine containers were filled before him. There was peace in the city; Cyrus

---

[1]In the Bible this king's name is also spelled, less correctly, Nebuchadnezzar.

[2]Translation by Mordechai Cogan, *The Raging Torrent: Historical Inscriptions from Assyria and Babylonia Relating to Ancient Israel* (Jerusalem: Carta, 2008), 203, 204.

[3]May/June.

[4]In this period, north Syria.

[5]November/December.

[6]January/February.

[7]February/March.

[8]I.e., Jehoiachin; see 2 Kings 24:10–16.

[9]I.e., Zedekiah; see 2 Kings 24:17.

---

[10]Ca. 4.25 gallons (15 liters), presumably of olive oil.

[11]Ca. 1 gallon (3.8 liters), presumably of olive oil.

[12]Translation by Mordechai Cogan, *The Raging Torrent: Historical Inscriptions from Assyria and Babylonia Relating to Ancient Israel* (Jerusalem: Carta, 2008), 211–212, 213–214.

[13]The New Year festival celebrating the god Marduk, at which *Enuma Elish* (Text 1) was recited.

[14]The same is reported for subsequent years.

proclaimed peace to Babylon in its totality. He
appointed Gubaru as governor of governors in
Babylon. From the month Kislev until the month
Adar, the gods of Akkad, which Nabonidus had
brought down to Babylon, returned to their cult
centers....

40. THE CYRUS CYLINDER

**This foundation inscription commemorates rebuild-
ing in Babylon, which the Persian king Cyrus II (the
Great) captured in 539 BCE. It is the most important
source for Cyrus's reign (559–530 BCE) and in general is consistent with the depiction of Cyrus in the
books of Ezra and Isaiah 40–55.[1]**

... [Marduk][2] surveyed and looked throughout all the lands, searching for a righteous king,
his heart's desire, whom he would support. He
called out his name: Cyrus, king of Anshan;[3]
he pronounced his name to be king over all the
world.[4] He made the land of Gutium[5] and all the
Umman-manda[6] bow in submission at his feet.
And he shepherded with justice and righteousness
all the black-headed people,[7] over whom he had
given him victory. Marduk, the great lord, who
nurses his people, looked with gladness upon his
good deeds and upright heart. He ordered him to
march to his city Babylon. He set him on the road
to Babylon, and like a companion and friend, he
went at his side. His vast army, whose number, like
the water of the river, cannot be known, marched
at his side fully armed. He made him enter his
city Babylon without fighting or battle; he saved
Babylon from hardship. He delivered Nabonidus,[8]
the king who did not revere him, into his hands.
All the people of Babylon, all the lands of Sumer
and Akkad, princes and governors, bowed to him

and kissed his feet. They rejoiced at his kingship
and their faces shone. Lord, by whose aid the dead
were revived and all who had been redeemed of
hardship and difficulty, they greeted him with
gladness and praised his name.

I am Cyrus, king of the world, great king,
mighty king, king of Babylon, king of Sumer and
Akkad, king of the four quarters, son of Cambyses,
great king, king of Anshan, grandson of Cyrus,
great king, king of Anshan, descendant of
Teispes, great king, king of Anshan, of an eternal line of kingship, whose rule Bel and Nabu[9]
love, whose kingship they desire for their heart's
pleasure.

When I entered Babylon in peaceful manner, I took up my lordly abode in the royal palace
amidst rejoicing and happiness. Marduk, the great
lord, allotted me a magnanimous heart as lover
of Babylon, and I daily attended to his worship.
My vast army moved about Babylon in peace; I
did not permit anyone to frighten the people of
Sumer and Akkad. I sought the welfare of the city
of Babylon and all its sacred centers. As for the
citizens of Babylon,...upon whom (Nabonidus)
imposed corvée, which was not the god's will
and not befitting them, I relieved their weariness
and freed them from their service. Marduk, the
great lord, rejoiced over my good deeds. He sent
gracious blessings upon me, Cyrus, the king who
worships him, and upon Cambyses, the son, my
offspring, and upon all my army, and in peace,
before him, we moved about.

By his exalted word, all the kings who sit upon
thrones throughout the world, from the Upper
Sea to the Lower Sea,[10] who live in districts far
off, the kings of the West, who dwell in tents, all
of them, brought their heavy tribute before me
and in Babylon they kissed my feet. From Babylon
to Ashur and Susa, Akkad, Eshnunna, Zamban,
Meturnu, Der, as far as the region of Gutium,
the sacred centers on the other side of the Tigris
whose sanctuaries had been abandoned for a long
time, I returned the gods to the places where they
once resided and I had them dwell in eternal

---

[1]Translation by Mordechai Cogan, *The Raging Torrent: Historical
Inscriptions from Assyria and Babylonia Relating to Ancient Israel*
(Jerusalem: Carta, 2008), 226–228.
[2]The chief god of Babylon; see Text 1.
[3]Persia.
[4]Cf. Isaiah 44:28–45:4.
[5]Media, east of Mesopotamia.
[6]The Medes.
[7]The native population of Mesopotamia.
[8]The last native Babylonian king, ruled 556–539 BCE; see Texts 39,
104, and 105.

---

[9]Bel is a title of Marduk, and Nabu, the god of wisdom, was
Marduk's son.
[10]I.e., from the Mediterranean Sea to the Persian Gulf.

abodes. I gathered all their inhabitants and returned them to their dwellings; and the gods of Sumer and Akkad, whom Nabonidus, to the anger of the lord of the gods, had brought into Babylon, at the command of Marduk, the great lord, in security I settled in their habitations, in pleasing abodes. May all the gods whom I settled in their sacred centers daily ask of Bel and Nabu that my days be long and may they intercede for my welfare. May they say to Marduk, my lord: "As for Cyrus, the king who reveres you, and Cambyses his son...." The people of Babylon praise my reign. I settled all the lands in peaceful abodes....[1]

---

[1] Cf. 2 Chronicles 36:22–23; Ezra 1:1–4.

Code of Hammurapi
At the top, Hammurapi, king of Babylon, receives the insignia of kingship from Shamash, the sun god and god of justice. Under the scene is the Code itself, written in Babylonian cuneiform. The stela is made of diorite and is over 7 feet (2.2 m) high. (See Text 41.)

4

LEGAL AND COMMERCIAL TEXTS

COLLECTIONS AND CODES

MANY COLLECTIONS OF Laws from the ancient Near East have survived. The most complete come from ancient Sumer in the late third millennium BCE and from Babylon, Assyria, and the land of the Hittites in Asia Minor in the second millennium BCE, and there are fragmentary collections from other periods and locations. Below are excerpts from Babylonian and Hittite collections.

MESOPOTAMIA
41. CODE OF HAMMURAPI

The most famous ancient Near Eastern collection of laws is known as the Code of Hammurapi,[1] king of Babylon ca. 1792–1750 BCE. The most complete version was found in Susa, in Persia, in the early twentieth century CE (see page 86), and is representative of other collections. The laws themselves are case laws, set in a poetic framework that describes how Hammurapi was given kingship by the gods in order to ensure justice throughout his territory.[2]

PROLOGUE

When the august god Anu, king of the Anunnaki, and the god Enlil, lord of heaven and earth, who determines the destinies of the land, allotted supreme power over all peoples to Marduk, the firstborn son of the god Ea, exalted him among the Igigi deities,[3] named the city of Babylon with its august name and made it supreme within the regions of the world, and established for him within it eternal kingship whose foundations are as fixed as heaven and earth, at that time the gods Anu and Enlil, for the enhancement of the well-being of the people, named me by name: Hammurapi, the pious prince, who venerates the gods, to make justice to prevail in the land, to abolish the wicked and the evil, to prevent the strong from oppressing the weak, to rise like the sun god Shamash over all humankind, to illuminate the land.

I am Hammurapi the shepherd, selected by the god Enlil....

[There follows a lengthy description of Hammurapi's relationship to the gods, cataloguing his piety and reiterating their choice of him.]

When the god Marduk commanded me to provide just ways for the people of the land (in

---

[1] A more correct spelling than the traditional "Hammurabi."
[2] Translation by Martha T. Roth, *Law Collections from Mesopotamia and Asia Minor* (Writings from the Ancient World 6; Atlanta, GA: Scholars Press, 2d ed., 1997), 76–134.

[3] A summary of the myth found in *Enuma Elish* (Text 1).

order to attain) appropriate behavior, I established
truth and justice as the declaration of the land,
I enhanced the well-being of the people. At that
time (I decreed):

LAWS

(1) If a man accuses another man of homicide
but cannot bring proof against him, his accuser
shall be killed.

(2) If a man charges another man with
practicing witchcraft but cannot bring proof
against him, he who is charged with witchcraft shall go to the divine River Ordeal, he
shall indeed submit to the divine River Ordeal;
if the divine River Ordeal should overwhelm
him, his accuser shall take full legal possession
of his estate; if the divine River Ordeal should
clear that man and should he survive, he who
made the charge of witchcraft against him shall
be killed; he who submitted to the divine River
Ordeal shall take full legal possession of his
accuser's estate.

(3) If a man comes forward to give false testimony in a case but cannot bring evidence for his
accusation, if that case involves a capital offense,
that man shall be killed.

(4) If he comes forward to give (false) testimony
for (a case whose penalty is) grain or silver, he
shall be assessed the penalty for that case....

(9) If a man who claims to have lost property
then discovers his lost property in another man's
possession, but the man in whose possession the
lost property was discovered declares, "A seller
sold it to me, I purchased it in the presence of
witnesses," and the owner of the lost property
declares, "I can bring witnesses who can identify
my lost property," (and then if) the buyer produces
the seller who sold it to him and the witnesses
in whose presence he purchased it, and also the
owner of the lost property produces the witness
who can identify his lost property—the judges
shall examine their cases, and the witnesses in
whose presence the purchase was made, and the
witnesses who can identify the lost property shall
state the facts known to them before the god, then
it is the seller who is the thief, he shall be killed;
the owner of the lost property shall take his lost
property, and the buyer shall take from the seller's

estate the amount of silver that he weighed and
delivered.[1]

(10) If the buyer could not produce the seller
who sold (the lost property) to him or the witnesses before whom he made the purchase, but
the owner of the lost property could produce
witnesses who can identify his lost property, then
it is the buyer who is the thief, he shall be killed;
the owner of the lost property shall take his lost
property.

(11) If the owner of the lost property could not
produce witnesses who can identify his lost property, he is a liar, he has indeed spread malicious
charges, he shall be killed.

(12) If the seller should die, the buyer shall take
fivefold the claim for that case from the estate of
the seller.

(13) If that man's witnesses are not available,
the judges shall grant him an extension until the
sixth month, but if he does not bring his witnesses
by the sixth month, it is that man who is a liar; he
shall be assessed the penalty for that case.

(14) If a man should kidnap the child of
another man, he shall be killed.[2] ...

(48) If a man has a debt lodged against him,
and the storm god Adad devastates his field or a
flood sweeps away the crops, or there is no grain
grown in the field due to insufficient water—in
that year he will not repay grain to his creditor; he
shall suspend performance of the contract and he
will not give interest payments for that year....

(117) If an obligation is outstanding against
a man and he sells or gives into debt service his
wife, his son, or his daughter, they shall perform service in the house of their buyer or of the
one who holds them in debt service for three
years; their release shall be secured in the fourth
year.[3] ...

(124) If a man gives silver, gold, or anything
else to another man for safekeeping and he denies
it, they shall charge and convict that man, and he
shall give twofold that which he denied.[4] ...

(129) If a man's wife should be seized lying with
another male, they shall bind them and cast them

---

[1]Cf. Exodus 22:7–15.
[2]Cf. Exodus 21:16; Deuteronomy 24:7.
[3]Cf. Exodus 21:2–11; Deuteronomy 15:12–18.
[4]Cf. Exodus 22:7–15.

into the water; if the wife's master allows his wife to live, then the king shall allow his subject (i.e., the other male) to live.[1]

(130) If a man pins down another man's virgin wife who is still residing in her father's house, and they seize him lying with her, that man shall be killed; that woman shall be released.[2]

(131) If her husband accuses his own wife (of adultery), although she has not been seized lying with another male, she shall swear (to her innocence by) an oath by the god and return to her home.

(132) If a man's wife should have a finger pointed at her in accusation regarding another male, although she has not been seized lying with another male, she shall submit to the divine River Ordeal for her husband.[3]...

(138) If a man intends to divorce his first-ranking wife who did not bear him children, he shall give her silver as much as was her bride-wealth and restore to her the dowry that she brought from her father's house, and he shall divorce her....

(145) If a man marries a *nadītu*,[4] and she does not provide him with children, and that man then decides to marry a *shugītu*,[5] that man may marry the *shugītu* and bring her into his house; that *shugītu* should not aspire to equal status with the *nadītu*.

(146) If a man marries a *nadītu*, and she gives a slave woman to her husband, and she (the slave) then bears children, after which that slave woman aspires to equal status with her mistress—because she bore her children, her mistress will not sell her; she shall place upon her the slave-hairlock, and she shall reckon her with the slave women.[6]...

(154) If a man should carnally know his daughter, they shall banish that man from the city.[7]...

(157) If a man, after his father's death, should lie with his mother, they shall burn them both....

(162) If a man marries a wife, she bears him children, and that woman goes to her fate, her father shall have no claim to her dowry; her dowry belongs only to her children....

(170) If a man's first-ranking wife bears him children and his slave woman bears him children, and the father during his lifetime then declares to the children whom the slave woman bore to him, "My children," and he reckons them with the children of the first-ranking wife—after the father goes to his fate, the children of the first-ranking wife and the children of the slave woman shall equally divide the property of the paternal estate; the preferred heir is a son of the first-ranking wife, he shall select and take a share first.[8]...

(195) If a child should strike his father, they shall cut off his hand.[9]

(196) If an *awīlu*[10] should blind the eye of another *awīlu*, they shall blind his eye.

(197) If he should break the bone of another *awīlu*, they shall break his bone.

(198) If he should blind the eye of a commoner or break the bone of a commoner, he shall weigh and deliver 60 shekels[11] of silver.

(199) If he should blind the eye of an *awīlu*'s slave or break the bone of an *awīlu*'s slave, he shall weigh and deliver one-half of his value (in silver).

(200) If an *awīlu* should knock out the tooth of another *awīlu* of his own rank, they shall knock out his tooth.

(201) If he should knock out the tooth of a commoner, he shall weigh and deliver 20 shekels of silver.[12]...

(206) If an *awīlu* should strike another *awīlu* during a brawl and inflict upon him a wound, that *awīlu* shall swear, "I did not strike intentionally," and he shall satisfy the physician.[13]

(207) If he should die from his beating, he shall also swear; if he[14] is a member of the *awīlu* class, he shall weigh and deliver 30 shekels of silver.[15]...

(209) If an *awīlu* strikes a woman of the *awīlu*-class and thereby causes her to miscarry her fetus, he shall weigh and deliver 10 shekels of silver for her fetus.

---

[1]Cf. Deuteronomy 22:22.
[2]Cf. Deuteronomy 22:23–27.
[3]Cf. Numbers 5:11–31.
[4]A priestess.
[5]A priestess of lower rank.
[6]Cf. Genesis 16:1–6; 21:9–14.
[7]Cf. Leviticus 19:6–18; 20:10–21; Deuteronomy 27:20–23.

[8]Cf. Deuteronomy 21:15–17.
[9]Cf. Exodus 21:15.
[10]A noble.
[11]A shekel weighed ca. 0.35 ounce (10 grams).
[12]Cf. Exodus 21:20–21, 23–25, 26–27; Leviticus 24:19–20; Deuteronomy 19:21.
[13]I.e., pay the physician's fee.
[14]The victim.
[15]Cf. Exodus 21:18–20; Numbers 35:9–28.

(210) If that woman should die, they shall kill his daughter.

(211) If he should cause a woman of the commoner class to miscarry her fetus by the beating, he shall weigh and deliver 5 shekels of silver.

(213) If he strikes an *awīlu's* slave woman and thereby causes her to miscarry her fetus, he shall weigh and deliver 2 shekels of silver.

(214) If that slave woman should die, he shall weigh and deliver 20 shekels of silver.[1] ...

(229) If a builder constructs a house for a man but does not make his work sound, and the house that he constructs collapses and causes the death of the householder, that builder shall be killed.

(230) If it should cause the death of a son of the householder, they shall kill a son of that builder.

(231) If it should cause the death of a slave of the householder, he shall give to the householder a slave of comparable value for the slave.

(232) If it should cause the loss of property, he shall replace anything that is lost; moreover, because he did not make sound the house which he constructed and it collapsed, he shall construct anew the house which collapsed at his own expense....

(250) If an ox gores to death a man while it is passing through the streets, that case has no basis for a claim.

(251) If a man's ox is a known gorer, and the authorities of his city quarter notify him that it is a known gorer, but he does not blunt its horns or control his ox, and that ox gores to death a member of the *awīlu*-class, he shall give 30 shekels of silver.[2]

(252) If it is a man's slave, he shall give 20 shekels of silver....

(266) If, in the enclosure, an epidemic should break out or a lion make a kill, the shepherd shall clear himself before the god, and the owner of the enclosure shall accept responsibility for him for the loss sustained in the enclosure.[3] ...

(282) If a slave should declare to his master, "You are not my master," he shall bring charge and

proof against him that he is indeed his slave, and his master shall cut off his ear.[4]

EPILOGUE

These are the just decisions which Hammurapi, the able king, has established and thereby has directed the land along the course of truth and the correct way of life....

In order that the mighty not wrong the weak, to provide just ways for the waif and the widow, I have inscribed my precious pronouncements upon my stela and set it up before the statue of me, the king of justice, in the city of Babylon, the city which the gods Anu and Enlil have elevated, within the Esagila,[5] the temple whose foundations are fixed as are heaven and earth, in order to render the judgments of the land, to give the verdicts of the land, and to provide just ways for the wronged....

Let any wronged man who has a lawsuit come before the statue of me, the king of justice, and let him have my inscribed stela read aloud to him, thus may he hear my pronouncements and let my stela reveal the lawsuit for him; may he examine his case, may he calm his (troubled) heart....

[*There follow instructions that no future king should alter the laws or deface the stela and a lengthy series of curses[6] if he does.*]

HITTITE
42. HITTITE LAWS

Collections of Hittite laws survive in several copies from the mid-seventeenth to the early twelfth centuries BCE and are relatively stable. The laws that follow have close parallels in biblical law.[7]

(IV) If a free man is found dead on another's property, the property owner shall give his property, house, and 60 shekels of silver.[8] If the dead

---

[1]Cf. Exodus 21:22–25.
[2]Cf. Exodus 21:28–36.
[3]Cf. Exodus 22:10–13; Genesis 31:39.

[4]Cf. Exodus 21:2–6.
[5]The temple of Marduk in Babylon.
[6]Similar to those in treaties; see Texts 43–51.
[7]Translation by Harry A. Hoffner, Jr., in Martha T. Roth, *Law Collections from Mesopotamia and Asia Minor* (Writings from the Ancient World 6; Atlanta, GA: Scholars Press, 2d ed., 1997), 218–237.
[8]A shekel weighed ca. 0.35 ounces (10 grams).

person is a woman, the property owner shall give no property but 120 shekels of silver. If the place where the dead person was found is not private property, but uncultivated open country, they shall measure 3 miles in all directions, and the dead person's heir shall take those same payments from whatever village is found to lie within that radius. If there is no village within that radius, the heir shall forfeit his claim.[1] . . .

(10) If anyone injures a person and temporarily incapacitates him, he shall provide medical care for him. In his place he shall provide a person to work on his estate until he recovers. When he recovers, his assailant shall pay him 6 shekels of silver and shall pay the physician's fee as well.[2] . . .

(17) If anyone causes a free woman to miscarry, if it is her tenth month, he shall pay 10 shekels of silver. If it is her fifth month, he shall pay 5 shekels of silver. He shall look to his house for it.

(18) If anyone causes a female slave to miscarry, if it is her tenth month, he shall pay 5 shekels of silver.[3] . . .

(28) If a daughter has been promised to a man, but another man runs off with her, he who runs off with her shall give to the first man whatever he paid and shall compensate him. The father and mother of the woman shall not make compensation. If her father and mother give her to another man, the father and mother shall make compensation to the first man. If the father and mother refuse to do so, they shall separate her from him.

(29) If a daughter has been betrothed to a man, and he pays a bride price for her, but afterward the father and mother contest the agreement, they shall separate her from the man, but they shall restore the bride price double.

(30) But if before a man has taken the daughter in marriage he refuses her, he shall forfeit the bride price which he has paid.

(31) If a free man and a female slave are lovers and live together, and he takes her as his wife, and they make a house and children, but afterward either they become estranged or they each find a new marriage partner, they shall divide the house

equally, and the man shall take the children, with the woman taking one child.

(32) If a male slave takes a free woman in marriage, and they make a home and children, when they divide their house, they shall divide their possessions equally, and the free woman shall take most of the children, with the male slave taking one child.

(33) If a male slave takes a female slave in marriage, and they have children, when they divide their house, they shall divide their possessions equally. The slave woman shall take most of the children, with the male slave taking one child. . . .

(70) If anyone steals an ox, a horse, a mule, or an ass, when its owner claims it, he shall take it in full. In addition, the thief shall give to him double.[4] He shall look to his house for it.

(71) If anyone finds an ox, a horse, or a mule, he shall drive it to the king's gate. If he finds it in the country, they shall present it to the elders. The finder shall harness it. When its owner finds it, he shall take it in full, but he shall not have the finder arrested as a thief. But if the finder does not present it to the elders, he shall be considered a thief.[5] . . .

(74) If anyone breaks the leg or horn of an ox, he shall take that ox for himself and give an ox in good condition to the owner of the injured ox. If the owner of the ox says: "I will take my own ox," he shall take his ox and the offender shall pay 2 shekels of silver.

(75) If anyone hitches up an ox, a horse, a mule, or an ass, and it dies, or a wolf devours it, or it gets lost, he shall give it in full. But if he says: "It died by the hand of a god," he shall take an oath to that effect.[6]

(76) If anyone impresses an ox, a horse, a mule, or an ass, and it dies at his place, he shall bring it and shall pay its rent also.[7] . . .

(79) If oxen enter another man's field, and the field's owner finds them, he may hitch them up for one day until the stars come out. Then he shall drive them back to their owner.[8] . . .

(105) If anyone sets fire to a field, and the fire catches a vineyard with fruit on its vines, if a vine,

---

[1] Cf. Deuteronomy 21:1–2.
[2] Cf. Exodus 21:18–19.
[3] Cf. Exodus 21:22.

[4] Cf. Exodus 22:4, 7, 9.
[5] Cf. Exodus 23:4; Deuteronomy 22:1–3.
[6] Cf. Exodus 22:10–13.
[7] Cf. Exodus 22:14–15.
[8] Cf. Exodus 22:5.

an apple tree, a pear tree, or a plum tree burns, he shall pay 6 shekels of silver for each tree. He shall replant the planting. And he shall look to his house for it. If it is a slave, he shall pay 3 shekels of silver for each tree.

(106) If anyone carries embers into his field, catches it while in fruit, and ignites the field, he who sets the fire shall himself take the burnt-over field. He shall give a good field to the owner of the burnt-over field, and he will reap it.[1]

(107) If a person lets his sheep into a productive vineyard, and ruins it, if it has fruit on the vines, he shall pay 10 shekels of silver for each 3,600 square meters. But if it is bare, he shall pay 3 shekels of silver.[2] . . .

(168) If anyone violates the boundary of a field and takes one furrow of the neighbor's field, the owner of the violated field shall cut off a strip of his neighbor's land .25 meters deep along their common boundary and take it for himself. He who violated the boundary shall give one sheep, 10 loaves, and one jug of . . . beer and reconsecrate the field.[3] . . .

(187) If a man has sexual relations with a cow, it is an unpermitted sexual pairing: he will be put to death.[4] They shall conduct him to the king's court. Whether the king orders him killed or spares his life, he shall not appear before the king.[5] . . .

(189) If a man has sexual relations with his own mother, it is an unpermitted sexual pairing.[6] If a man has sexual relations with his daughter, it is an unpermitted sexual pairing.[7] If a man has sexual relations with his son, it is an unpermitted sexual pairing.

(190) If a man has sexual relations with his stepmother, it is not an offense. But if his father is still living, it is an unpermitted sexual pairing.[8]

(191) If a free man sleeps with free sisters who have the same mother and with their mother—one in one country and the other in another, it is not an offense. But if it happens in the same

location, and he knows the women are related, it is an unpermitted sexual pairing.[9]

(192) If a man's wife dies, he may take her sister as his wife. It is not an offense.

(193) If a man has a wife, and the man dies, his brother shall take his widow as wife. If the brother dies, the father shall take her. When afterward his father dies, the father's brother shall take the woman whom he had.[10]

(194) If a free man sleeps with slave women who have the same mother and with their mother, it is not an offense. If brothers sleep with a free woman, it is not an offense. If father and son sleep with the same female slave or prostitute, it is not an offense.[11]

(195) If a man sleeps with his brother's wife while his brother is still alive, it is an unpermitted sexual pairing.[12] If a free man has a free woman in marriage and approaches her daughter sexually, it is an unpermitted sexual pairing.[13] If he has the daughter in marriage and approaches her mother or her sister sexually, it is an unpermitted sexual pairing.[14] . . .

(197) If a man seizes a woman in the mountains, it is the man's offense, but if he seizes her in the house, it is the woman's offense: the woman shall die.[15] If the woman's husband discovers them in the act, he may kill them without committing a crime.[16]

(198) If he brings them to the palace gate and says: "My wife shall not die," he can spare his wife's life, but he must also spare the lover and clothe his head.[17] If he says: "Both of them shall die," they shall roll the wheel.[18] The king may have them killed or he may spare them.

(199) If anyone has sexual relations with a pig or a dog, he shall die.[19] He shall bring him to the palace. The king may have them killed or he may

---

[1]Cf. Exodus 22:6.
[2]Cf. Exodus 22:5.
[3]Cf. Deuteronomy 19:14; 27:17.
[4]Cf. Exodus 22:19; Leviticus 18:23; 20:15–16; Deuteronomy 27:21.
[5]Apparently so the king would not be defiled.
[6]Cf. Leviticus 18:7–8; 20:11.
[7]Cf. Genesis 19:36.
[8]Cf. Genesis 35:22; 49:6; Leviticus 18:8; 20:11; 1 Corinthians 5:1–2.

[9]Cf. Leviticus 18:17.
[10]Cf. Genesis 38:8; Deuteronomy 25:5–10; Ruth 4:5.
[11]Cf. Amos 2:7.
[12]Cf. Leviticus 18:16; 20:21.
[13]Cf. Leviticus 18:17; 20:14.
[14]Cf. Leviticus 18:18.
[15]Cf. Deuteronomy 22:23–27.
[16]Cf. Leviticus 20:10; Deuteronomy 22:22.
[17]Meaning unclear.
[18]Meaning unclear.
[19]Cf. Exodus 22:19; Leviticus 18:23; 20:15–16; Deuteronomy 27:21.

spare them, but the human shall not approach the king.[1] If an ox leaps on a man,[2] the ox shall die; the man shall not die. They shall substitute one sheep for the man and put it to death. If a pig leaps on a man, it is not an offense.

(200) If a man has sexual relations with either a horse or a mule, it is not an offense, but he shall not approach the king, nor shall he become a priest. If anyone sleeps with an *arnuwalash*-woman,[3] and also sleeps with her mother, it is not an offense.

TREATIES

INTERNATIONAL TREATIES ARE a form of contract between the rulers of two countries, who may be either equals (in which case the treaty is often called a parity treaty) or in a superior-inferior relationship (a suzerainty treaty).

HITTITE

Some two dozen Hittite treaties are preserved, largely dating to the fourteenth and thirteenth centuries BCE. Most are suzerainty treaties between the Hittite king and one of his subject kings or vassals. Duplicates or near duplicates often exist in Hittite and Akkadian and are highly formulaic in nature; as a result, even though they are seldom complete, they can easily be restored.

43. TREATY BETWEEN SUPPILULIUMA I OF HATTI AND NIQMADDU II OF UGARIT

Dating to the mid-fourteenth century BCE, this treaty had been promised in an earlier letter (see Text 74).[4]

Thus says His Majesty, Suppiluliuma, Great King, King of Hatti, Hero:

When Itur-Addu, king of the land of Mukish; Addu-nirari, king of the land of Nuhashshi; and Aki-Teshub, king of Niya[5] were hostile to the authority of His Majesty, the Great King, their lord; assembled their troops; captured cities in the interior of the land of Ugarit; oppressed the land of Ugarit; carried off subjects of Niqmaddu, king of the land of Ugarit, as civilian captives; and devastated the land of Ugarit; Niqmaddu, king of the land of Ugarit, turned to Suppiluliuma, Great King, writing: "May Your Majesty, Great King, my lord, save me from the hand of my enemy! I am the subject of Your Majesty, Great King, my lord. To my lord's enemy I am hostile, and with my lord's friend I am at peace. The kings are oppressing me."[6] The Great King heard these words of Niqmaddu, and Suppiluliuma, Great King, dispatched princes and noblemen with infantry and chariotry to the land of Ugarit. And they chased the enemy troops out of the land of Ugarit. And they gave to Niqmaddu all of their civilian captives whom they took from the enemy. And Niqmaddu, king of the land of Ugarit ... honored the princes and noblemen very much. He gave them silver, gold, bronze, and ... He arrived ... in the city of Alalakh before His Majesty, Great King, his lord. ... And Suppiluliuma witnessed the loyalty of Niqmaddu.

Now Suppiluliuma, Great King, King of Hatti, has made the following treaty with Niqmaddu, king of the land of Ugarit, saying:

If in the future fugitives of the land of Nuhashshi, or of the land of Mukish, or of other lands, leave those lands and enter the land of Ugarit and the service of the king of Ugarit, no other king of another land shall take them from the control of Niqmaddu, king of the land of Ugarit, nor from the control of his sons or grandsons, forever. My Majesty, Great King, has made a treaty to this effect.

Furthermore, all of the land of Ugarit, together with its border districts, together with its mountains, together with its fields, together with ... up to Mount Igari-ayali, together with Mount

---

[1] Apparently so the king would not be defiled.
[2] In sexual arousal.
[3] A foreign woman, perhaps a captive.
[4] Translation by Gary Beckman, *Hittite Diplomatic Texts* (Atlanta, GA: Scholars Press, 2d ed., 1999), 34–36.

---

[5] Mukish (Alalakh), Nuhashshi, and Niya were city-states that neighbored Ugarit.
[6] Cf. 2 Kings 16:5–8.

Hadamgi, [. . .]itkitiya, Panishtai, Nakhati, Halpi and Mount Nana, Shalma, Gulbata, Zamirti, Sulada, Maraili, and Himulli.

[At this point the surviving texts are fragmentary. The treaty concludes as follows:]

Now Suppiluliuma, Great King, King of Hatti, Hero, has deeded by means of a sealed document, these border districts, cities, and mountains, to Niqmaddu, king of the land of Ugarit, and to his sons and grandsons forever. Now Niqmaddu is hostile to my enemy and at peace with my friend. He has put himself out greatly for My Majesty, Great King, his lord, and has observed the treaty and state of peace with Hatti. Now My Majesty, Great King, has witnessed the loyalty of Niqmaddu.

And whoever alters the words of this treaty tablet will transgress the oath. The Thousand Gods shall be aware of the perpetrator, beginning with the Storm God of Heaven, the Sun God of Heaven, the Storm God of Hatti, the Sun Goddess of Arinna, Hebat of Kizzuwatna, Ishtar of Alalakh, Nikkal of Numabbi, and the Storm God of Mount Hazzi.

44. NOTICE OF TRIBUTE TO BE PAID TO HATTI BY UGARIT

Written in Akkadian, this mid-fourteenth-century-BCE text was found at Ugarit and specifies the tribute due from Niqmaddu II, the vassal, to Suppululiuma, the Hittite king. It further serves to illustrate requirements of the treaty in Text 43. There is a closely related text in Ugaritic that apparently accompanied the tribute as an inventory.[1]

Thus says His Majesty, Suppululiuma, Great King, King of Hatti, Hero:

When all the kings of the land of Nuhashshi and the king of the land of Mukish were hostile to His Majesty, Great King, their lord, Niqmaddu, king of the land of Ugarit, was at peace with His Majesty, Great King, his lord, and not hostile. Then the kings of the land of Nuhashshi and the kings of the land of Mukish oppressed Niqmaddu, king of the land of Ugarit, saying: "Why are you not hostile to His Majesty along with us?" But Niqmaddu did not agree upon hostilities against His Majesty, Great King, his lord, and His Majesty, Great King, witnessed the loyalty of Niqmaddu. Now Suppiluliuma, Great King, King of Hatti, has thus made a treaty for Niqmaddu, king of the land of Ugarit: Your tribute for His Majesty, Great King, your lord, is as follows:

12 minas and 20 shekels[2] of gold and one golden cup one mina in weight as the primary portion of the tribute; four linen garments, one large linen garment, 500 shekels of blue-purple wool, and 500 shekels of red-purple wool for His Majesty, Great King, your lord.

One golden cup 30 shekels in weight, one linen garment, 100 shekels of blue-purple wool, 100 shekels of red-purple wool for the Queen.

One golden cup 30 shekels in weight, one linen garment, 100 shekels of blue-purple wool, 100 shekels of red-purple wool for the crown prince.

One golden cup 30 shekels in weight, one linen garment, 100 shekels of blue-purple wool, 100 shekels of red-purple wool for the chief scribe.

One golden cup 30 shekels in weight, one linen garment, 100 shekels of blue-purple wool, 100 shekels of red-purple wool for the *huburtanuri*.[3]

And the same for the second *huburtanuri*.

One linen garment, 100 shekels of blue-purple wool, 100 shekels of red-purple wool for the vizier.

One golden cup, one linen garment, 100 shekels of blue-purple wool, 100 shekels of red-purple wool for the *andubsalli*.[4]

There is no one else to pay among the noblemen in the entourage of His Majesty, Great King, his lord. On the day when Niqmaddu brings his tribute, Niqmaddu shall not be obligated for any other gift.

---

[1]Translation by Gary Beckman, *Hittite Diplomatic Texts* (Atlanta, GA: Scholars Press, 2d ed., 1999), 166–167.

[2]A shekel weighed ca. 0.35 ounce (10 grams), and a mina was probably 50 shekels.

[3]A high royal official.

[4]A high royal official.

And His Majesty, Great King, witnessed the loyalty of Niqmaddu, when he himself came and threw himself at the feet of His Majesty, Great King, his lord. And His Majesty, Great King, his lord, thus gave him this treaty. The Thousand Gods beginning with the Sun God of Heaven, the Sun Goddess of Arinna, the Storm God of Heaven, and the Storm God of Hatti shall be aware of the words written on this tablet. They will punish whoever alters the words of this tablet.

45. TREATY BETWEEN SHATTIWAZA OF MITANNI AND SUPPILULIU-MA I OF HATTI

Dating to the mid-fourteenth century BCE, this copy of the treaty was written as though originating in Mitanni, a Hurrian confederation in northern Mesopotamia and northern Syria. But the parallel version, written in Hatti, shows that this one too originated in the Hittite capital, not surprisingly since Mitanni was the vassal. The Mitanni version does not include the stipulations about mutual support and extradition of fugitives found in the Hittite version.[1]

Thus says Shattiwaza, son of Tushratta, king of the land of Mitanni: Before Shuttarna, son of Artatama, King of Hurri, altered the...of the land of Mitanni, King Artatama, his father, did wrong. He used up the palace of the kings, together with its treasures. He exhausted them in payment to the land of Assyria and to the land of Alshi. King Tushratta, my father, built a palace and filled it with riches, but Shuttarna destroyed it, and it became impoverished. And he broke the...of the kings, of silver and gold, and the cauldrons of silver from the bathhouse. And from the wealth of his father and his brother he did not give anyone in Mitanni anything, but he threw himself down before the Assyrian, the subject of his father, who no longer pays tribute, and gave him his riches as a gift.

Thus says Shattiwaza, son of King Tushratta: The door of silver and gold which King Shaustatar, my great-great-grandfather, took by force from the land of Assyria as a token of his glory and set up

in his palace in the city of Washshukkani[2]—to his shame Shuttarna has now returned it to the land of Assyria. All the utensils of the storehouse of gifts of silver and gold he gave to the land of Alshi. He exhausted the house of the king of the land of Mitanni, together with its treasures and its riches. He filled it with dirt. He destroyed the palace and exhausted the households of the Hurrians. He had the noblemen brought and extradited to the land of Assyria and the land of Alshi. They were turned over and impaled in the city of Taite. Thus he brought an end to the Hurrians. But Aki-Teshub fled before him and entered Babylonia. Two hundred chariots fled with him, and the King of Babylonia took away for himself the two hundred chariots and all the possessions of Aki-Teshub. He made Aki-Teshub assume the same rank as his chariot warriors. He conspired to kill him. He would have killed me, Shattiwaza, son of King Tushratta, too, but I escaped from his hands and called upon the gods of His Majesty, Suppiluliuma, Great King, King of Hatti, Hero, Beloved of the Storm God. They led me on a road without....The gods of the King of Hatti and the gods of the king of Mitanni cause me to reach His Majesty, Suppiluliuma, Great King, King of Hatti, Hero, Beloved of the Storm God.

At the Marassantiya River I fell at the feet of His Majesty, Suppiluliuma, Great King, King of Hatti, Hero, Beloved of the Storm God. The Great King took me by the hand and rejoiced over me and questioned me at length concerning all the customs of the land of Mitanni. And when he had heard exhaustively about the customs of the land of Mitanni, the Great King and Hero spoke as follows: "If I conquer Shuttarna and the troops of the land of Mitanni, I will not reject you but will adopt you as my son.[3] I will stand by you and place you on the throne of your father. And the gods know My Majesty, Suppiluliuma, Great King, King of Hatti, Hero, Beloved of the Storm God. He never goes back on the words which issue from his mouth." Thus says Shattiwaza, son of Tushratta: I rejoiced at the words of the King, my lord, which I heard. I, Prince Shattiwaza, spoke to the Great King, my lord: "If you, my lord, will

---

[1]Translation by Gary Beckman, *Hittite Diplomatic Texts* (Atlanta, GA: Scholars Press, 2d ed., 1999), 48–54.

[2]The capital of Mitanni; location uncertain.
[3]Cf. 2 Samuel 7:14; 2 Kings 16:7.

give me life, and the gods will stand by me, then Suppiluliuma, Great King, King of Hatti, Hero, Beloved of the Storm God, shall certainly not remove King Artatama from his royal throne. Let me stand as his designated successor, and let me rule the land of Mitanni. Shuttama treated the lands badly, but I will never do anything for ill."

And when I, Prince Shattiwaza, came before the Great King, I had only three chariots, two Hurrians, two other attendants, who set out with me, and a single outfit of clothes—which I was wearing—and nothing else. And the Great King took pity on me and gave me chariots mounted with gold, chariot horses with armor,...a tent of linen, servants of the...-house, two vessels of silver and gold, together with their cups of silver and gold, silver utensils of the bathhouse, a silver washbasin, festive garments of the woolworker—all this and everything of the craftsman. He ... me to Piyassili, his son, and the King entrusted me to the hand of Piyassili, to his chariotry, and to his troops. From the city of Carchemish where we arrived, we sent a messenger to the people of the city of Irrite, but Shuttarna had influenced the Hurrians with the riches of Tushratta and had united them. We sent to them in Irrite, and these Hurrians sent back to Piyassili: "Why are you coming? If you are coming for battle, come, but you shall not return to the land of the Great King!" When we heard the words of the people of Irrite, we—Prince Piyassili and Prince Shattiwaza—crossed the Euphrates and arrived at Irrite ready for battle.

And the gods of the Great King, King of Hatti, protected us, and the Hurrians whom Shuttarna had sent as protection to Irrite, as well as the chariotry and troops of the district of Irrite, gathered in wait for us. We reached Irrite, and the troops and chariotry which had sat within the city came out before us. We captured and destroyed....

[*The next section is damaged. It describes how Piyassili and Shattiwaza continued to battle with Shuttarna's forces and allies and finally defeated them.*]

A duplicate of this tablet is deposited in the land of Mitanni before the Storm God, Lord of the *kurinnu*[1] of Kahat. It shall be read repeatedly, forever and ever, before the king of the land of Mitanni

and before the Hurrians.[2] Whoever, before the Storm God, Lord of the *kurinnu* of Kahat, alters this tablet, or sets it in a secret location—if he breaks it, if he changes the words of the text of the tablet—in regard to this treaty we have summoned the gods of secrets and the gods who are guarantors of the oath. They shall stand together and listen and be witnesses: The Sun Goddess of Arinna, who governs kingship and queenship in Hatti, the Sun God, Lord of Heaven, the Storm God, Lord of Hatti, Sheri, Hurri, Mount Nanni, Mount Hazzi, the Storm God, Lord of the Market, the Storm God, Lord of the Army, the Storm God, Lord of Help, the Storm God of Pittiyarik, the Storm God of Nerik, the Storm God, Lord of the Ruin Mounds, the Storm God of Aleppo, the Storm God of Lihzina, the Storm God of Samuha, the Storm God of Hurma, the Storm God of Sarissa, the Storm God of Sapinuwa, the Storm God of Hisashapa, the Storm God of Tahaya, the Storm God of..., the Storm God of Kizzuwatna, the Storm God of Uda, the Tutelary Deity of Hatti, the Tutelary Deity of Karahna, Zithariya, Karzi, Hapantaliya, the Tutelary Deity of the Countryside, the Tutelary Deity of the Hunting Bag, Lelwani, Ea, Damkia, Telipinu of Tawiniya, Telipinu of Turmitts, Telipinu of Hanhana, the Proud Ishtar, Askasepa, the Grain-deity, the Moon God, Lord of the Oath, Ishara, Queen of the Oath, Hebat, Queen of Heaven, Hebat of Aleppo, Hebat of Uda, Hebat of Kizzuwatna, the War God, the War God of Hatti, the War God of Illaya, the War God of Arziya, Yarri, Lord of the Bow, Zappana, Hasamili, Hantitassu of Hurma, Abara of Samuha, Katahha of Ankuwa, the Queen of Katapa, Ammamma of Tahurpa, Hallara of Dunna, Huwassanna of Hupisna, the Lady of Landa, Kuniyawanni of Landa, the mountain-dweller gods, the mercenary gods, the male deities and female deities of Hatti, the male deities and female deities of the land of Kizzuwatna, Ereshkigal, the primeval deities—Nara, Namsara, Minki, Ammunki, Tuhusi, Ammizzadu, Alalu, Anu, Antu—Enlil, Ninlil, Belet-ekalli, the mountains, the rivers, the Tigris and the Euphrates, heaven and earth, the winds, and the clouds, they shall stand and listen and be witnesses to these words of the treaty.[3]

---

[1] A type of shrine.

[2] Cf. Deuteronomy 31:10–13.

[3] For the invocation of mountains and heaven and earth as witnesses, cf., e.g., Micah 6:1–2; Deuteronomy 30:19; Isaiah 1:2.

If you, Shattiwaza, and you Hurrians do not observe the words of this treaty, these gods of the oath shall destroy you, Shattiwaza, and you Hurrians, together with your land, together with your wives, together with your sons, and together with your possessions. They will draw you out like malt from its husk. As one does not get a plant from...so any other wife whom you might take in place of my daughter,[1] and you Hurrians, together with their wives and their sons, shall thus have no progeny. And these gods, lords of the oath, shall allot you poverty and destitution. And they shall overthrow your throne, Shattiwaza. And you, Shattiwaza—these oath gods shall snap you off like a reed, together with your land. Your name and your progeny by another wife whom you might take shall be eradicated from the earth. And you, Shattiwaza, together with your land, because of not delivering goodness and recovery among the Hurrians—you shall be eradicated. The ground shall be ice, so that you will slip. The ground of your land shall be a marsh...so that you will certainly sink and be unable to cross. You, Shattiwaza, and you Hurrians shall be the enemies of the Thousand Gods. They shall defeat you.

If you, Shattiwaza, and you Hurrians observe this treaty and oath, these gods shall protect you, Shattiwaza, together with the daughter of the Great King of Hatti, her sons and grandsons, and you Hurrians, together with your wives and your sons, and together with your land. And the land of Mitanni shall return to its previous state. It shall prosper and expand. And you, Shattiwaza, your sons and daughters by the daughter of the Great King, King of Hatti—they shall accept you for kingship for eternity.[2] Prolong the life of the throne of your father; prolong the life of the land of Mitanni.

The Storm God of Heaven and Earth, the Moon God and the Sun God, the Moon God of Harran, heaven and earth, the Storm God, Lord of the *kurinnu* of Kahat, the Storm God, Lord of Uhushuman, Ea, Lord of Wisdom, the Deity of Herds of Jurta, Anu and Antu, Enlil and Ninlil, the Mitra Gods, the Varuna gods, Indra, the Nasatya gods, the underground water-course, Shamanminuhi, the Storm God, Lord of

Washshukkani, the Storm God of the Temple Platform of Irrite, Nabarbi, Shuruhi, Ishtar, Ishtar, Star, Shala, Belet-ekalli, the Lady of the *ayakki*-shrine, Ishara, Partahi of Shuta, the mountains, the rivers, and the springs, the deities of heaven and earth. If I, Prince Shattiwaza, and the Hurrians do not observe the words of this treaty and of the oath, let me, Shattiwaza, together with my other wife, and us Hurrians, together with our wives, together with our sons, and together with our land—as a fir tree when it is felled has no more shoots, like this fir tree let me, Shattiwaza, together with any other wife whom I might take, and us Hurrians, together with our lands, together with our wives, and together with our sons, like the fir tree have no progeny.[3] As the water of a drainpipe never returns to its place, let us, like the water of a drainpipe, not return to our place. Let me, Shattiwaza, together with any other wife whom I might take, and the Hurrians, together with our lands, our wives, and our sons, like salt indeed have no progeny. Like a dissolved lump of salt let us not return to our place. I, Shattiwaza—if any other wife whom I might take...my throne shall be overthrown. If we do not observe this treaty and oath, the gods, lords of the oath, shall destroy us.

Thus says Prince Shattiwaza and indeed also the Hurrians: If we observe this treaty and oath of His Majesty, Suppiluliuma, Great King, King of Hatti, Hero, Beloved of the Storm God, the gods whose names we have invoked shall go with us, exalt us, protect us, and be good to us. Let our lord Shattiwaza go in front, and let us enjoy a bountiful harvest in his protection.[4] Let us experience goodness and peace. The Storm God, Canal Inspector of Heaven and Earth, shall be our helper for eternity. Let Shattiwaza, us Hurrians, and the land of Mitanni experience joy of heart and peace of mind for eternity. As His Majesty, Suppiluliuma, Great King, King of Hatti, Hero, Beloved of the Storm God, loves his lands, his troops, his sons, and his grandsons like his table-companions, he shall love us—me Shattiwaza, us Hurrians, and the land of Mitanni, together with our lands and together with our possessions, like these.

---

[1] In the Hittite version of the treaty, Suppiluliuma gave one of his daughters to Shattiwaza to be his highest-ranking wife.
[2] Cf. Psalm 89:29.

[3] Cf. Job 18:16; Text 131.
[4] Cf. Psalm 72:16.

One tablet of Kili-Teshub, of his treaty and his oath, complete.[1]

46. TREATY BETWEEN MURSILI II OF HATTI AND TUPPI-TESHUB OF AMURRU

Both Hittite and Akkadian versions exist of this late-fourteenth-century-BCE treaty between Hatti and Amurru, a small kingdom in northern Lebanon; this is the Hittite version.[2]

Thus says My Majesty, Mursili, Great King, King of Hatti, Hero, Beloved of the Storm God, son of Suppiluliuma, Great King, King of Hatti, Hero:

Aziru, your grandfather, Tuppi-Teshub, became the subject of my father. When it came about that the kings of the land of Nuhashshi[3] and the king of the land of Kinza[4] became hostile to my father, Aziru did not become hostile. When my father made war on his enemies, Aziru likewise made war. And Aziru protected only my father, and my father protected Aziru, together with his land. He did not seek to harm him in any way. And Aziru did not anger my father in any way. He always paid him the 300 shekels[5] of refined, first-class gold which he had imposed as tribute. My father died,[6] and I took my seat upon the throne of my father. But as Aziru had been in the time of my father, so he was in my time.

Then it happened that the kings of the land of Nuhashshi and the king of the land of Kinza became hostile to me, but your grandfather Aziru and your father Ari-Teshub [did not join] them. They supported me alone as overlord. And when Aziru became an old man and was no longer able to go on military campaign as he had always gone to war with infantry and charity, then Ari-Teshub likewise went to war with the infantry and chariotry of the land of Amurru. And my Majesty destroyed those enemies....

But when your father died, according to the request of your father, I did not cast you off.

Because your father had spoken your name before me during his lifetime, I therefore took care of you. But you were sick and ailing.[7] And although you were an invalid, I nonetheless installed you in place of your father. I made...your brothers and the land of Amurru swear an oath to you.

And as I took care of you according to the request of your father, and installed you in place of your father, I have now made you swear an oath to the King of Hatti and the land of Hatti, and to my sons and grandsons. Observe the oath and the authority of the King. I, My Majesty, will protect you, Tuppi-Teshub. And when you take a wife and produce a son, he shall later be king in the land of Amurru. And as you protect My Majesty, I will likewise protect your son. You, Tuppi-Teshub, in the future protect the King of Hatti, the land of Hatti, my sons, and my grandsons. The tribute which was imposed upon your grandfather and upon your father shall be imposed upon you: They paid 300 shekels of refined gold by the weights of Hatti, first-class and good. You shall pay it likewise. You shall not turn your eyes to another. Your ancestors paid tribute to Egypt, but you shall not pay it....

If...while the King of Egypt is hostile to My Majesty you secretly send your messenger to him, or you become hostile to the King of Hatti and cast off the authority of the King of Hatti, becoming a subject of the King of Egypt, you, Tuppi-Teshub, will transgress the oath.

Whoever is My Majesty's enemy shall be your enemy. Whoever is My Majesty's friend shall be your friend. And if any of the lands which are protectorates of the King of Hatti should become hostile to the King of Hatti, and if I, My Majesty, come against that land for attack, and you do not mobilize wholeheartedly with infantry and chariotry, and do not make war wholeheartedly and without hesitation on the enemy, you will transgress the oath. And if you commit some misdeed or...you think as follows: "Although I am under oath, either let them defeat the enemy, or let the enemy defeat them. I don't want to know anything about it."— you will transgress the oath. Or if you send a man off to that enemy to warn him as follows: "The infantry and chariotry of Hatti are now coming. Be on guard!"—you will transgress the oath.

---

[1] A colophon, or cataloging device.
[2] Translation by Gary Beckman, *Hittite Diplomatic Texts* (Atlanta, GA: Scholars Press, 2d ed., 1999), 59–64.
[3] Northwestern Syria east of Amurru.
[4] Qadesh on the Orontes River in northwestern Syria.
[5] Ca. 100 ounces (3 kilograms).
[6] Literally, "became a god."

---

[7] Perhaps a metaphor for political weakness.

As I, My Majesty, protect you, Tuppi-Teshub, be an auxiliary army for My Majesty and for Hatti. And if some evil matter arises in Hatti and someone revolts against My Majesty, and you hear of it, lend assistance together with your infantry and your chariotry. Take a stand immediately to help Hatti. But if it is not possible for you to lend assistance personally, send aid to the King of Hatti by either your son or your brother, together with your infantry and your chariotry. If you do not send aid to the king of Hatti by your son or your brother, together with your infantry and your chariotry, you will transgress the oath.

If some matter oppresses you, Tuppi-Teshub, or someone revolts against you, and you write to the King of Hatti, then the King of Hatti will send infantry and chariotry to your aid.

If Hittites bring you, Tuppi-Teshub, infantry and chariotry—because they will go up to your cities, Tuppi-Teshub must regularly provide them with food and drink. And if any Hittite undertakes an evil matter against Tuppi-Teshub, such as the plunder of his land or of his cities, or the removal of Tuppi-Teshub from kingship in the land of Amurru, he will transgress the oath.

Whatever civilian captives of the land of Nuhashshi and the land of Kinza my father carried off, or I carried off—if one of these civilian captive flees from me and comes to you, and you do not seize him and give him back to the King of Hatti, you will transgress the oath. And if you should even think as follows concerning a fugitive: "Come or go! Wherever you go, I don't want to know about you."—you will transgress the oath.

If someone should bring up before you, Tuppi-Teshub, evil matters against the King or against Hatti, you shall not conceal him from the King. Or if My Majesty speaks confidentially of some matters to you: "Perform these deeds or that deed," then make an appeal right there at that moment concerning whatever among those deeds you do not want to perform: "I cannot do this deed. I will not perform it." And when the King again commands, and you do not perform a deed of which you are capable, but rebuff the King, or if you do not observe the matter of which the King speaks to you confidentially, you will transgress the oath.

If some population or fugitive sets out, travels toward Hatti, and passes through your land, set them well on their way and point out the road to Hatti. Speak favorable words to them. You shall not direct them to anyone else. If you do not set them on their way and do not show them the road to Hatti, but direct them to the mountains—or if you speak evil words before them, you will transgress the oath.

Or if the King of Hatti beleaguers some country through battle, and it flees before him, and comes into your country—if you want to take anything, ask the King of Hatti for it. You shall not take it on your own initiative. If you take anything on your own initiative and conceal it, you will transgress the oath.

Furthermore, if a fugitive comes into your land in flight, seize him and turn him over.

[*The text is broken here. It resumes with the list of divine witnesses.*]

The Thousand Gods shall now stand for this oath. They shall observe and listen. The Sun God of Heaven, the Sun Goddess of Arinna, the Storm God of Heaven, the Storm God of Hatti, Sheri, Hurri, Mount Nanni, Mount Hazzi, the Storm God of the Market, the Storm God of the Army, the Storm God of Aleppo, the Storm God of Zippalanda, the Storm God of Nerik, the Storm God of Lihzina, the Storm God of the Ruin Mound, the Storm God of Hisashapa, the Storm God of Sahpina, the Storm God of Sapinuwa, the Storm God of Pittiyarik, the Storm God of Samuha, the Storm God of Hurma, the Storm God of Sarissa, the Storm God of Help, the Storm God of Uda, the Storm God of Kizzuwatna, the Storm God of Ishupitta, the Storm God of . . ., the Storm God of Arkata, the Storm God of Tunip, the Storm God of Aleppo resident in Tunip, Milku of the land of Amurru, the Tutelary Deity, the Tutelary Deity of Hatti, Zithariya, Karzi, Hapantaliya, the Tutelary Deity of Karahna, the Tutelary Deity of the Countryside, the Tutelary Deity of the Hunting Bag, Ea, Allatu, Telipinu of Turmitta, Telipinu of Tawaniya, Telipinu of Hanhana, Bunene, Askasepa, the Moon God, Lord of the Oath, Ishara, Queen of the Oath, Hebat, Queen of Heaven, Ishtar, Ishtar of the Countryside, Ishtar of Nineveh, Ishtar of Hattarina, Ninatta, Kulitta, the War God of Hatti, the War God of Illaya, the War God of Arziya, Yarri, Zappana, Hantitassu of Hurma, Abara of Samuha, Katahha of Ankuwa, the Queen of Katapa, Ammamma of Tahurpa, Hallara of Dunna, Huwassanna of Hupisna, Tapisuwa of Ishupitta, the Lady of Landa, Kuniyawanni of Landa, NIN.PISAN.PISAN[1] of Kinza, Mount Lebanon, Mount Shariyana, Mount Pishaisha, the mountain-dweller gods, the mercenary gods, Ereshkigal, the male deities and female deities of Hatti, the male deities and female deities of Amurru, all the primeval deities—Mara, Namsara, Minki, Tuhusi, Ammunki, Ammizzadu, Alalu, Antu, Anu, Apantu, Enlil, Ninlil—the mountains, the rivers, the springs, the great sea, heaven and earth, the winds, the clouds. They shall be witnesses to this treaty and to the oath.[2]

All the words of the treaty and oath which are written on this tablet—if Tuppi-Teshub does not observe these words of the treaty and of the oath, then these oath gods shall destroy Tuppi-Teshub, together with his person, his wife, his son, his grandsons, his household, his city, his land, and together with his possessions.

But if Tuppi-Teshub observes these words of the treaty and of the oath which are written on this tablet, then these oath gods shall protect Tuppi-Teshub, together with his person, his wife, his son, his grandsons, his city, his land, his household, his subjects, and together with his possessions.

47. TREATY BETWEEN HATTUSILI III OF HATTI AND RAMESES II OF EGYPT

Concluded in 1259 BCE, this treaty marked an end to the struggle between Egypt and Hatti for control of the Levant. Both Egyptian and Hittite versions of the treaty exist, although neither is complete. This is the Egyptian version; the silver tablet to which it refers no longer exists, so this text itself is a copy.[3]

The treaty which the Great Ruler of Hatti, Hattusili, the Hero, the son of Mursili, the Great Ruler of Hatti, the hero, the grandson of Suppiluliuma, the Great Ruler of Hatti, the hero, made upon a silver tablet, for Usinmare Setepenre,[4] the Great Ruler of Egypt, the Hero, the son of Menmare,[5] the Great Ruler of Egypt, the Hero, the grandson of Menpehtyre,[6] the Great Ruler of Egypt, the Hero: the good treaty of peace and of brotherhood, for inaugurating good peace and good brotherhood between us forever.

Now formerly, since eternity, as regards the relationship of the Great Ruler of Egypt with the Great Ruler of Hatti, God did not permit hostilities to arise between them, acting as by treaty. But in the time of Muwatalli, the Great Ruler of Hatti, my brother, he fought with Usimare Setepenre, the Great Ruler of Egypt. But now, as from today, see: Hattusili, the Great Ruler of Hatti, makes a treaty to reestablish the relationship which Re[7] made and which Seth[8] made—with the land of Egypt and the land of Hatti—to prevent hostilities ever arising between them again.

See, Hattusili, the Great Ruler of Hatti, binds himself by treaty with Usimare Setepenre, the Great Ruler of Egypt, beginning from today, in order to create good peace and good brotherhood between us eternally—he being in brotherhood and peace with me, and I being in brotherhood and peace with him, eternally.

Now when Muwatalli, the Great Ruler of Hatti, my brother, went to his fate, then Hattusili sat as Great Ruler of Hatti upon the throne of his father. See, I am with Rameses Meriamun, the Great Ruler of Egypt, we having made our peace and our brotherhood, it being even better than the peace and brotherhood which previously existed in the land.

See, I as the Great Ruler of Hatti am now with Usimare Setepenre, the Great Ruler of Egypt, in good peace and good brotherhood. It is the children's children of the Great Ruler of Hatti who shall be in brotherhood and peace with the children's children of Rameses Meriamun, the

---

[1]A Sumerian goddess whose Hittite or Semitic equivalent is unknown.

[2]For the invocation of mountains and heaven and earth as witnesses, cf., e.g., Micah 6:1–2; Deuteronomy 30:19; Isaiah 1:2.

[3]Translation by K. A. Kitchen, *Ramesside Inscriptions Translated and Annotated. Translations.* Volume II (Oxford: Blackwell, 1996), 80–84.

[4]Rameses II.

[5]Seti I.

[6]Rameses I.

[7]The Egyptian sun god.

[8]The Egyptian god of the desert and of the storm.

Great Ruler of Egypt, they enjoying our relationship of brotherhood and peace—the land of Egypt with the land of Hatti, in peace and brotherhood just like us eternally, and no hostility occurring between us eternally.

The Great Ruler of Hatti shall never trespass against the land of Egypt, to take anything from it. And Usimare Setepenre, the Great Ruler of Egypt, shall never trespass against the land of Hatti, to take anything from it.

As for the standing treaty which had been current in the time of Suppiluliuma, the Great Ruler of Hatti, and likewise the standing treaty which existed in the time of Muwatalli, the Great Ruler of Hatti, my brother[1]—I hold firm to it. See, Rameses Meriamun, the Great Ruler of Egypt, also holds firm to it, to the treaty which he has made together with us, beginning from today. We both hold firm to it, we shall remain within this regular relationship.

If some other foe should come against the territories of Usimare Setepenre, the Great Ruler of Egypt, and he sends word to the Great Ruler of Hatti, saying: "Come with me as ally against him!"—then the Great Ruler of Hatti shall act with him, and the Great Ruler of Hatti shall kill his enemy. But if the Great Ruler of Hatti has no wish to go, then he must send his troops and his chariotry, and they shall kill his foe.

Or, if Rameses Meriamun, the Great Ruler of Egypt, is angry with servants of his, and they commit a further offense against him, and he moves to kill them—then the Great Ruler of Hatti shall act with him, to eliminate anyone against whom such anger is directed.

Now, if some other foe should come against the Great Ruler of Hatti, then Usimare Setepenre, the Great Ruler of Egypt, shall act, and he shall come as ally to kill his foe. But if Rameses Meriamun has no wish to come, then he shall...send his troops and his chariotry, in making response to the land of Hatti.

Now, if servants of the Great Ruler of Hatti trespass against him, then Rameses Meriamun, the Great Ruler of Egypt, shall send to the Great Ruler of Hatti....

[*A broken passage about succession in Hatti follows.*]

If a great man of Egypt flees to the Great Ruler of Hatti, or else a town of those belonging to the lands of Rameses Meriamun, the Great Ruler of Egypt, also comes to the Great Ruler of Hatti—then the Great Ruler of Hatti shall not receive them, but the Great Ruler of Hatti shall have them brought back to Usimare Setepenre, the Great Ruler of Egypt, their master—life, prosperity, and health.

Or, if one man, or two men—who are unknowns—flee from the land of Egypt, and they come to the land of Hatti to become someone else's servant—then they shall not be left in the land of Hatti, they shall be brought back to Rameses Meriamun, the Great Ruler of Egypt.

Or, if a great man flees from the land of Hatti, and he comes to Usimare Setepenre, the Great Ruler of Egypt, or a town or a district or a...belonging to the land of Hatti, and they come to Rameses Meriamun, the Great Ruler of Egypt—then Usimare Setepenre, the Great Ruler of Egypt, shall not receive them, but Rameses Meriamun, the Great Ruler of Egypt, shall have them brought back to the Great Ruler of Hatti, and they shall not be left.

Likewise, if one man, or two men—who are unknowns—flee and come to the land of Egypt to become someone else's servants—then Usimare Setepenre, the Great Ruler of Egypt, shall not leave them so, he shall have them brought back to the Great Ruler of Hatti.

As for these words of the treaty which the Great Ruler of Hatti has made with Rameses Meriamun, the Great Ruler of Egypt, on this silver tablet—as for these terms, a thousand gods, of gods male and female belonging to the land of Hatti, together with a thousand gods, of gods male and female belonging to the land of Egypt—they are with me as witnesses who have heard these terms:

The Sun God, Lord of heaven, the Sun God of the town of Arinna, the Storm God,[2] Lord of heaven, the Storm God of Hatti, the Storm God of the town of Arinna the Storm God of the town of Zippalanda, the Storm God of the town of Pattiariq, the Storm God of the town of

---

[1] The scribe made an error and actually wrote "father."

[2] Here and following, literally, "Seth."

Hissaspa, the Storm God of the town of Saressa, the Storm God of the town of Aleppo, the Storm God of the town of Lihzina, the Storm God of the town of Hurma, the Storm God of the town of Nerik, the Storm God of the town of Sapinuwa, the Storm God of..., the Storm God of the town of Sahipina, Antaret of the Hatti-land, the god of Zitkharriya, the god of Karzis, the god of Halpantaliyas, the goddess of the town of Karahna, the goddess of the wastes, the goddess of Nineveh, the goddess of..., the god of Nenatti, the god of Kulitti, the goddess of Hebat, the Queen of Heaven, the gods, lords of the oath, the goddess, the lady of the earth, the lady of the oath, Ishkhara the lady, the mountains and rivers of the Hatti-land, the gods of the land of Qizzuwatna, Amun, Re, Seth, the gods male and female, the mountains and rivers of the land of Egypt, the Sky, the Earth, the great Sea, the winds, the clouds.[1]

Concerning these terms which are recorded upon this silver tablet for the land of Hatti and the land of Egypt: As for whoever shall not keep them—destroy his house, his land, and his servants.

As for whoever shall keep these terms which are recorded upon this silver tablet, be they in Hatti or be they Egyptians, and they do not act in neglect of them—the thousand gods of the land of Hatti together with the thousand gods of the land of Egypt shall act to cause him to flourish and to live, together with his household, his land, and his servants.

[There follow, apparently out of order, other stipulations concerning fugitives and a description of the state seals of Hatti.]

ARAMAIC
48. TREATY BETWEEN BAR-GAYAH AND MATIEL (THE SEFIRE TEXTS)

These texts were written in Aramaic on three fragmentary large stone stelas found in the village of Sefire, south of Aleppo in Syria. Dating to the mid-eighth century BCE, they apparently contain three versions of a treaty between Matiel, king of Arpad, a city north of Aleppo (see 2 Kings 18:34; Isaiah

10:9; Jeremiah 49:23), and Bar- (or Bir-) gayah, king of KTK, an unidentified (and unvocalizable) city. The same Matiel is also mentioned in Text 49, but Bar-gayah is otherwise unknown.

The treaty of Bar-gayah, king of KTK, with Matiel, the son of Attar-samak, the king of Arpad, and the treaty of the sons of Bar-gayah with the sons of Matiel, and the treaty of the sons of the sons of Bar-gayah and his offspring with the offspring of Matiel, the son of Attar-samak, king of Arpad, and the treaty of KTK with the treaty of Arpad, and the treaty of the lords of KTK with the treaty of the lords of Arpad, and the treaty of... with all Aram, and with Musur[2] and with his sons who will arise after him, and with the kings of all Upper and Lower Aram and with all who enter the house of the king and with....

This is the treaty which Bar-gayah cut[3] before...Mullesh, and before Marduk and Sarpanitu, and before Nabu and Tashmet,...and before Nergal and Las, and before Shamash and Nur, and before Sin..., and before Nikkar and Qadiah, and before all the gods of Rahbah and Adam,...of Aleppo, and before the Seven Gods, and before El and Elyan,[4] and before Heav[en and Earth...][5] and the springs, and before day and night—witnesses are all the gods.[6]...Open your eyes to look upon the treaty of Bar-gayah....

If Matiel, son of Attar-samak, king of Arpad, is false to...a ewe, then may she not get pregnant, and if seven nurses anoint [their breasts] and nurse a child, then may he not be satisfied, and if seven mares nurse a colt, then may he not be sat[isfied, and if seven] cows nurse a calf, then may he not be satisfied, and if seven ewes nurse a lamb, may he not be satisfied, and if seven....

And if Matiel is false (to Bar-gayah) or to his son or to his offspring, may his kingdom be like a kingdom of sand, a kingdom of sand,[7] as long

---

[1]For the invocation of mountains and heaven and earth as witnesses, cf., e.g., Micah 6:1–2; Deuteronomy 30:19; Isaiah 1:2.

[2]A kingdom north of Syria.
[3]Compare the biblical idiom "to cut [i.e., make] a covenant," although a different word for cutting is used here; see also later, page 103 and n. 4.
[4]Cf. Genesis 14:19, 22.
[5]For the invocation of heaven and earth as witnesses, cf., e.g., Deuteronomy 30:19; Isaiah 1:2.
[6]See earlier, pages 96, 99–100, 101.
[7]The repetition may be a scribal error. On the metaphor, cf. Matthew 7:26.

as Ashur rules. And may Hadad[1] pour out every kind of evil on the earth and in heaven, and every kind of trouble, and may he pour out on Arpad hailstones. And for seven years may the locust eat, and for seven years may the worm eat, and for seven years may…come up on the face of its land. And may grass not come out, so that no green is seen and no pasturage is seen. And may the sound of the lyre not be heard in Arpad,[2] but among its people the groan of affliction and the noise of crying and howling. And may the gods send every kind of devourer against Arpad and against its people. May the mouth of a snake eat, and the mouth of a scorpion, and the mouth of a bear, and the mouth of a panther. May the moth and the louse and…the throat of a serpent. May its pasturage be destroyed, made into a desert. And may Arpad become a tell…for the gazelle and the fox and the hare and the wildcat and the owl…and the magpie. May this city not be spoken of, nor

[other place names follow].

As this wax is burned in fire, so may Arpad and…be burned in fire. May Hadad sow them in salt and weeds, and may it not be spoken of. This…and…are Matiel and his person. As this wax is burned in fire, so may Matiel be burned in fire. And as this bow and these arrows are broken, so may Inurnta[3] and Hadad break the bow of Matiel and the bow of his nobles. And as this man of wax is blinded, so may Matiel be blinded. And as this calf is cut up,[4] so may Matiel be cut up and may his nobles be cut up. And as a prostitute is stripped bare, so may the wives of Matiel and the wives of his offspring and the wives of his nobles be stripped bare….[5]

[The rest of the first stela is badly damaged. It contains stipulations and blessings and concludes with more curses:]

Whoever does not keep the words of the inscription which is on this stela, and says, "I will

erase some of its words," or "I will overturn goodness and make it evil," on the day that he does so, may the gods overturn that man and his house and all that is in it, and may they make its lower part its upper part. And may his root not inherit a name.

[The second stela is badly damaged. Fragments of a third stela contain detailed stipulations:]

…or to your son or to your offspring or to one of the kings of Arpad, and speaks against me, or against my son, or against the son of my son, or against my offspring, likewise any man who burns hot and speaks evil against me…you must [not] accept such words from his hand; you must deliver them into my hands, and your son must deliver them to my son, and your offspring must deliver them to my offspring, and the offspring of any of the kings of Arpad must deliver them to me. Whatever is good in my eyes I will do to them. And if not, then you will be false to all the gods of the treaty which is in this inscription.

Now if a fugitive flees from me, one of my officials, or one of my brothers, or one of my eunuchs,[6] or one of the people who are under my control, and they go to Aleppo, you should not provide food to them, and you should not say to them, "Be still in your place," and you should not stir them up against me. You should placate them and return them to me. And if they do not dwell in your land, placate them there until I come and placate them. And if you stir them up against me, and provide food to them, and say to them, "Be still in your place, and do not return to his place," you will be false to this treaty.

And as for all the kings of my trade network, or anyone who is my ally, if I send my messenger to him for peace or for any of my business, or he sends his messenger to me, the road shall be open to me. You shall not overrule me in this, and you shall not assert authority over me concerning it. And if not, you will be false to this treaty.

And if any one of my brothers, or any one of the house of my father, or any one of my sons, or any one of my officers, or any one of my officials, or any one of the people who are under my

---

[1]The Aramean storm god.
[2]Cf. Ezekiel 26:13.
[3]Aramaic spelling of the name of the Mesopotamian god Ninurta, a god of war.
[4]Cf. Genesis 15:9–10; Jeremiah 34:18.
[5]Cf. Amos 7:17.

[6]Royal officials.

control, or any one of those who hate me, seeks my head to kill me and to kill my son and my offspring—if they kill me, you should come and avenge my blood at the hand of those who hate me. And your son should come and avenge my son's blood from those who hate him. And your son's son should come and avenge the blood of my son's son, and your offspring should come and avenge the blood of my offspring. And if it is a city, you should strike it with a sword. And if it is one of my brothers or one of my slaves or one of my officers or one of the people who are under my control, you should strike him and his offspring and his clan and his friends with a sword. And if not, then you will be false to all the gods of the treaty which is in this inscription.

And if it should arise in your heart and you raise on your lips to put me to death, or if it should arise in the heart of your son's son and he raises it on his lips to put to death my son's son, or if it should arise in the heart of your offspring and he raises it on his lips to put to death my offspring, or if it arises in the heart of the kings of Arpad, in whatever way a mortal[1] dies, you will be false to all the gods of the treaty which is in this inscription.

And if my son, who sits on my throne, quarrels with one of his brothers, or banishes him, you shall not send your tongue between them and say to him, "Kill your brother, or imprison him and do not release him." But if you make peace between them, he will not kill and he will not imprison. But if you do not make peace between them, you will be false to this treaty.

As for the kings of my trade network, if a fugitive of mine flees to one of them, or a fugitive of theirs flees and comes to me, if he has returned mine, I will return his and you should not prevent me. And if not, you will be false to this treaty.

You shall not send your tongue against my house or the sons of my sons or the sons of my brothers or the sons of my offspring or the sons of my people, and say to them: "Kill your lord and be his successor! For he is not better than you." Someone will avenge my blood. And if you do act treacherously against me or against my sons or against my offspring, you will be false to all the gods of the treaty which is in this inscription.

[The rest of the surviving part of the third stela concludes with a broken section about an unknown territory called Talayim and about bribery.]

MESOPOTAMIA

49. TREATY BETWEEN ASHUR-NIRARI V AND MATIEL

Matiel, the king of Arpad (see Text 48), is also the vassal in a partially preserved treaty with the Assyrian king Ashur-nirari V (ruled ca. 754–745 BCE). Some scholars think that this is the same ruler called Bar-gayah, king of KTK in Text 48; the two texts are similar in content.[2]

... May his land be reduced to a wasteland, may only an area of the size of a brick be left for him to stand upon, may nothing be left for his sons ... and the people of his land to stand upon. May Matiel ... together with the people of his land, be crushed like gypsum.

This spring lamb has not been brought out of its fold for sacrifice, nor for a banquet, nor for a purchase, nor for divination concerning a sick man, nor to be slaughtered ... : it has been brought to conclude the treaty of Ashur-nirari, king of Assyria, with Matiel. If Matiel sins against this sworn treaty, then, just as this spring lamb has been brought from its fold and will not return to its fold and not behold its fold again, so may, alas, Matiel, together with his sons, daughters, magnates, and the people of his land be ousted from his country, not return to his country, and not behold his country again.

This head is not the head of a spring lamb, it is the head of Matiel, it is the head of his sons, his magnates, and the people of his land. If Matiel should sin against this treaty, so may, just as the head of this spring lamb is cut off, and its knuckle placed in its mouth, ... the head of Matiel be cut off, and his sons. ...

This shoulder is not the shoulder of a spring lamb, it is the shoulder of Matiel, it is the shoulder of his sons. ... If Matiel should sin

---

[1]Literally, "son of man."

[2]Translation by Simo Parpola and Kazuko Watanabe, *Neo-Assyrian Treaties and Loyalty Oaths* (Helsinki: Helsinki University Press, 1988), 8–9, 11–12.

against this treaty, so may, just as the shoulder of this spring lamb is torn out . . . the shoulder of Matiel, of his son, his magnates, and the people of his land be torn out. . . .

If the Assyrian army goes to war at the orders of Ashur-nirari, king of Assyria, and Matiel, together with his magnates, his forces, and his chariotry, does not go forth in full loyalty, may Sin,[1] the great lord who dwells in Harran, clothe Matiel, his sons, his magnates, and the people of his land in leprosy like a cloak; may they have to roam the open country; and may there be no mercy for them. May there be no more dung of oxen, asses, sheep, and horses in his land.

May Adad,[2] the canal inspector of heaven and earth, put an end to Matiel's land, and the people of his land through hunger, want, and famine; may they eat the flesh of their sons and daughters, and may it taste as good to them as the flesh of spring lambs. May they be deprived of Adad's thunder so that rain become forbidden to them. May dust be their food, pitch their ointment, donkey urine their drink, papyrus their clothing, and may their sleeping place be in the dung heap.

If Matiel, his sons, or his magnates sin against this treaty of Ashur-nirari, king of Assyria, may his farmers not sing the harvest song in the fields, may no vegetation spring forth in the open country and see the sunlight, may women fetching water not draw water from the springs . . . .

If our death is not your death, if our life is not your life, if you do not seek the life of Ashur-nirari, his sons, and his magnates as your own life and the life of your sons and officials, then may Ashur,[3] father of the gods, who grants kingship, turn your land into a battlefield, your people to devastation, your cities into mounds,[4] and your house into ruins.

If Matiel sins against this treaty with Ashur-nirari, king of Assyria, may Matiel become a prostitute, his soldiers women, may they receive (a gift) in the square of their cities like any prostitute,[5] may one country push them to the next; may

Matiel's (sex) life be that of a mule, his wives extremely old; may Ishtar,[6] the goddess of men, the lady of women, take away their bow, bring them to shame, and make them bitterly weep: "Woe, we have sinned against the treaty of Ashur-nirari, king of Assyria."

[*More curses and a list of gods follow.*]

50. TREATY BETWEEN ESAR-HADDON, KING OF ASSYRIA, AND BAAL, KING OF TYRE

A fragmentary treaty from the early seventh century BCE, which describes the maritime trade of the Phoenician city of Tyre; compare Ezekiel 27. It includes the following stipulations and curses:[7]

If there is a ship of Baal or the people of Tyre that is shipwrecked off the land of the Philistines or within Assyrian territory, everything that is on the ship belongs to Esar-haddon, king of Assyria; however, one must not do any harm to any person on board the ship but must return them all to their country.

These are the ports of trade and the trade routes which Esar-haddon, king of Assyria, entrusted to his servant Baal: to Akko, Dor, to the entire district of the Philistines, and to all the cities within Assyrian territory on the seacoast, and to Byblos, the Lebanon, all the cities in the mountains, all these being cities of Esar-haddon, king of Assyria. . . .

May the great gods of heaven and earth, the gods of Assyria, the gods of Akkad and the gods of Eber-nari[8] curse you with an indissoluble curse.

May Baal-shamaim, Baal-malage, and Baal of Zaphon raise an evil wind against your ships to undo their moorings and tear out their mooring pole, may a strong wave sink them in the sea and a violent tide rise against you.

May Melqart and Eshmun deliver your land to destruction and your people to deportation; may they uproot you from your land and take away the

---

[1] The moon god.
[2] The storm god.
[3] The principal god of Assyria.
[4] Literally, "tells"; cf. Deuteronomy 13:17; Joshua 8:28; Jeremiah 49:2.
[5] Cf. Ezekiel 16:23–25.

[6] The principal goddess of Assyria.
[7] Translation by Simo Parpola and Kazuko Watanabe, *Neo-Assyrian Treaties and Loyalty Oaths* (Helsinki: Helsinki University Press, 1988), 25–26.
[8] The Assyrian province of "Beyond the (Euphrates) River."

food from your mouth, the clothes from your body, and the oil for your anointing,

May Astarte break your bow in the thick of battle and have you crouch at the feet of your enemy, may a foreign enemy divide your belongings.

Tablet of the treaty established with Baal of Tyre....

51. THE VASSAL TREATIES OF ESAR-HADDON

Several versions of this treaty have been found. In them, the Assyrian king Esar-haddon (ruled ca. 681–669 BCE) requires various subject kings to the east of Assyria to recognize Ashurbanipal as his successor. They include the most detailed curses of any surviving ancient treaties, curses that have been compared to those in Leviticus 26 and especially Deuteronomy 28.[1]

The treaty of Esar-haddon, king of the world, king of Assyria, son of Sennacherib, likewise king of the world, king of Assyria, with Humbaresh, city-ruler of Nahshimarti,[2] his sons, his grandsons, with all the Nahshimartians, the men in his hands, young and old, as many as there are from sunrise to sunset, all those over whom Esar-haddon, king of Assyria, exercises kingship and lordship, with you, your sons, and your grandsons who will be born in the days to come after this treaty, concerning Ashurbanipal, the great crown prince designate, son of Esar-haddon, king of Assyria, on behalf of whom he has concluded this treaty with you, in the presence of Jupiter, Venus, Saturn, Mercury, Mars, and Sirius; in the presence of Ashur, Anu, Enlil, Ea, Sin, Shamash, Adad, Marduk, Nabu, Nusku, Urash, Nergal, Mullissu, Sherua, Belit-ili, Ishtar of Nineveh, Ishtar of Arbela, the gods dwelling in heaven and earth, the gods of Assyria, the gods of Sumer and Akkad, all the gods of the lands.

[*There follows another list of gods, by whom the vassal is to swear.*]

This is the treaty which Esar-haddon, king of Assyria, has concluded with you, in the presence of the great gods of heaven and earth, on behalf of Ashurbanipal, the great crown prince designate, son of Esar-haddon, your lord, whom he has named and appointed to the crown-princeship.

When Esar-haddon passes away, you will seat Ashurbanipal, the great crown prince designate, upon the royal throne, and he will exercise the kingship and lordship of Assyria over you. You shall protect him in country and in town, fall and die for him. You shall speak with him in the truth of your heart, give him sound advice loyally, and smooth his way in every respect.

You shall not depose him nor seat anyone of his brothers, elder or younger, on the throne of Assyria instead of him.

You shall neither change nor alter the word of Esar-haddon, king of Assyria, but serve this very Ashurbanipal, the great crown prince designate, whom Esar-haddon, king of Assyria, your lord, has presented to you, and he shall exercise the kingship and dominion over you.

You shall protect Ashurbanipal, the great crown prince designate, whom Esar-haddon, king of Assyria, has presented and ordered for you, and on behalf of whom he has confirmed and concluded this treaty with you; you shall not sin against him, nor bring your hand against him with evil intent, nor revolt or do anything to him which is not good and proper; you shall not oust him from the kingship of Assyria by helping one of his brothers, elder or younger, to seize the throne of Assyria in his stead, nor set any other king or any other lord over yourselves, not swear an oath to any other king or any other lord.

If you hear any improper, unsuitable, or unseemly word concerning the exercise of kingship which is unseemly and evil against Ashurbanipal, the great crown prince designate, either from the mouth of his brothers, his uncles, his cousins, his family, members of his father's line; or from the mouth of magnates and governors, or from the mouth of the bearded and the eunuchs,[3] or from the mouth of any human being at all, you shall not conceal it but come and report it to Ashurbanipal, the great crown prince designate.

[1]Translation by Simo Parpola and Kazuko Watanabe, *Neo-Assyrian Treaties and Loyalty Oaths* (Helsinki: Helsinki University Press, 1988), 28–32, 33, 45–46, 48–49, 58.
[2]A city in Media, east of Assyria.

[3]Different ranks of royal officials.

If Esar-haddon, king of Assyria, passes away while his sons are minors, you will help Ashurbanipal, the great crown prince designate, to take the throne of Assyria, and you will help Shamash-shumu-ukin, his equal brother, the crown prince designate of Babylon, to ascend the throne of Babylon. You will reserve for him the kingship over the whole of Sumer, Akkad, and Karduniash.[1] He will take with him all the gifts that Esar-haddon, king of Assyria, his father, gave him; do not hold back even one....

If you hear any evil, improper, ugly word which is not seemly or good to Ashurbanipal, the great crown prince designate, son of Esar-haddon, king of Assyria, your lord, either from the mouth of his enemy or from the mouth of his ally, or from the mouth of his brothers or from the mouth of his uncles, his cousins, his family, members of his father's line, or from the mouth of your brothers, your sons, your daughters, or from the mouth of a prophet, an ecstatic, an inquirer of oracles, or from the mouth of any human being at all, you shall not conceal it but come and report it to Ashurbanipal, the great crown prince designate, son of Esar-haddon, king of Assyria.

[*Many more provisions describe in repetitious language any type of disloyalty to Ashurbanipal and forbid any alteration to the treaty. The curses follow:*]

May Ashur, king of the gods, who decrees the fates, decree an evil and unpleasant fate for you. May he not grant you long-lasting old age and the attainment of extreme old age.

May Mullissu, his beloved wife, make the utterance of his mouth evil, may she not intercede for you.

May Anu, king of the gods, let disease, exhaustion, malaria, sleeplessness, worries, and ill health rain upon all your houses.

May Sin,[2] the brightness of heaven and earth, clothe you with leprosy and forbid your entering into the presence of the gods or king. Roam the desert like the wild ass and the gazelle!

May Shamash,[3] the light of heaven and earth, not judge you justly. May he remove your eyesight. Walk about in darkness!

May Ninurta,[4] the foremost among the gods, fell you with his fierce arrow; may he fill the plain with your blood and feed your flesh to the eagle and the vulture.

May Venus, the brightest of the stars, before your eyes make your wives lie in the lap of your enemy; may your sons not take possession of your house, but a strange enemy divide your goods.

May Jupiter, exalted lord of the gods, not show you the entrance of Bel in Esagila; may he destroy your life.

May Marduk, the eldest son,[5] decree a heavy punishment and an indissoluble curse for your fate.

May Sarpanitu,[6] who grants name and seed, destroy your name and your seed from the land.

May Belet-ili,[7] the lady of creation, cut off birth from your land; may she deprive your nurses of the cries of little children in the streets and squares.

May Adad,[8] the canal inspector of heaven and earth, cut off seasonal flooding from your land and deprive your fields of grain, may he submerge your land with a great flood; may the locust who diminishes the land devour your harvest; may the sound of mill or oven be lacking from your houses, may the grain for grinding disappear from you; instead of grain may your sons and your daughters grind your bones; nay not even your first finger-joint dip in the dough, may the...of your bowls eat up the dough. May a mother bar the door to her daughter. In your hunger eat the flesh of your sons! In want and famine may one man eat the flesh of another; may one man clothe himself in another's skin; may dogs and swine eat your flesh; may your ghost have nobody to take care of the pouring of libations to him.

May Ishtar, lady of battle and war, smash your bow in the thick of battle, may she bind your arms, and have you crouch under your enemy.

---

[1]A name for Babylonia.
[2]The moon god.

[3]The sun god, and the god of justice; see page 86.
[4]A warrior god.
[5]Marduk, the chief god of Babylon (see Texts 1 and 41 [prologue]), was the oldest son of Ea.
[6]Marduk's goddess wife.
[7]The birth goddess.
[8]A storm god.

May Nergal,[1] hero of the gods, extinguish your life with his merciless sword, and send slaughter and pestilence among you.

May Mullissu,[2] who dwells in Nineveh, tie a flaming sword at your side.

May Ishtar, who dwells in Arbela, not show you mercy and compassion.

May Gula, the great physician, put sickness and weariness in your hearts and an unhealing wound in your body. Bathe in blood and pus as if in water!

May the Pleiades, the heroic gods, massacre you with their fierce weapons.

May Aramish[3] . . . .

May Bethel and Anat-bethel[4] hand you over to the paws of a man-eating lion.

May Kubaba, the goddess of Carchemish, put a serious venereal disease within you; may your urine drip to the ground like raindrops.

May all the great gods of heaven and earth who inhabit the universe and are mentioned by name in this tablet, strike you, look at you in anger, uproot you from among the living and curse you grimly with a painful curse. Above, may they take possession of your life; below, in the netherworld, may they make your ghost thirst for water. May shade and daylight always chase you away, and may you not find refuge in a hidden corner. May food and water abandon you; may want and famine, hunger and plague never be removed from you. Before your very eyes man dogs and swine drag the teats of your young women and the penises of your young men to and fro in the squares of Ashur; may the earth not receive your corpses but may your burial place be in the belly of a dog or a pig. May your days be dark and hour years dim, may darkness which is not to be brightened be declared as your fate. May your life end in exhaustion and sleeplessness. May an irresistible flood come up from the earth and devastate you; may anything good be forbidden to you, anything ill be your share; may tar and pitch be your food; may the urine of an ass be your drink, may naphtha be your ointment, may duckweed be your covering. May demon, devil, and evil spirit select your houses.

[*The text continues with the vassal's acceptance of the stipulations, followed by another set of curses. It concludes with the date (May 672 BCE) and this colophon:*]

18th day of Iyyar, eponymy of Nabu-bel-usur, governor of Dur-Sharruku. The treaty of Esar-haddon, king of Assyria, concluded on behalf of Ashurbanipal, the great crown prince designate of Assyria, and Shamash-shum-ukin, the crown prince designate of Babylon.

CONTRACTS

THE MANY PRIVATE contracts known from ancient sources are very similar. Here are some of particular interest for biblical interpretation.

52. MURASHU TABLET

Dating to the mid-fifth century BCE are the records of a banking firm in Nippur in Babylonia comprising several hundred tablets written in Babylonian. In the text that follows, as in others in the archive, several of the principals and witnesses have Jewish names, descendants of those exiled to Babylonia in the early sixth century.

Yadiyaw, the son of Banael; Yahunatan, Shamaon, and Ahiyaw, the sons of Yadiyaw; Satur, the son of Shabbatai; Baniya, the son of Amel-nana; Yigdalyaw, the son of Nana-iddin; Abda, the son of Apla; Nattun, the son of Shillim; and all their partners in Bit-gira; spoke freely to Ellil-shum-iddin, the son of Murashu, as follows:

"Rent to us for three years the Mares' Canal, from its inlet up to its outlet, and the tithed field which is on this canal, and the field which is to the left of the Milidu Canal, and the three marshes which are to the right of the Milidu Canal, except the field which drinks its waters from the Ellil Canal; and we will give you annually 700 *kur*[5] of barley according to the standard measure of Ellil-shum-iddin, and, as an annual gift, 2 grazing bulls and 20 grazing rams."

---

[1] A god of war, plague, and the underworld.
[2] A title of the goddess Ishtar.
[3] An obscure north Syrian deity.
[4] Deities also known from the Elephantine texts.

---

[5] A *kur* (cf. biblical "cor") was ca. four bushels.

Witnesses: Ninaku, dependent of Zatame; Ninib-nadin and Ellil-nadin-shum, sons of Ninib-eriba; Ardi-Ellil, son of Shuruktu-Ninib; Apla, son of Bel-balatsu-iqbi; El-zabad, son of Apla; Pilliyaw, son of Shillim; Minyamin, son of Baniya; Danna, son of Iddina; Shum-iddina, son of Adanu/Tattanu; Nushku-nadin, the scribe, son of Ardi-Gula.

Nippur, month of Ab, day 20, year 36[1] of Artaxerxes, king of the lands.

ELEPHANTINE PAPYRI

Several hundred papyri written in Aramaic give us a detailed look at a Jewish settlement at Elephantine, an island in the Nile in southern Egypt, called Yeb in the papyri. Elephantine was opposite the town called Syene (cf. Ezekiel 29:10; 30:6), a name preserved in modern Arabic as Aswan. The texts date to the second half of the fifth century BCE. (For other texts from Elephantine, see Texts 88, 91–93, and 195.)

53. MARRIAGE CONTRACT

In this text, Ananiah, a Jew in Elephantine, contracts to marry a slave-woman owned by Meshullam.

On the 18 of Ab [which is day 30 of] the month of Pharmouthi, in the year 16 of Artaxerxes the king,[2] Ananiah, son of Azariah, official of Yaho[3] the god who is in the fortress Yeb, spoke to Meshullam, son of Zakkur, an Aramean of Syene, of the detachment[4] of Varyazata, saying: "I have come to you to give me the woman named Tamet, your slave-woman, as a wife. She is my wife and I am her husband from this day and forever.[5] Tamet has brought me in her hand; 1 garment of wool, worth 7 shekels[6] of silver; 1 mirror, worth 7 and a half *hallurs*[7] of silver; 1 pair of sandals; 1 half cup of balsam oil; 6 cups of castor oil; 1 tray. All the silver and the value of the goods in silver is 7 shekels, 7 and a half *hallurs* of silver.

If tomorrow or a following day Anani should rise in the assembly and say, "I hate Tamet my wife,"[8] silver of hatred is on his head. He will give to Tamet 7 shekels of silver, and she will take out all that she brought in her hand, from straw to string. If tomorrow or a following day Tamet should rise and say: "I hate my husband Anani," silver of hatred is on her head. She will give to Anani 7 shekels of silver, but she will take out all that she brought in her hand, from straw to string. If tomorrow or on a following day Anani should die, Tamet will have control of all the goods which are between Anani and Tamet. If tomorrow or on a following day Tamet should die, Anani will have control over all the goods which are between Tamet and Anani.

And I, Meshullam, tomorrow or on a following day, will not be able to take Palti[9] away from under your heart, unless you expel his mother Tamet. And if I do take him away from you, I will give to Anani silver, 5 *karsh*.[10]

Nathan, son of Ananiah, wrote this document. And the witnesses thereto: Witness Nathan, son of Gaddul; Menahem, son of Zakkur; Gemariah, son of Mahseiah.

Tamet brought in her hand to Anani silver, 1 *karsh*, 5 shekels.[11]

Document of wife[hood which Anani wrote for Ta]met.[12]

54. TRANSFER OF REAL ESTATE FROM ANANIAH TO TAMET

In this letter, Ananiah transfers title of part of a house to his wife Tamet (see Text 53).

On the 25 of Tishri, which is day 25 of the month of Epeiph, in the year 31 of Artaxerxes the king,[13] Ananiah, son of Azariah, official of Yaho[14]

---

[1]429 BCE.

[2]449 BCE.

[3]An alternate spelling of the divine name Yahweh.

[4]Elephantine was a military colony.

[5]Cf. Hosea 2:16–20; contrast 2:2.

[6]A shekel weighed ca. 0.35 ounce (10 grams).

[7]A *hallur* was worth 1/40 of a shekel.

[8]A technical term connected with divorce; cf. Deuteronomy 22:13, 16; 24:3; Judges 15:2; Isaiah 60:15.

[9]Apparently the son of Tamet and Ananiah, who would have been considered Meshullam's property.

[10]A *karsh* was worth ten shekels.

[11]This line, written on the back of the document, is an addendum or correction.

[12]This line is a docket, or summary of the contents, which would have been visible on the outside of the rolled papyrus text.

[13]434 BCE.

[14]An alternate spelling of the divine name Yahweh.

the god who is in the fortress Yeb, spoke to the woman Tamet, his wife, saying:

"I give to you half of the large room and the chamber of the house which I bought from Ubil, daughter of Shatibara and from Bagazushta, Caspians of the fortress Yeb. I, Ananiah, give it to you in love. It is yours from today forever, and it is your children's whom you bore to me, after you.

And these are the dimensions of that house which I, Ananiah, give to you, Tamet:

From half of the large room and the chamber, from top to bottom: 11 cubits[1] by the measuring rod.

In width in cubits, from east to west: 7 cubits 1 h(and) by the measuring rod.

In area: 81 cubits.

Built is the lower (part of the) house, new, with beams and windows.

These are the boundaries of the house which I am giving to you:

Above it my—Ananiah's—portion is attached to it.

Below it, the temple of Yaho the god, and the street of the king between them.

To its east is the district of Khnum the god, and the street of the king is between them.

To its west the house of Shatibara, a Caspian, is attached to it.

This is the portion of the house whose measurements are written and whose boundaries. I, Ananiah, give it to you in love.

I, Ananiah, will not be able to bring suit against you in this matter. Moreover, neither will a son of mine or a daughter or a brother or a sister be able to sue you with regard to this house. And if I sue you with regard to this house, I will be required to give you silver, 5 karsh,[2] that is, five by the king's weight, silver, 2 q(uarters) to 1 karsh, and with no suit. And if another person brings suit against you, he will give you silver, 20 karsh, and the house is still yours.

But if you die at the age of 100 years,[3] my children, whom you bore to me, they will have control over it after your death. Moreover, if I, Anani, die at the age of 100 years, Palti and Yehoyishma, my two children, they will have control over my other portion, I, Anani. Another person—my mother or my father or another man—will not have control over the house, all of it, but only my children whom you bore to me. And a person who would take away my house after my death from Palti and Yehoyishma will give them silver, 10 karsh, by the king's weight, 2 q(uarters) to 1 karsh, and my house is theirs moreover, and there will be no suit.

Mauziah, son of Nathan, wrote at the dictation of Ananiah, son of Azariah, the (temple-) official. And the witnesses thereto: Gemariah, son of Mahseiah; Hoshaiah, son of Yathom; Mithrasarah, the Magian; Tata, the Magian.

Document of a house which Ananiah wrote for Tamet, his wife.

55. DOCUMENT OF MANUMISSION

In this text, Meshullam (see Text 53) promised that on his death his slave woman Tapmet[4] and their daughter Yehoyishma would be set free.

On the 20 of Siwan, which is the 7 of Phamenoth, in the year 38 of Artaxerxes the king:[5]

At that time Meshullam, son of Zakkur, a Jew of the fortress Yeb, of the detachment of Arpahu, spoke to the woman named Tapmet, his slave-woman, who has a mark on her right hand, like this: "Belonging to Meshullam,"[6] saying: "I have thought of you during my life. For freedom I have released you at my death, and I have released your daughter named Yehoyishma, whom you bore to me. My son or daughter, or my brother or sister, a close or distant relative, or a partner, or an associate, will not have control over you or over your daughter Yehoyishma, whom you bore to me. Such a person will not have control over you, to mark you or to sell you for payment of silver. Whoever rises against you or against your daughter Yehoyishma, whom you bore to me, he should give you a fine of silver, 50 karsh[7] by the king's weight,

---

[1]A cubit was ca. 18 inches (44 cm).
[2]A karsh weighed ca. 3.5 ounces (100 grams).
[3]Probably expressing the wish for a long life; it may have been bad luck to give a realistic age.

[4]Apparently an alternate spelling of Tamet (see Texts 53 and 54).
[5]427 BCE.
[6]As a slave, Tapmet was branded.
[7]A karsh weighed ca. 3.5 ounces (10 grams).

and you are released from shadow to the sun,[1] along with Yehoyishma, your daughter. No other man will have control over you or your daughter Yehoyishma, for you are released to the god."[2]

And Tapmet and her daughter say: "We will serve you as a son or a daughter provides for his father during your life and until your death. We will support Zakkur, your son, as a son provides for his father, as we have been serving you during your life. If we rise and say, 'We will not provide for you as a son provides for his father, or for Zakkur, your son, after your death,' we will be liable to you and to Zakkur, your son, a fine of silver, 50 *karsh* by the king's weight, refined silver, and there will be no lawsuit or legal process."

Haggai wrote this document in Yeb, at the dictation of Meshullam, son of Zakkur. And the witnesses thereto: Atrapharna, son of Nisaya, a Mede; witness: Micaiah, son of Ahyo; witness: Berechiah, son of Miphtah; Dallah, son of Gaddul.

Document of relinquishment which Meshullam, son of Zakkur, wrote for Tapmet and Yehoyishma.

COMMERCIAL TRANSACTIONS
SAMARIA OSTRACA

Written on pottery sherds, or ostraca, more than a hundred of these routine receipts were found in fill below the latest layer of occupation at Samaria, the capital of the northern kingdom of Israel, dating to the reign of Jeroboam II (788–747 BCE). Their content is unremarkable, but many of the personal names they contain are identical or similar to ones attested in the Bible (though not of the same individuals).

56. In the tenth year,[3] to Shamaryaw,[4] from Biryam,[5] a jar of (old) wine:

Gara (son of) Elisha, 2;
Uzza (son of) Qad-Bes, 1;
Eliba . . . , 1;
Baala (son of) Elisha, 1;
Yadayaw,[6] 1.

57. In the tenth year, to Gaddiyaw, from Azah:[7]

Abibaal, 2;
Ahaz, 2;
Sheba, 1;
Merib-baal, 1.

58. In the tenth year, from Sepher, to Gaddiyaw, a jar of fine[8] oil.

59. Baruch, greetings! . . .
Baruch, the shepherds paid attention . . .
3 (measures of) barley are to be counted . . . .

TELL QASILE OSTRACA

These ostraca, found at Tell Qasile near Tel Aviv, date to the late eighth century BCE.

60. Belonging to the king[9]: A thousand (measures of) oil and a hundred. (A)hiyahu.

61. Gold of Ophir[10] for Beth-horon,[11] sh(ekels) 30.[12]

ARAD OSTRACA

Excavations at this southern Judean site east of Beer-sheba uncovered nearly a hundred ostraca, written in ink on potsherds, and mostly dating to the late seventh or early sixth century BCE. More than a dozen are addressed to Elyashib, an official in the city (see also Text 72g), and concern allocation of supplies from Arad, at that time apparently a large fortress. The following are typical examples.

62. To Elyashib:
And now, give to the Kittim[13] wine: b(ath)[14] 3; and write the name of the day.[15]

---

[1] An obscure phrase, perhaps meaning "from slavery to freedom."
[2] Or "to God."
[3] I.e., 779 BCE.
[4] Biblical Shemariah.
[5] The location of this town is unknown.
[6] Biblical Jedaiah

[7] A town near Samaria.
[8] Literally, "washed."
[9] I.e., according to the royal measure. Alternatively, "For the king."
[10] Cf. 1 Chronicles 29:4; Sirach 7:18; see also 1 Kings 9:28; 22:48; Isaiah 13:12; Psalm 45:9; Job 22:24; 28:16. Ophir, most likely in southern Arabia (cf. Genesis 10:29), was a source of especially fine gold.
[11] Either for the temple (*beth*) of the god Horon or for delivery to the town of Beth-horon, north of Jerusalem.
[12] A shekel weighed ca. 0.35 ounces (10 grams).
[13] Probably Greek mercenaries.
[14] A bath was ca. 6 gallons (23 liters).
[15] Ezekiel 24:2.

And from the rest of the best flour, you should load 1 measure to make bread for them. From the wine of the mixing bowls you should give.

63. To Elyashib:

And now, give to the Kittim b(ath) 2 of wine for the four days...and 300 (loaves of) bread. And fill the homer[1] of wine and hand it over tomorrow—do not delay! And if there is still vinegar, then you should give it to them.

64. To Elyashib:

And now, give from the wine 3 b(aths). Now Hananyahu has commanded you to Beer-sheba with the load of a yoke of donkeys, and you should pack them with dough. And count the wheat and the bread and take for yourself....

Your brother Hananyahu sends greetings to Elyashib and to your house. I bless you by Yahweh.

And now: When I left your house, I sent the silver, 8 sh(ekels),[2] to the sons of Gaalyahu....

65. To my lord Elyashib:

May Yahweh seek your welfare!

And now, give to Shemaryahu ½ (measure), and to the Kerosite[3] you should give 1 (measure).

And as for the matter about which you commanded me, it is well. He is staying in the house of Yahweh.[4]

INSCRIBED JARS

Jars used for storing and transporting wine, oil, and other commodities were frequently inscribed or sealed to indicate their contents, volume, origin, or destination.

66. FROM HAZOR, MID-EIGHTH CENTURY BCE

To Peqah. Semadar.[5]

67. FROM LACHISH, EIGHTH CENTURY BCE

An indication of volume, according to the royal standard.

bath,[6] (according) to the king

68. FROM BEER-SHEBA, EIGHTH CENTURY BCE

Half(-measure), (according) to the king

69. FROM LACHISH, LATE SEVENTH OR EARLY SIXTH CENTURY BCE

Juice of black raisins

70. ROYAL (LMLK) JAR HANDLES

About two thousand jar handles stamped with a royal seal (either a four-winged scarab or a two-winged sun disk) and the notation indicating that the jar's contents are measured by the royal standard or that they are crown property. These date from the late eighth century BCE and are found mainly at sites in Judah. The inscriptions read "(According) to the king" followed by one of four city names: Hebron, Ziph, Socoh, and Mamshit.[7]

71. INSCRIBED HANDLES FROM GIBEON

Some sixty handles with inscriptions were found in excavations at the site of Gibeon (el-Jib), north of Jerusalem, twenty-seven of which include the name of the site (written gb'n). Dating to the early sixth century BCE, they come from the storage area of a functioning winery, and the inscriptions are the ancient equivalent of labels identifying the city and the specific estate from which the wine came. Here is a sample of the best preserved.

    a. Gibeon: Walled-estate[8] of Azaryahu
    b. Gibeon: Walled-estate of Amaryahu

---

[1] A homer was ca. 60 gallons (230 liters).
[2] A shekel weighed ca. 0.35 ounces (10 grams).
[3] Probably a descendant of Keros; see Ezra 2:44; Nehemiah 7:47.
[4] Either the Temple in Jerusalem or a local shrine.
[5] A rare word, occurring in the Bible only in Song of Solomon 2:13, 15; 7:13, where it means "(vine-)blossom." Here it may refer to a variety of grape from which the wine in the jar was made.

[6] A bath was ca. 6 gallons (23 liters).
[7] The vocalization and location of this place are uncertain.
[8] As in French "clos." The reading and interpretation, however, are disputed.

c. Gibeon: Walled-estate of Hananyahu son of Nera.

72. SEALS AND SEAL IMPRESSIONS

Many thousands of seals and seal impressions have been found in both licit and illicit excavations. The seals themselves, usually made of semiprecious stone, were carefully carved in a mirror image so that they left a readable impression. Seals were pierced, either for setting in a ring or for wearing on a cord or chain around the neck (cf. Song of Solomon 8:6). Typically seals contain the name of the owner of a seal and his or her father's names; sometimes a title is added as well. Most of the names occurring on seals and seal impressions are fairly standard; it is notable that some women, presumably upper class, also were able to seal documents in their own names. There are frequently also images on the seals along with the writing.

Seal impressions are found on clay (the only medium likely to survive), both tablets and jars and small lumps of clay (called bullae) attached to a string that wrapped a papyrus text.

Here is a sample of Hebrew seals and seal impressions whose provenance is known.

a. Belonging to Elyakim, servant of Yawkin (impressions of the same seal, dating to the late eighth century BCE, were found at Tell Beit Mirsim, Ramat Rahel, and Beth-shemesh)
b. Belonging to Shema, servant of Jeroboam[1] (from Megiddo, eighth century BCE)
c. Meshullam (son of) Ahimelech (from Lachish, late eighth century BCE)
d. Belonging to Nera (son of) Shebna (from Ramat Rahel, late eighth century BCE)
e. Belonging to Menahem (son of) Yobanah (from Ramat Rahel, late eighth century BCE)
f. Shephatyahu (son of) Asayahu (from Lachish, late eighth century BCE)
g. Belonging to Elyashib, son of Eshyahu (from Arad, late seventh century BCE; three different seals with the same

inscription were found; see also Texts 62–65)
h. Belonging to Yaazanyahu, servant of the king (from Tell en-Nasbeh [ancient Mizpah], ca. 600 BCE)
i. Belonging to Gealyahu, son of the king (from Beth-zur, ca. 600 BCE)
j. Belonging to Jehoaz (son of) Ahab (from Tell es-Safi, ca. 600 BCE)
k. Belonging to Jehocal,[2] son of Shelemiah, son of Shobi (from Jerusalem, early sixth century BCE)
l. Belonging to Gedaliah,[3] son of Pashur (from Jerusalem, early sixth century BCE)

73. WEIGHTS

Hundreds of weights have been found at excavations in Israel and Palestine. While a few are ceramic and metal, most are stone; the word "stone" in the Bible can also mean "weight" (e.g., Proverbs 11:1; 20.23; Micah 6:11). They are identified as weights by inscriptions in hieratic (Egyptian) numerals; just as we use Arabic numerals, Egyptian numerical symbols seem to have been widely used even by non-Egyptian speakers. Occasionally the unit of measurement is also inscribed, either written out in full or, more frequently, abbreviated.

The following units of measurement occur; many are also found in ostraca used as receipts (see Texts 56–65):

a. shekel (*šql*)	ca. 3.5 oz (10 gram)
b. neseph (*nṣp*)	probably $\frac{5}{6}$ shekel (not attested in the Bible)
c. pim (or payim) (*pym*)	$\frac{2}{3}$ shekel (1 Samuel 13.21)
d. beka (*bqʿ*)	$\frac{1}{2}$ shekel (Genesis 24.22; Exodus 38.26)
e. gera	$\frac{1}{20}$ (or $\frac{1}{24}$) shekel (Exodus 30:13; Leviticus 27:25; etc.)

---

[1]Jeroboam II, king of the northern kingdom of Israel, 788–747 BCE.

[2]Almost certainly the same individual mentioned in Jeremiah 37:3.
[3]Almost certainly the same individual mentioned in Jeremiah 38:1.

Sealed Document
A sealed document from Elephantine in Egypt (see page 109), dating to 404 BCE, that illustrates how letters could be sent. The Aramaic text was written on papyrus, then folded, tied with string, and sealed, with a summary of the contexts written on the outside. It is ca. 7.5 inches (30 cm) wide.

5

LETTERS

The invention of writing enabled communication at a distance, and from the third millennium BCE to the present people have corresponded by letters. Some ancient letters are official, from a ruler to his or her subjects, or from one ruler to another. Others are personal, from a private individual to another; many of these were ephemeral and were not meant to be saved.

Letters typically include identification of both the sender and the recipient, as well as opening and closing greetings, which frequently frame the body of the letter, its subject. Some ancient letters also include a date and the name of the scribe who actually wrote the letter down as it was dictated by the sender.

Other compositions that use the letter form are found elsewhere in this book, such as letters to and from the gods (see Texts 95 and 176) and letters concerning prophets (see Texts 171–75).

ROYAL CORRESPONDENCE
74. FROM SUPPILULIUMA I OF HATTI TO NIQMADDU II OF UGARIT

In this letter, dating to the mid-fourteenth century BCE and written in Akkadian, the Hittite king requests the king of Ugarit to attack Nuhashshi and Mukish, vassals of Mitanni that neighbored Ugarit. It anticipates the subsequent treaty between Hatti and Ugarit (see Text 43).[1]

Thus says My Majesty, Great King: Say to Niqmaddu:

While the land of Nuhashshi and the land of Mukish are hostile to me, you, Niqmaddu, shall not fear them. Trust in yourself! As previously your forefathers were at peace with Hatti and not hostile, now you, Niqmaddu, shall thus be hostile to my enemy and at peace with my friend. And if you, Niqmaddu, hear and observe these words of the Great King, your lord, then you shall surely experience the favor which the Great King, your lord, will show to you.

Now you, Niqmaddu, observe the peace treaty with Hatti. In the future you will see how the Great King deals with the kings of the land of Nuhashshi and the king of the land of Mukish, who renounced the peace treaty with Hatti and became hostile to the Great King, their lord. In the future, you, Niqmaddu, must trust in the words of the Great King, your lord.

And if all the kings release whatever troops they have for an attack on your land, you, Niqmaddu, shall not fear them. Send

---

[1]Translation by Gary Beckman, *Hittite Diplomatic Texts* (Atlanta, GA: Scholars Press, 2d ed., 1999), 125–126.

your messenger to me immediately. Let him come!

And if you, Niqmaddu, take the initiative and attack the troops of the land of Nuhashshi or the troops of the land of Mukish by the force of your arms, no one shall take them away from you. Or if perhaps, in the absence of troops of the land of Nuhashshi, the troops of the land of Mukish enter your land as fugitives, no one shall take them from you. Or if perhaps cities of your region somehow become hostile to you, and you do battle with them and defeat them, no one shall later take them away from you. Or if perhaps in the future the Great King defeats these kings, then the Great King will give you a sealed treaty tablet.

75. FROM PIHA-WALWI, A HITTITE ROYAL OFFICIAL, TO IBIRANU, KING OF UGARIT

Dating to the late thirteenth century BCE, this letter, written in Akkadian, reminds the king of Ugarit of his obligations as a vassal (see Text 43).[1]

Thus says Prince Piha-walwi: Say to my son Ibiranu:

At this moment all is well with His Majesty.

Why have you not come before His Majesty since you assumed kingship of the land of Ugarit? And why have you not sent your messengers? Now His Majesty is very angry about this matter. Now send your messengers quickly before His Majesty, and send the king's presents together with my presents.

76. FROM NAPTERA TO PUDU-HEBA

After the peace treaty between Egypt and Hatti in 1259 (see Text 47), cordial relations existed between the two countries, as this letter of the mid-thirteenth century BCE, written in Akkadian, illustrates. It was sent by the wife of Pharaoh Rameses II to the wife of the Hittite king Hattusili III.[2]

Thus says Naptera,[3] Great Queen of Egypt: Say to Pudu-Heba, Great Queen of Hatti, my sister:

I, your sister, am well. My land is well.

May you, my sister, be well! May your land be well! I have heard that you, my sister, wrote to me inquiring about my health, and that you are writing to me in regard to the relationship of good peace and the relationship of good brotherhood which exists between the Great King, the King of Egypt, and the Great King, the King of Hatti, his brother.

The Sun God and the Storm God will exalt you, and the Sun God will cause peace to thrive and will provide good brotherhood forever between the Great King, the King of Egypt, and the Great King, the King of Hatti, his brother. And I am likewise in a condition with peace and brotherhood with you, my sister.

I have now sent you a present as a gift of greeting for you, my sister. And may you, my sister, be informed about the present which I have sent to you in the care of Parihnawa, the messenger of the King:

One very colorful necklace of good gold, made up of twelve strands. Its weight is 88 shekels.[4]
One dyed cloak of byssus.
One dyed tunic of byssus.
Five dyed linen garments of good fine thread.
Five dyed linen tunics of good fine thread.
A grand total of twelve linen garments.

77. FROM RAMESES II TO HATTUSILI III

In this mid-thirteenth-century-BCE letter, written in Akkadian after the establishment of the treaty between Egypt and Hatti (see Text 47), the Pharaoh is replying to a request from the Hittite king for medical help in getting his aging sister pregnant.[5]

---

[1]Translation by Gary Beckman, *Hittite Diplomatic Texts* (Atlanta, GA: Scholars Press, 2d ed., 1999), 127.
[2]Translation by Gary Beckman, *Hittite Diplomatic Texts* (Atlanta, GA: Scholars Press, 2d ed., 1999), 129.
[3]Known in Egyptian sources as Nefertari.
[4]A shekel weighed ca. 0.35 ounce (10 grams).
[5]Translation by Gary Beckman, *Hittite Diplomatic Texts* (Atlanta, GA: Scholars Press, 2d ed., 1999), 137–138.

Thus says Wasumuaria-satepnaria,[1] Great King, King of Egypt, Son of the Sun God, Rameses, Beloved of Amun, Great King, King of Egypt:

Speak to Hattusili, Great King, King of Hatti, my brother:

Now I, the Great King, your brother, am well. May you, my brother, be very well!

Say to my brother: That which my brother wrote to me concerning his sister Matanazzi: "Let my brother send a man to prepare medicines for her, so that she might be caused to give birth." That is what my brother wrote to me.

Say to my brother: Now I, the King, your brother, know about Matanazzi, my brother's sister. She is said to be fifty or sixty years old. It is not possible to prepare medicines for a woman who has completed fifty or sixty years so that she might still be caused to give birth.

O that the Sun God and the Storm God might command, so that the ritual which will be performed will be carried out fully for my brother's sister!

And I, the King, your brother, shall send a competent incantation priest and a competent physician, and they will prepare medicines for her in order that she might give birth.

I have now sent a present to my brother in the care of this messenger:

... cloaks of byssus.
... tunics of byssus.

THE AMARNA LETTERS

This archive of several hundred clay tablets consists largely of correspondence sent during the fourteenth century BCE to Egyptian pharaohs of the Eighteenth Dynasty, especially Akhenaten (Amenophis IV). They were found at the site of Tell el-Amarna, which, under the ancient name Akhetaten, was the capital of Egypt at the time. The senders include kings of such major powers as Babylonia, Assyria, and Hatti and vassals in city-states, such as Byblos, Tyre, Akko, Megiddo, Gezer, Lachish, Shechem, Ashkelon, Damascus, and Jerusalem. The Amarna letters are written in Babylonian cuneiform, the lingua franca of the entire Near East during the second millennium BCE. The following three letters are representative.

78. FROM RIB-HADDA TO THE PHARAOH

In this letter, the ruler of Gubla (biblical Gebal; Byblos), on the Mediterranean coast north of Beirut, asks the Pharaoh for help.[2]

Rib-Hadda says to his lord, king of all countries, Great King, King of Battle: May the Lady of Gubla[3] grant power to the king, my lord. I fall at the feet of my lord, my Sun,[4] 7 times and 7 times.[5] Be informed that since Amanappa[6] reached me, all the Apiru[7] have at the urging of Abdi-Ashirta[8] turned against me. May my lord heed the words of his servant. Send me a garrison to guard the city of the king until the archers come out. If there are no archers, then all lands will be joined to the Apiru. Listen! Since Bit-Arha[9] was seized at the urging of Abdi-Ashirta, they have as a result been striving to take over Gubla and Batruna,[10] and thus all lands would be joined to the Apiru. There are two towns that remain to me, and they want to take them from the king. May my lord send a garrison to his two towns until the archers come out, and may something be given to me for their food. I have nothing at all. Like a bird in a cage,[11] so am I in Gubla. Moreover, if the king is unable to save me from his enemies, then all lands will be joined to Abdi-Ashirta. What is he, the dog,[12] that he takes the lands of the king for himself?

---

[1] The Akkadian transcription of two of Rameses's titles (Egyptian "Uset-maat-re Setepen-re").

[2] Translation by William L. Moran, *The Amarna Letters* (Baltimore, MD: Johns Hopkins University Press, 1992), 149 (EA 79).
[3] The goddess of Byblos, probably Athirat (biblical Asherah).
[4] A title of the kings of Egypt.
[5] Cf. Genesis 33:3.
[6] An Egyptian official.
[7] A socioeconomic group on the fringes of society that frequently caused problems for the rulers of the city-states of the Levant and refused to accept Egyptian authority. The earlier identification of the Apiru with the "Hebrews" of the Bible is now questioned.
[8] The ruler of Amurru in northwestern Syria.
[9] Location unknown.
[10] A town ca. 12 miles (20 km) north of Byblos.
[11] See Text 34, page 8.
[12] Cf. 1 Samuel 17:43; 2 Samuel 16:19; 2 Kings 8:13.

79. FROM LABAYU, THE RULER OF SHECHEM, TO THE PHARAOH[1]

To the king, my lord and my Sun:[2] Thus Labayu, your servant and the dirt on which you tread. I fall at the feet of the king my lord and my Sun, 7 times and 7 times.[3] I have obeyed the orders that the king wrote to me. Who am I that the king should lose his land on account of me? The fact is that I am a loyal servant of the king! I am not a rebel and I am not delinquent in duty. I have not held back my payments of tribute; I have not held back anything requested by my commissioner. He denounces me unjustly, but the king, my lord, does not examine my (alleged) act of rebellion. Moreover, when I entered Gazru,[4] I kept on saying, "Everything of mine the king takes, but what belongs to Milkilu?"[5] I know the actions of Milkilu against me! Moreover, the king wrote for my son. I did not know that my son was consorting with the Apiru.[6] I herewith hand him over to Addaya.[7] Moreover, how, if the king wrote for my wife, how could I hold her back? How, if the king wrote to me, "Put a bronze dagger in your heart and die," how could I not execute the order of the king?

80. FROM ABDI-HEBA, THE RULER OF JERUSALEM, TO THE PHARAOH[8]

Say to the king, my lord: Message of Abdi-Heba, your servant. I fall at the feet of the king, my lord, 7 times and 7 times.[9] Here is the deed against the land that Milkilu[10] and Shuardatu[11] did: against the land of the king, my lord, they ordered troops from Gazru,[12] troops from Gimtu,[13] and troops

from Qiltu. They seized Rubutu. The land of the king deserted to the Apiru.[14] And now, besides this, a town belonging to Jerusalem, Bit-Ninurta[15] by name, a city of the king, has gone over to the side of the men of Qiltu. May the king give heed to Abdi-Heba, your servant, and send archers to restore the land of the king to the king. If there are no archers, the land of the king will desert to the Apiru. This deed against the land was at the order of Milkilu and at the order of Shuardatu, together with Ginti. So may the king provide for his land.

81. FROM A ROYAL OFFICIAL TO KING ASHURBANIPAL

In this letter the writer asks the Assyrian king Ashurbanipal (ruled 669–627 BCE) for a position at court for his son, Urad-Gula. The letter is noteworthy because in flattering the king, he identifies him as the source of national prosperity (cf. Psalm 72).[16]

To the king my lord, from your servant Adad-shuma-usur. May it be well with the king my lord; may Nabu and Marduk bestow ever so many blessings upon the king my lord.

Ashur, king of the gods, nominated the king my lord for the kingship of the land of Assyria; Adad and Shamash have confirmed to the king my lord, through their truthful extispicy, the kingship of all lands.

The reign is propitious, truthful the days, the years are of justice. Rainfall is plentiful, spring floods surging, the economy is excellent. The gods are well disposed, there is much reverence for the divine, temples are prosperous, the great gods of heaven and the netherworld have been prayed to in the time of the king my lord. Old men dance, young men sing, women and girls are happy and joyful, women are being married and rings set upon them, they bear boys and girls, the newborn thrive.

The king my lord has given new life to the malefactor and the man condemned to death; you have released the man imprisoned for years; the

---

[1]Translation by William L. Moran, *The Amarna Letters* (Baltimore, MD: Johns Hopkins University Press, 1992), 307 (EA 254).

[2]A title of the kings of Egypt.

[3]Cf. Genesis 33:3.

[4]Biblical Gezer, ca. 35 miles (55 km) southwest of Shechem.

[5]The ruler of Gazru.

[6]See page 17, n. 7.

[7]The Egyptian commissioner.

[8]Translation by William L. Moran, *The Amarna Letters* (Baltimore, MD: Johns Hopkins University Press, 1992), 334 (EA 290).

[9]Cf. Genesis 33:3.

[10]The ruler of Gazru.

[11]The ruler of Qiltu (biblical Keilah), ca. 12 miles (20 km) southwest of Jerusalem.

[12]Biblical Gezer, ca. 20 miles (32 km) west-northwest of Jerusalem.

[13]Biblical Gath, ca. 25 miles (40 km) west-southwest of Jerusalem.

[14]See page 17, n. 7.

[15]Location unknown.

[16]Translation by Benjamin R. Foster, *Before the Muses: An Anthology of Akkadian Literature* (Bethesda, MD: CDL Press, 3d ed., 2005), 1015–1016.

man sick for many days has revived. The hungry are filled, the parched anointed, the naked clothed in a garment.[1]

Why should I and Urad-Gula, in the midst of them, be glum and downcast? Now the king my lord has displayed his love for Nineveh to the people, saying to the principal citizen: "Bring me your sons; let them be in my service." Urad-Gula is my son; he too should be with them in the service of the king my lord. We too should be joyful and dance along with the people and bless the king my lord.

My eyes dwell upon the king my lord. Of all those who serve in the palace, no one cares about me; there is no one of goodwill to me to whom I could give a present, who would accept it and take my part.

May the king my lord take pity upon his servant! Among all those people, may I not perish. May my ill-wishers not have what they look for!

82. FROM ADON, KING OF EKRON, TO PHARAOH NECO II

In this incomplete text, found at Saqqarah in Egypt, the writer asks for assistance to face the threat of an invasion by the Babylonians. It was written in Aramaic on papyrus, about 604 BCE, shortly before the Babylonian destruction of Ekron, a city ca. 22 miles (35 km) west of Jerusalem. The end of the letter is broken. (See also Text 37.)

To the lord of kings, Pharaoh; your servant Adon, king of Ekron. May the gods of the heavens and the earth, and Baal-shamayin,[2] the great god, seek the welfare of Pharaoh, the lord of kings, abundantly at all times, and may they lengthen the days of Pharaoh like the days of the heavens.... [The army of] the king of Babylon[3] has come and reached Aphek.[4]...For the lord of kings, Pharaoh, knows that your servant...to send troops to rescue me. Let him not abandon [me].... Your servant has kept his treaty obligations....

CORRESPONDENCE BETWEEN OFFICIALS
THE LACHISH LETTERS

More than a dozen letters and fragments of letters were found in the ruins of the gateway of this important fortress in southern Judah, destroyed by the Babylonians in their campaign of 588–586 BCE, which culminated in the destruction of Jerusalem. They seem to have been part of a military archive, but it is unclear whether they were sent to Lachish from elsewhere or whether they are copies of letters sent from Lachish. The letters are written in Hebrew on ostraca.

83. LACHISH LETTER 1

Although not strictly a letter, it was found with those that follow and therefore is placed here with others from the archive. Most of the names also occur in the Bible.

Gemaryahu son of Hissilyahu
Yaazanyahu son of Tobshillem
Hagab son of Yaazanyahu
Mibtahyahu son of Yirmiyahu[5]
Mattanyahu son of Neriyahu

84. LACHISH LETTER 2

To my lord Yaush: May Yahweh cause my lord to hear peaceful tidings today.

Who is your servant but a dog[6] that my lord remembers his servant? May Yahweh afflict those who report something which you do not know![7]

85. LACHISH LETTER 3

This text is written on both sides of the sherd.

Your servant Hoshayahu has sent to report to my lord Yaush: May Yahweh cause my lord to hear peaceful tidings and good tidings.

And now: may the ear of your servant be opened concerning the letter which you sent to your servant yesterday evening. Because the heart

---

[1]Cf. Job 31:19–20; Matthew 25:34–45.
[2]Literally, "lord of the heavens."
[3]Nebuchadrezzar II, who invaded the Levant in the late seventh and early sixth centuries BCE.
[4]One of several cities with this name on the Mediterranean coast.

[5]The Hebrew form of the name "Jeremiah."
[6]Cf. 2 Samuel 9:8; 2 Kings 8:13.
[7]The interpretation of the last sentence is uncertain.

of your servant has been sick since you sent it to your servant, and because my lord said, "You do not know how to read a letter." As Yahweh lives, no one has ever tried to read me a letter. And also, any letter which came to me I read, and afterward I could repeat everything.[1]

Now it has been reported to your servant, saying: "The commander of the army, Conyahu, son of Elnathan, has gone down to go to Egypt." And he has sent to take Hodavyahu, son of Ahiyahu, from here.

And as for the letter of Tobyahu, the servant of the king, which came to Shallum, son of Yada, from the prophet, saying: "Watch out!"—your servant has sent it to my lord.

86. LACHISH LETTER 4

In Jeremiah 34:7, Azekah and Lachish were the last Judean fortresses to survive prior to the Babylonian conquest of Jerusalem in 586 BCE. In one interpretation of the end of the following letter, Azekah had now fallen.

May Yahweh cause my lord to hear good tidings today.

And now, as for all that my lord instructed, your servant did it. I wrote on the tablet according to all that my lord instructed. With regard to Beth-Harapid: there is no one there. With regard to Semakyahu: Shemayahu seized him and sent him up to the city. But your servant cannot send the witness there today. Rather, in the morning. . . . And let (my lord) know that we are watching for the fire-signals of Lachish, according to all the signs that my lord gave. For we cannot see Azekah.

ARAMAIC LETTERS FROM EGYPT DATING TO THE PERSIAN PERIOD

87. FROM ARSAMES, SATRAP OF EGYPT, TO ARMAPIYA, A MILITARY OFFICER

Written in Aramaic on leather, this relatively mundane letter illustrates how Egypt was governed under Persian rule and introduces Arsames, who is also mentioned in the Elephantine papyri (see Text 88); the letter dates from the second half of the fifth century BCE.

From Arsames to Armapiya:

And now: Psamshek my deputy has sent to me, saying as follows: "Armapiya with the troops under his command do not listen to me in my lord's business, as I have instructed them."

Now Arsames says: As for the business of my house concerning which Psamshek will speak to you and the troops under your command, listen to him and do (it). Know this: if Psamshek sends me another complaint about you, you will be strictly called to account and officially reprimanded.

Bagasru is aware of this order. Ah-pipi is the scribe.

88. BETWEEN JEWISH LEADERS AT ELEPHANTINE AND THE GOVERNOR OF JUDAH

This and the following letter concern the destruction and rebuilding of the temple of Yahu (Yahweh) at Elephantine (Yeb). Other letters testify to tensions between the Jews at Elephantine and their neighbors in Syene, including the blockage of their well by the priests of the Egyptian deity Khnum. The first part of this letter (A) seems to be a draft, and perhaps only a copy of the second part (B) was sent. The text was written by two different scribes, with the change occurring in the middle of the first part.

a. (A) To our lord Bagavahya, governor of Judah, from your servants Jedaniah and his colleagues the priests in the fortress of Yeb. May the god of heaven give our lord abundant peace always, and may he grant you mercy before Darius the king[2] and the sons of his house a thousand times more than now. May he give you long life, and may you always be happy and strong.

Now your servant Jedaniah and his colleagues say as follows:

---

[1]The interpretation of the second half of this sentence is uncertain.

[2]Darius II, king of Persia, 424–405 BCE.

In the month of Tammuz in the year 14 of Darius the king,[1] when Arsames[2] left and went to the king, the priests of the god Khnum in the fortress of Yeb, in agreement with Vidranga, who was in charge here, said: "Let them remove the temple of the god Yahu which is in the fortress of Yeb." Then that wicked Vidranga sent a letter to Nafaina his son, who is head of the troops at the fortress of Syene, saying: "Let the temple which is in the fortress of Yeb be destroyed." Then Nafaina led Egyptians along with other troops to the fortress of Yeb with weapons. They entered the temple. They destroyed it to the ground, and they broke the stone columns that were there. They also destroyed the 5 stone gates, built of hewn stone, that were in the temple. And their standing doors and the bronze pivots of those doors, and the roof of cedar wood—all of these, with the rest of the fittings and the other things that were there—all of this they burned with fire. And the gold and silver basins and everything else that was in the temple they took for themselves. But from the days of the king of Egypt our fathers built this temple in the fortress of Yeb, and when Cambyses[3] entered Egypt, he found this temple built. Moreover, they destroyed all the temples of the gods of Egypt, but no one did any damage in this temple.

After this, we, with our wives and sons, put on sackcloth and fasted and prayed to Yahu the lord of heaven, who let us see our desire on Vidranga, that dog. They removed the chains from his feet[4] and all the possessions that he had acquired were ruined. All the men who had sought evil against this temple they killed and we saw our desire on them. Moreover, before this, when this evil was done to us, we sent a letter to our lord and to Jehohanan the high priest and his colleagues the priests in Jerusalem and to Avastana the brother of Anani and the nobles of the Judeans. They did not send a letter back to us.

Moreover, from the month of Tammuz in the year 14 of Darius the king and until this day we

have worn sackcloth and have fasted. Our wives were made like widows. We have not anointed ourselves with oil, nor have we drunk wine. Moreover, from then until today, year 17 of Darius the king, grain offerings, incense, and burnt offerings have not been made in this temple.

(B) Now, your servants Jedaniah and his colleagues and the Jews, all the citizens of Yeb, say as follows:

If it seems good to our lord, let him consider rebuilding this temple, since they are not permitting us to rebuild.[5] Look on your loyal friends in Egypt. Let a letter be sent from you to them concerning the temple of the god Yahu, that it be rebuilt in the fortress of Yeb as it had been built before. And grain offerings and incense and burnt offerings will be offered on the altar of the god Yahu in your name. And we will pray for you at all times, we, our wives, our sons, all the Jews who are here. If this is done, that is, the temple is rebuilt, then there will be righteousness for you before Yahu the god of the heavens, more than if a man were to offer to him burnt offerings and sacrifices worth 1,000 talents of silver and gold.

Thus we have sent to inform you. We also sent a letter concerning all these matters in our name to Delaiah and Shelemiah, sons of Sanballat, governor of Samaria.[6] Also, Arsames did not know anything about all that was done to us.

20 Marheshwan, year 17 of Darius.[7]

b. Official response to previous letter.

Memorandum. What Bagavahya and Delaiah said to me.

Memorandum: Let it be for you in Egypt, as follows.

Before Arsames, concerning the altar-house of the god of the heavens in the fortress of Yeb, which was built long ago, before Cambyses, which that wicked Vidranga destroyed in the year 14 of Darius the king. Let it be rebuilt in its former location, and let grain offerings and incense be offered on the altar just as was done before.

---

[1]June/July 410 BCE.
[2]See Text 87.
[3]King of Persia, 530–522 BCE.
[4]An obscure phrase, perhaps meaning that he was stripped of the symbols of power.

[5]Compare similar opposition in Ezra 4–6; Nehemiah 4.
[6]Cf. Nehemiah 2:10.
[7]25 November 407 BCE.

PERSONAL CORRESPONDENCE

89. FROM AN EGYPTIAN WORKER TO HIS SUPERVISOR

This ostracon, written in hieratic script, is from Deir el-Medina, a community that was responsible for the construction of Egyptian royal tombs in the vicinity of Thebes. It dates to the reign of Rameses II (thirteenth century BCE). The complaint resembles that in Text 90.[1]

Hormose to Pennebu:
When I was working in the granary of the Temple of Maat,[2] I became bedridden. The native of the necropolis community Reia, who is an apparitor[3] of the court, confiscated an undergarment (?) of six cubits,[4] which was not worn through, and he must also have confiscated one *khar*-measure[5] of emmer wheat and four temple baskets of coiled technique.

90. FROM AN ISRAELITE WORKER TO HIS SUPERVISOR

An ostracon from a late-seventh-century-BCE fortress (Mesad Hashavyahu) near Yavneh Yam, on the Mediterranean coast of Israel. Several details of the Hebrew text remain obscure. For biblical parallels, see Exodus 22:26–27; Deuteronomy 24:10–13; Amos 2:8.

May my lord the governor hear the word of his servant. Your servant was a reaper in Hazar-Assam. Your servant was reaping, and finished, and stored [the grain] a few days ago, before Sabbath.[6] When your servant had finished the reaping and storing a few days ago, Hoshayahu son of Shobay came and took the garment of your servant. When I finished my reaping a few days ago, he took the garment of your servant.

All my brothers, who were reaping with me in the heat of the sun, will answer for me. They will answer that I am truly innocent of guilt. Please return my garment. But if the governor does not (see fit to) return the garment of your servant, still, have mercy on me and return the garment of your servant and do not be silent.

91. CONCERNING PASSOVER

Dating to the early fifth century BCE, this ostracon from Elephantine gives instructions concerning family matters, including the celebration of Passover. The precise relationship of the sender to the recipient is unclear.

To Hoshayah: Greetings!
And now: Look after the children until Ahutab[7] comes. Do not entrust them to others. If their grain has been ground, knead for them 1 kab[8] until their mother comes.
Let me know when you will celebrate the Passover. Let me know too if the child is well.

92. CONCERNING REPAIR OF A GARMENT

This ostracon from Elephantine dates to the early fifth century BCE. The blessing by both Yaho (Yahweh) and the Egyptian god Khnum illustrates the syncretism of the religion of the Jews of Elephantine.

To my lord Mikayah from your servant Gaddul:
I send greetings and (wishes of) long life to you. I bless you by Yaho and by Khnum.
And now, send me the garment that is on you, so that it can be sewn.
I am sending the letter to greet you.

93. CONCERNING GROCERIES AND THE SABBATH

Dating to the early fifth century BCE, this ostracon from Elephantine gives instructions about a shipment of produce.

---

[1]Translation by Edward F. Wente, *Letters from Ancient Egypt* (Atlanta, GA: Scholars Press, 1990), 145, no. 194.
[2]The Egyptian goddess of truth and justice.
[3]An official.
[4]A cubit was ca. 18 inches (44 cm).
[5]A *khar* was about 85 quarts (77 liters).
[6]Or "quitting time."

[7]Their mother, mentioned later.
[8]About 1.2 quart (1.3 liter).

Greetings Yislah!

Now the vegetables I am sending tomorrow. Meet the boat tomorrow on Sabbath so that they don't spoil. As Yaho[1] lives, if (you do) not, I will take your life! Do not trust Meshullemet or Shemayah.

And now: send me the barley in exchange.... As Yaho lives, if (you do) not, I will take your life! ...

May you see my face and may I see your face (soon)!

---

[1] Alternate spelling of Yahweh.

Akhenaten and His Family Praying to the Aten
A limestone relief showing Pharaoh Akhenaten (ruled 1352–1336 BCE), his wife
Nefertiti, and one of their daughters praying to the solar disk. It is about 40
inches (102 cm) high. (See Text 94.)

6

HYMNS, PRAYERS, LAMENTS, AND RITUALS

HYMNS AND PRAYERS

EGYPT

94. HYMN TO THE ATEN (THE SUN DISK)

This famous hymn comes from the tomb built for Ay and his wife Tiyi at El-Amarna in Egypt. Ay was a high official during the reign of Akhenaten (Amenophis IV) and served as principal advisor to Akhenaten's successor Tutankhamun. When Tutankhamun's ten-year reign ended with his untimely death at the age of eighteen, Ay succeeded him and ruled as Pharaoh for four years (1327–1323 BCE). The hymn is presented as spoken by Ay and concludes with an encomium for Akhenaten and a prayer for his wife Nefertiti. It has striking parallels to Psalm 104.[1]

> Beautifully you appear from the horizon of
>   heaven, O living Aten who initiates life.
> For you are risen from the eastern horizon
>   and have filled every land with your
>   beauty.
> For you are fair, great, dazzling, and high over
>   every land,
> and your rays enclose the lands to the limit of
>   all you have made.

For you are Re,[2] having reached their limit
    and subdued them for your beloved son;[3]
for although you are far away, your rays are
    upon the earth and you are perceived.

When your movements vanish and you set in
    the western horizon,
the land is in darkness, in the manner of
    death.
People, they lie in bedchambers, heads covered
    up, and one eye does not see its fellow.
All their property might be robbed, although
    it is under their heads, and they do not
    realize it.
Every lion is out of its den, all creeping things
    bite.
Darkness gathers, the land is silent.
The one who made them is set in his horizon.

But the land grows bright when you are risen
    from the horizon.
Shining in the orb[4] in the daytime, you push
    back the darkness and give forth your rays.
The Two Lands[5] are in a festival of light—
    awake and standing on legs, for you have
    lifted them up:

[1]Translation by William J. Nurnane, *Texts from the Amarna Period in Egypt* (Atlanta, GA: Scholars Press, 1995), 113–116.

[2]The sun god.
[3]The Pharaoh.
[4]The Aten.
[5]Upper (southern) and Lower (northern) Egypt.

their limbs are cleansed and wearing clothes,
their arms are in adoration at your appearing.
The whole land, they do their work:
all flocks are content with their pasturage,
trees and grasses flourish,
birds are flown from their nests, their wings
    adoring your *ka*;[1]
all small cattle prance upon their legs.
All that fly up and alight, they live when you
    rise for them.
Ships go downstream, and upstream as
    well, every road being open at your
    appearance.
Fish upon the river leap up in front of you, and
    your rays are even inside the Great Green.[2]

O you who brings into being fetuses in
    women,
who makes fluid in people,
who gives life to the son in his mother's
    womb, and calms him by stopping his
    tears;
nurse in the womb, who gives breath to
    animate all he makes[3]
when it descends from the womb to breathe
    on the day it is born—
you open his mouth completely and make
    what he needs.
When the chick is in the egg, speaking in the
    shell,
you give him breath within it to cause him to
    live;
and when you have made his appointed time
    for him, so that he may break himself out
    of the egg,
he comes out of the egg to speak at his
    appointed time and goes on his two legs
    when he comes out of it.

How manifold it is, what you have made,
    although mysterious in the face of humanity,
O sole god, without another beside him!
You create the earth according to your wish,
    being alone—
people, all large and small animals,

all things which are on earth, which go on
    legs, which rise up and fly by means of
    their wings,
the foreign countries of Kharu[4] and Kush,[5]
    and the land of Egypt.
You set every man in his place, you make
    their requirements, each one having his
    food and the reckoning of his lifetime.
Their tongues differ in speech, their
    natures likewise. Their skins are distinct,
    for you have made foreigners to be distinct.
You make the inundations from the
    underworld,
and you bring it to the place you wish in order
    to cause the subjects to live,
inasmuch as you made them for yourself, their
    lord entirely, who is wearied with them,
the lord of every land, who rises for them,
the orb of the daytime, whose awesomeness is
    great!
As for all distant countries, you make their life:
you have granted an inundation in heaven,
    that it might come down for them
and make torrents upon the mountains, like
    the Great Green, to soak their fields with
    what suits them.

How functional are your plans, O lord of
    continuity!
An inundation in heaven, which is for the
    foreigners and for all foreign flocks which
    go on legs;
and an inundation when it comes from the
    underworld for the Tilled Land,[6]
while your rays nurse every field:
when you rise, they live and flourish for you.
You make the seasons in order to develop all
    you make:
the growing season to cool them, and heat so
    that they might feel you.

You made heaven far away just to rise in it, to
    see all you make,
being unique and risen in your aspects of
    being as "living Aten"—manifest, shining,
    far yet near.

---

[1]Life force.
[2]The Mediterranean Sea.
[3]Cf. Genesis 1:30; 7:22; Psalm 104:29.

[4]Western Asia, along the Mediterranean coast.
[5]Nubia (modern Sudan).
[6]Egypt.

You make millions of developments from
    yourself, you who are a oneness: cities,
    towns, fields, the path of the river.
Every eye observes you in relation to them, for
    you are Aten of the daytime above the earth.
When you have gone, nobody can exist.
You create their faces so that you might not see
    yourself as the only thing which you made.

You are in my heart, and there is none who
    knows you except your son, Neferkheprure-
    Waenre,[1]
for you make him aware of your plans and
    your strength.
The land develops through your action, just
    as you made them:[2]
When you have risen they live, but when you
    set they die. You are lifetime in your very
    limbs, and one lives by means of you.
Until you set, all eyes are upon your beauty
    but all work is put aside when you set on
    the western side.
You raise them up for your son, who issued
    from your limbs, the King of Upper and
    Lower Egypt, who lives on Maat,[3]
the Lord of the Two Lands, Neferkheprure-
    Waenre,
Son of Re, who lives on Maat, Lord of
    Crowns, Akhenaten, long in his lifetime:
and the King's Chief Wife, his beloved, the
    lady of the Two Lands, Nefernefruaten-
    Nefertiti—may she live and be young
    forever continually.

MESOPOTAMIA
95. LETTER-PRAYER TO NINMUG

Letter-prayers use the genre of the letter (see page 115); the addressee is the god or goddess whom the letter writer wants to hear his petition. This Babylonian letter to the goddess of truth and justice dates to the mid-eighteenth century BCE.[4]

Say to my lady Ninmug:
Thus says Ninurta-qarad, your servant:
Ishum will listen to what you say; intercede for
me with Ishum for the sin that I have committed. When you have interceded for me, I, radiant
with happiness, will bring Ishum an offering, and I
will bring you a sheep. When I sing praises before
Ishum, I will sing your praises as well.

96. HYMN TO ISHTAR

This Babylonian hymn to Ishtar (called Inanna in Sumerian; see Text 4), the goddess of love and war, concludes with a prayer for Ammiditana, king of Babylon in the mid-seventeenth century BCE.[5]

Sing of the goddess, most awe-inspiring
    goddess,
let her be praised, mistress of people, greatest
    of the Igigi.[6]
Sing of Ishtar, most awe-inspiring goddess,
let her be praised, mistress of women, greatest
    of the Igigi.

She is the joyous one, clad in loveliness,
she is adorned with allure, appeal, charm.
Ishtar is the joyous one, clad in loveliness,
she is adorned with allure, appeal, charm.

In her lips she is sweetness, vitality her mouth,
while in her features laughter bursts to bloom.
She is proud of the love-charms set on her
    head,
fair her hues, full-ranging, and lustrous her eyes.

The goddess, right counsel is hers,
she grasps in her hand the destinies of all that
    exist.
At her regard, well-being is born,
vigor, dignity, good fortune, divine protection.

Whispers, surrender, sweet shared captivation,
harmony too she reigns over as mistress.
The girl who invokes finds in her a mother,
among women one mentions her, invokes her
    name.

---

[1]A royal name of Akhenaten.
[2]People.
[3]The goddess of truth and justice.
[4]Translation by Benjamin R. Foster, *Before the Muses: An Anthology of Akkadian Literature* (Bethesda, MD: CDL Press, 3d ed., 2005), 219.

[5]Translation by Benjamin R. Foster, *Before the Muses: An Anthology of Akkadian Literature* (Bethesda, MD: CDL Press, 3d ed., 2005), 85–88.
[6]The assembly of the gods.

Who is it that could rival her grandeur?
Her attributes are mighty, splendid, superb.
Ishtar this is, who could rival her grandeur?
Her attributes are mighty, splendid, superb.

She it is who stands foremost among the gods,
her word is the weightiest, it prevails over
    theirs.
Ishtar stands foremost among the gods,
her word is the weightiest, it prevails over theirs.

She is their queen, they discuss her
    commands,
all of them bow down before her:
they go to her in radiance,
women and men fear her too.

In their assembly her utterance is noble,
    surpassing,
she is seated among them as an equal to Anu,
    their king,
she is wise in understanding, reflection,
    insight.
Together they make their decisions, she and
    her lord.

There they sit together on the dais
in the temple chamber, delightful abode,
the gods stand in attendance before them,
their ears awaiting what those mouths will
    command.

Their favorite king, whom their hearts love
    most,
ever offers in splendor his pure offerings,
Ammiditana offers in plenty before them
his personal pure libation of cattle and fatted
    stags.

She has asked of Anu her spouse
long life hereafter for him,
many years of life for Ammiditana
has Ishtar rendered to him as her gift.

By her command she gave him in
    submission
the four world regions at his feet,
the whole of the inhabited world
she harnessed to his yoke.

What she desires, this song for her pleasure
is indeed well suited to his mouth,
he performed for her Ea's[1] own words.
When he heard this song of her praise,
he was well pleased with him,
saying, "Let him live long,
may his own king[2] always love him."

O Ishtar, grant long life enduring to
    Ammiditana,
the king who loves you, long may he live.

97. PRAYER TO ANU

**Dating to ca. 1500–1200 BCE, this is a relatively rare
hymn to the head of the older generation of gods
(see Text 1).[3]**

O most great god, whose lustrations are pure
    in heaven,
O Anu, greatest lord, whose purifications are
    pure in heaven,
god of heaven, lord of heaven,
Anu, god of heaven, lord of heaven,
who releases the day, crowned lord, lord of signs,
dispeller of evil, wicked, and terrifying
    dreams, evil signs and portents,
may my wickedness, sin, and grave misdeed
be absolved with your life-giving incantation,
and all that I have committed or neglected
    against my personal god and my personal
    goddess be absolved.
May the angry hearts of my personal god and
    my personal goddess be reconciled to me,[4]
may your furious heart be calmed,
and your feelings be eased; have mercy!
Let me endow your temple richly, and anoint
    your door bolt with oil,
let me sound my lord's praises, let me ever
    exalt the greatness of your great divinity!

---

[1]Ea was the god of wisdom.
[2]Probably the chief god of Babylon
[3]Translation by Benjamin R. Foster, *Before the Muses: An Anthology
of Akkadian Literature* (Bethesda, MD: CDL Press, 3d ed., 2005),
640.
[4]See Text 100.

98. HYMN TO ISHTAR

Dating to ca. 1500–1200 BCE, this hymn to Ishtar (see Text 90) includes a prayer for help by an individual who believes he is under a spell.[1]

O pure Ishtar, lofty one of the Igigi,[2]
who makes battle, who brings about combat,
most stately and perfect of goddesses,
at your command, O Ishtar, humankind is
     governed.
The sick man who sees your face revives,
his bondage is released, he gets up instantly.
At your command, O Ishtar, the blind man
     sees the light,
the unhealthy one who sees your face
     becomes healthy.
I, who am very sick, I kneel, I stand before
     you,
I turn to you to judge my case, O torch of the
     gods,[3]
I have seen your face, may my bonds be
     released.
Do not delay, I am confused and anxious.
I live like one bastinadoed.
I did what you said to do, O Ishtar!
A sorcerer or sorceress
whom you know, but I do not know,
with magic rites of malice and assassination,
which they have worked in your presence,
have laid figurines of me in a grave,
have come to assassinate me!
They have worked in secret against me,
I work against them openly!
By your sublime command, which cannot be
     altered,
and your firm assent, which cannot be
     changed,
may whatever I say come true.
Let life come to me from your pure utterance,
may you be the one to say: "What a pity about
     him!"
O you who are the supreme goddess among
     the gods.

---

[1]Translation by Benjamin R. Foster, *Before the Muses: An Anthology of Akkadian Literature* (Bethesda, MD: CDL Press, 3d ed., 2005), 673–674.
[2]The assembly of the gods.
[3]Ishtar was identified with the planet Venus, the morning and evening star.

99. HYMN TO MARDUK

Dating to ca. 1500–1200 BCE, this hymn to Marduk, the chief god of Babylon (see Text 1), prays for forgiveness for sin that apparently caused illness.[4]

O Marduk, great lord, merciful god,
who grasps the hand of the fallen,
who releases the bound, revives the
     moribund,
for wrongdoing known or not known,
which I committed through carelessness,
     negligence, or malfeasance,
which against your great divinity,
I committed through carelessness, negligence,
     or malfeasance,
I bring my life before your great divinity.
May the soothing water be accepted by you,
may your angry heart be calmed.
May your sweet forgiveness,
your great absolution,
your mighty intelligence be mine,
let me sound the praises of your great divinity.

100. PRAYER TO A PERSONAL GOD

In Mesopotamian religion, as in other traditions worldwide, each individual was thought to have a personal god who looked after his or her well-being. This Babylonian text dates to ca. 1500–1200 BCE.[5]

O my god, my lord, who created my name,
guardian of my life, producer of my progeny,
O angry god, may your heart be calmed,
O angry goddess, be reconciled with me.
Who knows where you dwell, O my god?
Never have I seen your pure standing place or
     sleeping chamber.
I am constantly in great distress: O my god,
     where are you?
You who have been angry with me, turn
     toward me,
turn your face to the pure godly meal of fat
     and oil,

---

[4]Translation by Benjamin R. Foster, *Before the Muses: An Anthology of Akkadian Literature* (Bethesda, MD: CDL Press, 3d ed., 2005), 688.
[5]Translation by Benjamin R. Foster, *Before the Muses: An Anthology of Akkadian Literature* (Bethesda, MD: CDL Press, 3d ed., 2005), 721.

that your lips receive goodness. Command
    that I thrive,
command long life with your pure utterance.
Bring me away from evil that, through you, I
    be saved.
Ordain for me a destiny of long life,
prolong my days, grant me long life!

101. HYMN TO ENLIL

This hymn is a personal lament, similar to those for
cities (see Texts 107 and 108), but in this case of
an individual praying to Enlil, the storm god and
chief god of the city of Nippur. Although written in
Sumerian, it probably dates to the mid-first millennium BCE, having been written by scribes for whom
Sumerian continued to be a learned language.[1]

A storm cloud, it lies solidly grounded, its
    heart inscrutable—
his word, a storm cloud, lies solidly grounded,
    its heart inscrutable.
Great An's[2] word, a storm cloud, lies solidly
    grounded, its heart inscrutable.
Enlil's word, a storm cloud, lies solidly
    grounded, its heart inscrutable.
Enki's[3] word, a storm cloud, lies solidly
    grounded, its heart inscrutable.
Asalluhe's[4] word, a storm cloud, lies solidly
    grounded, its heart inscrutable.
Enbilulu's[5] word, a storm cloud, lies solidly
    grounded, its heart inscrutable.
Mudugasa's[6] word, a storm cloud, lies solidly
    grounded, its heart inscrutable.
Shiddukishara's[7] word, a storm cloud, lies
    solidly grounded, its heart inscrutable.
Lord Dikurmah's[8] word, a storm cloud, lies
    solidly grounded, its heart inscrutable.

His word which up above shakes the heavens,
his word which down below makes earth quake,
his word by which the Anunnaki[9] are
    perverted for him,
his word has no diviner, has no interpreter of
    dreams.

His word, the risen waters of a flood storm,
    has none who could oppose it;
his word, which shakes the heavens, makes
    earth quake,
his word enfolds like a huge burial mat
    mother and child.
The lord's word kills the marsh grass in its pools;
Asalluhe's word drowns the crop when on its
    stalks.
The lord's word, risen floodwaters, overflows
    the levees;
Asalluhe's word, huge waters, floods the
    breached quays;
his word lops off great *meshu*-trees;
his word lays everything to hand for the storm.
Enlil's word, sweeping on, no eye sees.

Of captivity in the mountains is his word;
of the mountains is his word.
Of the mountains is his word;
the mighty one's word is of the mountains.
Great An's word is of the mountains.
Enlil's word is of the mountains.
The warrior Asalluhe's word is of the
    mountains.
Lord Enbilulu's word is of the mountains.
The warrior Mudugasa's word is of the
    mountains.
Shiddukishara heir to Esagila's word is of the
    mountains.
Lord Dikurmah's word is of the mountains.

Let me take his word to a diviner, and that
    diviner is made a liar;
let me take his word to an interpreter of
    dreams, and that interpreter is made a liar.

When his word has been said to a lad amid
    wails, that lad mourns;
when his word has been said to a lass amid
    wails, that lass mourns.

---

[1]Translation by Thorkild Jacobsen, *The Harps That Once . . . :
Sumerian Poetry in Translation* (New Haven, CT: Yale University
Press, 1987), 478–484.
[2]The sky god and king of the older generation of gods (Akkadian
Anu).
[3]The father of Marduk, the chief god of Babylon (Akkadian Ea).
[4]The Sumerian name of Marduk.
[5]The god of rivers and irrigation canals.
[6]The son of Marduk, the scribe god; in Akkadian, Nabu.
[7]The record keeper of the assembly of the gods.
[8]The chief judge of the assembly of the gods.

[9]The assembly of the gods.

His word for its part walks softly, but for their
part the mountains are being destroyed;
his word for its part walks grandly, and for
their part the houses of the rebel regions
are battered down.

His word, a very brewing vat, is covered: who
is to know the inside of it?
His word, unbeknownst inside, stalks outside;
his word, unbeknownst outside, stalks inside.
His word is making people ill, is weakening
people;
his word—its drifting in the sky is
tantamount to an ailing country;
his word—its walking the earth is
tantamount to a scattered nation.
His word, a storm, removes from a household
of five, five exactly.
Asalluhe's word removes from a household of
ten, ten exactly.

His word scares me up above, worries me up
above;
Asalluhe's word is voiced down below, causes
me to shiver down below.
The lord's word—at which most bitterly I
moan—is of the mountains;
his word, which above shakes the heavens, is
of the mountains;
when it alights—as ever before—whither am
I to go?

Like a gale, like a gale, the mighty one,
like a gale the mighty one is shaking me.
The mighty one, the lord of all lands,
he of the unfathomable heart, of the effective
words,
whose commands are not to be
countermanded,
the mighty one, Enlil, whose pronouncements
are not to be changed.
This word, this storm, the destruction of the
byres, the uprooting of the folds,
the pulling up of my roots, the denuding of
my forests, the replacing of my rites for the
Anunnaki with the enemy's rites,
the locust-like denuding of my forests—
O lord of all lands, out of magnanimity may
you speak it not out!

The like of what is in the heart, may you
speak it not out!

You have cut off food from my insides,
and—to match—locked up my guts!

May you speak it not out, may you speak not
out: "Destruction!"

Like a lone reed, like a lone reed the mighty
one is shaking me,
the mighty one, the lord of all lands,
he of the unfathomable heart, of the effective
words,
whose commands are not to be countermanded,
Enlil, whose pronouncements are not to be
changed;
like embedded rushes, like embedded halfa
grass,
like a lone poplar planted on the riverbank,
like a dogwood tree planted on dry land,
like a lone tamarisk planted where there are
tempests,
like a lone reed the mighty one is shaking me!

102. CORONATION PRAYER

This prayer was written for the accession to the throne of the Assyrian king Ashurbanipal (ruled 669–627 BCE).[1]

May Shamash,[2] king of heaven and earth, elevate you to shepherdship of the four world regions. May Ashur,[3] who bestows the scepter, prolong your days and your years.... Just as grain, and silver, oil, cattle, and the salt of Bariku[4] are desirable, so too may the name of Ashurbanipal, king of Assyria, be desirable to the gods. May they grant him speaking and hearing, truth and justice.

May the resident of Ashur obtain 30 kor[5] of grain for 1 shekel of silver, may the resident of Ashur obtain 30 quarts of oil for 1 shekel of silver, may the resident of Ashur obtain 30 minas of wool for 1

---

[1]Translation by Benjamin R. Foster, *Before the Muses: An Anthology of Akkadian Literature* (Bethesda, MD: CDL Press, 3d ed., 2005), 815–816.
[2]The sun god.
[3]The chief god of Assyria, corresponding to Marduk in Babylon.
[4]A special delicacy.
[5]A kor was ca. 6.5 bushels (230 liters).

shekel of silver.[1] May the great listen when the lesser speak, may the lesser listen when the great speak, may harmony and peace be established in Ashur.

May they protect the life of Ashurbanipal, king of Assyria. May they give him a just scepter to enlarge his land and people. May his reign be ever renewed, may they establish his royal throne forever. May they bless him day, month, and year, may they make his reign outstanding. During his years, may the rain from heaven and the flood from the underground depths be unfailing.

Grant to Ashurbanipal, king of Assyria, our lord, long days, many years, a strong weapon, a long reign, years of abundance, a good name, and reputation, contentment, happiness, good repute, and first rank among kings.

Anu[2] has given his crown, Enlil[3] has given his throne, Ninurta[4] has given his weapon, Nergal[5] has given his splendor, Nusku[6] has sent wise counselors to stand in attendance upon him.

He who shall speak insolence or falsehood to the king, be he important, he will die violently; be he rich, he will become poor. He who shall harbor evil against the king in his heart, Erra[7] will call him to account in a plague. He who thinks disrespectful thoughts of the king, his foundations will be a cyclone, his possessions will be empty air.

Assemble, all ye gods of heaven and netherworld, bless Ashurbanipal, king, counselor man! Deliver the weapon of combat and battle into his hand. Give him the people of this land, that he serve as their shepherd.

103. PRAYER OF ASHURBANIPAL

In this text, the Assyrian king Ashurbanipal (ruled 669–627 BCE) recalls his careful collection of texts from all over his empire and prays to Nabu, the god of wisdom and writing.[8]

I, Ashurbanipal, king of the universe, king of Assyria, on whom Nabu and Tashmetu[9] have bestowed vast intelligence, who acquired penetrating acumen for the most recondite details of scholarly erudition, no predecessors of whom among kings having any comprehension of such matters, I wrote down on tablets Nabu's wisdom, the impressing of each and every cuneiform sign, and I checked and collated them. I placed them for the future in the library of the temple of my lord Nabu, the great lord, at Nineveh,[10] for my life and for the well-being of my soul, to avoid disease, and to sustain the foundations of my royal throne. O Nabu, look joyfully and bless my kingship forever! Help me whenever I call upon you! As I traverse your house, keep constant watch over my footsteps. When this work is deposited in your house and placed in your presence, look upon it and remember me with favor!

104. PRAYER OF NABONIDUS TO SIN

Discovered in the ruins of the ziggurat at Ur, this foundation text is a prayer to the moon god illustrating the almost obsessive devotion to that deity of Nabonidus, the last king of Babylon (ruled 556–539 BCE); see also Texts 39, 40, and 105.[11]

O Sin, my lord god, king of heaven and netherworld, god of gods, who dwell in the great heavens, as you joyfully enter this temple, may there be upon your lips words favorable to Esagila, Ezida, and Ekishnugal,[12] the temples of your great divinity,[13] and instill reverence for your great divinity in the hearts of your people, lest they do wrong against your great divinity. May its foundation last like heaven. Save me, Nabonidus, from wrongdoing against your great divinity, grant me the gift of a life long of days. Instill as well in the heart of

---

[1]A shekel weighed ca. 0.35 ounce (10 grams), and a mina was probably 50 shekels.

[2]The sky god and king of the older generation of gods.

[3]The storm god.

[4]The warrior god, son of Enlil.

[5]The god of the underworld.

[6]God of light, Enlil's chief of staff.

[7]God of plague.

[8]Translation by Benjamin R. Foster, *Before the Muses: An Anthology of Akkadian Literature* (Bethesda, MD: CDL Press, 3d ed., 2005), 831.

[9]The goddess wife of Nabu.

[10]The capital city of Assyria.

[11]Translation by Benjamin R. Foster, *Before the Muses: An Anthology of Akkadian Literature* (Bethesda, MD: CDL Press, 3d ed., 2005), 863.

[12]The principal temples of Marduk in Babylon, Nabu in Borsippa, and Sin at Ur.

[13]The wording implies that when Marduk and Nabu were worshiped, it was really Sin.

Belshazzar, my firstborn son, my offspring, reverence for your great divinity. May he commit no wrongdoing, may he enjoy the delights of living in full measure.

105. PRAYER OF NABONIDUS TO GOD MOST HIGH

This Aramaic text, found on one of the Dead Sea Scrolls (4Q242), dates to the first century BCE, but it preserves an older tradition. It is a fictitious prayer of Nabonidus, the last king of Babylon, written from a Jewish perspective, and is comparable to the Prayer of Manasseh in the Apocrypha. Nabonidus lived in Tema (spelled Teman in this text) in northern Arabia for several years of his reign (see Text 39), while his son Belshazzar was coregent in Babylon (553–543 BCE). His absence is reflected in Daniel 4:15–16, 13–26, but there it is attributed to Nebuchadnezzar. About half of the text is missing and has been conjecturally restored.[1]

The words of the prayer which Nabonidus, king of Babylon, the great king, prayed when he was stricken with an evil disease by the decree of God in Teman. I Nabonidus was stricken with an evil disease for seven years, and from that time I was like unto a beast and I prayed to the Most High and, as for my sin, he forgave it. A diviner—who was a Jew of the exiles—came to me and said: "Recount and record these things in order to give honor and greatness to the name of God Most High." And thus I wrote: "I was stricken with an evil disease in Teman by the decree of the Most High God, and, as for me, seven years I was praying to gods of silver and gold, bronze, iron, wood, stone, and clay, because I was of the opinion that they were gods."[2]

106. PRAISE OF BABYLON

This fragment of a late Babylonian text is reminiscent of the psalms that speak of Zion as Yahweh's beautiful home.[3]

The citizens of Babylon are freed from service by Enlil:[4]
whoever shall put harm in their way, he shall bear the onus for them.
Nippur is the lord's city, Babylon is his favorite,
Nippur and Babylon have but one mind!
Babylon is full of joy to behold.
The resident of Babylon will live a long life.
Babylon is sweet to the taste as a date from Dilmun![5]

CITY LAMENTS

AT THE END of the third millennium BCE, the powerful Third Dynasty of Ur, which ruled southern Mesopotamia, came to an abrupt end, and its principal cites were destroyed, in part at least because of invaders from several directions. Thereafter, laments for the ruined cities were composed in Sumerian; these have often been compared to the poems in the biblical book of Lamentations. But there are no exact parallels in subsequent Mesopotamian literature, so a direct influence may not be present. The laments survive in multiple copies, all from the early second millennium BCE. The most complete have as their subject the cities of Ur, Sumer, and Nippur; less well-preserved laments also exist for other cities.

107. LAMENT FOR UR[6]

To overturn the appointed time, to forsake the preordained plans,
the storms gather to strike like a flood.
To overturn the divine decrees of Sumer,
to lock the favorable reign in its abode,
to destroy the city, to destroy the temple,
to destroy the cattle pen, to level the sheepfold,
that the cattle not stand in the pen,
that the sheep not multiply in the fold,

---

[1]Translation by Frank Moore Cross, "Fragments of the Prayer of Nabonidus," in *Leaves from an Epigraphist's Notebook: Collected Papers in Hebrew and West Semitic Paleography and Epigraphy* (Harvard Semitic Studies 51; Winona Lake, IN: Eisenbrauns, 2003), 180.
[2]Cf. Daniel 4:33–37.
[3]Translation by Benjamin R. Foster, *Before the Muses: An Anthology of Akkadian Literature* (Bethesda, MD: CDL Press, 3d ed., 2005), 879.

[4]The chief god of Nippur.
[5]A far-off place, probably somewhere in the Persian Gulf, famous for its dates.
[6]Translated by Piotr Michalowski, *The Lamentation over the Destruction of Sumer and Ur* (Winona Lake, IN: Eisenbrauns, 1989), 37–69.

that its watercourses carry brackish water,

that weeds grow in the fertile fields,

that mourning plants grow in the steppe,

that the mother does not seek out her child,

that the father does not say, "Oh, my dear wife!"

that the junior wife not take joy in his embrace,

that the young child not grow vigorous on her knee,

that the wet nurse not sing lullabies,

to change the location of kingship,

to defile the rights and decrees,

to take away kingship from the land,

to cast the eye of the storm on all the land,

to forsake the divine decrees by the order of An[1] and Enlil,[2]

after An had frowned upon all the lands,

after Enlil had looked favorably on an enemy land,

after Nintu[3] had scattered the creatures she had created,

after Enki[4] had altered the course of the Tigris and Euphrates,

after Utu[5] had cast his curse on the roads and highways,

in order to forsake the divine decrees of Sumer, to change its preordained plans,

to alienate the divine decrees of the reign of kinship of Ur,

to defile the Princely Son[6] in his temple Ekishnugal,

to break up the unity of the people of Nanna, numerous as ewes,

to change the food offerings of Ur, the shrine of magnificent food offerings,

that its people no longer dwell in their quarters, that they be given over to live in an inimical place,

that the soldiers of Shimashki and Elam,[7] the enemy, dwell in their place,

that its shepherd be captured by the enemy, all alone,

that Ibbi-Sin[8] be taken to the land of Elam in fetters,

that from the mountain Zabu, which is on the edge of the sea-land, to the borders of Anshan,[9]

like a bird that has flown its nest, he not return to his city,

that on the two banks of the Tigris and Euphrates bad weeds grow,

that no one set out for the road, that no one seek out the highway,

that the city and its settled surroundings be razed to ruins,

to slaughter its numerous black-headed people,

that the hoe not attack the fertile fields, that seed not be planted in the ground,

that the song of the one tending the oxen not resound on the plain,

that butter and cheese not be made in the cattle pen, that dung not be laid on the ground,

that the shepherd not enclose the sacred sheepfold with a fence,

that the sound of churning not resound in the cattle pen,

to decimate the animals of the steppe, to finish off all living things,

that the four-legged creatures of Shakan[10] not lay dung on the ground,

that the marshes be so dry as to be full of cracks, that it not have any new seed,

that saghul-reeds grow in the canebreak, that they be covered by a stinking morass,

that there be no new growth in the orchards, that it all collapse by itself—

the city of Ur is a great charging aurochs, confident in its own strength,

it is the primeval city of lordship and kingship, built on sacred ground—

to quickly subdue it like a sacred ox, to bow its neck to the ground,

---

[1] The sky god and king of the older generation of gods (Akkadian Anu).

[2] The chief god of the city of Nippur.

[3] The birth goddess.

[4] The god of fresh water and wisdom (Akkadian Ea).

[5] The sun god (Akkadian Shamash).

[6] I.e., Nanna, the moon god.

[7] Regions to the east of Mesopotamia.

[8] The last king of the Third Dynasty of Ur, who ruled at the end of the third millennium BCE.

[9] A major city in Elam.

[10] A goddess of small cattle.

the gods An, Enlil, Enki, and Ninmah[1]
   decided its fate.
Its fate, which cannot be changed, who can
   overturn it—
who can oppose the commands of An and
   Enlil?
An frightened the very dwelling of Sumer, the
   people were afraid,
Enlil blew an evil storm, silence lay on the city,
Nintu bolted the door of the storehouses of
   the land,
Enki blocked the water in the Tigris and
   Euphrates,
Utu took away the pronouncement of equity
   and justice,
Inanna[2] handed over victory in strife and
   battle to a rebellious land,
Ningirsu[3] wasted Sumer like milk poured to
   the dogs.
Revolt descended upon the land, something
   that could not be known,
something unseen, which had no name,
   something that could not be fathomed.
The lands were confused in their fear,
the god of that city turned away, its shepherd
   vanished.
The people, in fear, breathed only with
   difficulty,
the storm immobilizes them, the storm does
   not let them return,
there is no return for them, the time of
   captivity does not pass.
This is what Enlil, the shepherd of the black-
   headed people, did:
Enlil, to destroy the loyal household, to
   decimate the loyal man,
to put the evil eye on the son of the loyal one,
   on the first born,
Enlil then sent down Gutium[4] from the
   mountains.
Their advance was as the flood of Enlil that
   cannot be withstood,
the great storm of the plain filled the plain, it
   advanced before them,

the teeming plain was destroyed, no one
   moved about there.
The dark time was roasted by hailstones and
   flames,
the bright time was wiped out by a shadow.
On that bloody day, mouths were crushed,
   heads were crashed,
the storm was a harrow coming from above,
   the city was struck as by a hoe.
On that day, the heavens rumbled, the earth
   trembled, the storm worked without
   respite,
the heavens were darkened, they were covered
   by a shadow, the mountains roared,
the sun lay down at the horizon, dust passed
   over the mountains,
the moon lay at the zenith, the people were
   afraid. . . .
Ibbi-Sin was sitting in anguish in the palace,
   all alone.
In the Enamtila, the palace of his delight, he
   was crying bitterly.
The devastating flood was leveling
   everything,
like a great storm it roared over the earth,
   who could escape it? . . .
The temple of Kish, Hursagkalama, was
   destroyed,
Zababa[5] took an unfamiliar path away from
   his beloved dwelling,
Mother Bau[6] was lamenting bitterly in her
   Urukug,
"Alas the destroyed city, my destroyed
   temple!" bitterly she cries.

[In the following section, one goddess after another utters the refrain in the previous line, as various cities
are destroyed. Then the affliction of Ur is related in
detail. Finally the moon god Sin (also called Nanna)
questions his father Enlil:]

   "O father who begot me, why have you turned
      away from Ur, the city that was built for you?
   O Enlil, why have you turned away from Ur,
      the city that was built for you?

---

[1] A title of Nintu, the birth goddess.
[2] The goddess of love and war (Akkadian Ishtar).
[3] A war god and son of Enlil.
[4] A region to the east of Mesopotamia.

---

[5] The patron god of the city of Kish.
[6] The goddess of the city of Lagash.

The boat with first-fruit offerings no longer
brings the first-fruit offerings to the father
who begot me,
its food offerings can no longer be brought to
Enlil in Nippur....
My father who begot me, my city, which is all
alone, return to your embrace,
Enlil, my city of Ur, which is all alone, return
to your embrace,
my Ekishnugal, which is all alone, return to
your embrace!
May you bring forth offspring in Ur, may you
multiply its people,
may you restore the divine decrees of Sumer
that have been forgotten!"
Oh, the righteous temple, the righteous
temple! Oh, its people, its people!
Enlil then answers his son Sin:
"There is lamentation in the haunted city,
mourning reeds grow there,
in its midst there is lamentation, mourning
reeds grow there,
in it the population pass their days in sighing.
My son, the Noble Son..., why do you
concern yourself with crying?
O Nanna, the Noble Son..., why do you
concern yourself with crying?
The judgment of the assembly cannot be
turned back,
the word of An and Enlil knows no
overturning,
Ur was indeed given kingship but it was not
given an eternal reign.
From time immemorial, since the land was
founded, until the population multiplied,
who has even seen a reign of kingship that
would take precedence forever?
The reign of its kingship had been long
indeed but had to exhaust itself.
O my Nanna, do not exert yourself in vain,
leave your city!"
Then, upon hearing this, His Majesty, the
Noble Son, became distraught,
Lord Ashimbabbar, the Noble Son, grieved,
Nanna, who loves his city, left his city,
Sin took an unfamiliar path away from his
beloved Ur....
The trees of Ur were sick, the reeds of Ur
were sick,

laments sounded all along its city wall.
Daily there was slaughter before it.
Large axes were sharpened in front of Ur,
the spears, the arms of battle, were being
launched,
the large bow, javelin, and siege-shield gather
together to strike,
the barbed arrows covered its outer side like a
raining cloud,
large stones, one after another, fell with great
thuds.
Daily the evil wind returns to attack the city.
Ur, which had been confident in its own
strength, stood ready for slaughter,
its people, oppressed by the enemy, could not
withstand their weapons.
Those in the city who had not been felled by
weapons, died of hunger,
hunger filled the city like water, it would not
cease,
this hunger contorts people's faces, it twists
their muscles.
Its people are as if surrounded by water, they
gasp for breath,
its king breathed heavily in his palace, all
alone,
its people dropped their weapons, their
weapons hit the ground,
they struck their necks with their hands and
cried.
They sought counsel with each other, they
searched for clarification,
"Alas, what can we say about it, what more
can we add to it?
How long until we are finished off by this
catastrophe?
Ur—inside it there is death, outside it there
is death,
inside it we are being finished off by famine,
outside it we are being finished off by Elamite[1]
weapons.
In Ur the enemy has oppressed us, oh, we are
finished!"

[*A lengthy description of the city's destruction follows,
including the defilement of its temples.*[2]]

---

[1]Elam was a region east of Mesopotamia.
[2]Cf. Jeremiah 52:17–23.

In grief Sin approached his father, the father who begot him.
"O father, who begot me, how long will the enemy eye be cast upon my account, how long...?"

* * *

Enlil then provides a favorable response to his son:
"My son, the city that was built for you in joy and prosperity, it was given to you as your reign,
the destroyed city, the great wall, the walls with broken battlements: all this is part of the appointed reign....
Ur shall be rebuilt in splendor, may the people bow down to you,
there is to be bounty at its base, there is to be grain,
there is to be splendor at its top, the Sun will rejoice there!
Let an abundance of grain embrace its table,
May Ur, the city whose fate was pronounced by An, be restored for you!"
Having pronounced his blessing, Enlil raised his head toward the heavens, saying:
"May the land, north and south, be organized for Nanna,
may the roads of the land be set in order for Sin!
Like a cloud hugging the earth, they shall submit to him,
by order of An and Enlil abundance shall be bestowed!"
Father Nanna stood in his city of Ur with head raised high once again,
the hero Sin entered into the Ekishnugal.
Ningal[1] refreshed herself in her sacred living quarters,
in Ur she entered into her Ekishnugal.

[*The poem describes the mourning in the city and then gives pleas for the gods to restore it. It ends with a prayer to Nanna:*]

O Nanna, your kingship is sweet, return to your place!

May a good abundant reign be long lasting in Ur!
Let its people lie down in safe pastures, let them copulate!...
O Nanna—oh, your city! Oh, your temple! Oh, your people!

108. LAMENT FOR ISIN

In this lament for the Sumerian city of Isin, its principal goddess Nininsina and other lesser goddesses describe the desolation of their temples and ask Enlil that the city be restored. [2]

The august dog-headed one, Nininsina, am I;
the matron of the chief treasury, Nintinugga, am I;
Hedibkug, matron of the inner chamber, am I;
Ninashte, mistress of Larak, am I;
matron of this house, Ezina, the laden, silvern ear of grain, am I;
daughter of this house, a lady, am I, Gunura;
mistress of Ningingar, the holy place, am I.

This my house, where good food is not eaten anymore;
this my house, where good drink is not drunk anymore;
my house, where good seats are not sat in;
my house, where good beds are not lain in;
my house, where holy stone jars are not eaten from;
my house, where holy bronze cups are not drunk from;
my house, where holy serving tables are not carried,
where from holy pitchers water is not poured.
Where holy kettledrums are not set up,
where holy harps are not played,
where to holy timbrels wailings are not wailed,
where holy sistrums are not jingled sweetly.
Where my reed pipes emit not loud notes,
where lutes are not held.
Where the elegist is not calming my heart,
where the anointed ones[3] sing not for joy.

---

[1]The goddess wife of Sin.

[2]Translation by Thorkild Jacobsen, *The Harps That Once...: Sumerian Poetry in Translation* (New Haven, CT: Yale University Press, 1987), 475–477.
[3]The priests.

My house, where no happy husband lives
    with me,
my house, where no sweet child dwells with me,
my house, through which I, its mistress, never
    grandly pass—
never grandly pass, in which I dwell no more.

My father, may it be restored!
When? May it be restored!
You decreed it!
My father Enlil, may it be restored!
When? May it be restored!
You decreed it!

I—let me go into my house, let me go in,
let me lie down, let me lie down!
I—let me go into my storehouse, let me go in,
let me lie down, let me lie down,
I—let me lie down to sleep in my house,
its sleep was sweet,
I—let me lie down in my house, let me lie
    down,
its bed was good,
I—let me sit down on the chair,
its chair was good.
A tambourine lament of Gula.[1]

OTHER SUMERIAN
LAMENTS

CLOSELY RELATED TO the Sumerian city laments
are texts known as "harp songs" (balags), more than
three dozen of which are known, preserved in multiple copies from the early second millennium to as late
as the second century BCE. They were used in various
rituals, including for the destruction of a temple prior
to its reconstruction and possibly also at funerals.
This genre is notable for its use of repetition.

109. THE RAGING SEA WILL
NOT BE CALMED[2]

[The beginning is not preserved.]

A lament, woe! A lament, woe! If only I
    could hold back the sighs!
Lord of my city, great mountain, Enlil,[3] a
    lament, woe!
Lord of my city, great mountain, lord of the
    lands, a lament, woe!
In the steppe a wail! Its young man is sobbing.
A song in the storehouse! Its young woman is
    sobbing.
Its young man shakes at the wail.
Its young woman shakes at the wail.

Wild ox, honored one, wild ox, when your
    name is against the lands,
great mountain, father Enlil, wild ox, when
    your name is against the lands,
shepherd of the black-headed, wild ox, when
    your name is against the lands,
when your name is in the land,
when it is in the land of Elam,[4]
when it is to the very horizon of heaven,
when it is to the edge of the earth!

You are exalted! You are exalted!
Enlil, you are exalted!
Enlil, in all the lands, you are exalted!
You place your neck in your lap. You are
    exalted!
You take counsel in your own heart! You are
    exalted!
From its throat even the bird pours out "Woe!"
For its throat even the girgilu-bird pours out
    "Woe!"
when he who has turned away from the
    nation
among his black-headed causes necks to droop
    sadly over shoulders.

Wild ox, honored one, wild ox, when your
    name is against the lands,
great mountain, father Enlil, wild ox, when
    your name is against the lands,
shepherd of the black-headed, wild ox, when
    your name is against the lands,
when your name is in the land,
when it is in the land of Elam,

---

[1]A concluding note by the scribe. Gula was a goddess of healing,
here identified with Nininsina.
[2]This is the ancient title of the work. Translated by Mark E. Cohen,
The Canonical Lamentations of Ancient Mesopotamia. Volume I
(Potomac, MD: Capital Decisions Limited, 1988), 381–384.

[3]The chief god of the city of Nippur.
[4]Located in the mountains east of Mesopotamia.

when it is to the very horizon of heaven,
when it is to the edge of the earth!

How long? How long?
Enlil, how long?
Enlil, how long in the lands?
Shepherd of the black-headed, how long?
In their very midst the crow....
At the word of Enlil, the crow....
The honored one who has scattered men from
    the nation,
father Enlil, has caused the black-headed to
    be carried off.

Wild ox, honored one, wild ox, when your
    name is against the lands,
great mountain, father Enlil, wild ox, when
    your name is against the lands,
shepherd of the black-headed, wild ox, when
    your name is against the lands,
when your name is in the land,
when it is in the land of Elam,
when it is to the very horizon of heaven,
when it is to the edge of the earth!

Change your mind! Change your mind!
Enlil, change your mind!
Enlil in the land, change your mind!
Shepherd of the black-headed, change your
    mind!
Change your mind! Change it! Speak to him!
Heart be calm! Be calm! Speak to him!

The bull is at rest. When will he rise up?
Enlil is at rest. When will he rise up?
In Nippur, at the Duranki,[1] when will he
    rise up?
In Nippur, at that place where fates are
    decided, when will he rise up?
At that house, set up as the life of the nation,
    when will he rise up?
Set up as the life of the lands, when will he
    rise up?

Let the resting bull arise!
Let resting Enlil arise!

Let the resting bison arise!
From among the fattened oxen with the bent
    legs let him arise!
From among the good...of the *gadalallu*-
    priests let him arise!
From among the meal-fed goats let him
    arise!
From among the fat-tailed, banded sheep let
    him arise!

The rising bull gazes about.
The rising Enlil gazes about.
In Nippur, at Duranki, he gazes about.
In Nippur, at that place where the fates are
    determined, he gazes about.
You are killing us! You are destroying us!

The bull, when rising, scrapes the very
    heavens!

● ● ●

Heaven cannot bear the word of the lord.
Heaven and earth cannot bear the word of
    Enlil.
Heaven and earth cannot bear just one hand
    of the lord.
Earth cannot bear just one foot of Enlil.

His fate! A wail! A wail!...A wail! A wail!
The fate of great An![2] A wail! A wail!
The fate of Enlil! A wail! A wail!
The lofty fate of the Ekur![3] A wail! A wail!
His fate which causes the heavens to tremble!
    A wail! A wail!
His fate which is as beautiful as the earth! A
    wail! A wail!
His word is the wail of the nation, the life of
    the lands.
The word of great An is the wail of the
    nation, the life of the lands.
The word of Enlil is the wail of the nation,
    the life of the lands.
The word of the lord afflicts the young man
    with woe; that young man moans.

---

[1]Literally, the meeting place of heaven and earth; a title for the temple of Enlil at Nippur.

[2]The sky god and head of the older generation of gods (Akkadian Anu).

[3]The temple of Enlil in Nippur.

His word afflicts the young woman with woe;
that young woman moans.

[*The rest of the text is poorly preserved or missing.*]

110. HE IS A STORM: AT THE HOWLING[1]

[*The beginning is not preserved.*]

The wail is from anger; it is also from outrage.
The word of great An[2] is from anger; it is also
from outrage.
The word of Enlil[3] is from anger; it is also
from outrage.
The word of the great hero is from anger; it is
also from outrage.
The exalted word of Ishkur is from anger; it is
also from outrage.
The word of Ugude is from anger; it is also
from outrage.
The word of Ugurara is from anger; it is also
from outrage.[4]
On account of this the heavens trembled, the
earth shook.
The heavens continually rumbled, the earth
continually shook.
The sun lay at the horizon.
The moon stopped still in the midst of the sky.
In the sky the great lights disappeared.
An evil storm...the nation.
A deluge swept over the lands.
The reed bed dried up in its own pool.
The crops were drowned on their stalks.
The houses leaned off their pillars.
The city lay off its foundation.
The nation was destroyed right off its very
foundation.
The cattle pen was scattered along with its
cows.
The sheepfold was torn out along with its
sheep.

The house along with its nest was carried off.
Expressing divine anger, the deluge swept on.
The flood gored even the highlands and the
lowlands which had been secure.
The city along with its houses....

• • •

May his heart be calm in his house! May his
liver be pacified!
May the brickwork of his Nippur calm him![5]
May the brickwork of the Ekur pacify him!
May the Kiur, the great place, calm him!
May the shrine Enamtila pacify him!
May the brickwork of Sippar calm him!
May the Ebabbar pacify him!
May the brickwork of Tintir calm him!
May the brickwork of the Esagila pacify him!
May the brickwork of Borsippa calm him!
May the brickwork of the Ezida pacify him!
May the shrine Emahtila calm him!
May the Etemenanki pacify him!
May the Edaranna calm him!
May the brickwork of the Eugalgal pacify him!
May the shrine Enamhea calm him!
May the brickwork of the Epada pacify him!
May the shrine Euttash calm him!
May the Ehenuna pacify him!

• • •

111. THE GOD MANIFEST[6]

The god manifest, who stands at the
mountain,
he, Shulpae,[7] who manifests himself, who
stands at the mountain,
who manifests himself for the lustrous lady...,
the huge dragon, he who manifests himself at
dawn,
he who destroyed the cattle pen, who
manifests himself,
he who uprooted the sheepfold, who manifests
himself,

---

[1]This is the ancient title of the work. Translated by Mark E. Cohen, *The Canonical Lamentations of Ancient Mesopotamia*. Volume II (Potomac, MD: Capital Decisions Limited, 1988), 435–436.

[2]The sky god and king of the older generation of gods (Akkadian Anu).

[3]The chief god of the city of Nippur.

[4]Ishkur, Ugude, and Ugurara are titles of Enlil.

[5]The following lines mention various cities and the temples to Enlil in them.

[6]This is the ancient title of the work. Translated by Mark E. Cohen, *The Canonical Lamentations of Ancient Mesopotamia*. Volume II (Potomac, MD: Capital Decisions Limited, 1988), 736–737.

[7]The divine husband of Ninhursag, a mother goddess.

who devastated Sumer, who manifests himself,
the great dragon, he who killed the black-
    headed, who manifests himself,
a violent storm which spills the seed in the
    cattle pen, who manifests himself,
a violent storm which spills the seed in the
    sheepfold, who manifests himself,
he is the venom of the *mushatur*-snake which
    is hurled against a man,
the venom of a scorpion which is not visible
    to a man,
a flood which erupts in the night,
a net stretched over the sea,
from whose interstices no fish escapes,
a talon which seizes a calf,
legs which pin a man,
a dangerous ford which sheep cannot cross,
a dangerous shore where sheep can neither
    drink nor ford over,
a lion which snatches a cow from the cowherd,
a powerful one which snatches a sheep from
    the shepherd,
a strong one which seizes a bull,
a storm which seizes a bull in its mouth.

Your word being infallible,
… what can one know about you?
Shulpae, what can one know about you?
His utterance! What can one know
    about you?
His additional pronouncements! What can
    one know about you?

May he who understands his heart
utter a prayer to the lord!
May he who understands the heart of great An,[1]
who understands the heart of Enlil,[2] may he
    utter a prayer!

• • •

RITUALS

MANY TEXTS DESCRIBING rituals are known from
throughout the ancient Near East. The following
sample illustrates some of the main types. Other
rituals are found in Chapter 7.

MEDICAL TEXTS

One type of ritual was associated with the practice of medicine, often carried out in temples. The
following first-millennium-BCE Babylonian texts are
representative.

112. FOR HEADACHE[3]

Headache, applied in heaven, removed in the
    netherworld,
which sapped the strength of the strong
    young man,
which has not returned her energy to the
    beautiful young woman,
which has set upon the sick man,
Ishtar, without whom no one has relaxation
    or delight, made it come down from the
    mountain.
It drew near the limbs of the afflicted man;
the man stands saying "Alas!"
Who will remove it? Who will cast it out?
Ishtar, daughter of Sin,
Enkum, son of Enlil,
Asalluhi, son of Enlil:[4]
Let them cast it out from the body of the
    afflicted man!

[*There follow instructions that the man be rubbed with
pure butter.*]

113. FOR A WOMAN WHO HAS
SUFFERED MISCARRIAGE[5]

O pure kiln, great daughter of Anu,[6]
within whom the fire flares into being,
within whom valiant Girra[7] has taken up his
    dwelling,

---

[1]The sky god and king of the older generation of gods.
[2]The chief god of the city of Nippur.

[3]Translation by Benjamin R. Foster, *Before the Muses: An Anthology
of Akkadian Literature* (Bethesda, MD: CDL Press, 3d ed., 2005),
975.
[4]Various deities are invoked before the remedy is applied.
[5]Translation by Benjamin R. Foster, *Before the Muses: An Anthology
of Akkadian Literature* (Bethesda, MD: CDL Press, 3d ed., 2005),
979.
[6]The sky god and head of the older generation of gods.
[7]The god of fire.

you are sound, your equipment is sound,
whether you be empty or full, you are sound.
But when I conceive, I cannot bring to term
    what is within me.
Please give me your soundness,
take away my distress!
Let no imperfect vessel come out from you;
so too for me, may what is within me thrive,
may I see my baby,
may I find acceptance in the house wherein I
    dwell!

114. GARLIC FOR SICKNESS

A kind of sympathetic magic is prescribed here.[1]

As this garlic is peeled off and thrown into
    the fire,
and Girra[2] burns it up with fire,
which will not be cultivated in a garden patch,
which will not be hard by a ditch or canal,
whose roots will not take hold in the ground,
whose sprout will not come forth nor see the
    sun,
which will not be used for the repast of god
    or king,
so may the curse, something evil, revenge,
    interrogation,
the sickness of my suffering, wrongdoing,
    crime, misdeed, sin,
the sickness that is in my body, flesh, and
    sinews,
be peeled off like this garlic.
May Girra burn it with fire this day,
may the wicked thing go forth, that I may see
    light.

115. FOR TOOTHACHE[3]

After Anu[4] created heaven,
heaven created earth,

earth created rivers,
rivers created watercourses,
watercourses created marshland,
marshland created the worm.
The worm came crying before Shamash,[5]
before Ea[6] his tears flowed down:
"What will you give me, that I may eat?
What will you give me, that I may suck?"
"I will give you a ripe fig and an apple."
"What are a ripe fig and apple to me?
So set me to dwell between teeth and jaw,
that I may suck the blood of the jaw,
that I may chew on the bits of food stuck in
    the jaw."
Insert the peg, take hold of the foot.[7]
Because you said this, worm,
may Ea strike you with the might of his hand!

[*There follows a recipe for a potion of beer, oil, and
herbs to be applied to the tooth.*]

OTHER RITUAL TEXTS
116. INSTRUCTIONS FOR TEMPLE OFFICIALS

**Multiple copies of this mid-second-millennium-BCE
Hittite text have been found.[8]**

[*The beginning is broken.*]

Furthermore, let those who prepare the daily
bread be clean; let them be washed and cleansed;
let their hair and fingernails be removed, and let
them have on clean clothes. If not, let them not
prepare it. Let those who propitiate the heart and
soul of the gods prepare them. And let the baker's
house in which they prepare them be swept and
sprinkled. Furthermore, let not a pig or a dog
approach the door of the place of the broken bread.

Is the disposition of men and of the gods at
all different? No! Even in this matter somewhat

---

[1]Translation by Benjamin R. Foster, *Before the Muses: An Anthology
of Akkadian Literature* (Bethesda, MD: CDL Press, 3d ed., 2005),
994.

[2]The god of fire.

[3]Translation by Benjamin R. Foster, *Before the Muses: An Anthology
of Akkadian Literature* (Bethesda, MD: CDL Press, 3d ed., 2005),
995.

[4]The sky god and father of the older generation of gods.

---

[5]The sun god.

[6]The god of wisdom.

[7]The dentist is to remove the tooth, or perhaps its nerve.

[8]Translation by Edgar H. Sturtevant and George Bechtel, *A Hittite
Chrestomathy* (Philadelphia, PA: Linguistic Society of America,
University of Pennsylvania, 1935), 149–151.

different? No; but their disposition is quite the same. When a slave stands before his master, he is washed and he has on clean clothes; and either he gives him something to eat, or he gives him something to drink. And he, his master, eats and drinks something and he is relaxed in spirit and he is favorably inclined to him. If, however, the slave is ever dilatory, and is not observant, there is a different disposition toward him. And if ever a slave vexes his master, either they kill him or they injure his nose, his eyes, or his ears; or the master calls him to account and also his wife, his sons, his brother, his sister, his relatives by marriage, and his family, whether it be a male slave or a female slave. Then they revile him in public, and they consider him nothing at all. And if ever he dies, he does not die alone, but his family is included with him.

If then, on the other hand, anyone vexes the feelings of a god, does the god punish him alone for it? Does he not punish his wife, his children, his descendants, his family, his slaves male and female, his cattle, his sheep, and his harvest from it, and remove him utterly? Now, of your own accord, be very much afraid of the word of a god.

Further: there is a festival of the month, a festival of the year, a festival for *ayalas*,[1] a festival of the autumn, a festival of the spring, a festival of the thunder, a rain festival, a festival of *pudahas*, a festival of *isuwas*, a festival of *issalas*, a festival of the drinking horn, festivals of the pure priest, festivals of the old men, festivals of the mothers of god,[2] a festival of *dahis*, festivals of the men of the east, festivals of *pulas*, festivals of *hahratar*, or whatever festival there is in behalf of Hattusa. If you do not perform them set up with all the cattle, sheep, bread, beer, and wine, and you, temple officials, accept pay from those who give it, you will cause the festival to fall short of the desire of the god.

Or if you take it, when it has been set up, and do not bring it right to the gods themselves, and you carry it away from them to your houses, and your wives, your children, and your slaves eat it up, or if, on the other hand, a relative by marriage or a good citizen comes to you, and you give it to such a person—if you take it from the god himself, and

do not bring it straight to him, and share by share you give it away, then let this charge of division lie against you with a capital penalty. Do not divide it. But whoever divides it, let him die; let there be no pardon for him.[3]

[*More prohibitions against taking what belongs to the god follow.*]

Now you who are temple officials in the temple, be very careful of the reputation of the precinct. At nightfall promptly go down into the town; and eat and drink, and if thoughts of a woman overcome anyone, let him sleep with a woman. And as long as the omens are favorable for them, let them stay. Afterward let each come up to the temple to spend the night, whoever is a temple official—great priests, small priests, and all…priests—and whoever else opens the temple door. Let them severally not neglect to spend the night up in the temple. Furthermore, at night let patrolmen be chosen, and let them patrol all night. Outside in the precinct let the keepers watch; but inside in the temples let the temple officials patrol all night; and let them not sleep. Now from night to night let one important priest be in command of the patrolmen. And besides, of those who are priests, let someone be doorkeeper; let him guard the temple. Let no one spend the night in his own house with his wife; and whomsoever they find down in his own house, it is a capital offense for him. Now of your own accord guard the temples diligently; and do not sleep. Furthermore, let the precinct be divided among you; then the one in whose part of the precinct sin occurs shall die; let him not be pardoned.

[*Several more sections of regulations follow, and the text ends with this conclusion:*]

The first tablet of the duties of all the temple officials, of the kitchen workers of the gods, of the farmers of the gods, and of the cowherds of the gods, and the shepherds of the gods, is finished.

---

[1] Stag.
[2] Probably priestesses.

[3] Cf. 1 Samuel 2:12–17, 29.

117. GOD AND SACRIFICE LISTS FROM UGARIT

a. This list of gods in Ugaritic is one of several of the genre from Ugarit; similar lists are found elsewhere. They served as a kind of checklist rubric so that priests would not forget any deity during prayers or sacrifices. Many of the deities occur in the Ugaritic myths and epics (see Chapters 1 and 2).

The god of the father[1]
El[2]
Dagan[3]
Baal of Zaphon[4]
Baal
Baal
Baal
Baal
Baal
Baal
Earth and Heaven
The Kotharat[5]
Moon
Zaphon[6]
Kothar[7]
Pidray[8]
Athtar[9]
Mountains and Deeps
Asherah[10]
Anat[11]
Sun
Arsay[12]
Usharaya[13]
Astarte[14]

The gods who help Baal
Resheph[15]
Dadmish[16]
The Assembly of the Gods
Sea
Uthatu[17]
Kinnor[18]
Kings[19]
Shalim[20]

b. This list of sacrifices illustrates how the god list in the previous text would have been used.

On the fourteenth (day of the month) the king will wash himself pure.
On the day of fullness, they will slaughter bulls to Moon.
On the tenth (day of the month), a sacrifice for Baal of Zaphon: two ewes and a city dove; and two kidneys and a ram for . . . ; and a liver and a ram for Shalim; and a bull-liver and a ram for Baal of Zaphon; a ewe for Zaphon as a burnt offering.
And as peace offerings, the same.
And in the temple of Baal at Ugarit, . . . and a neck (?);
for the god of the father, a cow; for El, a ram; for Baal, a ram; for Anat of Zaphon, a bull and a ram; for Pidray, a ram as a burnt offering.
And as a peace offering: for the god of the father, a ram; for Baal of Ugarit, a ram; for Baal of Aleppo, a ram; for Moon, a ram; for Anat of Zaphon, a bull and a ram; for Pidray, a ram; for Dadmish, a ram.
And in the window (?): for the god of the father, a ram; for Baal, a bull and a ram; for Dagan, a ram, for the gods who help Baal, a ram; for Anat, a ram; for Resheph, a ram as a peace offering.

[*The text continues in the same vein.*]

---

[1] I.e., the deified ancestor(s), probably of the royal house; see further Text 127.
[2] The head of the Ugaritic pantheon.
[3] The god of grain and father of the storm god Baal; see also Judges 16:23; 1 Samuel 5:1–7.
[4] Zaphon, a prominent mountain north of Ugarit, was the home of the storm god Baal.
[5] Birth goddesses.
[6] The deified mountain home of Baal.
[7] The craftsman of the gods.
[8] A minor goddess, Baal's attendant, whose name means "misty."
[9] The morning star.
[10] The goddess wife of the high god El.
[11] The goddess of war and sister of the storm god Baal.
[12] A minor goddess, Baal's attendant, whose name means "earthy."
[13] An underworld goddess.
[14] A goddess of love often associated with the storm god Baal.

[15] A god of plague.
[16] Probably a goddess of healing.
[17] Apparently a divinized censer used in ritual.
[18] Apparently a divinized lyre used in ritual.
[19] Probably the deified deceased kings of the dynasty; see Text 127.
[20] The god of dusk.

118. MARSEILLES TARIFF

Found in Marseilles, France, in 1844, this late-fourth-century-BCE Punic list, or tariff, of sacrificial distributions was actually written in Carthage in North Africa. Although it is broken, much can be restored because of similar texts, especially from Carthage. Its detailed prescriptions are similar to those in Leviticus 1–7.

Temple of Baal of Zaphon. The tariff of the payments which the thirty men who are in charge of the payments set up in the time of the officials Hilles-Baal, the suffete,[1] son of Bod-Tinnit, son of Bod-Eshmun, and Hilles-Baal, the suffete, son of Bod-Eshmun, son of Hilles-Baal, and their colleagues:

In the case of an ox, whether a whole-offering or a . . . -offering or a whole peace-offering, for the priests: ten 10 (shekels[2] of) silver each; and in the case of a whole-offering, there goes to them in addition to this payment flesh weighing three hundred; and in the case of a . . . -offering, knuckles and joints, but the skin and the ribs and the feet and the rest of the flesh go to the one making the sacrifice.

In the case of a calf whose horns are lacking . . . or a deer, whether a whole-offering or a . . . -offering or a whole peace-offering, for the priests: 5 (shekels of) silver each; and in the case of a whole-offering, there goes to them in addition to this payment flesh weighing one hundred fifty 150; and in the case of a . . . -offering, knuckles and joints, but the skin and the ribs and the feet and the rest of the flesh go to the one making the sacrifice.

In the case of a ram or a goat, whether a whole-offering or a . . . -offering or a whole peace-offering, for the priests: three-quarters of (a shekel of) silver

and 2 zars[3] each; and in the case of a . . . -offering, there goes to them in addition to this payment knuckles and joints, but the skin and the ribs and the feet and the rest of the flesh go to the one making the sacrifice.

In the case of a bird, domesticated or wild, whether a whole peace-offering or a purification-offering or a divination-offering, for the priests: three-quarters of (a shekel of) silver and 2 zars each, but the flesh goes to the one making the sacrifice.

In the case of another bird-offering, whether holy first-fruits or hunting-sacrifice or oil-sacrifice, to the priests: 10 aguras[4] (of silver) each. . . .

In every . . . -offering which is brought before the gods, there goes to the priests knuckles and joints. . . .

For a cake and for milk and for fat and for every sacrifice which a man sacrifices as a meal-offering, . . .

For every sacrifice which someone poor in cattle or poor in birds sacrifices, nothing goes to the priests. . . .

Every clan and every family and every drinking guild of the gods and all men who sacrifice . . . these men shall make payment for each sacrifice in accord with what is set in this document. . . .

Every payment not set in this tablet shall be given according to the document which . . . and Hilles-Baal, son of Bod-Eshmun and their colleagues [wrote].

Every priest who takes a payment contrary to what is set in this tablet will be fin[ed . . . .]

Everyone who offers a sacrifice who does not give . . . the payment . . . .

---

[1] A title of leadership in Carthage. The word is related to the older Semitic word for "ruler, judge" (Hebrew *shophet*).
[2] A shekel weighs ca. 0.35 ounce (10 grams).

[3] A smaller but otherwise unknown weight.
[4] Perhaps the same as Hebrew *gera*, ca. 9 grains (0.6 gram).

Funerary Stela of Kuttamuwa
Found in 2008 at Zincirli in southern Turkey, this monument shows the deceased at his mortuary feast. Made of basalt, it is 39 inches (99 cm) high and 28 inches (72 cm) wide, and dates to the mid-eighth century BCE. (See Text 133.)

7

BURIAL TEXTS

FUNERARY TEXTS

EGYPT

Hundreds of Egyptian funerary texts are known, because they were widely used for many centuries with essentially the same content: to ensure that the deceased would find their way into the next life, in the West, where the sun sets. These texts fall into three chronological groups, although they are related in content: the Pyramid Texts from the Old Kingdom (ca. 2700–2200 BCE), the Coffin Texts from the Middle Kingdom (ca. 2100–1750 BCE), and the Book of the Dead from the New Kingdom (ca. 1550–1100 BCE). Here is a selection.

119. STELA OF INTEF

Intef was a royal official of the twentieth century BCE. He was buried in the major necropolis of Abydos in southern Egypt, where the deity known as "Foremost of the Westerners," the god of the underworld identified with Osiris, was worshipped. The assertions of good behavior resemble the "negative confessions" in Text 123 and the characteristics of a wise person (see Chapter 11).[1]

Kissing the earth to the Foremost of the
    Westerners,
seeing the beauty of Wepwawet,[2] by the
    Chamberlain Intef;
he says:
"Now as for this chapel I have made in the
    desert of Abydos—
O this land of shelter,
the walls to which the Lord to the Limit
    ordained,
a place excellent since the time of Osiris,
which Horus[3] founded for his forefathers,
which the stars in heaven serve,
the mistress of the sunfolk,
to whom the great ones in Busiris[4] come,
the equal to On[5] in blessedness, with which
    the Lord to the Limit is content—
an invocation offered for the blessed one,
the Chamberlain Intef, begotten of Senet!

"I was silent with the wrathful,
    one who mingled with the ignorant, for
    the sake of quelling aggression.

---

[1]Translation by R. B. Parkinson, *Voices from Ancient Egypt: An Anthology of Middle Kingdom Writings* (London: British Museum Press, 1991), 61–63.

[2]A wolf or jackal deity, associated with Anubis, the god of mummification and cemeteries.
[3]The divine son and successor of Osiris; see Text 12.
[4]A city in northern Egypt that was a center for the worship of Osiris.
[5]Also known as Heliopolis, a center for the worship of the sun god.

I was cool, free from haste,
  knowing the outcome, one who foresaw
  what would come.
I was a speaker in occasions of wrath,
  who knew the phrases about which there is
  anger.
I was lenient, hearing my name,
  toward one who told me the state of his
  heart.
I was collected, kind, merciful,
  who quieted the weeper with a kind word.
I was one who was generous to his
  dependent,
  who did what was excellent for his equal.
I was one exact in the house of his lord,
  who knew flattery when spoken.
I was generous, open-handed,
  a lord of provisions, free from neglect.
I was a friend to the little,
  sweet of charm to the have-not.
I was the carer of the hungry who was
  without goods,
  open-handed to the poor.
I was wise for him who was not,
  one who taught a man what was excellent
  for him.
I was an exact one of the king's house,
  who knew what was said in every office.
I was one who hearkened, hearing Truth,
  who passed over matters of no concern.
I was one sweet to the house of his lord,
  remembered for his successful deeds.
I was good within the offices,
  patient and free from priggishness.
I was good, not short-tempered,
  not one who seizes a man for a remark.
I was righteous, the likeness of a balance,
  truly exact like Thoth.[1]
I was firm-footed, excellent of counsel,
  one faithful to his benefactor.
I was wise, one who taught himself wisdom,
  who took counsel so as to be asked for
  counsel.
I was one who spoke in the office of Truth,
  cleverly spoken in occasions of anxiety."

---

[1]The scribe god and patron of scribes, who presided over the weighing of the soul of the dead person on a balance scale.

BOOK OF THE DEAD

Although handwritten, "books of the dead" were mass-produced for tombs from the late second millennium to the late first millennium BCE. They vary considerably in order and content, suggesting that the scroll itself had a magical function. A complete papyrus, the Papyrus of Ani, is the most well-known example. Dating to the mid-thirteenth century BCE, it is a kind of illuminated manuscript, a scroll originally nearly eighty feet long. (It was cut into thirty-seven pieces in the late nineteenth century CE for shipment to England.) Like most other versions of the Book of the Dead, the Papyrus of Ani opens with a series of hymns put into the mouth of the deceased.

120. HYMN TO THE SUN GOD RE[2]

Worship of Re when he rises in the eastern horizon of the sky, by Ani.

He says: "Hail to you, you having come as Khepri,[3] even Khepri who is the creator of the gods. You rise and shine on the back of your mother (the sky), having appeared in glory as King of the gods. Your mother Nut shall use her arms on your behalf in making greeting. The Manu-mountain[4] receives you in peace, Maat[5] embraces you at all seasons. May you give power and might in vindication—and a coming forth as a living soul to see Harakhti—to the ka[6] of Ani."

He says: "O all you gods of the Soul-mansion who judge sky and earth in the balance, who give food and provisions; O Tatenen, Unique One, creator of mankind; O Southern, Northern, Western, and Eastern Enneads,[7] give praise to Re, Lord of the Sky, the Sovereign who made the gods. Worship him in his goodly shape when he appears in the Day-bark.[8] May those who are

---

[2]Translation by Raymond O. Faulkner, in *The Egyptian Book of the Dead: The Book of Going Forth by Day* (San Francisco, CA: Chronicle Books, 1994), Plate 1.
[3]A solar deity, depicted as a scarab beetle.
[4]I.e., the West, where the sun sets and then illumines the underworld.
[5]The goddess of truth and justice.
[6]Life force.
[7]The Ennead was the nine principal gods of Egypt, whose constituents varied from region to region.
[8]The sun was thought to travel across the sky in a large boat during the day and then through the underworld at night.

above worship you, may those who are below worship you, may Thoth[1] and Maat write to you daily; your serpent-foe has been given over to the fire and the rebel-serpent is fallen, his arms are bound, Re has taken away his movements, and the Children of Impotence[2] are nonexistent. The Mansion of the Prince is in festival, the noise of shouting is in the Great Place, the gods are in joy when they see Re in his appearing, his rays flooding the lands. The Majesty of this noble god proceeds, he has entered the land of Manu, the land is bright at his daily birth, and he has attained his state of yesterday. May you be gracious to me when I see your beauty, having departed from upon earth. May I smite the Ass, may I drive off the rebel-serpent, may I destroy Apophis[3] when he acts, for I have seen the Abdju-fish in its moment of being and the Inet-fish piloting the canoe on its waterway. I have seen Horus[4] as helmsman, with Thoth and Maat beside him, I have taken hold of the bow-warp of the Night-bark and the stern-warp of the Day-bark. May he grant that I see the sun-disk and behold the moon unceasingly every day; may my soul go forth to travel to every place which it desires; may my name be called out, may it be found at the board of offerings; may there be given to me loaves in the Presence of the Followers of Horus, may a place be made for me in the solar bark on the day when the god ferries across, and may I be received into the presence of Osiris in the Land of Vindication." For the *ka* of Ani.

121. THE WEIGHING OF THE HEART

The illustration for the following section shows Anubis, the jackal god, weighing the deceased's heart on a balance scale against a feather, with Thoth, the scribe god, recording the result.[5]

Chapter for not letting Ani's heart create opposition against him in the God's Domain.

"O my heart which I had from my mother! O my heart which I had from my mother! O my heart of different ages! Do not stand up as a witness against me, do not be opposed to me in the tribunal, do not be hostile to me in the presence of the Keeper of the Balance, for you are my *ka*[6] which was in my body, the protector who made my members hale. Go forth to the happy place whereto we speed; do not make my name stink to the Entourage who make men. Do not tell lies about me in the presence of the god; it is indeed well that you should hear!"

Thus says Thoth, judge of truth, to the Great Ennead[7] which is in the presence of Osiris:[8] "Hear this word of very truth. I have judged the heart of the deceased, and his soul stands as a witness for him. His deeds are righteous in the great balance, and no sin has been found in him. He did not diminish the offerings in the temple, he did not destroy what has been made, he did not go about with deceitful speech while he was on earth."

Thus says the Great Ennead to Thoth who is in Hermopolis: "This utterance of yours is true. The vindicated Osiris Ani[9] is straightforward, he has no sin, there is no accusation against him before us, Ammit shall not be permitted to have power over him.[10] Let there be given to him the offerings which are issued in the presence of Osiris, and may a grant of land be established in the Field of Offerings as for the Followers of Horus."

Thus says Horus, son of Isis: "I have come to you, O Wennefer,[11] and I bring Ani to you. His heart is true, having gone forth from the balance, and he has not sinned against any god or any goddess. Thoth has judged him in writing which has been told to the Ennead, and Maat the great

---

[1] The scribe god and patron of scribes.
[2] Evil spirits.
[3] A serpent enemy of the sun god.
[4] The divine son and successor of Osiris, who ruled the earth as his father ruled the underworld.
[5] Translation by Raymond O. Faulkner, in *The Egyptian Book of the Dead: The Book of Going Forth by Day* (San Francisco, CA: Chronicle Books, 1994), Plate 3.

[6] Life force.
[7] The nine principal gods of Egypt.
[8] The divine king of the underworld.
[9] When a person died, he or she became identified as Osiris, the god who had been restored to life in the underworld.
[10] Ammit was the monster deity who gobbled up the heart if it failed the balance test.
[11] A title of Osiris.

has witnessed. Let there be given to him bread and beer which have been issued in the presence of Osiris, and he will be forever, like the Followers of Horus."

Thus says Ani: "Here I am in your presence, O Lord of the West. There is no wrongdoing in my body, I have not wittingly told lies, there has been no second fault. Grant that I may be like the favored ones who are in your suite, O Osiris, one greatly favored by the good god, one loved of the Lord of the Two Lands, Ani, vindicated before Horus."

122. Hymn to Osiris[1]

Worship of Osiris, Lord of Eternity, Wennefer.

"Harakhti multiple of forms and great of shapes, Ptah-Sokar, Atum in Heliopolis, Lord of the Shetyt-shrine, who enriches Memphis; these are the gods who govern the Duat;[2] they protect you when you go to rest in the Lower Sky. Isis embraces you in peace and drives away the adversary from your path. Turn your face to the West that you may illumine the Two Lands with fine gold. Those who were asleep stand up to look at you; they breathe the air, they see your face like the shining of the sun-disk in its horizon, their hearts are at peace because of what you have done, for to you belong eternity and everlasting."

123. Negative Confession

In Chapter 125 of the Book of the Dead, the deceased declares his innocence in a list of things he has not done. This is often compared to Job 31; see also Text 119.[3]

To be said on reaching the Hall of the Two Truths so as to purge N[4] of any sins committed and to see the face of every god:

"Hail to you, great God, Lord of the Two Truths! I have come to you, my Lord, I was brought to see your beauty. I know you, I know the names of the forty-two gods, who are with you in the Hall of the Two Truths, who live by warding off evildoers, who drink of their blood, on that day of judging characters before Wennefer.[5] Lo, your name is "He-of-Two-Daughters," and "He-of-Maat's-Two-Eyes." Lo, I come before you, bringing Maat[6] to you, having repelled evil for you.

"I have not done crimes against people;
I have not mistreated cattle;
I have not sinned in the Place of Truth.[7]
I have not known what should not be known;
I have not done any harm.
I did not begin a day by exacting more than my due;
my name did not reach the bark of the mighty ruler.[8]
I have not blasphemed a god;
I have not robbed the poor.
I have not done what a god abhors;
I have not maligned a servant to his master.
I have not caused pain;
I have not caused tears.
I have not killed;
I have not ordered to kill;
I have not made anyone suffer.
I have not damaged the offerings in the temples;
I have not depleted the loaves of the gods;
I have not stolen the cakes of the dead.
I have not copulated nor defiled myself.
I have not increased nor reduced the measure;[9]
I have not diminished the *arura*,[10]
I have not cheated in the fields.
I have not added to the weight of the balance;

[1]Translation by Raymond O. Faulkner, in *The Egyptian Book of the Dead: The Book of Going Forth by Day* (San Francisco, CA: Chronicle Books, 1994), Plate 19.
[2]A term for the underworld.
[3]Translation by Miriam Lichtheim, *Ancient Egyptian Literature* (Berkeley, CA: University of California Press, 1976; 2006), 2.124–32.
[4]The name of the deceased was given here.

[5]A title of Osiris.
[6]The goddess of truth and justice.
[7]A temple.
[8]The sun god in his boat crossing the heavens.
[9]Cf. Amos 8:5.
[10]A measure of area, ca. 2/3 acre (1/4 hectare).

I have not falsified the plummet of the scales.

I have not taken milk from the mouth of children;

I have not deprived the cattle of their pasture.

I have not snared birds in the reeds of the gods;

I have not caught fish in their ponds.

I have not held back water in its season;

I have not dammed a flowing stream;

I have not quenched a needed fire.

I have not neglected the days of meat offerings;

I have not detained cattle belonging to the god;

I have not stopped a god in his procession.

"I am pure, I am pure, I am pure, I am pure!

I am pure as is pure that great heron in Hanes.[1]

I am truly the nose of the Lord of Breath, who sustains all the people, on the day of completing the Eye[2] in On,[3] in the second month of winter, last day, in the presence of the lord of this land. I have seen the completion of the Eye in On!

No evil shall befall me in this land, in this Hall of the Two Truths; for I know the names of the gods in it, the followers of the great God!

[*There follow addresses to the forty-two gods mentioned at the beginning, again proclaiming the deceased's innocence:*]

"O Wide-of-stride who comes from On: I have not done evil.

O Flame-grasper who comes from Kheraha: I have not robbed.

O Long-nosed who comes from Khmun: I have not coveted.

O Shadow-eater who comes from the cave: I have not stolen.

O Savage-faced who comes from Rostau: I have not killed people.

O Lion-Twins who come from heaven: I have not trimmed the measure.

O Flint-eyed who comes from Khem: I have not cheated.

O Fiery-one who comes backward: I have not stolen a god's property.

O Bone-smasher who comes from Hnes: I have not told lies.

O Flame-thrower who comes from Memphis: I have not seized food.

O Cave-dweller who comes from the West: I have not sulked.

O White-toothed who comes from the Lakeland: I have not trespassed.

O Blood-eater who comes from the slaughterplace: I have not slain sacred cattle.

O Entrail-eater who comes from the tribunal: I have not extorted.

O Lord of Maat who comes from Maaty: I have not stolen bread rations.

O Wanderer who comes from Bubastis: I have not spied.

O Pale-One who comes from On: I have not prattled.

O Villain who comes from Anjdty: I have contended only for my goods.

O Fiend who comes from the Slaugherhouse: I have not committed adultery.

O Examiner who comes from Min's temple: I have not defiled myself.

O Chief of the nobles who comes from Imu: I have not caused fear.

O Wrecker who comes from Huy: I have not trespassed.

O Disturber who comes from the sanctuary: I have not been violent.

O Child who comes from the nome[4] of On: I have not been deaf to Maat.

O Foreteller who comes from Wensi: I have not quarreled.

O Bastet who comes from the shrine: I have not winked.

O Backward-faced who comes from the pit: I have not copulated with a boy.

---

[1] Later Heracleopolis, in southern Egypt.
[2] The eye of Horus, or the sun.
[3] Later Heliopolis.

[4] An administrative subdivision of ancient Egypt.

O Flame-footed who comes from the Dusk: I have not been false.

O Dark-one who comes from darkness: I have not reviled.

O Peace-bringer who comes from Sais: I have not been aggressive.

O Many-faced who comes from Djefet: I have not had a hasty heart.

O Accuser who comes from Utjen: I have not attacked and reviled a god.

O Horned-one who comes from Siut: I have not made many words.

O Nefertem who comes from Memphis: I have not sinned, I have not done wrong.

O Timeless-one who comes from Tjebu: I have not made trouble.

O Willful-One who comes from Tjebu: I have not waded in water.

O Flowing-one who comes from Nun: I have not raised my Voice.

O Commander of people who comes from his shrine: I have not cursed a god.

O Benefactor who comes from Huy: I have not been boastful.

O Nehebkau who comes from the city: I have not been haughty.

O High-of-head who comes from the cave: I have not wanted more than I had.

O Captor who comes from the graveyard: I have not cursed god in my town.

"Hail to you, gods! I know you, I know your names. I shall not fall in fear of you; you shall not accuse me of crime to this god whom you follow! No misfortune shall befall me on your account! You shall speak rightly about me before the All-Lord, for I have acted rightly in Egypt. I have not cursed a god, I have not been faulted.

"Hail to you, gods in the Hall of the Two Truths, who have no lies in their bodies, who live on maat[1] in On, who feed on their rightness before Horus in his disk. Rescue me from Babi,[2] who feeds on the entrails of nobles, on that day of the great reckoning. Behold me, I have come to you, without sin, without guilt, without evil, without a witness against me, without one whom I have wronged. I live on maat, I feed on maat, I have done what people speak of, what the gods are pleased with; I have contented a god with what he wishes. I have given bread to the hungry, water to the thirsty, clothes to the naked, a ferryboat to the boatless.[3] I have given divine offerings to the gods, invocation-offerings to the dead. Rescue me, protect me, do not accuse me before the great god!

"I am one pure of mouth, pure of hands, one to whom "Welcome" is said by those who see him; for I have heard the words spoken by the Donkey and the Cat, in the house of the Open-mouthed;[4] I was a witness before him when he cried out, I saw the splitting of the ished-tree in Rostau.[5] I am one who is acquainted with the gods, one who knows what concerns them. I have come here to bear witness to maat, to set the balance in right position among the dead.

"O you who are high upon your standard Lord of the atef-crown,[6] who is given the name "Lord of Breath": rescue me from your messengers, who inflict wounds, who mete out punishment, who have no compassion, for I have done maat for the Lord of maat! I am pure, my front is pure, my rear is pure, my middle has been in the well of maat, no limb of mine is unclean. I have washed in the well of the South, I have halted at the town of the North, in the meadow of the grasshoppers, where the crew of Re bathes by day and by night, where the gods enjoy passing by day and by night."

[*The gods of successive entryways now interrogate the deceased:*]

"Let him come," they say to me;
"Who are you?" they say to me;
"What is your name?" they say to me.

---

[1] Truth.

[2] The baboon god.

[3] Cf. Isaiah 58:7; Ezekiel 18:7; Job 22:7; 31:16–20; Tobit 4:16; Matthew 25:34–45.

[4] A reference to the punishment of Seth, Osiris's brother, in the form of a donkey, by the cat goddess Mafdet.

[5] References to myths of victories of Horus and Re.

[6] The feathered crown of Osiris.

"'I am the stalk of the papyrus, 'He-Who-Is-in-the Moringa'[1] is my name."
"What have you seen there?"
"The Leg and the Thigh."
"What did you say to them?"
"I have witnessed the acclaim in the land of the Fenkhu."[2]
"What did they give you?"
"A firebrand and a faience column."
"What did you do with them?"
"I buried them on the shore of the pool Maaty, at the time of the evening meal."
"What did you find there on the shore of the pool Maaty?"
"A scepter of flint whose name is 'Breath-giver.'"
"What did you do to the firebrand and the faience column, when you had buried them?"
"I lamented over them, I took them up, I extinguished the fire, I broke the column, threw it in the pool."
"Come then, enter the gate of this Hall of the Two Truths, for you know us."

"I shall not let you enter through me," says the beam of this gate, "unless you tell my name."
"'Plummet-of-the-Place-of-Truth' is your name."
"I shall not let you enter though me," says the right leaf of this gate, "unless you tell my name."
"'Scale-pan-That-Carries-*maat*' is your name."
"I shall not let you enter through me," says the left leaf of this gate, "unless you tell my name."
"'Scale-pan-of-Wine' is your name."
"I shall not let you pass over me," says the threshold of this gate, "unless you tell my name."
"'Ox-of-Geb' is your name."
"I shall not open for you," says the bolt of this gate, "unless you tell my name."

"'Eye-of-Sobk-Lord-of-Bakhu' is your name."
"I shall not open for you, I shall not let you enter by me," says the keeper of this gate, "unless you tell my name."
"'Breast-of-Shu-Given-Him-to-Guard Osiris' is your name."
"We shall not let you pass over us," say the cross-timbers, "unless you tell our name."
"'Offspring-of-Renenutet' is your name."
"You know us, pass over us."

"You shall not tread upon me," says the floor of this hall.
"Why not, since I am pure?"
"Because we do not know your feet, with which you tread on us; tell them to me."
"'Who-Enters-before-Min' is the name of my right foot, '*Wnpt*-of-Nephthys' is the name of my left foot."
"Tread upon us, since you know us."

"I shall not announce you," says the guard of the Hall, "unless you tell my name."
"'Knower-of-Hearts Examiner-of-Bellies' is your name."
"To which god present shall I announce you?"
"Tell it to the Interpreter of the Two Lands."
"Who is the Interpreter of the Two Lands?
"It is Thoth."[3]

"Come," says Thoth, "why have you come?"
"I have come here to report."
"What is your condition?"
"I am free of all wrongdoing, I avoided the strife of those in their day, I am not one of them."
"To whom shall I announce you?"
"To him whose roof is of fire, whose walls are living cobras, the floor of whose house is in the flood."
"Who is he?"
"He is Osiris."
"Proceed, you are announced: the Eye is your bread, the Eye is your beer, the Eye is your offering on earth," so says he to me.

---

[1]A title of Osiris. The next several sentences refer to aspects of the myth of Osiris.
[2]The Phoenicians.

[3]The scribe of the gods who oversees the weighing of the heart (see Text 121).

[*There follow rubric-like instructions and a prom-
ise that the scroll will be effective if they are carried
out:*]

This is the way to act toward the Hall of the
Two Truths. A man says this speech when he is
pure, clean, dressed in fresh clothes, shod in white
sandals, painted with eye-paint, anointed with the
finest oil of myrrh. One shall offer to him beef,
fowl, incense, bread, beer, and herbs. And you
make this image in drawing on a clean surface in
red paint mixed with soil on which pigs and goats
have not trodden.

He for whom this scroll is recited will prosper,
and his children will prosper. He will be the friend
of the king and his courtiers. He will receive
bread, beer, and a big chunk of meat from the
altar of the great god. He will not be held back at
any gate of the West. He will be ushered in with
the kings of Upper and Lower Egypt. He will be a
follower of Osiris.

Effective a million times.

124. FOR GOING OUT INTO
THE DAY

**From another version of the Book of the Dead ("The
Theban Recension").**[1]

"The doors of the sky are opened for me, the
doors of the earth are opened for me, the door-
bolts of Geb are opened for me, the shutters of
the sky-windows are thrown open for me. It is
he who guarded me who releases me, who binds
his hand onto me and thrusts his hand to me on
earth, the mouth of the Pelican[2] is opened for
me, the mouth of the Pelican is given to me, and
I go out into the day to the place where I desire
to be.[3]

"May I have power in my heart, may I have
power in my heart, may I have power in my
arms, may I have power in my legs, may I have

power in my mouth, may I have power in all my
members, may I have power over invocation-
offerings, may I have power over water, may I
have power over air, may I have power over the
waters, may I have power over the streams, may
I have power over riparian lands, may I have
power over the men who would harm me, may
I have power over the women who would harm
me in the God's Domain, may I have power over
those who would give orders to harm me upon
earth."

A god replies: "Surely it will be according to
what you say to me. You shall live on the bread
of Geb,[4] and you shall not eat what you detest.
You shall live on bread of white emmer and
beer of red barley of Hapi[5] in the pure place;
you shall sit under the branches of the tree of
Hathor[6] who is preeminent in the wide solar
disk when she travels to Heliopolis bearing the
script of the divine words, the book of Thoth.[7]
You shall have power in your heart, you shall
have power in your heart, you shall have power
in your mouth, you shall have power in your
arms, you shall have power over water, you
shall have power over the waters, you shall
have power over the streams, you shall have
power over riparian lands, you shall have power
over the men who would harm you, you shall
have power over the women who would harm
you in the God's Domain, you shall have power
over those who would give orders to harm you
on earth or in the God's Domain. Raise yourself upon your left side, put yourself upon your
right side, sit down and stand up, throw off
your dust, may your tongue and your mouth be
wise."

As for whoever knows this book, he shall go out
into the day, he shall walk on earth among the
living and he shall never suffer destruction. A
matter a million times true.

---

[1]Translation by Raymond O. Faulkner, in *The Egyptian Book of
the Dead: The Book of Going Forth by Day* (San Francisco, CA:
Chronicle Books, 1994), 107, no. 68.
[2]A goddess of the underworld.
[3]Cf. Text 182, pages 188–189.

[4]The god of the earth.
[5]One of the four sons of the god Horus.
[6]The goddess of love, often depicted as a cow.
[7]The scribe of the gods.

125. A *SHABTI* INSCRIPTION

Shabtis were figurines buried with the deceased who would perform manual labor for the deceased in the next life.[1]

"O *shabti*, allotted to me, if I be summoned or if I be detailed to do any work which has to be done in the God's Domain; if indeed obstacles are implanted for you therewith as a man at his duties, you shall detail yourself for me on every occasion of making arable the fields, of flooding the banks, or of conveying sand from east to west; 'Here am I,' you shall say."

126. CARPENTRAS STELA

This incomplete Aramaic inscription was published in 1704, the first in modern times. It is located in the museum of the town of Carpentras, in southeastern France, perhaps brought there from Egypt by a member of the town's large Jewish community. It dates to the fourth century BCE and, although written in Aramaic, is fully Egyptian in content, as is the relief above it, one panel of which shows the body of the deceased flanked by the gods Horus and Anubis. The inscription, in quasi-poetic form, illustrates the use of Aramaic in Egypt (see also Texts 53–55, 87, 88, and 195).

Blessed be Tabi, daughter of Tahapi, the one devoted to the god Osiris.
Anything evil she did not do, and the slander of a man she did not say there.[2]
Before Osiris be blessed; from Osiris receive water. Serve the Lord of the Two Truths,[3] and among the favored ones....

UGARIT
127. ROYAL FUNERARY TEXT

This Ugaritic text is bristling with difficulties, but from what can be understood it is important evidence for

the deification and probably the worship of dead ancestors at Ugarit, at least of the royal family. In it, the Rephaim, the "shades" among whom were the dead kings of Ugarit (cf. Isaiah 14:9), are summoned to welcome Niqmaddu to the underworld; this is Niqmaddu III, the father of Ammurapi, the last king of Ugarit, who ruled in the late thirteenth century BCE. The text ends with a sacrifice for the new king—"The king is dead; long live the king!" as it were—and for the city, which ironically was destroyed soon after. Another Ugaritic text, not translated here, includes a broken list of the kings of Ugarit, each of whom is identified as divine.

Book of the Sacrifice of the Shades.
You have been called, O Rephaim of the
   earth,
   you have been called, O Assembly of
      Ditan:
( ),[4] the Rapha, has been called;
   ( ), the Rapha, has been called;
   ( ) has been called;
   ( ) has been called
The ancient Rephaim have been called:
   you have been called, O Rephaim of the
      earth,
   you have been called, O Assembly of
      Ditan.
Ammishtamru the king has been called;
   Niqmaddu the king has also been called.
O throne of Niqmaddu, may you be wept
   over,
   and may tears be shed over his footstool.
Before him, let the king's table be wept
   over:
   let it swallow its tears: desolation and
      desolation of desolations!
Let Sun burn,
   and let Lady Light burn!
On high Sun cries out:
"After your lords, from the throne,
   after your lords, go down to the earth,
   go down to the earth and fall in
      the dust.
Under ( ),

[1]Translation by Raymond O. Faulkner, in *The Egyptian Book of the Dead: The Book of Going Forth by Day* (San Francisco, CA: Chronicle Books, 1994), 101, no. 6.
[2]Presumably in the world of the living, if this interpretation is correct.
[3]A dual form of the Egyptian word Maat.

[4]Here and in the following lines, unintelligible names of dead kings of the dynasty are found.

under ( ),
> under the ancient Rephaim;
under Ammishtamru the king,
> under Niqmaddu the king also."
One, offer a sacrifice;
> two, offer a sacrifice;
> three, offer a sacrifice;
> four, offer a sacrifice;
> five, offer a sacrifice;
> six, offer a sacrifice;
> seven, offer a sacrifice.
You should present a bird of a well-being
> (sacrifice):
> a well-being (sacrifice) for Ammurapi,
> and a well-being (sacrifice) for his son;
a well-being (sacrifice) for Tharyelli,[1]
> a well-being (sacrifice) for her house;
a well-being sacrifice for Ugarit,
> a well-being sacrifice for its gates.

PHOENICIAN
128. AHIRAM SARCOPHAGUS

One of the earliest Phoenician inscriptions known, this text dates to the early tenth century BCE. It is carved on the edge of the lid of a large stone coffin that held the remains of a king of Gebal (Byblos).

The chest that Ittobaal,[2] the son of Ahiram,[3] king of Gebal, made for Ahiram his father, when he placed him in eternity. And now if any king among kings or governor among governors or army commander attacks Gebal and opens this chest, may the scepter of his rule be stripped, may the throne of his kingship be overthrown, and may rest flee from Gebal. As for him, may his inscription be erased....

129. AHIRAM GRAFFITO

This text was written in the shaft of the tomb where the sarcophagus (see Text 128) was found. Its reading and interpretation are debated:

---

[1]The queen.
[2]Also the name (biblical Ethbaal) of the father of Jezebel, wife of Ahab, king of Israel (1 Kings 16:31).
[3]Also the name of kings of Tyre, in the shorter form Hiram.

For your information: Behold, one will perish below this!

130. TABNIT

This inscription is carved on the lid of a reused Egyptian sarcophagus that had been imported to the Phoenician coastal city of Sidon. It memorializes Tabnit, king of Sidon and priest of the goddess Astarte in the mid-fifth century BCE. His father was Eshmunazor I, and his son was Eshmunazor II (see Text 131).

I, Tabnit, priest of Astarte, king of the Sidonians, son of Eshmunazor, priest of Astarte, king of the Sidonians, rest in this casket. Whoever you are, any person, who finds this casket, do not, do not open my lid, and do not disturb me.[4] For they have not put silver with me, they have not put gold with me, or anything valuable. I alone lie in this casket. Do not, do not open my lid and do not disturb me, for that is an abomination to Astarte. And if you do open my lid and do disturb me, may you not have any seed among the living under the sun[5] or a resting place with the Rephaim.[6]

131. ESHMUNAZOR

This inscription is carved on the lid of another Egyptian sarcophagus that had been imported to Sidon. It memorializes Eshmunazor II, son of Tabnit (see Text 130), a king of Sidon in the mid-fifth century BCE.

In the month of Bul,[7] in the fourteenth (14) year of the reign of King Eshmunazor, king of the Sidonians, son of King Tabnit, king of the Sidonians, King Eshmunazor, king of the Sidonians, said:

---

[4]Cf. 1 Samuel 28:15.
[5]Cf. Ecclesiastes 4:15; 6:12; 9:9.
[6]In general, as here, the Rephaim are the dead in their shadowy existence in the underworld (cf. Psalm 88:10; Proverbs 2:18; 21:16; Job 26:5); sometimes the specifically denoted dead royalty or ancestors (see Text 127 and Isaiah 14:9).
[7]As in Hebrew (1 Kings 6:38), the eighth month (October/November).

I was snatched away before my time,[1] the son of a limited number of days...an orphan, the son of a widow. And I lie in this coffin and in this tomb in the place that I built.

Whoever you are, any king or any person, do not open this resting place, and do not look for anything in it, for they have not put anything in it, and do not take away this coffin of my resting place and move me from this resting place to another resting place. Even if people tell you, do not listen to their talk. As for any king or any person who opens up this resting place, or who takes away the coffin of my resting place or who moves me from this resting place, may he not have a resting place with the Rephaim,[2] and may he not be buried in a tomb, and may he not have a son or seed in his place. And may the holy gods deliver up him to a mighty king who will rule over him to cut him off—the king or person who opens up this resting place or who takes away this coffin, or the seed of that king or those persons. May he not have a root below or fruit above[3] or any renown among those who live under the sun.[4] For I should be pitied; I was snatched away before my time, the son of a limited number of days...an orphan, the son of a widow am I.

For I, Eshmunazor, the king of the Sidonians, the son of King Tabnit, king of the Sidonians, son of the son of King Eshmunazor, the king of the Sidonians, and my mother, Immi-astart, priestess of Astarte[5] our lady, the queen, daughter of King Eshmunazor, king of the Sidonians, we built the house of the gods, the house of Astarte, in Sidon, the land of the sea, and we installed Astarte in the Mighty Heavens.[6] We built the temple of Eshmun,[7] the holy prince, at the spring of...on the mountain, and installed him in the Mighty Heavens. We built houses for the gods of the Sidonians in Sidon, the land of

the sea, a house for Baal of Sidon and a house for Astarte, name of Baal.[8] Moreover, the lord of kings[9] gave us Dor and Joppa,[10] the lands of Dagon,[11] the mighty lands, which are in the plain of Sharon, in return for the great deeds that I did, and we incorporated them within the boundary of the land to belong to the Sidonians forever.

Whoever you are, any king or any person, do not open up my lid, and do not uncover my lid and do not move me from this resting place and do not take away the coffin of my resting place, lest the holy gods deliver them up and cut off that king or those persons and their seed forever.

132. BATNOAM

This early- to mid-fourth-century-BCE text is an example of a burial inscription for a woman. Batnoam was the queen mother of the king of Gebal (Byblos).

In this chest lie I, Batnoam, mother of King Azbaal, king of Gebal, son of Paltibaal, priest of the Mistress, in a robe and a headdress and a gold muzzle on my mouth,[12] just like the queens who were before me.

SAMAL
133. KUTTAMUWA

Discovered in 2008, this well-preserved and elaborately carved monument (see page 146) is a funerary stela in the distinctive dialect of the kingdom of Samal (see also Text 35), which is very close to the Phoenician used in Text 26. Dating to the mid- to late eighth century BCE, its archaeological context is a mortuary room or chapel, probably connected with regular rituals on behalf of the dead, perhaps ancestor worship.

---

[1] Cf. Ecclesiastes 7:17.
[2] See page 156, n. 6.
[3] Cf. Isaiah 37:31; Amos 2:9.
[4] See Ecclesiastes 4:15; 6:12; 9:9.
[5] The goddess-wife of the storm god Baal.
[6] The name of the shrine.
[7] The patron god of Sidon, a god of healing, whose name is found in the name of the dead king Eshmunazor.

[8] That is, Baal's "other self"; the same epithet is used in Ugaritic texts.
[9] Cf. Daniel 2:47.
[10] Cities on the Mediterranean coast south of Sidon.
[11] The god of grain, associated with Baal.
[12] Perhaps to prevent demons from entering the mouth.

I am Kuttamuwa, servant of Panamuwa,[1] who had this stela made for myself while I was alive. And I put it in my eternal chamber and I established a feast in this chamber: a bull for Hadad of [ ],[2] and a ram for [ ],[3] and a ram for Shamash,[4] and a ram for Hadad of the vineyards, and a ram for Kubaba,[5] and a ram for myself[6] who is on this stela. And now, if any of my sons or of the sons of someone else makes this chamber his own, let him take the best of this vineyard as an offering each year. He should also sacrifice for myself, and should provide for me a libation.

HEBREW

134. SILWAN

On a ridge in Jerusalem southeast of the city of David were many tombs from the Iron Age and later. On one is a burial inscription of a royal official, dating to the late eighth century BCE. Although the official's name is not fully preserved, he may have been Shebna, who was condemned for having cut a tomb in the rock (Isaiah 22:15–19).

This [is the tomb of _____-]yahu who is over the house.[7] Here there is no silver or gold, only [his bones] and the bones of his maidservant with him. Cursed be the person who opens this.

135. EL-QOM

Two inscriptions from a tomb cave in the Judean hill country west of Hebron, dating to the late eighth and early seventh centuries BCE, respectively. The first is badly damaged.

a.   Uriyahu the rich[8]: his inscription.
     Blessed be Uriyahu by Yahweh, and from his enemies, by his Asherah,[9] he has delivered him.
     By Oniyahu.
     By his Asherah.
b.   To Ophay son of Natanyahu this chamber (belongs)

136. KETEF HINNOM

In a large burial cave on the outskirts of Jerusalem, two silver amulets were found along with other grave goods. Discovered in 1979, the tomb was in use for some time, beginning in the late seventh century BCE, which is when the amulets are most likely dated. The two amulets contain versions of the "Priestly Blessing," also found in a slightly different form in Numbers 6:24–26. They may have been personal possessions of the deceased, or they may have been included in the tomb as a blessing for the deceased in the afterlife.

a.   . . . the covenant and mercy to those who love him and those who keep. . . .[10]
     For in him is redemption, for Yahweh is our restorer and a rock.
     May Yahweh bless you and may he keep you.
     May Yahweh make [his] face [shi]ne. . . .
b.   May . . . be blessed by Yahweh, the helper and the rebuker of [evi]l. May Yahweh bless you; may he keep you. May Yahweh make his face shine on you and give you peace.

PERSIAN

137. MAUSOLEUM OF CYRUS

According to the second-century-CE Greek historian Arrian, quoting the fourth-century-BCE historian Aristobulus of Cassandreia's *History of Alexander*, this text was written on the mausoleum of Cyrus II

---

[1]Probably Panamuwa II (ruled ca. 743–732 BCE), or perhaps his grandfather Panamuwa I.

[2]The text is unclear; perhaps an unidentifiable geographical name.

[3]An unidentifiable deity.

[4]The sun god.

[5]An Anatolian goddess.

[6]Others take this word (*nbš*; cf. Heb. *npš*) to mean "soul"; it can also mean "monument."

[7]That is, roughly, the "royal steward," the title of Shebna (Isaiah 22:15), and of other royal officials (1 Kings 4:6; 16:9; 18:3; 2 Kings 18:18).

[8]Reading uncertain.

[9]The interpretation of this word is disputed. It may refer to the goddess Asherah, understood as the divine consort of Yahweh (see also Texts 153 and 154). An alternative is to understand it as a common noun, referring to the wooden pole that symbolized the goddess (see, e.g., Deuteronomy 16:21; 2 Kings 23:6).

[10]Cf. Deuteronomy 7:9; Daniel 9:4; Nehemiah 1:5.

(the Great), king of Persia from 559 to 530 BCE (see Text 40). The mausoleum still stands at Pasargadae in Iran, but it has no inscription on it.

O man, I am Cyrus, son of Cambyses, who established the empire of the Persians and ruled Asia. Do not begrudge me this memorial.

Pyrgi Dedicatory Inscription
Written on gold leaf, this Phoenician inscription was found at Pyrgi in Italy in
1964. Dating to ca. 500 BCE, it is 7.5 inches (19 cm) high and 3.5 inches (9 cm)
wide. (See Text 148.)

COMMEMORATIVE AND DEDICATORY TEXTS

THESE TEXTS ARE of two types. Some were monuments erected to commemorate an event or a person and, like the burial texts in Chapter 7, often include a description of the person's accomplishments, a blessing on the person, and sometimes a warning not to remove or deface the monument. Others are texts written on votive offerings and also often include blessings.

ARAMAIC

138. TELL FEKHERIYE

This bilingual Aramaic and Assyrian inscription was found in northeastern Syria in 1979. Carved on the statue of the ruler named in the text, it dates to mid-ninth century BCE. This is the Aramaic version.

The image of Haddu-yithi[1] which he set up before Hadad of Sikan:[2] the canal-inspector of the heavens and the earth, who sends down wealth and gives pasture and watering places to all the land; and who gives calm and offering bowls to all the gods his brothers; the canal-inspector of all rivers, who makes all lands luxurious; the merciful god to whom prayer is good, who dwells in Sikan;

the great lord, the lord of Haddu-yithi, king of Guzan, son of Sas-nuri,[3] king of Guzan.[4] For the preservation of his life[5] and for the lengthening of his days and for the increase of his years, and for the peace of his house and for the peace of his seed and for the peace of his people, and for removal of sickness from him, and for the hearing of his prayer, and for the taking of the words of his mouth: he set it up and gave it to him.

And whoever afterward, if it is worn, should set it up anew, may he put my name on it. And if this person removes my name from it and puts his name, may Hadad the warrior be his accuser.[6]

The statue of Haddu-yithi, king of Guzan and of Sikan and of Azran, for exalting and . . . his throne and for the lengthening of his life and in order that the words of his mouth be good to the gods and to the people. This image he made, better than before; before Hadad who dwells in Sikan, the lord of Habur, he set up his statue. And whoever removes my name from the vessels of the temple of Hadad my lord, may Hadad my lord not accept his food and water from his hand; and may

---

[1]The name means "Hadad is my salvation." Hadad was the Aramean storm god, equivalent to Adad in Mesopotamia and Baal in Ugaritic and Phoenician.
[2]Sikan was the ancient name of Tell Fekheriye.

[3]In the Assyrian text his name is Shamash-nuri.
[4]Guzan was the capital of Haddu-yithi's small kingdom in northeastern Syria.
[5]Literally, "for the life of his soul."
[6]Although what follows is found on the same line of text, its content suggests that it is a new inscription, perhaps on the occasion of the statue's rededication.

Sala,[1] my lady, not accept his food and water from his hand; and may he sow and may he not reap;[2] and may he sow a thousand measures, but take only a half-measure from it;[3] and may a hundred ewes suckle a lamb, but may it not be satisfied; and may a hundred cows suckle a calf, but may it not be satisfied; and may a hundred women suckle a child, but may it not be satisfied; and may a hundred women bake bread in an oven, but may they not fill it;[4] and may his people glean barley from a refuse pit and may they eat; and may pestilence, the staff of Nergal,[5] not be cut off from his land.

139. ZAKKUR

This Aramaic text is written on a stela found near Aleppo in northern Syria, dating to the early eighth century BCE, and commemorating a victory over other kings in the region. Although it is badly damaged, it is especially important for its mention of oracles from the god Baal-Shamayin (see further Chapter 10).

The stela which Zakkur, king of Hamath[6] and Luash, set up for Iluwer[7] . . . :

I am Zakkur, king of Hamath and Luash. I am a humble man.[8] But Baal-shamayin[9] [rescued] me, and stood with me, and made me king over Hadrak.[10] And Bar-Hadad, son of Hazael, king of Aram,[11] united against me s[even]teen kings: Bar-Hadad and his army, and Bargash and his army, and the king of Que and his army, and the king of Amuq and his army, and the king of Gurgum and his army, and the king of Samal[12] and his army, and the king of Miliz and his army . . . seven[teen kings]. And all of these kings laid siege to Hadrak. And they raised a wall

higher than the wall of Hadrak, and they dug a moat deeper than its moat.

And I lifted my hands to Baal-shamayin, and Baal-shamayin answered me and Baal-shamayin [spoke] to me through seers[13] and through diviners, and Baal-shamayin [said] to me: "Do not be afraid! For I made [you] king and I . . . with you, and I will rescue you from all [these kings who] have laid siege to you. . . ."

[*The rest is badly damaged.*]

140. BAR-RAKIB

This text is from Samal, in northwestern Syria. Written in Aramaic rather than in the local Samal dialect (like Texts 26 and 133) or Phoenician (like Text 35), it dates to the second half of the eighth century BCE.

I am Bar-Rakib, son of Panamuwa,[14] king of Samal, servant of Tiglath-pileser,[15] lord of the four (quarters) of the earth. Because of the righteousness of my father and my righteousness, my lord Rakib-El[16] and my lord Tiglath-pileser seated me on the throne of my father. And the house of my father labored, more than all others. And I ran at the wheel of my lord, the king of Assyria, in the midst of powerful kings, owners of silver and owners of gold. And I took over my father's house, and made it better than the house of any of the powerful kings. And my brothers the kings desired everything good in my house. Now my fathers, the kings of Samal, had no good house. There was the house of Kilamuwa, and it was their winter house and a summer house. But I built this house.

141. DASKYLEION

This mid-fifth-century-BCE text is from southern Turkey.

These are the images of Elnapp, son of Ishi.

---

[1]Hadad's goddess-wife.
[2]Cf. Micah 6:15, and compare the curses in Texts 45, 48, 49, and 51.
[3]Cf. Deuteronomy 28:38.
[4]Cf. Leviticus 26:26.
[5]A god of plague and of the underworld.
[6]The capital city of a kingdom in central-western Syria.
[7]A title of Baal.
[8]This may refer to his piety, like Numbers 12:3, or, less likely, to his nonroyal origins.
[9]Literally, "lord of the heavens."
[10]Mentioned in Zechariah 9:1.
[11]The Ben-Hadad of 2 Kings 13:3, 24.
[12]See introduction to Text 26.

[13]The same word used in 2 Samuel 24:11; Amos 7:12; etc.
[14]See Text 144.
[15]King of Assyria ca. 745–727 BCE.
[16]His patron deity. Rakib-El is probably a title of Hadad/Baal, meaning "the divine rider"; cf. the epithet "rider on the clouds," page 19, and Psalm 68:4, 33; Issiah 19:1.

He made them for himself.[1] I adjure you by Bel and Nebo:[2]

Whoever passes on this way, let him not do damage.

142. KESEÇEK KÖYÜ

This mid-fifth-century-BCE text is also from southern Turkey.

This relief Nanast erected before Adrason. May he protect his monument.[3] And whoever does anything evil to this relief, may Shahar[4] and Shamash[5] punish him.

143. SARAÏDIN.

This mid-fifth-century-BCE text is also from southern Turkey.

I am Wassawanes, son of Appuwwassi, son of the son of Wassawanes, and my mother is Aswalkarti. And when I was hunting here, in this place I used to eat breakfast.

SAMAL

144. PANAMUWA

This badly damaged mid-eighth-century-BCE text, inscribed on a statue of the storm god Hadad, is written in the local dialect of Samal, like Texts 26 and 133. Other texts from this site (modern Zincirli in southern Turkey) were written in Aramaic (see Text 140) and Phoenician (see Text 26). Samal was the capital city of the kingdom of Yaudi.

I am Panamuwa, son of Qarli, king of Yaudi, who erected this statue for Hadad. In my youth, the gods Hadad and El[6] and Resheph[7] and Rakib-El[8] and Shamash[9] stood with me, and Hadad and El and Rakib-El and Shamash and Resheph put the scepter of authority in my hand. And Resheph stood with me. And whatever I grasped with my hand...and whatever I asked from the gods, they used to give me....[A] land of barley...a land of wheat[10] and a land of garlic....[T]hey worked the land....

I also sat on the seat of my father, and Hadad gave into my hand the scepter of auth[ority. I also cut of]f sword and slander from the house of my father, and in my days too, Yaudi ate and drank....

[*Several badly damaged lines follow.*]

I erected this statue of Hadad and the place for Panamuwa, son of Qarli, king of Yaudi.

[*The rest of the inscription, also badly damaged, elaborates what Hadad had done for the king and promises blessings on his sons who pray for him after his death and curses on those who do not.*]

PHOENICIAN

145. YEHIMILK

A dedicatory inscription for the building of a temple, by Yehimilk, king of the Phoenician city of Gebal (Byblos), dating to the tenth century BCE. See also Text 146.

The house that Yehimilk, king of Gebal, built. It was he who restored all the ruins of these buildings. May Baal-shamem[11] and the lady of Gebal and the assembly of the holy gods of Gebal lengthen the days[12] of Yehimilk and his years over Gebal. For he is a righteous king and an upright king[13] before the holy gods of Gebal.

146. YEHAWMILK

A dedicatory inscription of a mid-fifth-century-BCE king of Gebal (Byblos). See also Text 145.

I am Yehawmilk, king of Gebal, son of Yaharbaal, son of the son of Urimilk, king of Gebal, whom the Lady, Mistress of Gebal, made king over Gebal. I called upon my Lady, the Mistress of

---

[1]Or "his soul," or "his monument."
[2]Bel and Nebo were originally Babylonian deities, corresponding to Marduk and his son Nabu.
[3]Or "his soul," or "his life."
[4]The god of dawn.
[5]The sun god.
[6]The high god and original head of the pantheon.
[7]A god of plague and death.
[8]Probably a title of Hadad/Baal, meaning "the divine rider"; cf. the epithet "rider on the clouds," page 19, and Psalm 68:4, 33.
[9]The sun god.

[10]Cf. Deuteronomy 8:8.
[11]Literally, "lord of the heavens."
[12]Cf. Exodus 20:12; 1 Kings 3:14.
[13]Cf. Psalm 32:11; Proverbs 11:6.

Gebal, and she heard my voice. And I made for my Lady, the Mistress of Gebal, this bronze altar which is in this courtyard, and this gold gate which is opposite my gate, and this gold winged-disk which is in the stone which is over this gold gate, and this portico and its columns and the capitals which are on them, and its roof. I, Yehawmilk, king of Gebal, made them for my Lady, the Mistress of Gebal, when I called upon my Lady, the Mistress of Gebal, and she heard my voice and was beneficent to me.

May the Mistress of Gebal bless Yehawmilk, king of Gebal, and grant him life and lengthen his days and his years over Gebal, for he is a righteous king. And may the Lady, the Mistress of Gebal, give him favor in the eyes of the gods and in the eyes of the people of this land, and favor of the people of this land.[1]

Whoever you are, any king or any person, who continues to do work on this altar, and on this gold gate, and on this portico, you should put my name, Yehawmilk, king of Gebal, with yours on that work. And if you do not put my name with yours or if you remove this work, and…expose its foundation, may the Lady, the Mistress of Gebal, destroy that man and his seed in the presence of all the gods of Gebal.

147. BODASTART

This inscription commemorates the construction of a temple to the god Eshmun[2] by Bodastart, king of Sidon in the late fifth century BCE, perhaps the cousin or brother of Eshmunazor II (see Text 131). The various titles of Sidon refer either to districts of the city or to temples within it.

King Bodastart, the king of the Sidonians, son of the son of King Eshmunazor, king of the Sidonians, in Sidon-of-the-Sea, the Mighty Heavens, the Land of the Reshephs, Sidon the Ruler, which he built. And Sidon the Prince, this house, he built for his god, for Eshmun, the Holy Prince.

148. PYRGI

Found at Pyrgi, north of Rome in Italy, this text, dating to ca. 500 BCE, is written in Phoenician on

gold leaf (see page 160); an Etruscan version was also found. Although the reading of the text is clear, its meaning is less so.

To the Lady, to Astarte,[3] this holy place, which Thebariye Velanas, king of Kaysriye, made and which he gave in the month of the sacrifice of the sun on the day of the oblation in the temple. And I built it, because Astarte requested it from my hand, in the year 3 of my reign, in the month Kirar, on the day of the burial of the deity.[4] And may the years during which the deity will be in his house, may they be as many years as these stars.[5]

AMMONITE
149. THE TELL SIRAN BOTTLE

Found near Amman, Jordan, this tiny metal bottle (ca. 3.9 inches [10 cm] high) contains a complete dedicatory text. Dating to ca. 600 BCE, it is one of a handful of Ammonite texts, and the only one fully preserved.

The works of Amminadab, king of the sons of Ammon,[6] son of Hissalel, king of the sons of Ammon, son of Amminadab, king of the sons of Ammon:

The vineyard and the gardens and the enclosure (?) and cistern.[7]

May he rejoice and be glad for many days and far-off years.

HEBREW
150. SILOAM TUNNEL

This rare example of an Israelite monumental inscription is a now incomplete text found inscribed on the wall of Hezekiah's Tunnel in Jerusalem, dating to the end of the late eighth century BCE (see 2 Kings 20:20; 2 Chronicles 32:30).

…the piercing. And this is the account of the piercing. While…were still…the axe, each man toward his neighbor, and while there were still three

---

[1]The last phrase may be an erroneous repetition by the scribe.
[2]The patron god of Sidon, a god of healing, whose name is found in the name of the king's grandfather Eshmunazor.

[3]The goddess of love.
[4]Perhaps a dead king; "the deity" in the next sentence may have the same meaning.
[5]Genesis 15:5; 22:17; 26:4. An alternate translation is "like the stars of El"; cf. Isaiah 14:13.
[6]The Ammonites.
[7]Cf. Ecclesiastes 2:4–6.

cubits[1] to the piercing, [there was hear]d the voice of a man calling to his neighbor, because there was a crack in the rock, on the right and on the left. And on the day of the piercing, the hewers struck, each man toward his neighbor, ax against ax, and the waters flowed from the source[2] to the pool, one thousand two hundred cubits, and one hundred cubits was the rock above the heads of the hewers.

151. EKRON

This dedicatory inscription, dating to the early seventh century BCE, is from Ekron, one of the cities of the Philistine pentapolis. Although sometimes identified as Philistine, the language of this short text is very close to Hebrew.

The house that Ikausu,[3] son of Padi,[4] son of Yasid, son of Ada, son of Yair, ruler of Ekron, built for Pitgayah,[5] his lady. May she bless him and guard him and lengthen his days and bless his land.

KUNTILLET AJRUD

In the northern Sinai desert, at a fortress that also served as a caravanserai, graffiti and inscriptions were found on storage jars and on wall plaster. The material dates to ca. 800 BCE.

152. ON A STORE BOWL, A VOTIVE OFFERING

For Obadyaw, son of Adna: May he be blessed by Yahweh.

153. ON A STORAGE JAR

Saying of (Ashyahu the king[6]): Say to Yehallel and to Yawasa and to . . . : I bless you by Yahweh of Samaria and by his Asherah.[7]

154. ON A SECOND STORAGE JAR

a. . . . by Yahweh of the Teman and by his Asherah.[8] . . . Everything which he asks from the compassionate god . . . may Yahweh give to him according to his heart.

b. Saying of Amaryaw: Say to (my) lord: Are you well? I have blessed you by Yahweh of Teman and by his Asherah.[9] May he bless and keep you[10] and may he be with my lord.

155. ON PLASTER, A FRAGMENT OF A HYMN

. . . in earthquake. And when El[11] shines forth . . .

. . . and the mountains will melt and the hills will crush . . .

. . . earth. The Holy Ones of the Most High[12] . . .

. . . the blessed of Baal[13] on the day of batt[le] . . .

. . . for the name of El on the day of batt[le]. . . .

156. KHIRBET BEIT LEI

Several graffiti were scratched on the walls of a cave at Khirbet Beit Lei in the southern Judean hills. Dating to the early sixth century BCE they were perhaps written by refugees during the Babylonian campaigns. The texts are very difficult to read, and their interpretation is disputed.

a. Yahweh is the god of all the earth. The hills of Judah belong to the god of Jerusalem.[14]

b. Pay heed, O Yah, compassionate god! Forgive, Yah, Yahweh!

c. Save, O Yahweh!

---

[1]A cubit was ca. 18 inches (44 cm).

[2]The Gihon Spring.

[3]The same name as Achish, the Philistine king of Gath (1 Samuel 21:10); see also Text 36.

[4]The king mentioned in Sennacherib's account of his campaign in 701 BCE; see page 80.

[5]An otherwise unknown goddess.

[6]If the reading is correct, Ashyahu may be a variant form of the name of Joash (Jehoash), king of the northern kingdom of Israel ca. 800–784 BCE.

[7]The interpretation of this word is disputed. It may refer to the goddess Asherah, understood as the divine consort of Yahweh (see also

Texts 154 and 136). An alternative is to understand it as a common noun, referring to the wooden pole that symbolized the goddess (see, e.g., Deuteronomy 16:21; 2 Kings 23:6).

[8]See page 158, n. 9.

[9]See page 158, n. 9.

[10]Cf. Numbers 6:24 and see Text 129a.

[11]Or "God."

[12]The text has not been fully published, and this is a conjectural interpretation; cf. Daniel 7:18, etc.

[13]Or "the lord," as a title of Yahweh.

[14]An alternate reading is: "I am Yahweh your god. I will look with favor on the cities of Judah and I will redeem Jerusalem."

Wife of Nebamun

A fragment of a painting in an Egyptian tomb that shows Hatshepsut, the wife of Nebamun, accompanying her husband on a hunt for birds. Her image, which is ca. 7.5 inches (30 cm) high, is painted in vivid colors on white plaster and shows her ornately dressed. Nebamun was a temple official during the reign of Amenhotep III in the mid-fourteenth century BCE.

9

LOVE POETRY

MESOPOTAMIA

We have few actual love poems from the ancient Near East similar to the Song of Solomon in the Bible. From Mesopotamia, we find texts expressing love between a male and a female; some have a ritual setting, either the marriage of the god Dumuzi and the goddess Inanna (see Text 4) or a sacred marriage between a king and a priestess, as in the texts here, several of which have at the end a scribal note suggesting the ritual use of these highly erotic poems. Occasionally Shu-Sin (Shu-Suen), a king of the Third Dynasty of Ur (ruled ca. 2000 BCE) is named, suggesting that the female speaker is the queen.[1]

157

> Man of my heart, my beloved one,
> O! that to make your charms,
>   which are sweetness, are honey,
>   still more sweet—
>
> Lad of my heart, my beloved one,
> O! that to make your charms,
>   which are sweetness, are honey,
>   still more sweet,

---

[1]Translations by Thorkild Jacobsen, *The Harps That Once . . . : Sumerian Poetry in Translation* (New Haven, CT: Yale University Press, 1987), 88–94.

you, my own lord and sergeant at arms
    would march against me!
Man, I would flee from you
    —into the bedroom.

O! that you, my own lord and sergeant at arms
    would mark against me!
Lad, I would flee from you
    —into the bedroom.

O! that you would do,
    all the sweet things to me,
my sweet dear one,
    you bring that which will be honey sweet!

In the bedroom's honey-sweet corner
let us enjoy over and over
    your charms and your sweetness!

Lad, o! that you would do,
    all the sweet things to me,
my sweet dear one,
    you bring that which will be honey sweet!

Man who has become attracted to me,
speak to my mother,
    she would let you!
She has worn down my father.

She knows where you would be happy
to sleep, man, in our house until morning,

she knows where your heart would rejoice;
to sleep, lad, in our house till morning!

When you fell in love with me,
could you have but done, lad,
　　your sweet thing to me!

O! my lord and good genius,
　　my lord and guardian angel,
My Shu-Sin, who does Enlil's
　　heart good,
the place where, could you but do
　　your sweet thing to me,
where, could you but
　　—like honey—
　　put in your sweetness!

O squeeze it in there for me!
　　As one would flour into the
　　measuring cup!

O pound it and pound it in there for me!
　　As one would flour into the
　　old dry measuring cup!

A dialogue pertaining to Inanna.[1]

158

[*This poem is incomplete.*]

* * *

O our son-in-law, as you let day slip by,
O our son-in-law, as you let night fall,
you now let the moonlight turn in,
the stars all wane!

O our son-in-law, as you let day slip by,
O our son-in-law, as you let night fall,
you now let the moonlight turn in,
the stars all wane,
I now unfasten for you bolt and pure lock
　　from the door. Run! Come quickly!

* * *

There is the watch on its round of the wall![2]
　　When the patrol has passed,
O our son-in-law, when the patrol has gone
　　to rest,

seize the twilight by the hand, whatever such
　　there still be,
they have unleashed daylight!
　　Come to our house quickly!

* * *

159

[*This poem is in dialogue format.*]

"O my fair one of locks!
　　O my fair one of locks!
Sweet one, tree well grown!
　　O my fair one of locks!
O my fair one of locks!
　　—like a date palm!
O my fair one of shaggy neck
　　—like the date fibers!

"Man, who for your locks
　　are acclaimed in the assembly,
my sweet one, who kisses
　　our garment bosoms in greeting,
lad, who for your locks
　　are honored in the assembly,
my brother of handsome visage,
　　who kisses our garment bosoms in greeting!

"O my lapis lazuli beard!
　　O my roped locks!
My one with beard mottled
　　like a slab of lapis lazuli,
my one with locks arranged ropewise!
You are my turban pin,
　　my gold I wear,
my trinket fashioned
　　by a cunning craftsman,
my trinket worked on
　　by a cunning craftsman!"

"My beloved bride makes my fame appear in
　　all mouths!
As sweet as her words are her private parts,
and as sweet as her private parts are her words."

* * *

"You are truly a sweet one to talk with!
You are truly one producing
　　a reign of pleasant days!
You are truly one establishing

---

[1] A concluding note by the scribe.
[2] Cf. Song of Solomon 5:7.

prime counsel and honest judgment!
You are truly one establishing
    purity and clean hands![1]

"Beloved of Enlil,
may the heart of your personal god,
    should it become embittered,
    again relax!
Come with the sun!
    Go with the sun!
May your personal god
    light the way for you,
have hod carriers and pickaxe carriers
    even it for you!"

160

My wool being lettuce, he will water it,
it being box-grown lettuce, he will water it
and touch the *dubdub*-bird in its hole!

My nurse has worked at me mightily,
has done my wool up in a stag-arrangement,
has gently combed it,
and is straightening my "May He Come"
    breast-shields.

Let him come! Into my wool, it being
    the most pleasant of lettuces,
I shall with arousing glances
    induce the brother to enter.
I shall make Shu-Sin—all ready—
show himself a lusty man,
Shu-Sin, to whom my allure be without end!
Shu-Sin, whose allure to me will never change!

●   ●   ●

You are truly our lord! You are truly our lord!
Silver wrought with lapis lazuli! You are truly
    our lord!
You are truly our farmer bringing in much grain!

He being the apple of my eye, being the lure
    of my heart,
may days of life dawn for him! May Shu-Sin
    live long years!

A dialogue pertaining to Inanna.[2]

161

Vigorously he sprouted,
    vigorously he sprouted and sprouted,
    watered it—it being lettuce!
In his black garden of the desert bearing
    much yield
    did my darling of his mother,
my barley stalk full of allure in its furrow,
    water it—it being lettuce,
did my one—a very apple tree bearing fruit at
    the top—
    water it—it being a garden!
The honey-sweet man, the honey-sweet
    man,
    was doing sweet things to me!
My lord, the honey-sweet man, the godly
    one,
    my darling of his mother,
his hands honey-sweet, his feet honeying,
    was doing sweet things to me!
His limbs being sweet, sweet honey,
    he was doing sweet things to me!

O my one who of a sudden was doing sweet
    things
    to the whole insides up to the navel,
    my darling of his mother,
my desert-honey loins, darling of his mother,
    you watered it—it being lettuce!

EGYPT

The best-preserved ancient Near Eastern love poems are Egyptian texts from the late second millennium BCE, a sample of which is given here. These texts are often compared to the biblical Song of Solomon, also a collection of love poems, and like it, not spontaneous declarations of love, but literary works, like Shakespeare's sonnets and many similar poems in world literature. Although there is no evidence of a direct relationship between the Egyptian and biblical collections, in both the lovers call each other "brother" and "sister" and describe each other's physical beauty in detail. Such descriptions are also found in the Genesis Apocryphon, one of the Dead Sea Scrolls, which catalogs the beauty of Sarah, Abraham's wife. Psalm 45, a hymn for a royal wedding, also has some similarities to these collections.

---

[1] I.e., ritual purity.
[2] A concluding note by the scribe.

162[1]

Beginning of the sayings of the great happiness.[2]
The One, the sister without peer,
the handsomest of all!
She looks like the rising morning star
at the start of a happy year.
Shining bright, fair of skin,
lovely the look of her eyes,
sweet the speech of her lips,
she has not a word too much.
Upright neck, shining breast,
hair true lapis lazuli;
arms surpassing gold,
fingers like lotus buds.
Heavy thighs, narrow waist,
her legs parade her beauty;
with graceful steps she treads the ground,
captures my heart by her movements.
She causes all men's necks
to turn about to see her;
joy has he whom she embraces,
he is like the first of men!
When she steps outside she seems
like that other One.[3]

My brother torments my heart with his voice,
he makes sickness take hold of me;
he is neighbor to my mother's house,
and I cannot go to him!
Mother is right in charging him thus:
"Give up seeing her!"
It pains my heart to think of him,
I am possessed by love of him.
Truly, he is a foolish one,
but I resemble him;
he knows not my wish to embrace him,
or he would write to my mother.
Brother, I am promised to you
by the Gold[4] of women!
Come to me that I may see your beauty,
father, mother will rejoice!

My people will hail you all together,
they will hail you, O my brother!

163[5]

Seven days since I saw my sister,
and sickness invaded me;
I am heavy in all my limbs,
my body has forsaken me.
When physicians come to me,
my heart rejects their remedies;
the magicians are quite helpless,
my sickness is not discerned.
To tell me "She is here" would revive me!
Her name would make me rise;
her messenger's coming and going,
that would revive my heart!
My sister is better than all prescriptions,
she does more for me than all medicines;
her coming to me is my amulet,
the sight of her makes me well!
When she opens her eyes my body is young,
her speaking makes me strong;
embracing her expels my malady—
seven days since she went from me!

164[6]

O that you came to your sister swiftly!
Like a swift envoy of the king;
the heart of his lord frets for his message,
his heart is anxious to hear it.
All stables are held ready for him,
he has horses at the stations;
the chariot is harnessed in its place,
he may not pause on the road.
When he arrives at his sister's house,
his heart will jubilate!

O that you came to your sister swiftly!
Like a horse of the king;
picked from a thousand steeds of all kinds,
the choicest of the stables.
It is singled out in its feed,
its master knows its paces;

---

[1]Translation by Miriam Lichtheim, *Ancient Egyptian Literature* (Berkeley, CA: University of California Press, 1976; 2000), 2.182–83.
[2]An introductory note by the scribe.
[3]Perhaps the sun, or the goddess of the morning star mentioned at the beginning.
[4]Probably a reference to the goddess Hathor.

[5]Translation by Miriam Lichtheim, *Ancient Egyptian Literature* (Berkeley, CA: University of California Press, 1976; 2000), 2.185.
[6]Translation by Miriam Lichtheim, *Ancient Egyptian Literature* (Berkeley, CA: University of California Press, 1976; 2000), 2.186–87.

when it hears the sound of the whip,
there's no holding it back.
There's no chief of charioteers who could
     overtake it. [1]
Sister's heart is aware:
he is not far from her!

O that you came to your sister swiftly,
like a bounding gazelle in the wild;[2]
its feet reel, its limbs are weary,
terror has entered its body.
A hunter pursues it with his hounds,
they do not see it in its dust;
it sees a resting place as a trap,
it takes the river as road.
May you attain her hiding place,
before your hand is kissed four times;
as you pursue your sister's love,
the Golden[3] gives her to you, my friend!

165[4]

I passed by her house in the dark,
I knocked and no one opened;
a good night to our doorkeeper,
Bolt, I will open!
Door, you are my fate,
you are my own good spirit;
our ox will be slaughtered inside,
Door, do not show your strength!
We'll offer a longhorn to the bolt,
a shorthorn to the lock,
a wild goose to the doorposts,
its fat to the key.
And the choice cuts of our ox
are for the carpenter's boy;
so he'll make for us a bolt of reeds,
and a door of woven grass.
Now any time the brother comes, he'll find
     her house is open;
he'll find a bed laid with fine sheets,
a lovely girl is with them.[5]

The girl will tell me: "My house here,
its owner is the mayor's son!"

166[6]

I shall lie down at home
and pretend to be ill;
then enter the neighbors to see me,
then comes my sister with them.
She will make the physicians unneeded,
she understands my illness![7]

167[8]

My heart thought of my love of you,
when half of my hair was braided;
I came at a run to find you,
and neglected my hairdo.
Now if you let me braid my hair,
I shall be ready in a moment.

168[9]

My sister's love is on yonder side,
the river is between our bodies;
the waters are mighty at flood-time,
a crocodile waits in the shallows.
I enter the water and brave the waves,
my heart is strong on the deep;
the crocodile seems like a mouse to me,
the flood as land to my feet.
It is her love that gives me strength,
it makes a water-spell for me;
I gaze at my heart's desire,
as she stands facing me!

My sister has come, my heart exults,
my arms spread out to embrace her;
my heart bounds in its place,
like the red fish in its pond.
O night, be mine forever,
     now that my queen has come!

[1]Cf. Song of Solomon 1:9.
[2]Cf. Song of Solomon 2:9, 17; 8:14.
[3]Probably a reference to the goddess Hathor.
[4]Translation by Miriam Lichtheim, *Ancient Egyptian Literature* (Berkeley, CA: University of California Press, 1976; 2000), 2.188.
[5]Cf. Song of Solomon 5:2–5.

[6]Translation by Miriam Lichtheim, *Ancient Egyptian Literature* (Berkeley, CA: University of California Press, 1976; 2000), 2.189.
[7]Cf. 2 Samuel 13:1–6.
[8]Translation by Miriam Lichtheim, *Ancient Egyptian Literature* (Berkeley, CA: University of California Press, 1976; 2000), 2.191.
[9]Translation by Miriam Lichtheim, *Ancient Egyptian Literature* (Berkeley, CA: University of California Press, 1976; 2000), 2.193.

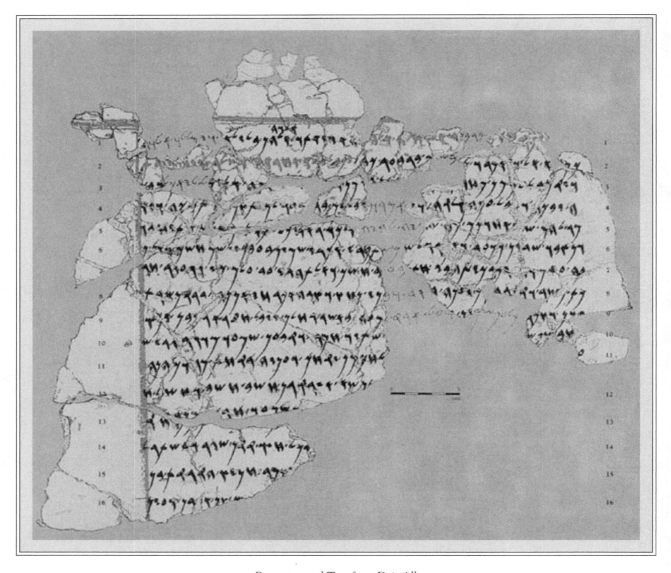

Reconstructed Text from Deir Alla
Found at Deir Alla in the Jordan Valley, this text was written in black and red
ink on wall-plaster. Dating to ca. 700 BCE, it describes a vision of the prophet
Balaam. A complete line is ca. 12 inches (31 cm) long. (See Text 180.)

10

PROPHETIC TEXTS

The phenomenon of prophecy was widespread in the ancient Near East, as texts of a variety of genres from different places and different periods attest.

EGYPT

169. The Prophecy of Neferti

Although set several centuries earlier, this text was written during the reign of Pharaoh Amenemhet I (ruled ca. 1963–1934 BCE) as a kind of propaganda piece for his reign, which marked the restoration of stability after the upheavals of the First Intermediate Period.[1]

Now, there was once a time when the Majesty of the Dual King Snefru,[2] the justified, was the worthy king of this entire land. On one of those days, the Council of the Residence entered into the Great House[3] to pay their respects. They then went out, having paid their respects, as was their daily custom. And his Majesty said to the functionary who was beside him: "Go, bring me the Council of the Residence, who have just left here from today's respects!" And they were ushered in to him immediately.

And they were once again prostrate in front of his Majesty. And his Majesty said to them: "Lads! Look, I've had you called to make you seek me out a son of yours who is a man of understanding, a brother of yours who is a clever man, a friend of yours who can achieve a perfect deed, who will tell me a few perfect words, choice verses, which my Majesty will be entertained to hear."

And they once again prostrated themselves in front of his Majesty. And they said to his Majesty: "Bastet[4] has a chief lector priest, sovereign, our lord, called Neferti. He is a strong-armed commoner, a scribe with clever fingers. He is a wealthy man, who has greater riches than any of his equals. O let him be brought for your Majesty to see!" And his Majesty said: "Go, bring him to me!" And he was ushered in to him immediately. And he was prostrate in front of his Majesty.

And his Majesty said: "Come now, Neferti, my friend, and tell me a few perfect words, choice verses, which my Majesty will be entertained to hear!" And the lector priest Neferti said: "Of what has happened, or of what will happen, sovereign, my lord?" And his Majesty said: "But of what will

---

[1] Translation by R. B. Parkinson, *The Tale of Sinuhe and Other Ancient Egyptian Poems 1940–1640 BC* (Oxford World's Classics; Oxford: Oxford University Press, 1997; 2009), 134–139.

[2] Also spelled Snofru; ruled ca. 2575–2551 BCE.

[3] Here, and repeatedly in the text that follows, following Egyptian protocol, the formula "life, prosperity, health" was added by the scribe. I have omitted it.

[4] A lioness goddess.

happen, for today happens and then is passed by!"
Then he stretched his hand out to a box of writing
equipment. Then he took for himself a roll and a
palette. And he was writing down what the lector
priest Neferti said.

He was a sage of the east; he belonged to Bastet
in her orient.[1] He was a child of the Heliopolitan
nome.[2] He ponders the happenings in the land.[3]
He recalls the sad state of the east, the Asiatics
journeying in their strength, terrorizing the hearts
of the harvesters, and seizing the cattle from plowing. He says:

"Stir, my heart,
and beweep this land, in which you began,
for silence is what overwhelms!
Look, what should be denounced will be
    respected,
and look, the official will be laid low in the
    land!
Do not tire! Look, this is in front of you!
May you attend to what is before you!
Look, there will be no officials in the affairs
    of the land,
and what is done will be what is undone.
May the Sun God begin to recreate!
For the land has been ruined entirely, no
    remnant exists.
Not even the total of one fingernail will
    survive its fate.

"Destroyed is this land, and no one cares
    about it,[4]
no one speaks out, no one sheds tears.
What is this land like?
For the sun is covered, and will not shine for
    folk to see.
They will not stay alive, when clouds cover.[5]
And everyone will be numb for lack of it.
I will say what is in front of me; I prophesy
    nothing that will not come.

"And the river of Egypt is dry,
so that water is crossed on foot;
water will be sought for ships to sail on,

for its course has become a sandbank.[6]
The bank will be a flood,
and the water's place will be what was once
    the bank's.
The south wind will oppose the north wind;
there is no sky with a single wind.
An alien bird will breed
in the lagoons of the Delta,
having made its nest upon its neighbors,
and the people will have to approach it
    through want.

"Destroyed indeed are those things of
    happiness—the fishpools,
which were full of people gutting fish,
which overflowed full of fish and fowl;[7]
all happiness has fled, and the land is laid low
    with pain,
by those feeding Syrians who go throughout
    the land.
Enemies have arisen in the East!
Asiatics have come down to Egypt;
a secure stronghold is lacking: someone else is
    close by without the guards hearing;
a ladder will be waited for in the night,
the stronghold will be entered,
and slumber in the eyes will be swept away
just as the sleeper says, 'I am awake!'

"And the flock of the foreign countries will
    drink
at the river of Egypt.
They will cool themselves on their banks,
lacking anything to make them fearful.
This land will go to and fro;
the consequence is unknown, and what will
    happen is hidden,
like the saying, 'See how the hearer is deaf!
The mute takes the lead!'
I will show you the land in catastrophe,
what should not happen, happening:
arms of war will be taken up,
and the land will live by uproar.

"Arms will be made out of copper;[8]
bread will be asked for with blood;

---

[1] I.e., her rising in the east.
[2] An administrative subdivision of ancient Egypt.
[3] I.e., in the future.
[4] Cf. Isaiah 24:1.
[5] Cf. Ezekiel 30:18; 32:7–8; Amos 8:9.

[6] Cf. Isaiah 19:5; Ezekiel 30:12.
[7] Cf. Isaiah 19:8.
[8] Perhaps instead of copper being used for tools and the like.

a sick man will be laughed out loud;
death will not be wept at;
the night will not be spent fasting for death,
for a man's heart is concerned only with
　　himself.
Mourning will not be done today,
for the heart has turned away from it entirely.
A man will sit and bow his back
while one person is killing another.
I shall show you a son as a foe,
a brother as an enemy,
a man killing his own father.

"Every mouth is full of 'I want!',
all goodness has fled.
The land is ruined, though laws are decreed
　　against it,
for destruction is what is done,
and loss is what is found,
and what is done is undone:
a man's belongings have been taken from him,
　　and given to someone who was an outsider.
I shall show you the lord in sorrow,
and the outsider at peace,
the man who did nothing, helping himself,
and the man who did something, in want.[1]
With hatred, they will give something
only to silence a mouth that speaks,
and answer a phrase with an arm thrusting a
　　stick,
and speak back by killing.

"To the heart, spoken words seem like fire;
what comes from the mouth cannot be
　　endured.
Shrunk is the land—many its controllers.
It is bare—its taxes are great.
Little is the grain—large is the measure,
and it is poured out in rising amounts.
The sun god separates himself from mankind.
He will rise when it is time,
but no one knows when midday occurs, no
　　one can distinguish his shadow.
No one's face is bright when he is glimpsed;
no one's eyes are moist with water.
He is in the sky, but like the moon.
His times of nightfall will not stray,

but his rays on the face
are now a thing of the past.

"I will show you the land in calamity,
the weak man as the lord of force,
and he who did the greeting greeted.
I will show you the lowermost uppermost,
the man who followed after, now the man
　　leading a generation.
They will live in the necropolis.
The wretched will make riches;
the great will beg to exist.
Only the poor will eat bread, while forced
　　laborers are exultant.
The land will have no Heliopolitan nome,
the birthplace of every god.[2]

"In fact, a king from the south will come,
called Ameny.[3]
He is the son of a woman of Bowland;[4]
he is a child of Southern Egypt.
He will take the White Crown; he will uplift
　　the Red Crown.[5]
He will unite the Two Powers;[6] he will appease
　　the Two Lords[7] with what they wish,
with the Field-circler grasped,
and the Oar in motion.[8]
The people of his time will be joyful,
and the gentleman will make his name,
for eternity and all time!
Those who fall into evil and plot rebellion
have felled their own speech for fear of him.
Asiatics will fall to his slaughtering,
and Libyans will fall to his flame.
Rebels belong to his rage,
and malcontents to his awesomeness.
The uraeus[9] which is on his forehead
now quiets the malcontents for him.

---

[1] Cf. Ecclesiastes 10:6–7.

[2] Heliopolis, earlier On, was the center of the worship of Re, the sun god, and hence the place where all the gods originated.
[3] I.e., Amenemhet I, the first king of Dynasty 12, after the First Intermediate Period.
[4] Nubia, or southern Egypt.
[5] The crowns of Upper and Lower Egypt, respectively.
[6] Nekhbet and Wadjet, goddesses of Upper and Lower Egypt, respectively.
[7] Seth and Horus, the gods of Upper and Lower Egypt, respectively; they desire its unification.
[8] Royal ceremonial objects.
[9] The cobra symbol.

"And The Walls of the Ruler[1] will be built.
There will be no letting Asiatics come down
	to Egypt,
so that they will ask for water as suppliants
	do, to let their flocks drink.
Truth[2] will return to its proper place,
with Chaos driven outside.
He who will witness, and who will follow the
	king, will be joyful!
The sage will pour an offering of wine for me,
	when he sees that what I have said has come
	about."

So it ends, from start to finish, as found in
	writing.[3]

170. WENAMUN

In this eleventh-century-BCE text, an Egyptian official,
Wenamun, reports of his commercial trip to coastal
cities to the north, including Dor, then under the control of the Tjeker (one of the Sea Peoples, of whom the
biblical Philistines are another), Tyre, and Byblos (biblical Gebal), as well as to the island of Cyprus. In the
surviving parts of the report, Wenamun describes the
troubles he encountered on his journey, often with
comic touches; whether this is an actual report or a
literary composition is debated. The repeated mis-
treatment Wenamun received reflects the weakness of
Egypt in this period. In the course of his adventures,
Wenamun arrived at Byblos; this excerpt is set there.[4]

The Prince of Byblos sent word to me, saying,
"Get out of my harbor!" And I sent word back
to him, saying, "Where should I go?... If you can
locate a ship to transport me, let me be taken back
to Egypt." I spent twenty-nine days in his harbor
while he daily spent time sending word to me, saying, "Get out of my harbor!"
	Now when he offered to his gods, the gods
took possession of a page from the circle of his
pages and put him in an ecstatic state.[5] He told
him, "Bring the god up! Bring the envoy who is

carrying him! It is Amun[6] who sent him forth. It
is he who had him come." For when the ecstatic
became ecstatic that night, I had located a
freighter headed for Egypt and had already loaded
all my possessions into it but, so as to prevent
another eye from seeing the god, I was waiting for
darkness to fall that I might put him aboard.
	The harbor master came to me, saying, "Stay
until tomorrow, so the prince says." And I said to
him, "Are you the one who daily has spent time
coming to me to say, 'Get out of my harbor!'?
Are you now telling me to stay tonight so that
the freighter I located might first depart and you
might then return and say 'Move on!'?" And he
went and told it to the prince, and the prince sent
word to the captain of the freighter, saying, "Stay
until tomorrow, so the prince says."

MESOPOTAMIA
MARI LETTERS

Prophets figure in several dozen letters from the
city-state of Mari, on the Euphrates River in eastern
Syria, most from the reign of Zimri-Lim, who ruled ca.
1775—1760 BCE. The letters are written in Akkadian
(Babylonian) cuneiform. Some of the terms for those
who received divine messages are unique to Mari,
and their meanings are not fully understood.

171. TO ZIMRI-LIM FROM NUR-SIN

Nur-Sin, a royal official apparently stationed in
the city of Alahtum (probably Alalakh, in southern
Turkey), somewhat reluctantly reports an oracle of a
prophet of the storm god Adad, who has requested
both a sacrifice and transfer of real estate to Adad.[7]

To Zimri-Lim, king of Mari.
Speak to my lord: Thus Nur-Sin, your servant:
Once, twice, even five times have I written to
my lord about the delivery of the *zukrum*[8] to Adad
and about the estate that Adad, lord of Kallassu,[9]

---

[1] A line of fortresses in the eastern Delta built by Amenemhet I.
[2] Literally, Maat.
[3] A concluding note by the scribe.
[4] Translation by Edward F. Wente, in *The Literature of Ancient Egypt: An Anthology of Stories, Instructions, Stelae, Autobiographies, and Poetry* (ed. W. K. Simpson; New Haven, CT: Yale University Press, 3d ed., 2003), 118–119.
[5] Cf. 1 Samuel 10:10; 19:20–24.

[6] Wenamun was a priest of the temple of the god Amun, a manifes-tation of the sun god Re, and he had brought with him a statue of the god to ensure his safety.
[7] Translation by Martti Nissinen, *Prophets and Prophecy in the Ancient Near East* (Atlanta, GA: Society of Biblical Literature, 2003), 18–20.
[8] Probably a commemorative ritual that included sacrifice.
[9] A city near Aleppo, or perhaps a district of the city itself; its patron deity was the storm god Adad,

demands from us. Concerning the delivery of the *zukrum* to Adad, Alpan said to me in the presence of Zu-hadnim, Abi-shadi, and Zulhan as follows: "Sacrifice the *zukrum* with oxen and cows! My lord, in the presence of all the people, told me to sacrifice the *zukrum,* saying: 'Never shall he break an agreement with me!'" I have imposed witnesses on him. My lord should know this.

Through oracles, Adad, lord of Kallassu, would stand by, saying: "Am I not Adad, lord of Kallassu, who raised him[1] in my lap and restored him to his ancestral throne? Having restored him to his ancestral throne, I again gave him a residence. Now, since I restored him to his ancestral throne, I may take the estate away from his patrimony as well. Should he not deliver the state, I—the lord of the throne, territory and city—can take away what I have given! But if, on the contrary, he fulfills my desire, I shall give him throne upon throne, house upon house, territory upon territory, city upon city. I shall give him the land from the rising of the sun to its setting."

This is what the prophets said, and in the oracles he[2] was standing by all the time. Another matter: a prophet of Adad, lord of Kallassu, demands the area of Alahtum to be his estate. My lord should know this.

Previously, when I was still residing in Mari, I would convey every word spoken by a prophet or prophetess to my lord. Now, living in another land, would I not communicate to my lord what I hear and they tell me? Should anything ever not be in order, let not my lord say: "Why have you not communicated to me the word which the prophet spoke to you when he was demanding your area?" Herewith I communicate it to my lord. My lord should know this.

Moreover, a prophet of Adad, lord of Aleppo, came with Abu-halim and spoke to him as follows: "Write to your lord the following: 'Am I not Adad, lord of Aleppo, who raised you on my lap and restored you to your ancestral throne? I do not demand anything from you. When a wronged man or woman cries out to you, be there and judge their case. This only I have demanded from you. If you do what I have written to you and

heed my word, I will give you the land from the rising of the sun to its setting, your land greatly increased!'"

This is what the prophet of Adad, lord of Aleppo, said in the presence of Abu-halim. My lord should know this.

172. TO ZIMRI-LIM FROM INIB-SHINA

This letter to the king from his sister, who was also a priestess of the storm god Adad, contains a proverb (see page 194) also quoted in two other letters.[3]

Speak to my star: Thus Inib-shina:

Some time ago, Shelebum, the *assinnu,*[4] delivered to me an oracle and I communicated it to you. Now, a *qammatum*[5] of Dagan[6] of Terqa came and spoke to me. She said:

"The peacemaking of the man of Eshnunna[7] is false: beneath straw water runs. I will gather him into the net that I will knot. I will destroy his city and I will ruin his wealth, which comes from time immemorial."[8]

This is what she said to me. Now, protect yourself! Without consulting an oracle do not enter the city! I have heard people saying: "He is always distinguishing himself." Do not try to distinguish yourself!

173. TO ZIMRI-LIM FROM SHIBTU

In this letter to the king, his wife reports about oracles from prophets concerning a planned military campaign.[9]

---

[1] I.e., the king.
[2] I.e., Adad.

[3] Translation by Martti Nissinen, *Prophets and Prophecy in the Ancient Near East* (Atlanta, GA: Society of Biblical Literature, 2003), 28.
[4] Probably a transvestite, especially in ritual contexts; perhaps also a castrato.
[5] A type of female prophet.
[6] An important West Semitic god; in Ugaritic, the god of grain and father of the storm god Baal. See also Judges 16:23; 1 Samuel 5:1–7.
[7] The king of Eshnunna, a city on the Diyala River ca. 200 miles (325 km) southeast of Mari.
[8] In another letter to Zimri-Lim, the same proverb is interpreted to mean: "They keep on sending to you messages of friendship, they even send their gods to you, but in their hearts they are planning something else" (Nissinen, p. 31).
[9] Translation by Martti Nissinen, *Prophets and Prophecy in the Ancient Near East* (Atlanta, GA: Society of Biblical Literature, 2003), 39–40.

Speak to my lord: Thus Shibtu, your servant:

Concerning the campaign my lord is planning, I gave drink to male and female persons to inquire about signs. The oracle is extremely favorable to my lord. Likewise, I inquired of male and female about Ishme-Dagan.[1] The oracle is unfavorable to him. The report concerning him goes: "He will be placed under the feet of my lord."[2]

They said: "My lord has raised a *humashum*![3] Raising the *humashum* against Ishme-Dagan, he says: 'I will beat you with the *humashum*! Wrestle as much as you can, I shall win the match!'"

I said: "Will my lord come near to a conflict?" They answered: "There will be no armed conflict! For as soon as his[4] auxiliaries arrive they[5] will be scattered. The head of Ishme-Dagan will be cut off and placed under the feet of my lord, saying: 'The army of Ishme-Dagan is large, but even if his army is large, his auxiliaries have scattered it. My auxiliaries are Dagan, Shamash, Itur-Mer, Belet-ekallim, and Adad, the Lord of decisions, who go beside my lord.'"[6]

Perhaps my lord would say this: "She has made them speak by fraudulent means." But I did not make them speak anything. They speak voluntarily—they could resist as well! They say: "The auxiliaries of Ishme-Dagan are prisoners. When they fall into deceit and distress with him, they will not take heed of his word. Before my lord's arrival, his army will be dissipated."

174. TO ZIMRI-LIM FROM YARIM-ADDU

In this letter one of Zimri-Lim's officials reports on the location of Ishme-Dagan, king of Ekallatum and Zimri-Lim's enemy (see Text 173).[7]

Speak to my lord: Thus Yarim-Addu, your servant:

Concerning the report of Ishme-Dagan's going up to Ekallatum, which my lord has heard repeatedly, he in no way went up to Ekallatum. It is a product of rumors about him that keep circulating around him.

A prophet of Marduk stood at the gate of the palace,[8] proclaiming incessantly: "Ishme-Dagan will not escape the hand of Marduk. That hand will tie together a sheaf and he will be caught in it." This is what he kept proclaiming at the gate of the palace. Nobody said anything to him.

Directly he stood at the gate of Ishme-Dagan, proclaiming incessantly in the midst of the whole citizenry as follows: "You went to the ruler of Elam to establish peaceful relations; but when there was a peaceful relationship, you had the treasures of Marduk and the city of Babylon delivered to the ruler of Elam.[9] You exhausted my magazines and treasuries without returning my favors. And now you are going off to Ekallatum? He who dissipates my treasures must not demand from me more!" As he kept proclaiming this in the midst of the whole citizenry, nobody said anything to him.

[*The end of the letter is broken.*]

175. TO ZIMRI-LIM, FROM AN UNKNOWN SENDER

The top edge of the tablet is broken.[10]

Speak to my lord: Thus … your servant:

A prophet [of Dagan] came to me and spoke as follows. This is what he said: "Verily, what shall I give that belongs to Zimri-Lim? Give me one lamb and I shall eat it!"

I gave him a lamb and he devoured it raw in front of the city gate.[11] He assembled the elders in front of the gate of Saggaratum[12] and said: "A devouring will take place! Give orders to the cities

---

[1] King of Ekallatum on the Tigris River in Assyria.

[2] Cf. Joshua 10:24; 1 Kings 5:3; Psalms 8:6; 47:3; etc.

[3] Perhaps referring to a concrete object, in a kind of symbolic gesture or sign-act.

[4] I.e., Zimri-Lim's.

[5] The troops of Ishme-Dagan.

[6] Various deities accompany Zimri-Lim's army.

[7] Translation by Martti Nissinen, *Prophets and Prophecy in the Ancient Near East* (Atlanta, GA: Society of Biblical Literature, 2003), 73–74.

[8] Presumably the palace of Hammurapi, with whom Ishme-Dagan, the king of Ekallatum, had taken refuge.

[9] Elam was a kingdom east of Mesopotamia. Cf. 2 Kings 18:15.

[10] Translation by Martti Nissinen, *Prophets and Prophecy in the Ancient Near East* (Atlanta, GA: Society of Biblical Literature, 2003), 38.

[11] The eating of a raw (or perhaps live) lamb is a sign-act.

[12] Probably located ca. 50 miles (80 km) north of Mari.

to return the taboo material. Whoever commits an act of violence shall be expelled from the city. And for the well-being of your lord Zimri-Lim, clothe me in a garment."

This is what he spoke to me. For the sake of the well-being of my lord, I clothed him in a garment.

Now, I have recorded the oracle that he spoke to me and sent it to my lord. He did not utter his oracle in private, but he delivered his oracle in the assembly of the elders.

176. AN ORACLE FROM ESHNUNNA

This is a direct report of an oracle, like many of the oracles of biblical prophets ("Thus says the LORD"). The oracle comes from the goddess Kititum, a manifestation of the goddess Ishtar at Eshnunna, and was sent to its king Ibalpiel, a contemporary of Zimri-Lim of Mari and Hammurapi of Babylon in the first half of the eighteenth century BCE.[1]

King Ibalpiel.
Thus Kititum:
The secrets of the gods lie before me. Because the invocation of my name is ever in your mouth, I shall reveal to you, one by one, the secrets of the gods.[2]

At the advice of the gods, by the decision of Anu,[3] the country is given to you to rule. The sandals of the Upper Country and the Lower Country you will loosen.[4] The treasures of the Upper Country and the Lower Country you will have at your disposal. Your trade will not slow down. Wherever in a country your hand has reached, . . . peace. . . .

The foundations of your throne I, Kititum, shall make firm. With a protective spirit I have provided you. Let your attention be mine.

NEO-ASSYRIAN ORACLES

More than two dozen oracles, mostly of the goddess Ishtar, are preserved on Assyrian tablets, dating to the reigns of Esar-haddon (681–669 BCE) and Ashurbanipal (669–627 BCE). The prophetic speaker of the oracle is usually named.

177. TO ESAR-HADDON[5]

Esar-haddon, king of the lands, fear not! What is the wind that has attacked you, whose wings I have not broken? Like ripe apples your enemies will continually roll before your feet.

I am the great Lady, I am Ishtar of Arbela[6] who throw your enemies before your feet. Have I spoke to you any words that you could not rely upon?

I am Ishtar of Arbela, I will flay your enemies and deliver them up to you. I am Ishtar of Arbela, I go before you and behind you.

Fear not! You have got cramps, but I, in the midst of wailing, will get up and sit down.

By the mouth of Issar-la-tashiyat, a man from Arbela.

178. TO ESAR-HADDON[7]

Fear not, Esar-haddon! I am Bel,[8] I speak to you! I watch over the supporting beans of your heart. When your mother gave birth to you, sixty Great Gods stood there with me, protecting you. Sin[9] stood at your right side, Shamash[10] at your left. Sixty Great Gods are still standing around you; they have girded your loins.

Do not trust in humans! Lift up your eyes and focus on me! I am Ishtar of Arbela. I have reconciled Ashur to you. I protected you when you were a baby. Fear not; praise me!

Is there an enemy that has attacked you, while I have kept silent? The future shall be like the

[1] Translation by William L. Moran, "An Ancient Prophetic Oracle," in *The Most Magic Word: Essays on Babylonian and Biblical Literature* (ed. R. S. Hendel; Washington, DC: Catholic Biblical Association of America, 2002), 140–147; originally published in *Biblische Theologie und gesellschaftlicher Wandel: Für Norbert Lohfink SJ* (ed. G. Braulik et al.; Freiburg: Herder, 1993), 252–259.
[2] Perhaps a reference to the proceedings of the divine council; cf. 1 Kings 22:19–23.
[3] The sky god and head of the pantheon.
[4] Cf. Ruth 4:8; Deuteronomy 25:9.

[5] Translation by Martti Nissinen, *Prophets and Prophecy in the Ancient Near East* (Atlanta, GA: Society of Biblical Literature, 2003), 102–103.
[6] A major Assyrian city in northern Iraq; modern Irbil.
[7] Translation by Martti Nissinen, *Prophets and Prophecy in the Ancient Near East* (Atlanta, GA: Society of Biblical Literature, 2003), 105.
[8] Literally "lord," a title of Ashur, the chief god of Assyria.
[9] The moon god.
[10] The sun god.

past! I am Nabu, the Lord of the Stylus.[1]
Praise me!

By the mouth of the woman Baya, a man[2] from Arbela.

179. TO ESAR-HADDON[3]

I am Ishtar of Arbela! Esar-haddon, king of Assyria!

In Ashur, Nineveh, Calah, and Arbela[4] I will give endless days and everlasting years to Esar-haddon, my king.

I am your great midwife, I am your excellent wet nurse.[5] For endless days and everlasting years I have established your throne under the great heavens.[6]

I keep watch in a golden chamber in the middle of heaven, I let a lamp of amber shine in front of Esar-haddon, king of Assyria,[7] I guard him like the crown on my own head.

Fear not, king! I have spoken to you, I have not slandered you! I have inspired you with confidence, I have not caused you to come to shame! I will lead you safely across the River.

Esar-haddon, legitimate heir,[8] son of Mullissu![9] With a sharp dagger in my hand I will put an end to your enemies. Esar-haddon, king of Assyria—cup filled with lye, axe of two shekels!

Esar-haddon, in Ashur I will give you endless days and everlasting years! Esar-haddon, in Arbela I will be your effective shield!

Esar-haddon, legitimate heir, son of Mullissu! I keep thinking of you, I have loved you greatly! I hold you by your curl in the great heavens.

I make smoke go up on your right, I light a fire on your left.

---

[1] Nabu, the son of Ashur, was the god who wrote the tablet of destinies, like the biblical "book of life."

[2] Perhaps a scribal error, or an indication that the person's gender orientation was ambiguous, like the *assinnu* (see page 177, n. 4). The name Baya could be given to either a male or a female.

[3] Translation by Martti Nissinen, *Prophets and Prophecy in the Ancient Near East* (Atlanta, GA: Society of Biblical Literature, 2003), 106–107.

[4] The principal cities of Assyria.

[5] Cf. Numbers 11:12; Psalm 22:9–10.

[6] Cf. 2 Samuel 7:13; Psalms 89:29, 36.

[7] Cf. Psalm 132:17.

[8] Esar-haddon was not the oldest of his father Sennacherib's sons, and so his right to the throne had been challenged.

[9] Mullissu, also known as Ninlil, was the divine wife of the god Ashur. On the divine sonship of kings, cf. 2 Samuel 7:14; Psalms 2:7; 89:26.

[*The end of the tablet is broken.*]

TRANSJORDAN
180. DEIR ALLA

At a site on the east side of the Jordan Valley were found fragments of wall plaster with texts in red and black ink. Dating to ca. 700 BCE, the texts are in a language not conclusively identified, but probably a local dialect related to Ammonite and other Transjordanian languages as well as to Aramaic. They mention the Transjordanian seer Balaam, the subject of Numbers 22–24. The fragments have been reassembled in two "combinations," whose relationship to each other is unclear.[10]

a. The account of Balaam son of Beor who was a seer[11] of the gods. The gods came to him in the night, and he saw a vision like an oracle[12] of El. Then they said to Balaam son of Beor: Thus he will do.... And Balaam arose the next day... but he was not able to... and he wept grievously. And his people came up to him and said to him: "Balaam, son of Beor, why are you fasting and crying?" And he said to them: "Sit down! I will tell you what the Shaddayin[13] have done. Now, come, see the works of the gods! The gods gathered together; the Shaddayin took their places as the assembly.[14] And they said...: 'Sew up, bolt up the heavens in your cloud, ordaining darkness instead of eternal light! And put the dark...seal on your bolt, and do not remove it forever! For the swift reproaches the griffin-vulture and the voice of vultures sings out.... The swallow tears at the dove, and the sparrow... and instead of the rod, it is the staff that is led. The whelps of the fox... laughs at the wise. And the poor woman prepares myrrh while the priestess... for the prince a tattered loincloth. The respected one now respects others and

---

[10] Translation by Jo Ann Hackett, *The Balaam Text from Deir 'Allā* (Chico, CA: Scholars Press, 1984), 29–30.

[11] The same word used in 2 Samuel 24:11; Amos 7:12; etc.

[12] Literally, "burden," a term also used for prophetic pronouncements in the Bible (e.g., Isaiah 13:1; Zechariah 9:1; 12:1; Malachi 1:1).

[13] The assembly of the gods, named for their leader, El Shadday (cf. Genesis 17:1; Exodus 6:3; Numbers 24:4, 16; etc.)

[14] Like biblical prophets, Balaam claims to have witnessed the proceedings of the divine assembly, the council of the gods; cf. 1 Kings 22:19–23; Jeremiah 23:18.

the one who gave respect is now respected...and the deaf hear from afar...and a fool sees visions....'"

b....Let him cross over to the House of Eternity,...the house where the traveler does not rise and the bridegroom does not rise, the house...and the worm from the tomb, from those who have arisen among human beings, and from the graves of....

As for counsel, it is not you with whom he will take counsel, or for advice, will he not ask advice from one residing...?

You will cover him with one garment. If you hate him, he will falter....

You will lie down on our eternal bed to perish....

Death will take the newborn child, the suckling....

The Gezer Calendar
Probably a scribal exercise, this text, from Gezer in Israel, was written in an
early form of the Hebrew alphabet, and describes the agricultural seasons. It is
about 4.5 inches (11.5 cm) high. (See Text 200.)

WISDOM LITERATURE

Wisdom literature is the most universal type of ancient Near Eastern literature, not surprisingly since it deals with the human condition. Using a variety of genres, scribes focused on the meaning of life, from its most mundane aspects to the relationship of the gods to men and women, and especially the problem of suffering and evil. For this reason, wisdom literature is usually not concerned with historical events and personalities. Texts at the end of this chapter include scribal exercises.

EGYPT

181. SATIRE ON THE TRADES

Like Sirach 38:24–39:11, this text compares other professions with that of the scribe, easily the best. The description of other trades gives a remarkable glimpse of daily life in ancient Egypt. It concludes with proverbial advice to the young scribe-to-be. Found in many copies, probably because it was part of the scribal curriculum, it originally dates to the early second millennium BCE. (For other scribal reflections on their profession, see Texts 186 and 193.)[1]

Beginning of the instruction made by the man of Sile, whose name is Dua-khety, for his son, called Pepi, as he journeyed south to the residence, to place him in the school for scribes, among the sons of the magistrates, with the elite of the residence. He said to him:

> I have seen many beatings—set your heart on
>   books!
> I have watched those seized for labor—there's
>   nothing better than books!
> It's like a boat on water.
>
> Read the end of the *Kemit*-Book,[2]
> you'll find this saying there:
> A scribe at whatever post in town, he will not
>   suffer in it;
> as he fills another's need, he will not lack
>   rewards.
> I don't see a calling like it of which this saying
>   could be said.
>
> I'll make you love scribedom more than your
>   mother,
> I'll make its beauties stand before you;
> it's the greatest of all callings, there's none
>   like it in the land.
>
> Barely grown, still a child, he is greeted, sent
>   on errands;

---

[1]Translation by Miriam Lichtheim, *Ancient Egyptian Literature* (Berkeley, CA: University of California Press, 1976; 2000), 1.185–91.

[2]A book of instructions used in scribal education, known from other sources.

hardly returned he wears a gown.
I never saw a sculptor as envoy, nor is a
    goldsmith ever sent;
but I have seen the smith at work at the
    opening of his furnace;
with fingers like the claws of a crocodile, he
    stinks more than fish roe.

The carpenter who wields an adze, he is
    wearier than a field laborer;
his field is the timber, his hoe the adze.
There is no end to his labor, he does more
    than his arms can do,
yet at night he kindles light.
The jewel-maker bores with his chisel in hard
    stone of all kinds;
when he has finished the inlay of the eye, his
    arms are spent, he's weary;
sitting down when the sun goes down, his
    knees and back are cramped.

The barber barbers till nightfall,
he betakes himself to town, he sets himself up
    in his corner,
he moves from street to street, looking for
    someone to barber.
He strains his arms to fill his belly, like the
    bee that eats as it works.

The reed-cutter travels to the Delta to get
    arrows;
when he has done more than his arms
    can do,
mosquitoes have slain him, gnats have
    devoured him,
he is quite worn out.

The potter is under the soil, though as yet
    among the living;
he grubs in the mud more than a pig, in order
    to fire his pots.
His clothes are stiff with clay, his girdle is in
    shreds;
if air enters his nose, it comes straight from
    the fire.
He makes a pounding with his feet, and is
    himself crushed;
he grubs the yard of every house and roams
    the public places.

I'll describe to you also the mason:
his loins give him pain;
though he is out in the wind, he works
    without a cloak;
his loincloth is a twisted rope and a string in
    the rear.
His arms are spent from exertion, having
    mixed all kinds of dirt;
when he eats bread with his fingers, he has
    washed at the same time.

The carpenter also suffers much....
The room measures ten by six cubits.[1]
A month passes after the beams are laid....
And all its work is done.
The food which he gives to his household,
it does not suffice for his children.

The gardener carries a yoke, his shoulders are
    bent as with age;
there's a swelling on his neck and it festers.
In the morning he waters vegetables, the
    evening he spends with the herbs,
while at noon he has toiled in the orchard.
He works himself to death more than all
    other professions.

The farmer wails more than the guinea fowl,
    his voice is louder than the raven's;
his fingers are swollen and stink to excess....
When he reaches home at night, the march
    has worn him out.

The weaver in the workshop, he is worse off
    than a woman;
with knees against his chest, he cannot
    breathe air.
If he skips a day of weaving, he is beaten fifty
    strokes;
he gives food to the doorkeeper, to let him see
    the light of day.

The arrow-maker suffers much as he goes out
    to the desert;
more is what he gives his donkey than the
    work it does for him.
Much is what he gives the herdsmen, so
    they'll put him on his way.

---

[1] A cubit was ca. 18 inches (44 cm).

When he reaches home at night, the march
　　has worn him out.

The courier goes into the desert, leaving his
　　goods to his children;
fearful of lions and Asiatics, he knows himself
　　only when he's in Egypt.
When he reaches home at night, the march
　　has worn him out;
be his home of cloth or brick, his return is
　　joyless.

The stoker, his fingers are foul, their smell is
　　that of corpses;
his eyes are inflamed by much smoke, he
　　cannot get rid of his dirt.
He spends his days cutting reeds, his clothes
　　are loathsome to him.

The cobbler suffers much among his vats
　　of oil;
he is well if one's well with corpses; what he
　　bites is leather.

The washerman washes on the shore with the
　　crocodile as neighbor;
"Father, leave the flowing water," says his son,
　　his daughter;
it is not a job that satisfies. . . .
His food is mixed with dirt, no limb of his is
　　clean.
He is given women's clothes. . . .
He weeps as he spends the day at his
　　washboard. . . .
One says to him, "Soiled linen for you. . . ."

The bird-catcher suffers much as he watches
　　out for birds;
when the swarms pass over him, he keeps
　　saying, "Had I a net!"
But the god grants it not, and he's angry with
　　his lot.

I'll speak of the fisherman also: his is the
　　worst of all the jobs;
he labors on the river, mingling with the
　　crocodiles.
When the day of reckoning comes, he is full
　　of lamentations;

he does not say, "There's a crocodile," fear has
　　made him blind.
Coning from the flowing water, he says,
　　"Mighty god!"

See, there's no profession without a boss,
except for the scribe; he is the boss.
Hence if you know writing, it will do better
　　for you
than those professions I've set before you,
　　each more wretched than the other.
A peasant is not called a man—beware of it!

Lo, what I do in journeying to the residence,
lo, I do it for love of you.
The day in school will profit you;
its works are forever. . . .
I'll tell you also other things, so as to teach
　　you knowledge.
Such as:
If a quarrel breaks out, do not approach the
　　contender!
If you are chided . . . and don't know how to
　　repel the heat,
call the listeners to witness, and delay the
　　answer.

When you walk behind officials, follow at a
　　proper distance.
When you enter a man's house, and he's busy
　　with someone before you,
sit with your hand over your mouth.
Do not ask him for anything, only do as he
　　tells you,
beware of rushing to the table!

Be weighty and very dignified, do not speak of
　　secret things:
who hides his thought shields himself.
Do not say things recklessly, when you sit
　　with one who's hostile.
If you leave the schoolhouse when midday is
　　called, and go roaming in the street,
all will scold you in the end.
When an official sends you with a message,
　　tell it as he told it,
don't omit, don't add to it.
He who neglects to praise, his name will not
　　endure;

he who is skilled in all his conduct, from him
　　nothing is hidden,
he is not opposed anywhere.

Do not tell lies against your mother, the
　　magistrates abhor it.
The descendant does what is good, his actions
　　all emulate the past.
Do not consort with a rowdy, it harms you
　　when one hears of it.
If you have eaten three loaves, drunk two jugs
　　of beer,
and the belly is not sated, restrain it!
When another eats, don't stand there, beware
　　of rushing to the table!
It is good if you are sent out often, and hear
　　the magistrates speak.
You should acquire the manner of the
　　wellborn, as you follow in their steps.
The scribe is regarded as one who hears, for
　　the hearer becomes a doer.
You should rise when you are addressed, your
　　feet should hurry when you go;
do not trust.
Associate with men of distinction, befriend a
　　man of your generation.

Lo, I have set you on god's path,
a scribe's Renenet[1] is on his shoulder on the
　　day he is born....
Lo, no scribe is short of food and of riches
　　from the palace.
The Meskhenet[2] assigned to the scribe, she
　　promotes him in the council.
Praise god for your father, your mother, who
　　set you on the path of life!
This is what I put before you, your children
　　and their children.

It has come to a happy conclusion.[3]

182. DIALOGUE OF A MAN
WITH HIS SOUL

**Dating to the early second millennium BCE, this
remarkably modern-sounding text wrestles with the**

issue of whether the afterlife is to be preferred to the
present. It is cast in the form of a dialogue between a
man and his *ba*, that essential part which would survive in the world to come. The beginning of the text,
which survives in only one copy, is broken.[4]

I opened my mouth to my soul, to answer
　　what he said:
"This is all too much for me today! My soul
　　has disagreed with me!
Now this is beyond all exaggeration; this is
　　like leaving me alone!
My soul should not depart! He should stand
　　up for me about this! ...
He may be far from my body, from the net of
　　ropes,
but it shall not come about that he manages
　　to escape on the Day of Pain.
Look, my soul is misleading me—though I do
　　not listen to him,
is dragging me to death—though I have not
　　yet come to it,
is throwing me on the fire to burn me up! ...
He should stay close to me on the Day of Pain!
He should stand on that side, like a praise-
　　singer does
(this is the way to set off so as to return safely)!
O my soul, foolish to belittle the sorrow
　　which is due to life,
you who constrain me toward death, when I
　　have not yet come to it—
make the West[5] pleasant for me! Is this pain?
Life is a transitory time: the trees fall.
Trample on evil, put my misery aside!
May Thoth,[6] who appeases the gods, judge me!
May Khonsu,[7] who writes very truth, defend me!
May the Sun God, who controls the bark,
　　listen to my speech!
May Isdes[8] in the Sacred Chamber defend me!
For my need is pressing, a weight he has
　　placed on me.
It would be a sweet relief, if the gods drove off
　　the heaviness of my body!"

---

[1]The goddess of fortune.
[2]The birth goddess.
[3]A concluding note by the scribe.

[4]Translation by R. B. Parkinson, *The Tale of Sinuhe and Other
Ancient Egyptian Poems 1940–1640 BC* (Oxford World's Classics;
Oxford: Oxford University Press, 1997; 2009), 155–160.
[5]The afterlife.
[6]The scribe god and patron of scribes; see Text 121.
[7]The moon god.
[8]A baboon deity who was one of Thoth's assistants.

What my soul said to me:
"Aren't you a man?
—so you're alive, but to what good?
You should ponder life, like a lord of riches."

I said:
"So I haven't passed away yet, but that's not
    the point!
Indeed, *you* are leaping away—and you'll be
    uncared for,
with every desperado saying, 'I will seize you!'
Now, when you are dead, but with your name
    still living,
that place is an alighting place, attractive to
    the heart.
The West, an inescapable voyage, is a harbor.
If my soul listens to me, without
    wrongdoing,
with his heart in accord with mine, he will
    prosper.
I shall make him reach the West,
like someone in a pyramid at whose burial a
    survivor has waited.
I will make a cool shelter for your corpse,
so that you will make another soul in oblivion
    envious!
I will make a cool shelter, so that you will not
    be too cold,
and will make another soul who is scorched
    envious!
I shall drink at the river lip; I shall raise a
    shady spot,
so that you will make another soul who is
    hungry envious.
But if you constrain me toward death in *this*
    manner,
you will find nowhere to alight in the West!
Be patient, my soul, my brother,
until an heir exists who will make offerings
    of food,
and will wait at the grave on the day of
    burial,
and make ready a bed of the necropolis!"

My soul opened his mouth to me, to answer
    what I said:
"If you call burial to mind, it is heartbreak;
it is bringing the gift of tears, causing a man
    misery;

it is taking a man away from his house, and
    throwing him on the high ground.
You will not come up again to see the
    sunlight!
They who built in granite, who constructed
    pavilions in fair pyramids, as fair works,
so that the builders should become gods—
their altar stones have vanished,
like the oblivious ones' who have died on the
    shore for lack of a survivor,
when the flood has taken its toll, and the
    sunlight likewise,
to whom only the fish at the water's edge speak.
Listen to me! Look, it is good to listen to men!
Follow the happy day! Forget care!

"A commoner plows his plot;
he loads his harvest onto a boat and tows it
    along, for his feast day is approaching,
and he has seen the darkness of a north wind
    arise.
He watches in the boat as the sun goes down,
and gets out with his wife and children,
and they perish by a pool, infested by night
    with a swarm of crocodiles.
And at last he sits down, and argues, saying:
'I am not weeping for that other,
although she has no way out of the West to be
    on earth another time;
but I shall ponder on her children, crushed in
    the egg,
who saw the face of Khenty[1] before they had
    lived.'

"A commoner asks for dinner.
His wife says to him: 'It's for suppertime.'
He goes outside to relieve himself for a
    moment.
He is like another man as he turns back to his
    house,
and though his wife pleads with him, he does
    not hear her, after he has relieved himself,
and the household is distraught."

I opened my mouth to my soul, to answer
    what he said to me:
"Look, my name reeks,

---

[1] A crocodile god.

look, more than the smell of bird-
        droppings on summer days when the sky
        is hot.
Look, my name reeks,
    look, more than the smell of a haul of
        spiny fish on a day of catching when the
        sky is hot.
Look, my name reeks,
    look, more than the smell of birds, more
        than a clump of reeds full of waterfowl.
Look, my name reeks,
    look, more than the smell of fishermen,
        than the creeks of the pools they have
        fished.
Look, my name reeks,
    look, more than the smell of crocodiles,
        more than sitting under the river edges
        with a swarm of crocodiles.
Look, my name reeks,
    look, more than a woman about whom lies
        are told to her man.
Look, my name reeks,
    look, more than a healthy child about
        whom they say: 'He belongs to someone
        who hates him.'
Look, my name reeks,
    look, more than a port of the sovereign
        that utters treason behind his back.

"Who can I talk to today?
    For brothers are bad, the friends of today
        do not love.
Who can I talk to today?
    For hearts are selfish, and every man is
        stealing his brother's belongings.
Who can I talk to today?
    Mercy has perished, and the fierce man has
        descended on everyone.
Who can I talk to today?
    For they are contented with bad, and
        goodness is thrown down everywhere.
Who can I talk to today?
    He who should enrage a man with his bad
        deed makes everyone laugh with his evil
        crime.
Who can I talk to today?
    They plunder, and every man is taking his
        fellow.
Who can I talk to today?

For the wrongdoer is an intimate friend,
    and the brother with whom one dealt
    has become an enemy.
Who can I talk to today?
    The past is not remembered, and no one
        helps him who gave help then.
Who can I talk to today?
    For brothers are bad, and one turns to
        strangers for honesty.
Who can I talk to today?
    People are expressionless, and every man's
        face is downturned against his brothers.
Who can I talk to today?
    For hearts are selfish, and no man's heart is
        reliable.
Who can I talk to today?
    There are no just men, and the land is left
        over to the doers of injustice.
Who can I talk to today?
    An intimate friend is lacking, and one
        turns to an unknown man to protest.
Who can I talk to today?
    There is no one who is content, and he
        with whom one walked is no more.
Who can I talk to today?
    I am weighed down with misery for want of
        an intimate friend.
Who can I talk to today?
    For wrong roams the earth; there is no end
        to it.

"Death is to me today
    like a sick man's recovery,
    like going out after confinement.
Death is to me today
    like the smell of myrrh,
    like sitting under a sail on a windy day.
Death is to me today
    like the smell of flowers,
    like sitting on the shores of Drunkenness.
Death is to me today
    like a well-trodden path,
    like a man's coming home after an
        expedition.
Death is to me today
    like the sky's clearing,
    like a man grasping what he did not know
        before.
Death is to me today

like a man's longing to see home,
having spent many years in captivity.

"But There[1] a man is a living god,
punishing the wrongdoer's action.
But There a man stands in the bark,
distributing choice offerings from it to the
temples.
But There a man is a sage
who cannot, when he speaks, be stopped
from appeal to the Sun God."

What my soul said to me:
"Throw complaint over the fence, O my
partner, my brother!
May you make offering upon the brazier, and
cling to life by the means you describe.
Yet love me here, having put aside the West,
and also still desire to reach the West, your
body making landfall!
I shall alight when you are weary;
so we shall make harbor together!"

So it ends, from start to finish, as found in
writing.[2]

183. SONG OF THE HARPER

**Several similar Egyptian texts were written for use
in tombs, where there is often an image of a harper
who was singing them. They originally date from
the early second millennium BCE but were copied by
scribes for centuries after. They sometimes include
surprisingly skeptical views of the afterlife and in
some ways resemble the sentiments of Ecclesiastes
(Qoheleth). The example given here is identified as
from the tomb of Intef; several pharaohs of this name
are known from the Middle Kingdom (first half of the
second millennium BCE); it is preserved on a papyrus
from the late second millennium BCE that also contains love poems (see Texts 162–168).[3]**

The song which is in the chapel of King Intef,
justified in front of the singer with the harp:

Fortunate is this prince, for happy was his
fate, and happy his ending.
One generation passes away, and the next
remains,
ever since the time of those of old.[4]
The gods who existed before me rest (now) in
their tombs,
and the blessed nobles are also buried in their
tombs.
But as for these builders of tombs, their places
are no more.
What has become of them?
I have heard the words of Imhotep and
Hordedef,[5]
whose maxims are repeated intact as proverbs.
But what of their places?
Their walls are in ruins, and their places are
no more,
as if they had never existed.[6]
There is no one who returns from beyond
that he may tell of their state,
that he may tell of their lot,
that he may set our hearts at ease
until we make our journey to the place where
they have gone.
So rejoice your heart!
Absence of care is good for you;
follow your heart as long as you live.
Put myrrh on your head,
dress yourself in fine linen,
anoint yourself with the exquisite oils which
are only for the gods.
Let your pleasures increase, and let not your
heart grow weary.
Follow your heart and your happiness,
conduct your affairs on earth as your heart
dictates,
for that day of mourning will surely come
for you.[7]
The Weary-Hearted[8] does not hear their
lamentations,
and their weeping does not rescue a man's
heart from the grave.

---

[1]In the afterlife.
[2]A concluding note by the scribe.
[3]Translation by Vincent A. Tobin, in *The Literature of Ancient Egypt: An Anthology of Stories, Instructions, Stelae, Autobiographies, and Poetry* (ed. W. K. Simpson; New Haven, CT: Yale University Press, 3d ed., 2003), 332–333.

[4]Cf. Ecclesiastes 1:4; Sirach 14:16–18; *Iliad* 6.146–49.
[5]Notable figure of the Old Kingdom (early third millennium BCE).
[6]Cf. Ecclesiastes 1:11.
[7]Cf. Ecclesiastes 8:7–10; 11:9–10.
[8]An epithet of Osiris, the god of the underworld.

Refrain:
Enjoy pleasant times, and do not weary
   thereof.
Behold, it is not given to any man to take his
   belongings with them,
behold, there is no one departed who will
   return again.

184. INSTRUCTION OF AMENEMHET

**Although using the genre of instruction, this text is
a pseudo-autobiographical account of how Pharaoh
Amenemhet I (1963–1934 BCE) was assassinated (see
also Text 169).[1]**

Beginning of the teaching made by the Majesty
of the Dual King, Sehotepibre, the son of Re,
Amenemhet, the justified, when he spoke in a
revelation to his son, the Lord of All. He said:

"Rise as a god!
Listen to what I tell you,
that you may be king of the land, and rule the
   Banks, increasing the good.

Concentrate against subjects who prove
   nonexistent,
in whose respect no faith can be placed!
Do not approach them when you are alone!
Trust no brother! Know no friend!
Make for yourself no intimates—this is of no
   avail!

You should sleep with your own heart
   watching over you,
for a man will have no supporters on the Day
   of Pain.
I gave to the beggar, I raised the orphan,[2]
and I made the man who had not end up like
   someone who had.

It was someone who ate my food who caused
   trouble;[3]
someone to whom I had given help was
   raising plots with it;

someone clad in my fine linen was looking at
   me as if needy;
someone anointed with my myrrh was
   pouring water in return.

O my living images, my partners among men,
make for me mourning, such as was never
   heard before!—
the greatest fighting, such as was never seen
   before!
When one fights in the arena, forgetful of the
   past,
the goodness of someone who ignores what
   should be known is of no avail.

It was after supper, when darkness had fallen,
   and I had spent a happy time.
I was lying on my bed, since I was tired, and
   my heart had begun to follow sleep.
When the weapons at my disposal were
   wielded, I had become like a worm of the
   necropolis.

As I came to, I woke to fighting,
and I found it was an attack of the
   bodyguard.
If I had quickly taken weapons in my hand,
I would have made the back-turners retreat
   with a charge.
But no one is strong in the night; no one can
   fight alone;
no success will come without help.

Look, my passing happened when I was
   without you,
when the entourage had not yet heard that
   I would hand over to you,
when I had not yet sat with you, that I might
   make plans for you;
for I was not prepared for it, I did not foresee it,
and my heart had not thought of servants'
   negligence.

Had women ever before commanded troops?
Are people of tumult ever brought up in the
   Residence?
Is water that destroys the fields ever let forth?
Do commoners ever bring folly on themselves
   by their actions?

[1]Translation by R. B. Parkinson, *The Tale of Sinuhe and Other Ancient Egyptian Poems 1940–1640 BC* (Oxford World's Classics; Oxford: Oxford University Press, 1997; 2009), 206–208.
[2]Cf. Job 29:12.
[3]Cf. Psalm 41:9.

Since my birth, evil had not come near me;
my deeds as a strong hero were inimitable.

I strode to Elephantine, and I traveled to the
Marshes;[1]
I stood firm on the limits of the land, having
seen its midst.
I attained the limits of strength with my
strong arm, and my manifestations.

I was a maker of grain, beloved of Nepri.[2]
The Nile-flood[3] honored me on every plain.
No one hungered in my years; no one thirsted
then.
Men could relax through what I had done,
and told of me.
All that I decreed was as it should be.
I tamed lions, and I captured crocodiles.
I subdued Nubians, and I captured Medjai.[4]
I made the Syrians[5] do the dog-walk.

I made myself a mansion adorned with gold;
its portals were of lapis lazuli, with walls of
silver,
a floor of sycamore, doors of copper, bolts of
bronze,
made for all time, prepared for eternity.
I know, for I was the lord of it, of all!

But now the children of the masses are in the
street,
the wise saying: 'It is so!'
The fool saying: 'It is not!'
for he cannot know anything, lacking regard
for you.
O Senwosret,[6] my son!
My feet are departing, but my very heart
draws near, and my eyes are looking for
you,
to whom the children of a happy time, beside
the sun-folk, offer praises!

Look, I made a beginning, so that I might
secure the end for you.
I alone have brought to harbor my heart's
desire for you:
you wearing the white crown,[7] divine
progeny!
This is as it should be, as I began it for you.
I have descended into the bark of the Sun God.[8]
Ascend to the kingship created aforetime,
for it is what I achieved, in the midst of all
this!
Raise your monuments, endow your tomb
shaft!
May you fight for the wisdom of the wise-
hearted,
for you loved him beside your Majesty, life,
prosperity, health."

So it ends, from start to finish, as found in
writing.[9]

185. INSTRUCTION OF AMENEMOPE

This collection, dating from the late second millennium BCE, is one of the best preserved of Egyptian instructions. It consists of a lengthy introduction, followed by thirty chapters of proverbs, generally arranged thematically. It was clearly familiar to the compilers of the book of Proverbs, which in fact refers to "thirty sayings" (Proverbs 22:20); many of the proverbs in Proverbs 22:17–24:22 have close parallels in Amenemope, as the following excerpts show.[10]

The beginning of the instruction about life,
the guide for well-being,
all the principles of official procedure,
the duties of the courtiers;
to know how to refute the accusation of one
who made it,
and send back a reply to one who wrote;
to set one straight on the paths of life,
and make him prosper on earth;

[1]From southern Egypt to the Nile Delta.
[2]God of grain.
[3]Literally, Hapi, the god of the annual inundation of the Nile.
[4]Another term for Nubians.
[5]Literally, the Asiatics.
[6]Amenemhet's successor, also known as Seostris I, ruled ca. 1943–1898 BCE.

[7]The crown of Upper (southern) Egypt.
[8]Gone to the afterlife.
[9]A concluding note by the scribe.
[10]Translation by William Kelly Simpson, in *The Literature of Ancient Egypt: An Anthology of Stories, Instructions, Stelae, Autobiographies, and Poetry* (New Haven, CT: Yale University Press, 3d ed., 2003), 224–243.

to let his heart settle down in its chapel,
as one who steers him clear of evil;
to save him from the talk of others,
as one who is respected in the speech of men.
Written by the superintendent of the land,
    experienced in office,
the offspring of a scribe of the Beloved Land[1] ...
Amenemope, the son of Kanakht,
whose verdict is acquitted in the Ta-wer nome.[2]
For his son, the youngest of his children,
the least of his family. ...

Give your ears and hear what is said,
give your mind over to their interpretation:
It is profitable to put them in your heart,
but woe to him who neglects them.[3]

Beware of stealing from a miserable man,
and of raging against a cripple.[4]
Do not stretch out your hand to strike an old
    man,
nor snip at the words of an elder.

The hotheaded man in the temple
is like a tree grown in an enclosed space;
in a moment is its loss of foliage.
It reaches its end in the carpentry shop;
it is floated away from its place,
or fire is its funeral pyre.
The truly temperate man sets himself apart,
he is like a tree grown in a sunlit field,
but it becomes verdant, it doubles its yield,
it stands before its owner;
its fruit is something sweet, its shade is pleasant,
and it reaches its end in a grove.[5]

Do not displace the surveyor's marker on the
    boundaries of the arable land,
nor alter the position of the measuring line;
do not be covetous for a single cubit[6] of land,
nor encroach upon the boundaries of a widow.
One who transgresses the furrow shortens a
    lifetime,

one who seizes it for fields
and acquires by deceptive attestations, [7]
will be lassoed by the might of the Moon.[8]
To one who has done this on earth, pay
    attention,
for he is an oppressor of the feeble;
he is an enemy worthy of your overthrowing;
life is taken from his eye;
his household is hostile to the community,
his storerooms are broken into,
his property is taken away from his children,
and his possessions are given to someone else.[9]
Take care not to topple over the boundary
    marks of the field,
not fearing that you will be brought to court;
man propitiates God by the might of the Lord
when he sets the boundaries of the arable land.
Desire then to make yourself prosper,
and take care for the Lord of All;
do not trample on the furrow of someone else,
their good order will be profitable for you.
So plow the fields, and you will find whatever
    you need,
and receive the bread from your own
    threshing floor:
Better is a bushel which God gives you
than five thousand deceitfully gotten. ...
Better, then is poverty in the hand of God
than riches in the storehouse;
better is bread when the mind is at ease
than riches with anxiety.[10]

Do not fraternize with the hot-tempered man,
nor approach him to converse.
Safeguard your tongue from talking back to
    your superior,
and take care not to offend him.
Do not allow him to cast words only to entrap
    you,
and be not too free in your replies.[11]

Do not covet the property of the dependent
nor hunger for his bread;

---

[1] I.e., Egypt.
[2] The district that included Abydos, in southern Egypt.
[3] Cf. Proverbs 22:17.
[4] Cf. Proverbs 22:22–23.
[5] Cf. Psalm 1; Jeremiah 17:5–8.
[6] A cubit was ca. 18 inches (44 cm).

[7] Cf. Deuteronomy 19:14; 27:17; Job 24:2; Proverbs 22:28; 23:10–11; Hosea 5:10.
[8] Cf. Psalm 122:6.
[9] Cf. Job 20:21.
[10] Cf. Psalm 37:16; Proverbs 15:16; 16:8; 28:6.
[11] Cf. Proverbs 22:24–25.

the property of the dependent is an
    obstruction to the throat,
it makes the gullet throw it back.[1]

Do not lead a man astray with reed pen on
    papyrus:
it is the abomination of God.
Do not witness a false statement,
nor remove a man (from the list) by your
    order;
do not reckon with someone who has
    nothing,
nor make your pen be false.
If you find a large debt against a poor man,
make it into three parts;
release two of them and let one remain:
you will find it a path of life;
you will pass the night in sound sleep;
in the morning you will find it like good news.
Better it is to be praised as one loved by men
than wealth in the storehouse;
better is bread when the mind is at ease
than riches with trouble.

Do not defraud a person in the law court,
nor put aside the just man.
Do not pay attention to garments of white,
nor scorn one in rags.
Take not the bribe of the strong man,
nor repress the weak for him.

Do not eat a meal in the presence of a
    magistrate,
nor set to speaking first.
If you are sated, pretend to chew,
enjoy yourself with your saliva.
Look at the cup in front of you,
and let it suffice your need.[2]

Do not laugh at a blind man nor taunt a
    dwarf,
neither interfere with the condition of a
    cripple;
do not taunt a man who is in the hand of
    God,
nor scowl at him if he errs.

Man is clay and straw,
and God is his potter;[3]
he overthrows and he builds daily,
he impoverishes a thousand if he wishes.
But he makes a thousand into officials
when he is in his hour of life.
How fortunate is he who reaches the West,[4]
when he is safe in the hand of God.

Mark for yourself these thirty chapters:
They please, they instruct,
they are the foremost of all books;
they teach the ignorant.
If they are read before an ignorant man,
he will be purified (of his ignorance) through
    them.
Fill yourself with them; put them in your mind
and get men to interpret them.
As for a scribe who is experienced in his
    position,
he will find himself worthy of being a courtier.[5]

186. IN PRAISE OF SCRIBES

Like Sirach 39:1–11, this text asserts that being a scribe gives a special kind of immortality, surprisingly much more enduring than that promised by the elaborate Egyptian burial traditions. It dates to ca. 1300 BCE. (See also Texts 181 and 193.)[6]

As for those scribes and sages
from the time which came after the gods[7]
—those who could foresee what was to come,
    which happened—
their names endure for eternity,
although they are gone, although they
    completed their lifetimes and all their
    people are forgotten.

They did not make pyramids of bronze,
with stelae of iron;
they recognized not how heirs last as children,

---

[1]Cf. Proverbs 23:6–8.
[2]Cf. Proverbs 23:1–3; Sirach 31:12–14.

[3]Cf. Job 10:9; Isaiah 64:8; Jeremiah 18:5–10; etc.
[4]The afterlife.
[5]Cf. Proverbs 22:29.
[6]Translation by R. B. Parkinson, *Voices from Ancient Egypt: An Anthology of Middle Kingdom Writings* (London: British Museum Press, 1991), 149–150.
[7]I.e., after humans had been created.

with offspring pronouncing their names;
they made for themselves heirs
as writings and the Teachings they made.

They appointed for themselves the book as
    the lector-priest,
the writing board as Beloved Son,[1]
the Teachings as their pyramids,
the pen as their baby,
the stone surface as wife.
From the great to the small
are given to be his children:
the scribe, he is their head.

Doors and mansions were made: they have
    fallen,
their funerary priests leaving,
while their stelae are covered with earth,
their chambers forgotten.
Yet their names are still pronounced over
    their rolls
which they made, from when they were.
How good is the memory of them and what
    they made—
for the bounds of eternity.

Be a scribe! Put it in your heart,
that your name shall exist like theirs!
The roll is more excellent than the carved
    stela,
than the enclosure which is established.
These act as chapels and pyramids
in the heart of him who pronounces their
    names.
Surely a name in mankind's mouth
is efficacious in the necropolis!

A man has perished: his corpse is dust,
and his people have passed from the land;
it is a book which makes him remembered
in the mouth of a speaker.
More excellent is a roll than a built house,
than a chapel in the West.[2]
It is better than an established villa,
than a stela in a temple.

Is there any like Hordedef?
Is there another like Imhotep?
There is none among our people like
    Neferti,[3]
or Khety their chief.
I shall make you know the name of
    Ptahemdjehuty and Khakheperresonbe.
Is there another like Ptahhotep,
or likewise, Kaires?

These sages, who foretold what come—
what came from their mouths happened—
one benefits from the lines written in their
    books.
To them the offspring of others are given,
to be heirs as if their own children.
They hid from the masses their magic,
which is read from their Teachings.
Departing life has made their names
    forgotten;
it is writings which make them remembered.

MESOPOTAMIA

187. PROVERBS

**Here is a sampling of proverbs collected by scribes
in bilingual texts, containing both Sumerian and
Akkadian versions.[4]**

When you exert yourself, your god is yours. When
    you do not exert yourself, your god is not
    yours.
It is not wealth that is your support. It is your god.
A people without a king is like sheep without a
    shepherd.[5]
A people without a foreman is like water without
    a canal inspector.
Laborers without a supervisor are like a field with-
    out a plowman.
A house without an owner is like a woman with-
    out a husband.
The command of the palace is like Anu's: it may
    not be set aside.

---

[1]A person in charge of the funerary rituals, as Horus was for his
father Osiris.
[2]The afterlife.

[3]See Text 169. Most of the other scribes named here are not attested
elsewhere.
[4]Translations by W. G. Lambert, *Babylonian Wisdom Literature*
(Oxford: Clarendon, 1960), 230–271.
[5]Cf. 1 Kings 22:17.

Like Shamash's, the king's word is sure, his com-
   mand is unequalled, and his utterance cannot be altered.[1]
Commit no crime, and fear of your god will not
   consume you.
Slander no one, and then grief will not reach your
   heart.
Has she become pregnant without intercourse?
   Has she become fat without eating?
A wound without a doctor is like hunger without
   food.
Last year I ate garlic; this year my inside burns.
The scribal art is the mother of orators and the
   father of scholars.
A thing which has not occurred since time
   immemorial: a young girl broke wind in her
   husband's bosom.
The will of a god cannot be understood; the way
   of a god cannot be known. Anything of a
   god is difficult to find out.
You find something, but it gets lost. You throw something away, but it is preserved indefinitely.
Flesh is flesh, blood is blood. Alien is alien, foreigner is indeed foreigner.

188. ADVICE TO A PRINCE

Dating to the early first millennium BCE, this text gives
instructions to a Babylonian king on how he should
rule and the divinely imposed consequences if he
does not do so justly.[2]

If a king does not heed justice, his people
will be thrown into chaos, and his land will be
devastated.
   If he does not heed the justice of the land, Ea,[3]
king of destinies, will alter his destiny and will not
cease from hostilely pursuing him.
   If he does not heed his nobles, his life will be
cut short.
   If he does not heed his advisor, his land will
rebel against him.
   If he heeds a rogue, the status quo in his land
will change.

If he heeds a trick of Ea, the great gods in
unison and in their just ways will not cease from
prosecuting him.
   If he improperly convicts a citizen of Sippar,[4]
but acquits a foreigner, Shamash,[5] judge of heaven
and earth, will set up a foreign justice in his land,
where the princes and judges will not heed justice.
   If citizens of Nippur are brought to him for
judgment, but he accepts a present and improperly convicts them, Enlil,[6] lord of the lands, will
bring a foreign army against him to slaughter his
army, whose princes and chief offices will roam his
country.
   If he takes the silver of the citizens of Babylon
and adds it to his own coffers, or if he hears a lawsuit involving men of Babylon but treats it frivolously, Marduk,[7] lord of heaven and earth, will set
his foes upon him, and will give his property and
wealth to his enemy.
   If he imposes a fine on the citizens of Nippur,
Sippar, or Babylon, or if he puts them in prison,
the city where the fine was imposed will be completely overturned, and a foreign enemy will make
his way into the prison in which they were put.
   If he mobilized the whole of Sippar, Nippur,
and Babylon, and imposed forced labor on the
people, exacting from them a corvée at the her-
ald's proclamation, Marduk, the sage of the gods,
the prince, the counselor, will turn his land over
to his enemy so that the troops of his land will do
forced labor for his enemy; for Anu,[8] Enlil, and Ea,
the great gods, who dwell in heaven and earth,
in their assembly affirmed the freedom of those
people from such obligations.
   If he gives the fodder of the citizens of Sippar,
Nippur, and Babylon to his own steeds, the steeds
who eat the fodder will be led away to the enemy's
yoke, and those men will be mobilized with the
king's men when the national army is conscripted.
Mighty Ea, who goes before his army, will shatter
his front line and go at his enemy's side. . . .
   If the advisor or chief office of the king's presence denounces them and so obtains bribes from

---

[1]Anu was the sky god; Shamash was the sun god.
[2]Translation by W. G. Lambert, *Babylonian Wisdom Literature*
(Oxford: Clarendon, 1960), 113, 115.
[3]The god of the subterranean fresh waters and of wisdom; often a
trickster.

[4]Sippar, Nippur, and Babylon were principal cities of Babylonia.
[5]The sun god and chief god of Sippar.
[6]The chief god of Nippur.
[7]The king of the gods and chief deity of Babylon; see Text 1.
[8]The sky god and head of the older generation of gods.

them, at the command of Ea, king of the Apsu,
the advisor and chief officer will die by the sword,
their place will be covered over as a ruin, the wind
will carry away their remains, and their achieve-
ments will be given over to the storm wind.

If he declares their contracts void, or alters
their inscribed stela, sends them on a campaign,
or press-gangs them into hard labor, Nabu,[1] scribe
of Esagila,[2] who organizes the whole of heaven and
earth, who directs everything, who ordains kingship, will declare the treaties of his land void, and
will decree hostility.

If either a shepherd, or a temple overseer, or a
chief officer of the king, who serves as temple overseer of Sippar, Nippur, or Babylon, imposes forced
labor on them in connection with the temples of
the great gods, the great gods will quit their dwellings in their fury and will not enter their shrines.

189. THE BABYLONIAN THEODICY

Although it exists in several copies, this work is not
fully preserved. It originally consisted of twenty-
seven stanzas of eleven lines each. The first syllable of each line in a stanza is the same, a technique
similar to that found in Psalm 119. Moreover, the
twenty-seven syllables thus used form an acrostic,
identifying the writer: "I am Saggil-kinam-ubbib, the
incantation priest, worshiper of god and the king."
From other sources we know that this person was
active in the late twelfth and early eleventh centuries
BCE, the probable date of composition, although it is
possible that the attribution is pseudonymous. The
genre of the poem is a dialogue between a sufferer
and his friend; in it, the sufferer asserts that despite
his piety, his personal god has not rewarded him; it
thus resembles in both form and content the poetic
dialogues between Job and his friends in the book
of Job.[3]

I (Sufferer)

[The beginning is broken.]

Where is the wise man of your caliber?
Where is the scholar who can compete with
    you?
Where is the counselor to whom I can relate
    my grief?
I am finished. Anguish has come upon me.
I was a youngest child; fate took my father;
my mother who bore me departed to the Land
    of No Return.
My father and mother left me without a
    guardian.

II (Friend)
Respected friend, what you say is gloomy.
You let your mind dwell on evil, my dear fellow.
You make your fine discretion like an imbecile's;
you have reduced your beaming face to
    scowls.
Our fathers in fact give up and go the way of
    death.
It is an old saying that they cross the river
    Hubur.[4]
…Whose favorite is the fattened rich man?
He who waits on his god has a protecting
    angel,
the humble man who fears his goddess
    accumulates wealth.

III (Sufferer)
My friend, your mind is a river whose spring
    never fails,
the accumulated mass of the sea, which
    knows no decrease.
I will ask you a question; listen to what I say.
Pay attention for a moment; hear my words.
My body is a wreck, emaciation darkens me,
my success has vanished, my stability has gone.
My strength is enfeebled, my prosperity has
    ended,
moaning and grief have blackened my
    features.
The grain of my fields is far from satisfying me;
my wine, the life of mankind, is too little for
    satiety.
Can a life of bliss be assured? I wish I knew
    how!

---

[1] Son of the god Marduk and the scribe of the gods.
[2] The principal temple of Marduk in Babylon.
[3] Translation by W. G. Lambert, *Babylonian Wisdom Literature*
(Oxford: Clarendon, 1960), 71–89.

[4] Like the Styx in Greek mythology, the river that was the boundary
of the underworld, which the dead needed to cross.

[*Stanza IV and the beginning and end of Stanza V are incomplete.*]

V (Sufferer)

.....

The savage lion who devoured the choicest
    flesh,
did it bring its flour offering to appease the
    goddess's anger?
The nouveau riche who has multiplied his
    wealth,
did he weigh out precious gold for the goddess
    Mami?[1]
Have I held back offerings? I have prayed to
    my god,
I have pronounced the blessing over the
    goddess's regular sacrifices....

VI (Friend)
O palm, tree of wealth, my precious brother,
    endowed with wisdom, jewel of gold,
you are as stable as the earth, but the plan of
    the gods is remote.
Look at the superb wild ass on the plain;[2]
the arrow will follow the gorer who trampled
    down the fields.
Come, consider the lion that you mentioned,
    the enemy of cattle.
For the crime that the lion committed the pit
    awaits him.[3]
The opulent nouveau riche who heaps up goods
will be burned at the stake by the king before
    his time.
Do you wish to go the way these have gone?
Rather seek the lasting reward of your god!

VII (Sufferer)
Your mind is a north wind, a pleasant breeze
    for the people.
Choice friend, your advice is fine.
Just one word I would put before you.
Those who neglect the god go the way of
    prosperity,
while those who pray to the goddess are

impoverished and dispossessed.[4]
In my youth I sought the will of my god;
with prostration and prayer I followed my
    goddess.
But I was bearing a profitless corvée as a yoke.
My god decreed instead of wealth destitution.
A cripple is my superior, a lunatic outstrips me.
The rogue has been promoted, but I have
    been brought low.

VIII (Friend)
My reliable fellow, holder of knowledge, your
    thoughts are perverse.
You have forsaken right and blaspheme
    against your god's designs.
In your mind you have an urge to disregard
    the divine ordinances.
...the sound rules of your goddess.

[*The rest of Stanza VII is broken; Stanzas IX–XI are missing; Stanzas XII–XXI are broken.*]

XXII (Friend)
...As for the rogue whose favor you seek,
his...soon vanishes.
The godless cheat who has wealth,
a death-dealing weapon pursues him.
Unless you seek the will of the god, what luck
    have you?
He that bears his god's yoke never lacks food,
    though it be sparse.
Seek the kindly wind of the god,
what you have lost over a year you will make
    up in a moment.

XXIII (Sufferer)
I have looked around society, but the
    evidence is contrary.
The god does not impede the way of a devil.
A father drags his boat along the canal,
while his first-born lies in bed.
The first-born son pursues his way like a lion,
the second son is happy to be a mule driver.
The heir stalks along the road like a bully,
the younger son will give food to the
    destitute.

---

[1] The mother goddess.
[2] Cf. Job 39:5–8.
[3] See page 42.
[4] Cf. Job 27.

How have I profited that I have bowed down
    to my god?
I have to bow beneath the base fellow that
    meets me;
the dregs of humanity, like the rich and
    opulent, treat me with contempt.

XXIV (Friend)

O wise one, O savant, who masters
    knowledge,
in your anguish you blaspheme the god.
The divine mind, like the center of the
    heavens, is remote;
knowledge of it is difficult; the masses do not
    know it.
Among all creatures whom Aruru[1] formed
the prime offspring is altogether....
In the case of a cow, the first calf is lowly,
the later offspring is twice as big.
A first child is born to the weakling,
but the second is called a heroic warrior.
Though a man may observe what the will of
    the god is, the masses do not know it.

XXV (Sufferer)

Pay attention, my friend, understand my ideas.
Heed the choice expressions of my words.
People extol the word of a strong man who is
    trained in murder,
but bring down the powerless who have done
    no wrong.
They confirm the wicked whose crime is...,
yet suppress the honest man who heeds the
    will of his god.
They fill the storehouse of the oppressor with
    gold,
but empty the larder of the beggar of its
    provisions.
They support the powerful, whose... is guilt,
but destroy the weak and drive away the
    powerless.
As for me, the penurious, a nouveau riche is
    pursuing me.

XXVI (Friend)

Narru, king of the gods,[2] who created mankind,

and majestic Zulammar,[3] who dug out their
    clay,
and mistress Mami, the queen who fashioned
    them,[4]
gave perverse speech to the human race.[5]
With lies, not truth, they endowed them
    forever.
Solemnly they speak in favor of a rich man,
"He is a king," they say, "riches go at his
    side." But they harm a poor man like a
    thief,
they lavish slander upon him and plot his
    murder,
making him suffer evil like a criminal,
    because he has no protection,
terrifyingly they bring him to his end, and
    extinguish him like a flame.

XXVII (Sufferer)

You are kind, my friend; behold my grief.
Help me; look on my distress; know it.
I, though humble, wise, and a suppliant,
have not seen help and succor for one
    moment.
I have trodden the square of my city
    unobtrusively,
my voice was not raised, my speech was kept
    low.
I did not raise my head, but looked at the
    ground,
I did not worship even as a slave in the
    company of my associates.
May the god who has thrown me off give
    help,
For the shepherd Shamash[6] guides the people
    like a god.

190. "I WILL PRAISE THE LORD OF WISDOM"

Sometimes called the "Poem of the Righteous
Sufferer," its opening words (in Akkadian, *ludlul bēl
nēmeqi*) indicate that this is a hymn in which an individual (named "Shubshi-meshre-Shakkan" in Tablet

---

[1]The birth goddess who created humans beings from clay; cf. Text
14, page 46.
[2]A name of Enlil.

[3]A name of Ea.
[4]A variant version of the creation of humans; see Text 1, page 13,
and Text 14, page 46.
[5]Cf. Genesis 11:7–9.
[6]The sun god.

III) thanks Marduk, the chief god of Babylon, for having rescued him. While the poem raises the issue of undeserved suffering, it is more comparable to individual psalms of thanksgiving in the Bible than to the books of Job and Ecclesiastes. It does share with the book of Job a detailed description of the sufferer's physical and social woes and a restoration of well-being after a divine revelation. Although many copies of this late-second-millennium-BCE work survive, none is complete.[1]

I

I will praise the lord of wisdom, judicious god,
enraged in the night, in the daylight calming,
Marduk, the lord of wisdom, judicious god,
enraged in the night, in the daylight calming,
whose fury, like a storm blast, makes a
    wasteland,
whose breath is, like the dawn wind, pleasing.
In his rage he is irresistible, a very deluge is
    his wrath,
his is a pardoning mind, his a forgiving heart.
The full weight of whose hands the heavens
    cannot support,
whose soft palm saves a man about to die,
Marduk, the full weight of whose hands the
    heavens cannot support,
whose soft palm saves a man about to die.
When he is angry, many are the graves to be
    opened,
when he pities, from the tomb he raises the
    fallen.
He frowns, and Life-force and Lady Fortune
    go far away.
He looks with favor, and to the one he had
    rejected his god[2] comes back again.
Terrible is his...punishment to the one still
    not absolved.
He is moved to mercy, and suddenly the god
    is like a mother,
hastening to treat his loved one tenderly,
and behind, like a cow with her calf, back and
    forth, round about he goes.

Sharp are the barbs of his whip, the body
    pierce and pierce.
His bandages are cool, giving life to death
    itself.
He commands, and makes one give offense.
On this day of redress, absolved are guilt and
    sin.
It is he who ever saves, provides that a case be
    heard.
Through his holy spell are shivers and chills
    released—
healer of Adad's thrusts, of Erra's wound,[3]
reconciler of god and goddess enraged.
The exalted lord sees into the heart of the
    gods,
never does a god know his way.
Exalted Marduk sees into the heart of the gods,
no god, whoever he be, can learn his plan.
As heavy as is his hand, so merciful is his
    heart.
As savage as are his weapons, so healing is his
    spirit.
Against his will, who could cool his wound?
Would he not, which one relieves his thrusts?
I will glorify his fury, which like...
He took pity on me, and suddenly how he
    gave me life.
I will have the people learn adoration...
His good invocation I will teach the land.

● ● ●

My god has forsaken me and disappeared,
my goddess has failed me and keeps at a
    distance.
The benevolent angel who walked beside me
    has departed,
my protecting spirit has taken to flight, and is
    seeking someone else.
My strength is gone; my appearance has
    become gloomy;
my dignity has flown away, my protection
    made off.
Fear omens beset me.
I am got out of my house and wander outside.
The omen organs are confused and inflamed
    for me every day.

---

[1]Lines 1–40 of Tablet I are adapted from the translation of William L. Moran, "The Babylonian Job," in *The Most Magic Word: Essays on Babylonian and Biblical Literature* (ed. R. S. Hendel; Washington, DC: Catholic Biblical Association, 2002), 199–200. The remaining excerpts are from W. G. Lambert, *Babylonian Wisdom Literature* (Oxford: Clarendon, 1960), 33–61.
[2]That is, his personal god, not Marduk.

[3]Adad is a storm god; Erra is a god of plague.

The omen of the diviner and dream priest
   does not explain my condition.
What is said in the street portends ill for me.
When I lie down at night, my dream is
   terrifying.
The king, the flesh of the gods, the sun of his
   people,
his heart is enraged with me, and cannot be
   appeased.
The courtiers plot hostile action against me,
they assemble themselves and give utterance
   to impious words.
Thus the first, "I will make him pour out his
   life."
The second says, "I will make him vacate his
   post." On this wise the third, "I will seize
   his position."
"I will take over his estate," says the fourth. . . .
The clique of seven have assembled their
   forces,
merciless like a demon, equal to . . . .
One is their flesh, united in purpose.
Their hearts rage against me, and they are
   ablaze like fire.
They combine against me in slander and lies.

•   •   •

My lofty head is bowed down to the ground,
dread has enfeebled my robust heart. . . .
I, who strode along as a noble, have learned
   to slip by unnoticed.
Though a dignitary, I have become a slave.
To my many relations I am like a recluse. . . .
My friend has become foe,
my companion has become a wretch and a
   devil.
In his savagery my comrade denounces me,
constantly my associates furbish their
   weapons.
My intimate friend has brought my life into
   danger;
my slave has publicly cursed me in the
   assembly. . . .
When an acquaintance sees me, he passes by
   on the other side.
My family treats me as an alien.[1]

The pit awaits anyone who speaks well of me,
while he who utters defamation of me is
   promoted. . . .
I have no one to go at my side, nor have I
   found a helper.

•   •   •

II
I survived to the next year; the appointed
   time passed.
As I turn round, it is terrible, it is terrible;
my ill luck has increased, and I do not find
   the right.
I called to my god, but he did not show his face,
I prayed to my goddess, but she did not raise
   her head.
The diviner with his inspection has not got to
   the root of the matter,
nor has the dream priest with his libation
   elucidated my case.
I sought the favor of the zaqiqu-spirit,[2] but he
   did not enlighten me;
and the incantation priest with his ritual did
   not appease the divine wrath against me.
What strange conditions everywhere!
When I look behind, there is persecution,
   trouble.
Like one who has not made libations to his god,
nor invoked his goddess at table,
does not engage in prostration, nor takes
   cognizance of bowing down;
from whose mouth supplication and prayer is
   lacking,
who has done nothing on holy days, and
   despised sabbath,
who in his negligence has despised the gods'
   rites,
has not taught his people reverence and
   worship,
but has eaten his food without invoking his god,
and abandoned his goddess by not bringing a
   flour offering,
like one who has grown torpid and forgotten
   his lord,
has frivolously sworn a solemn oath by his
   god, like such a one do I appear.

---

[1]Cf. Job 19:19.

[2]A deity who caused dreams.

For myself, I gave attention to supplication
   and prayer:
to me prayer was discretion, sacrifice my rule.
The day for reverencing the god was joy to my
   heart;
the day of the goddess's procession was profit
   and gain to me.
The king's prayer—that was my joy,
and the accompanying music became a
   delight for me.
I instructed my land to keep the god's rites,
and provoked my people to value the goddess's
   name.
I made praise for the king like a god's,
and taught the people reverence for the palace.
I wish I knew that these things were pleasing
   to one's god!
What is proper to oneself is an offense to
   one's god,
what in one's own heart seems despicable is
   proper to one's god.
Who knows the will of the gods in heaven?
Who understands the plans of the underworld
   gods?
Where have mortals learned the way of a god?
He who was alive yesterday is dead today.
For a minute he was dejected, suddenly he is
   exuberant.
One moment people are singing in exaltation,
another they groan like professional
   mourners.
Their condition changes like opening and
   shutting the legs.
When starving they become like corpses,
when replete they vie with their gods.
In prosperity they speak of scaling heaven,
under adversity they complain of going down
   to hell.
I am appalled at these things; I do not
   understand their significance.
As for me, the exhausted one, a tempest is
   driving me!
Debilitating Disease is let loose upon me:
an Evil Wind has blown from the horizon,
Headache has sprung up from the surface of
   the underworld....
They caused fever in my limbs and made my
   fat quake.
My lofty stature they destroyed like a wall,

my robust figure they laid down like a bulrush,
I am thrown down like a bog plant and cast
   on my face.
The *alu*-demon[1] has clothed himself in my
   body as with a garment;
sleep covers me like a net.
My eyes stare, but do not see,
my ears are open, but do not hear.
Feebleness has seized my whole body,
concussion has fallen on my flesh.
Paralysis has gripped my arms,
impotence has fallen on my knees,
my feet forget their motion.

• • •

My hunger is prolonged, my throat stopped up.
When grain is served, I eat it like stinkweed,
beer, the life of mankind, is distasteful to me.
My malady is indeed protracted.
Through lack of food my countenance is
   changed,
my flesh is flaccid, and my blood has ebbed
   away.
My bones have come apart, and are covered
   only with my skin.
My tissues are inflamed, and have caught
   the...disease.
I take to a bed of bondage; going out is a pain;
my house has become my prison.
My arms are stricken—which shackles my
   flesh;
my feet are limp—which fetters my person.

• • •

I spend the night in my dung like an ox,
and wallow in my excrement like a sheep.
My complaints have exposed the incantation
   priest,
and my omens have confounded the diviner.
The exorcist has not diagnosed the nature of
   my complaint,
nor has the diviner put a time limit on my
   illness.
My god has not come to the rescue in taking
   me by the hand,

---

[1] A night demon that caused seizures.

nor has my goddess shown pity on me by
    going at my side.
My grave was waiting, and my funerary
    paraphernalia ready,
before I had died lamentation for me was
    finished.
All my country said, "How he is crushed!"
The face of him who gloats lit up when he
    heard,
the tidings reached her who gloats, and her
    heart rejoiced....

III

• • •

Day and night alike I groan,
in dream and waking moments I am equally
    wretched.
A remarkable young man of outstanding
    physique,
massive in his body, clothed in new garments—
...he stood over me,
...and my body was numbed....
A second time I saw a dream,
and in my night dream which I saw
a remarkable young man...
holding in his hand a tamarisk rod of
    purification—
"Laluralimma, resident of Nippur,
has sent me to cleanse you."
The water he was carrying he threw over me,
pronounced the life-giving incantation, and
    rubbed my body.
A third time I saw a dream.
and in my night dream which I saw—
...a young woman of shining countenance,
a queen of..., equal to a god....
She said, "Be delivered from your very
    wretched state,
whoever has seen a vision in the night time."
In the dream Urnindinlugga, the
    Babylonian...,
a bearded young man with a turban on his head.
An incantation priest, carrying a tablet:
"Marduk has sent me.
To Shubshi-meshre-Shakkan[1] I have brought
    prosperity."

He (Marduk) had entrusted me into the
    hands of my ministrant.
In waking hours he sent the message
and showed his favorable sign to my peoples.
In the protracted malady....
My illness was quickly over and my fetters
    were broken.
After the mind of my Lord had quietened
and the ear of merciful Marduk was appeased,
after he had received my prayers...
and his pleasant smile....

• • •

He made the wind bear away my offenses....

• • •

My clouded eyes, which were cloaked in a
    deathly shroud—
he drove it a thousand leagues away and
    lightened my vision.
My ears which were clogged and blocked like
    a deaf man's—
he removed their wax and opened my hearing.
My nose, whose breathing was choked by the
    onset of fever—
he soothed its affliction and now I breathe
    freely....

• • •

IV
...The Lord took hold of me,
the Lord set me on my feet,
the Lord gave me life,
he rescued me from the pit,
he summoned me from destruction....
He who smote me,
Marduk, he restored me.
He smote the hand of my smiter,
it was Marduk who made his weapon fall....

• • •

The Babylonians saw how Marduk restores to
    life,
and all quarters extolled his greatness:
"Who thought that he would see his sun?
Who imagined that he would walk along his
    street?

---

[1]The Babylonian name of the speaker.

Who but Marduk restores his dead to life?
Apart from Sarpanitum,[1] which goddess
　grants life?
Marduk can restore life from the grave,
Sarpanitum knows how to save from
　destruction.
Wherever the earth is laid, and the heavens
　are stretched out,
wherever the sun god shines, and the fire god
　blazes,
wherever the water flows and wind blows,
creatures whose clay Aruru[2] took in her
　fingers,
those endowed with life, who stride along,
mortals, as many as there are, give praise to
　Marduk!

• • •

191. A DIALOGUE OF PESSIMISM

This first-millennium-BCE satirical dialogue, written in Akkadian, is a series of exchanges between a master and his servant or slave. The best preserved of the ten or so segments follow.[3]

"Slave, listen to me."
"Here I am, sir, here I am."
"Quickly, fetch me the chariot and hitch it up so that I can drive to the open country."
"Drive, sir, drive. A hunter gets his belly filled. The hunting dogs will break the prey's bones, the hunter's falcon will settle down, and the fleeting wild ass...."
"No, slave, I will by no means drive to the open country."
"Do not drive, sir, do not drive. The hunter's luck changes: the hunting dog's teeth will get broken, the home of the hunter's falcon is in...wall, and the fleeting wild ass has the uplands for its lair."

"Slave, listen to me."
"Here I am, sir, here I am."
"I will lead a revolution."

"So lead, sir, lead. Unless you lead a revolution, where will your clothes come from? Who will enable you to fill your belly?"
"No, slave, I will by no means lead a revolution."
"The man who leads a revolution is either killed, or flayed, or has his eyes put out, or is arrested, or is thrown into jail."

"Slave, listen to me."
"Here I am, sir, here I am."
"I am going to love a woman."
"So love, sir, love. The man who loves a woman forgets sorrow and fear."
"No, slave, I will by no means love a woman."
"Do not love, sir, do not love. Woman is a pitfall—a pitfall, a hole, a ditch. Woman is a sharp iron dagger that cuts a man's throat."

"Slave, listen to me."
"Here I am, sir, here I am."
"Quickly, fetch me water for my hands, and give it to me, so that I can sacrifice to my god."
"Sacrifice, sir, sacrifice. The man who sacrifices to his god is satisfied with the bargain: he is making loan upon loan."
"No, slave, I will by no means sacrifice to my god."
"Do not sacrifice, sir, do not sacrifice. You can teach your god to run after you like a dog, whether he asks of you rites, or 'Do not consult your god,' or anything else."

"Slave, listen to me."
"Here I am, sir, here I am."
"I am going to make loans as a creditor."
"So make loans, sir, make loans. The man who makes loans as a creditor—his grain remains his grain, while his interest is enormous."
"No, slave, I will by no means make loans as a creditor."
"Do not make loans, sir, do not make loans. Making loans is like loving a woman; getting them back is like having children. They will eat your grain, curse you without ceasing, and deprive you of the interest on your grain."

"Slave, listen to me."
"Here I am, sir, here I am."
"I will perform a public benefit for my country."

---

[1]A mother goddess who is Marduk's wife.
[2]The birth goddess who created humans beings from clay; cf. Text 14, page 46.
[3]Translation by W. G. Lambert, *Babylonian Wisdom Literature* (Oxford: Clarendon, 1960), 145–149.

"So perform, sir, perform. The man who per-
forms a public benefit for his country, his deeds are
placed in the ring of Marduk."[1]

"No slave, I will by no means perform a public
benefit for my country."

"Do not perform, sir, do not perform. Go up on
the ancient ruin heaps and walk about; see the
skulls of high and low. Which is the malefactor,
and which is the benefactor?"[2]

"Slave, listen to me."

"Here I am, sir, here I am."

"What then is good?"[3]

"To have my neck and your neck broken and
to be thrown into the river is good. 'Who is so tall
as to ascend to the heavens? Who is so broad as to
compass the underworld?'"[4]

"No, slave, I will kill you and send you first."

"And my master would certainly not outlive me
by even three days!"

192. A DRINKING SONG

**Originally written in Sumerian, this Akkadian version
of a drinking song in praise of beer dates from the
mid-second millennium BCE. It draws on wisdom literature and has themes similar to those in the book
of Ecclesiastes.[5]**

Plans are made by Enki,[6]
lots are drawn by the gods' will.
From former days only empty air remains:
whenever has aught been heard from any who
went before?
These kings were superior to those, and
others to them.
Your eternal abode is above their homes,[7]
it is far away as heaven: whose hand can
reach it?
Like the depths of the earth, no one knows
anything of it.

The whole of life is but the twinkling of an eye;
the life of humankind is surely not forever.
Where is King Alulu, who reigned for 36,000
years?[8]
Where is King Etana, who went up to heaven?[9]
Where is Gilgamesh, who sought life like
Ziusudra?[10]
Where is Huwawa,[11] who was seized and
knocked to the ground?
Where is Enkidu, who showed forth strength
in the land?
Where is Bazi? Where is Zizi?[12]
Where are the great kings from former days
until now?
They will not be begotten again, they will not
be born again.
How far did a life without glamour transcend
death?
Fellow, I will teach you truly who your god is:
Cast down unhappiness in triumph, forget the
silence of death!
Let one day of happiness make up for 36,000
years of the silence of death!
Let the beer goddess rejoice over you as if you
were her own child!
That is the destiny of humankind.

193. IN PRAISE OF SCRIBES

**This bilingual text, in Sumerian and Akkadian, is a
promotion of the scribal profession by one of its
practitioners. All copies date to the first millennium
BCE, when it was probably written; Sumerian was no
longer spoken but was used as a scholarly and liturgical language.[13]**

The scribal art is the mother of the eloquent,
father of the erudite;
the scribal art is enjoyable, one can never
have enough of its charms.

[1]Marduk was the chief god of Babylon. The meaning of the phrase is unclear.
[2]Cf. Ecclesiastes 9:1–3.
[3]Cf. Ecclesiastes 6:11.
[4]A proverbial saying; cf. Deuteronomy 30:11–14.
[5]Translation by Benjamin R. Foster, *Before the Muses: An Anthology of Akkadian Literature* (Bethesda, MD: CDL Press, 3d ed., 2005), 769–770.
[6]The god of fresh water and wisdom.
[7]Because of the nature of tells, graves of later generations lie higher than the houses of their ancient predecessors.

[8]See Text 20, page 65 (Alulim).
[9]A legendary king of Kish (see page 65) who went up to heaven on the back of an eagle.
[10]Ziusudra was the Sumerian name of Utnapishtim; see page 42.
[11]The monster whom Gilgamesh and Enkidu killed; see page 42. His Akkadian name was Humbaba.
[12]Two kings of Mari.
[13]Translation by Benjamin R. Foster, *Before the Muses: An Anthology of Akkadian Literature* (Bethesda, MD: CDL Press, 3d ed., 2005), 1023; cf. Sirach 38:24–39:11; Texts 181 and 186.

The scribal art is not easy to learn, but he who
    masters it will no longer be intimidated by it.
Strive after the scribal art and it will surely
    enrich you;
work hard at the scribal art and it will bring
    you wealth.
Do not be careless in the scribal art, do not
    neglect it;
the scribal art is the abode of beauty, of the
    secret lore of Amanki.[1]
Work ceaselessly at it and it will reveal its
    secret lore to you;
do not neglect it, lest you be ill spoken of.
The scribal art is a good lot, one of wealth
    and plenty.
When you are a youngster, you suffer; when
    you are mature, you prosper.
The scribal art is the nexus of all wisdom:
Pour yourself into it, then draw from its
    excellence.
To learn Sumerian is the highest learning,
    the standard form, the dialect form,
to write a stela, to measure a field, to balance
    accounts....
    ...the palace....
The scribe shall be its servitor; he shall call
    others for forced labor!

HURRIAN

194. THE SONG OF RELEASE

Dating to the mid-second millennium BCE, this multipart
and incomplete text is known in several copies both
in the original Hurrian and in Hittite translation.[2]

I will tell of Teshub,[3] the Great King of Kummi.
I will praise the young woman Allani[4] at the
Bolts of the Netherworld. In addition to them I
will speak of the young woman Ishara,[5] a skilled
goddess, famous for her wisdom....

---

[1]A ritual name used for Enki, the god of wisdom.
[2]Translation by Harry A. Hoffner, Jr., *Hittite Myths* (Writings from
the Ancient World 2; Atlanta, GA: Scholars Press, 2d ed., 1998),
67–73.
[3]The Hurrian storm god, whose home was Kummi.
[4]The Hurrian goddess of the underworld.
[5]Another Hurrian goddess of the underworld, often identified with
Mesopotamian Ishtar.

A mountain expelled a deer from its body. The
deer went over to another mountain. It grew fat,
became discontented, and began to curse the new
mountain: "If only fire would burn up the mountain on which I am grazing! If only Teshub would
strike it with his lightning, and the resulting fire
would burn up the mountain!"

Now when the mountain heard this, his heart
became sick within him, and he cursed the deer in
return: "Why does the deer which I have fattened
now curse me in return? Let the hunters fell the
deer. Let fowlers take it. Let hunters take its meat,
and let fowlers take its hide."

But this is not a deer, it is a human being. That
man: he who ran away from his own city has
arrived in another country. When he became discontented, he began to plot evil in return against
his new city. And the city's gods have made him
accursed.

Leave that tale, and I will tell you another tale.
Hear my message: I will tell you an instructive
example.

There is a deer. It grazes those pastures which
are on the near side of a river. And it constantly
sets its eyes also on those pastures on the far side.
It did not care for the pastures on the near side
which it already had, and it did not achieve the
one on the far side.

But this is not a deer. It is a human being. That
man, whom his lord makes into a border commander, they made him a border commander in that
district, but he constantly set his eyes on a second
district.

The gods chose a wise course of action regarding that man; so that he did not care for that first
district, but he did not achieve the second district.

Leave that story, and I will tell you another
story. Listen to my message, and I will tell you an
instructive example.

A coppersmith cast a cup for his own glory. He
cast it and finished it. He provided it with attachments and engraved it. He made them gleam on it
with brilliance.

Then the foolish copper cup began to curse
in return him who had cast it: "If only the hand
of him who cast me would be broken. If only his
right arm muscle would be paralyzed."

When the coppersmith heard that, he was pained at heart, and the coppersmith began to say to himself: "Why does this copper which I have cast curse me in return?"[1]

So the coppersmith pronounced a curse on the cup: "May Teshub strike this cup and tear off its attachments. May the cup fall into an irrigation ditch, may the attachments fall into the river."

This is not a cup, but a human being. It is that son who is hostile toward his father. He grew up and reached adulthood, and no longer looks at his father. He it is whom his father's gods have made accursed.

Leave that tale, and I will tell you another tale. Hear my instructions; I will tell you an instructive example.

A dog ran off with a *kugulla*-bread from in front of an oven. He pulled it out of the oven and dropped it in oil. In oil he dropped it and sitting down he began to eat it.

This is not a dog but a human being: he whom his lord makes lord of an administrative unit. He took increased tribute behind the back of that city. He became very discontented. He no longer looks after the city. The citizens managed to inform on him before his lord. He began to pour out before his lord those items of tribute which he was continually swallowing.

[*The next parable, omitted here, is identical except that it names another animal.*]

Leave that tale, and I will tell you another tale. Hear the instructions, and I will tell you an instructive example.

A builder built a tower for glory and dug its foundations deep down to the Sun Goddess of the Netherworld. He brought its battlements up near to the sky.[2]

The foolish wall began to curse the one who built it: "If only the arm of him who built me would be broken, if only his right arm muscle would be paralyzed!"

The builder heard and became sad at heart. The builder said to himself: "Why is the wall which I built cursing me?" Then the builder uttered a curse on the tower: "Let Teshub strike the tower, let him expose its foundation stones upon it, let its . . . fall down into the ditch, let its brickwork fall down into the river."

This is not a tower, but a human being: that son who is hostile toward his father. He grew up and reached maturity. He no longer regards his father. Therefore, his father's gods have made him accursed.

[*Another parable, now incomplete, follows. The next part of the composition describes a feast given by Allani for Teshub.*]

When Teshub went, he set out to go to the palace of Allani. A chair was set up for him. When Teshub, the king, came in from outside, Teshub sat down high on a throne whose surface measured one *iku*[3] of field measure. He raised his feet on a stool whose surface measured seven *tawalla*-measures.

Teshub and Suwaliyat (also known as Tasmisu)[4] went down to the Dark Netherworld, and Allani girded herself for work. She goes back and forth in front of Teshub, and Allani made a fine feast at the Bolts of the Netherworld.

She slaughtered 10,000 cattle before great Teshub: 10,000 cattle she slaughtered. She slaughtered 30,000 fat-tailed sheep. But there was no counting the goat kids, lambs, and adult goats, so many were slaughtered.

The bakers made their wares ready. And the cupbearers came in. The cooks took up the brisket portions. And they brought them in with bowls as mortars. The mealtime arrived, and Teshub, the king, sat down to eat. But she seated the Primeval Deities[5] on Teshub's right.

Allani stepped up in front of Teshub as a cupbearer. The fingers of her hands were long. Her four fingers were placed under the animal-shaped vessel, and flavorfulness was in the vessel from which she gave her guests drink.

---

[1]Cf. Isaiah 29:16; 45:9–10.
[2]Cf. Genesis 11:1–4.

[3]About an acre. The superhuman size of deities is also found in architecture, as in the deity's footprints in the temple at Ain Dara in Syria, which are over 3 feet (1 meter) long.
[4]Tasmisu was Teshub's brother; his Hittite name was Suwaliyat.
[5]The older gods, whom Teshub had banished to the underworld.

[*The rest of the tablet is broken, as is the remainder of the cycle, consisting of only tangentially related tales.*]

ARAMAIC

195. AHIKAR

The story of Ahikar (also spelled Ahiqar), a wronged courtier who was restored to royal favor, was a popular one in the Near East. Versions of the story are known in several ancient languages, and a late version occurs in some manuscripts of the medieval Arabic collection *A Thousand and One Nights*. Variants of the plot are also widespread. One is in the book of Tobit, which also refers to Ahikar several times (Tobit 1:21–22; 2:10). The oldest text known is one of the Aramaic papyri from Elephantine in Egypt (see also page 109), which dates to the fifth century BCE. Like later versions, it has two distinct parts.

The first part is a prose tale, which tells how Ahikar, a scribe and high official in the courts of the Assyrian kings Sennacherib (705–681 BCE) and Esar-haddon (681–669 BCE), adopted his nephew Nadin (called Nadab in Tobit 11:18; 14:10) as his heir. At Ahikar's request, Esar-haddon appointed Nadin to succeed his adopted father. But Nadin falsely accused his father of treason, and Esar-haddon ordered Ahikar arrested and executed. He was rescued by his executioner, whom Ahikar himself had similarly saved from a false charge. Here the Aramaic version breaks off, but in later versions (see also Tobit 14:10), Ahikar is eventually restored and his adopted son is punished. Because the prose tale is poorly preserved, it is not translated here.

The second part of the text is a collection of proverbs, many in poetic parallelism, only loosely linked with the tale. Thus, although the intended audience of the proverbs is frequently addressed as "my son," that designation occurs in many other proverb collections, including the book of Proverbs, and was a conventional way of addressing not just an actual son, but a student or an apprentice. This collection seems originally to have been independent, like some of the smaller collections in the book of Proverbs, in which there are also parallels to individual proverbs in *Ahikar*. Like other such collections, too, they are in an almost random order,

with similar topics occasionally treated in clusters. A selection of the better-preserved proverbs follows.[1]

Indeed, she is precious to the gods;
her kingdom is eternal.
She has been established by Shamayin;[2]
Yea, the Holy Lord has exalted her.[3]

My son, do not curse the day
until you have seen the night.

Above all else, guard your mouth;[4]
and as for what you have heard, be discreet!
For a word is a bird,
and he who releases it is a fool.

A king's word is gentle, but keener
and more cutting than a double-edged dagger.

Here is a difficult thing before you:
do not stand opposed to the king.
His anger is swifter than lightning;
look out for yourself!
Let him not kindle it against your words,
lest you depart before your time.

When a royal command is given you,
it is a burning fire.
Execute it at once,
lest it flare up against you and singe your
    hands.
But rather let the king's command
be your heart's delight.

How can logs strive with a fire,
meat with a knife,
or a man with a king?

---

[1]Translation by James M. Lindenberger, *The Aramaic Proverbs of Ahiqar* (Baltimore, MD: Johns Hopkins University Press, 1983). At Professor Lindenberger's suggestion (personal commuunication), the order of the proverbs has been rearranged to follow B. Porten and A. Yardeni, *Textbook of Aramaic Diocuments from Anceient Egypt*, Vol. 3 (Jerusalem: The Hebrew University of Jerusalem, 1993), 36–49.
[2]A short form of the title "Baal Shamayn," "the Lord of the Heavens."
[3]Cf. Proverbs 8:22–31; Wisdom of Solomon 7:25–8:4; Sirach 24:1–7.
[4]Cf. Psalm 141:3; Proverbs 4:23; Sirach 22:27.

The king's tongue is gentle,
but it breaks a dragon's ribs.[1]
It is like death, which is invisible.

A king is like the Merciful,
even his voice is haughty.
Who is there who could withstand him,
but one with whom El[2] is?

A king is as splendid to see as Shamash;[3]
and his majesty is glorious,
to them that tread the earth in peace.

A good container keeps a thing within it,
but a broken one lets it out.[4]

The bramble sent a message to the
    pomegranate as follows:[5]
"Dear Pomegranate, what good are all your
    thorns to him who touches your fruit?"
The pomegranate replied to the bramble:
"You are nothing but thorns to him who
    touches you!"

Do not draw your bow
and shoot your arrow at the righteous man,[6]
lest the gods come to his aid
and turn it back against you.

Hear, O my son:
harvest any harvest,
and do any job;
then you may eat your fill
and provide for your children.

Do not take a heavy loan from an evil man.
But if you take a loan (at all), give yourself no
    peace until you have repaid it.

Do not despise that which is your lot,
nor covet some great thing which is withheld
    from you.

Whoever takes no pride in his father's and
    mother's name,
may Shamash not shine on him,[7]
for he is an evil man.

My distress is my own fault,
before whom will I be found innocent?
My own son spied out my house,
what shall I say to strangers?
He was a false witness against me,
who then will declare me innocent?
My poisoner came from my own house,
before whom can I press my complaint?

I have carried sand and hauled salt,
but there is nothing more burdensome than
    debt.

I have carried straw and lifted bran,
but there is nothing taken more lightly than
    a foreigner.

A sword stirs up quiet waters
between good neighbors.
If a young man utters great words
they will soar up above him
when his utterance exalts the gods.
If he is beloved of the gods
they will give him something worthwhile to say.

The stars in the sky are so numerous
that no one knows their names.
Just so, no one knows man.

Once upon a time a leopard came upon a she-goat
who was cold. The leopard said to the goat, "Why
won't you let me cover you with my pelt?" The
goat replied to the leopard, "Why should I do that
my lord? Don't take my hide away from me! For (as
they say) 'A leopard does not greet a gazelle except
to suck its blood.'"

Spare not your son from the rod;
otherwise can you save him from wickedness?

If I beat you, my son, you will not die;
but if I leave you alone, [you will not live].[8]

---

[1]Cf. Proverbs 25:15; Sirach 28:17.
[2]The head of the pantheon, one of whose epithets was "merciful."
[3]The sun god.
[4]Cf. Sirach 21:14.
[5]For a similar fable of dispute between plants, see Judges 9:8–15; 2 Kings 14:9.
[6]Cf. Psalm 11:2.
[7]Cf. Proverbs 20:20.
[8]Cf. Proverbs 23:13–14.

A blow for a serving-boy, a rebuke for a slave-
girl,
and for all your servants, discipline!

There are two things which are good,
and a third which is pleasing to Shamash:
one who drinks wine and shares it,
one who masters wisdom [and observes it],
and one who hears a word but tells it not.
Now that is precious to Shamash.

From heaven the peoples are favored;
Wisdom is of the gods.

ABECEDARIES

School exercises include writing of the alphabet.
Such abecedaries have survived from the late second
millennium BCE onward, and the order of the letters
of the alphabet is remarkably conservative regard-
less of the language in which the alphabet is being
used. In the following examples, scholarly transliter-
ation is used.

196. UGARITIC ABECEDARY

From the late second millennium BCE.

'a b g ǵ d h w z ḥ ṭ y k š l
m ḍ n ẓ s 'p ṣ q r ṯ
ǵ t 'i 'u ṡ

HEBREW ABECEDARIES

The presence of these exercises at relatively insignificant sites is an important datum for the spread of
literacy in ancient Israel. All three vary from the traditional Hebrew alphabet (as well as from the Ugaritic
in the previous reading and from later Greek) in the
order of the letters pe and 'ayin; the same sequence
is found in some biblical acrostic poems.[1] Other vari-
ations in order may also reflect alternate tradition or
may simply be a beginning scribe's mistakes.

197. IZBET SARTAH

This is the last line of an otherwise obscure text dating to ca. 1100 BCE; the script is very early Hebrew,
or perhaps Proto-Hebrew or Canaanite.

'b g d h w ḥ z ṭ y k l m n s p 'ṣ q r š t

198. TEL ZAYIT

Early to mid-tenth century BCE.

'b g d w h ḥ z ṭ y l k m n s p 'ṣ
q r š t

199. KUNTILLET AJRUD

Ca. 700 BCE (see Texts 152–155).

. . . ṭ y k l m n s p 'ṣ q r š t

200. GEZER CALENDAR

This agricultural calendar, inscribed on a limestone
tablet, was excavated at Gezer in Palestine in 1908.
Dating to the tenth century BCE, it was probably a
school exercise.

Two months gathering	[September-October]
two months planting	[November-December]
two months late sowing	[January-February]
(one) month cutting flax	[March]
(one) month reaping barley	[April]
(one) month reaping and measuring (grain)	[May]
two months pruning	[June-July]
(one) month summer fruit	[August]

---

[1] Psalm 10:6–8 (Hebrew); Lamentations 2; 3; 4.

INDEX OF BIBLICAL REFERENCES